CW01513217

Yankee Sailors
in British Gaols

Yankee Sailors in British Gaols

Prisoners of War at Forton and Mill, 1777–1783

Sheldon S. Cohen

DELAWARE

Newark: University of Delaware Press
London: Associated University Presses

Associated University Presses
440 Forsgate Drive
Cranbury, NJ 08512

Associated University Presses
25 Sicilian Avenue
London WC1A 2QH, England

Associated University Presses
P.O. Box 338, Port Credit
Mississauga, Ontario
Canada L5G 4L8

The paper used in this publication meets the requirements
of the American National Standard for Permanence of Paper
for Printed Library Materials Z39.48-1984.

Library of Congress Cataloging-in-Publication Data

Cohen, Sheldon S. (Sheldon Samuel), 1931–
    Yankee sailors in British gaols : prisoners of war at Forton and Mill, 1977–1783 / Sheldon S. Cohen.
        p.   cm.
    Includes bibliographical references and index.
    ISBN 0-87413-564-8 (alk. paper)
    1. United States—History—Revolution, 1775–1783—Prisoners and prisons, British.   2. Forton Gaol.   3. Mill Gaol.   4. Prisoners of war—United States—History—18th century.   5. Prisoners of war—Great Britain—History—18th century.   I. Title.
E281.C7   1995
973.3'71—dc20   95-2448
                                                                           CIP

Contents

Preface

"It's as though you aren't your own timekeeper anymore; they keep the time for you for almost everything." The elderly Englishman was reminiscing to me about his British army service and about being taken prisoner by General Erwin Rommel's Afrika Korps. He had spent almost four years in captivity before his release in 1945. Recalling this period, the former soldier commented that his lengthy confinement did not include any significant maltreatment. Nonetheless, the loss of personal freedom, the boredom, the frustrations, and above all, the uncertainty that accompanied his long detention had changed him indelibly.

The memories of this British army veteran are of a relatively recent time. Nevertheless they reflect a universal consequence of belligerency—prisoners of war. Indeed the issue of prisoners of war is an ancient by-product of conflict. It has been noted in the Bible and in Homer's narratives and in the history of the Peloponnesian and the Punic Wars. More recently, scholars have focused considerable study on American servicemen, both military and naval, during World War II, Korea, and Vietnam. Such writings have provided considerable insight into the manner in which American prisoners were treated during the contentious conflicts of this century.

But the United States also experienced several earlier wars stretching back over two centuries to the American Revolution. The hostilities that occurred during the eight years following the Lexington-Concord engagements in April 1775 exposed several thousand revolutionaries to varying durations of British captivity. The great majority of these prisoners were detained in America, and their incarcerations, on land or on offshore prison ships such as the infamous *Jersey,* have been well documented. Yet approximately three thousand rebels—mostly seamen—endured captivity thousands of miles away, in Great Britain. A fraction of these men were interned in scattered locales in England, Scotland, Wales, and Ireland. The great majority of them, however, were sent to England's two principal detention centers, Forton Gaol near Portsmouth and Mill Gaol near Plymouth.

The Americans incarcerated in Great Britain were noteworthy as this nation's first servicemen imprisoned abroad. There is much else to their story aside from this distinction. How these men, serving under circumstances different from those of contemporary wars, reacted to captivity, both as individuals and as a group, reveals much about Americans of this long-past era. There is also the story of how they were dealt with by their adversaries. (In later wars, U.S. servicemen have often been maltreated by their captors.) Last, in this often-overlooked episode from the War of Independence, there is the chronicle of the various ways that American governmental representatives, their European allies, and even some sympathetic Englishmen worked for the relief and release of imprisoned rebels in Great Britain.

A comprehensive account of Americans detained within the closed societies of Forton and Mill prisons has never been written. There have been several published works—primarily articles—which have offered general portrayals of the operation of these two detention centers or the rebel inmates sent to them. These earlier writings, however, often are outdated and sometimes are inaccurate or incomplete. Also, none of them fully incorporates the considerable, widely scattered manuscript material available in a multitude of public and private repositories across Great Britain and the United States. These sources include the vast holdings of England's Public Record Office (Kew) and National Maritime Museum (Greenwich), America's Library of Congress, and documents held in the editorial offices of the Benjamin Franklin Papers at Yale University. They also comprise historical documents from the more modest holdings of the Portsmouth City Record Office; the West Devon Record Office; and the New London, Connecticut, County Historical Society.

My own work on these American prisoners of the Revolution has three principal objectives. First, by combining manuscript material from the aforementioned repositories with an array of existing secondary sources, this book is designed to offer a comprehensive portrait of these little-remembered mariners, their experiences in captivity, and the disparate individuals who assisted them. This study also intends to represent the ways in which these incarcerated seamen exhibited characteristics that were indigenous to their New World culture. Third, and perhaps most significant historically, the ensuing chapters will examine the role that these often inarticulate Yankee captives played in the struggle for freedom of the United States.

Acknowledgments

I have noted in my preface that by combining historical material from Great Britain and the United States, a scholar can elucidate many lesser known, yet meaningful episodes from this nation's beginnings. My ensuing work intends to illustrate this precept. Concurrently, I would have found it difficult to assemble the multitude of primary and secondary sources forming the foundation of my project without the generous assistance, consideration, and support of many individuals and repositories on both sides of the Atlantic. Complementing my courteous friends, were other benefactors: fellow scholars, including Dr. Brooke Hindle, my thesis advisor and a naval officer in World War II; the administration of Loyola University of Chicago and its history department chaired by Professor Joseph Gagliano; editors; friends; and especially indulgent family members. They, too, deserve my inestimable appreciation for their valued criticism, encouragement, suggestions, and patience.

First I would like to thank three colleagues who very kindly took of their own time to examine, criticize, and assess my original manuscript. Dr. John Alexander, professor of American colonial history at the University of Cincinnati, provided a close and very beneficial evaluation of my writing. Professor Alexander, who contributed several articles during the 1960s dealing with the American captives at Forton and Mill, was able to offer particularly cogent advice on the tone and direction of this work. Dr. Michael Crawford, Head of the Early History Branch of the Naval Historical Center in Washington, D.C., is another recognized American colonial historian who very generously took the time to review my study. Dr. Crawford's extensive familiarity with naval history was extremely valuable, especially in correcting my gaffes in naval terminology. Also, I am indebted to Dr. Barbara Oberg, editor of *The Papers of Benjamin Franklin,* for taking the time from her busy schedule to read my manuscript. I hope that my account of the various means employed by Dr. Franklin to aid his countrymen imprisoned in Britain will be of some benefit to Dr. Oberg and her very thoughtful staff.

Next in order I would like to offer my appreciation to several individuals and repositories in the United Kingdom who assisted the formative process of my manuscript. Foremost among my British benefactors was Sarah Quail, City Records Officer at the Portsmouth Records Office. Mrs. Quail graciously supplied this inquiring American with a wealth of descriptive and chronological data concerning the topographical and antiquarian features of the Portsmouth-Gosport region. She also offered many enlightening facts regarding the religious, social, economic, and political characteristics of eighteenth-century Hampshire. Also in Portsmouth, the Reverend John Sturges, retired minister of the John Pounds Unitarian Chapel, furnished me with worthwhile facts concerning the history of his former pastorate, plus a few long-standing tales about the activities of the Reverend Thomas Wren. David Kemp of the Gosport Museum supplied me with relevant documents and information about the existence of the town's Haslar Naval Hospital and nearby Forton Prison and Forton Barracks. In London, Robin Hartley-Russell very kindly donated copies of his family papers that dealt with his ancestor David Hartley's involvement in matters connected with the American prisoners interned in Britain.

Unfortunately, I did not have the pleasure of personally thanking three Britons whose searches and correspondence brought further depth to my study. Several instructive letters from Elisabeth Stuart and Paul Brough, archivists at the West Devon Record Office in Plymouth, illuminated my understanding of the physical features surrounding Mill Prison in Devon. Both individuals also provided me with maps showing the precise locale of Mill (Millbay) Prison and useful information concerning dissenter meeting houses in Devon at the time of the American Revolution. L. C. Jarman from Braithwaite in the northern English county of Cumbria sent me information dealing with the family background and early life of the Reverend Thomas Wren of Portsmouth.

I must also offer my appreciation to several British repositories whose staffs were most courteous and receptive to me during the course of my research. In the London area, I would like to give credit to the Public Record Office in Kew and at Chancery Lane, the British Library, the Guildhall Library, Dr. Williams's Library, and the National Maritime Museum in Greenwich. Outside of London the following locales deserve my appreciation: The Gloucestershire Record Office, The Berkshire Record Office, The Gosport Museum, The Hampshire Record Office, The Portsmouth City Record Office, and the West Devon Record Office.

Moving to this side of the Atlantic, I would like to acknowledge those locales that supplied me with materials for completing my project. Some of the published primary source material, such as the *Papers of Benjamin Franklin* and *Naval Documents of the American Revolution,* along with secondary works dealing with the revolutionary era, were readily available through Loyola's Cudahy Library and the Northwestern University Library. However, it was Chicago's prestigious Newberry Library that held the most extensive and lucrative sources of printed books, monographs, journals, newspapers, government records, and other historical materials that dealt with the captive Yankees in England. The voluminous holdings of the Newberry also provided me with many useful works concerning the vicinities surrounding both prisons, including an invaluable 1775 guidebook describing Portsmouth and Gosport. I am greatly indebted to the staffs at all of these institutions.

Several locations and several individuals beyond the Chicago area also gave noteworthy assistance. Foremost among these repositories were the *Papers of Benjamin Franklin* housed at the Yale University Sterling Memorial Library. At the time I completed this manuscript, thirty volumes of this monumental historical project had been published. I have already expressed my gratitude to Dr. Barbara Oberg, editor of this invaluable historical endeavor. However, I would also like to offer my thanks for the special consideration given my research needs by staff members Kate Ohno, Ellen R. Cohn, Claude A. Lopez, Dr. Jonathan R. Dull, and the late Catherine M. Prelinger and Dorothy Bridgewater. I shall always appreciate the welcome attention and consideration they gave to me at the Sterling Library.

Before continuing my credits beyond New Haven, Connecticut, I would like to pay homage to some Yale faculty members who indirectly provided the incentives for this project. Many years ago, distinguished historians from this institution, including Professors Howard R. Lamar and the late Lewis P. Curtis, David M. Potter, and Hajo Holborn, first whetted my appetite to seek meanings "in Clio's realms." I shall always be indebted to them as I will be to Dean Richard B. Sewall from Yale's English Department who supplied me with the confidence to express my thoughts in a comprehensible manner. They are recalled today as giants—every one!

Other resource centers in the United States must also be given acknowledgments. The following sites very generously allowed me to quote from yet unpublished Benjamin Franklin Manuscripts: the American Philosophical Society, the Historical Society of Pennsylvania, the University of Pennsylvania Library, the William Clements Library at the University of Michigan, the Massachusetts

Historical Society, the National Archives, and the Library of Congress. Other American locales that provided useful data were the Connecticut Historical Society, the New London (Connecticut) Historical Society, the Essex Institute, New England Historical and Genealogical Society, Maryland Historical Society, Naval Historical Center (Washington, D.C.), New Hampshire Historical Society, New-York Historical Society, Philadelphia Maritime Museum, South Carolina Historical Society, University of South Carolina, Henry Laurens Papers, and the Virginia State Library.

Research facilities, benefactors, and colleagues aside, I would finally like to express my gratitude on a more personal level. It was truly the assistance, patience, support, and understanding of my wife, Kayla, that brought this project to its completion. Whatever its merits, this book is most affectionately dedicated to her.

Yankee Sailors
in British Gaols

1

Antecedents

For Massachusetts seaman Timothy Connor, arriving in the harbor of Portsmouth, England, on 1 May 1777 was not cause to celebrate a long journey's end. Connor had sailed from Cape Cod the previous February on the sixteen-gun privateer brig *Rising States,* commanded by Captain James Thompson. Her objective had been to seize unsuspecting British merchant vessels plying the eastern Atlantic and to sell them as prizes in Europe.[1] At first, all had gone well for the Yankee privateer in spite of a damaging storm. Three ships were taken off the French coast, and part of the crew had been detached to sail the prizes to French ports. Then disaster struck. On 15 April, *Rising States* was chased and taken by the seventy-four gun ship of the line HMS *Terrible.* Connor and thirty-eight shipmates were placed under marine guards, from whom they often had to beg scraps of food. Their officers were subjected to repeated, often menacing interrogations. Twenty-three days later, *Terrible* reached Spithead and the following day, her anchorage in Portsmouth harbor. The occasion was marked by a solitary gesture of magnanimity from the royal frigate's captain, Richard Bickerton—when he had the officers of *Rising States* served a dinner with a bottle of wine and some beer to drink.[2]

It was not until 13 and 14 June that all of the captives from *Rising States* were transported to Portsmouth town itself, where they first underwent examinations at the Royal Hospital. The repressive treatment endured on board *Terrible* ended as the anxious and disheveled Americans debarked at the seaport's docks on those late spring days. They must have appeared as a sorry lot to spectators. Seaman Connor wrote that he and many of his comrades had even "sold what trifles we had to get supplied with provisions." Soon afterward, *Rising States*' fate was determined when the captured brig was sold to a Portsmouth merchant who renamed the vessel *Charming Molly* and had her refitted—this time as a British privateer.[3]

1780 England and The North Coast of France

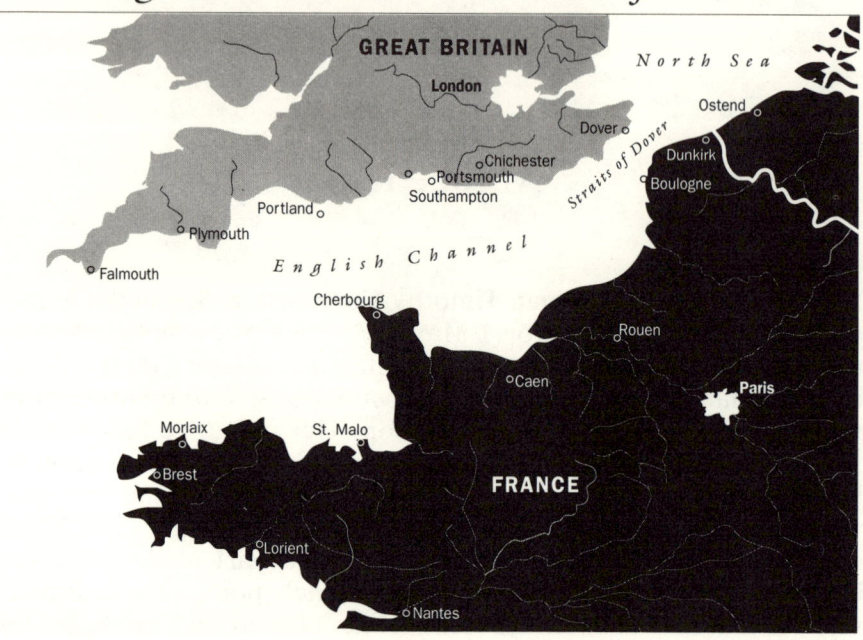

Map of Southern England and Northern France 1780. Composed by Loyola University of Chicago Graphic Arts Department.

Although Connor did not mention it, the Americans' personal discomforts were likely augmented by concerns about their status. This point was driven home to them when they were all arraigned before an unsympathetic Portsmouth justice. This British magistrate made his sentiment clearly known: the Americans standing before him were "pirates," "damned rebels," "traitors" to His Majesty King George III, and were deserving of no leniency. He quickly completed the formalities, ordering that the accused be remanded to the newly reopened gaol at nearby Forton.[4]

The judge's ruling was promptly executed. The Americans were removed from the courtroom under strong guard. From there, they were transported across the narrow width of Portsmouth Harbor to the town of Gosport. Upon reaching this hamlet, the closely guarded officers and crewmen of *Rising States* trudged uphill for another mile. Awaiting them at a pleasant rural crossroad were the forbidding gates of their destination, Forton Gaol. Although it mattered little to the band of detainees, they were the first Americans to be imprisoned in this English prison.[5]

Meanwhile, 165 miles to the west, in Devon, somewhat similar events had befallen Samuel Cutler, another Massachusetts seaman. Like Timothy Connor, Cutler had followed the rebel cause by serving aboard a privateer. Cutler's ship was the brig *Dalton,* and he was appointed clerk to her skipper, Captain Eleazar Johnson.[6] *Dalton,* with its 120-member crew, had sailed from Newburyport on 15 November 1776, also intent on seizing British prizes. Unlike *Rising States,* however, *Dalton* was unable to capture any vessels on her maiden Atlantic cruise. Then, on the day before Christmas, her voyage ended abruptly near the Azores. She was detected by the sixty-four gun HMS *Raisonable,* and after several hours' chase, Captain Johnson surrendered to the British warship.[7]

Cutler and his fellow Americans spent considerably more time on board British warships than did Seaman Connor. Following their capture, the unhappy crew from *Dalton* were transported to Plymouth harbor. There, in January 1777, they were transferred to HMS *Bellisle,* where Cutler wrote, "We were met with better usage," adding that they had been robbed by *Raisonable*'s crew while in confinement. Although *Bellisle*'s captain provided better treatment for the Americans, the other unpleasantness of shipboard confinement continued. For the next three months the prisoners were conveyed to a number of British frigates docked at Plymouth. Simultaneously, other captured rebel sailors were being added to their ranks. On 7 May 1777, Cutler wrote that the total number of American prisoners with him had now reached 180. He also noted that serious illness, including smallpox and dysentery, had already sent many among their ranks to the hospital.[8]

The British government already had plans for the ultimate disposition of these captured rebel seamen, but the dangers of contagion in close shipboard confinement caused them to act more speedily. To Cutler, this fact was evident throughout May, as small numbers of the Americans were taken to shore and reportedly committed to a prison he referred to as "Mill."[9] Eventually the time came for the ship's clerk and other *Dalton* crewmen to be moved under guard from the frigate to Plymouth itself. There, after a sequence of events not unlike that which Timothy Connor experienced several days later in Portsmouth, Samuel Cutler recounted the details of his own commitment.

> June 3 [1777] Tuesday
> Fifth remove. Nine Americans—myself included in the numbers—sent on shore to the Fountain Tavern for examination. We were escorted by seven soldiers and four midshipmen before three justices at the above tavern, appointed on purpose to examine the prisoners. After four hours examination together and separately, we were delivered to two constables and seven soldiers to be committed to Mill Prison for High Treason. At 4 P.M., 3rd June 1777, I arrived at Mill Prison within quarter a mile of Plymouth town.[10]

Cutler and Connor were among the first of about three thousand Americans, mostly naval personnel, who would find themselves committed to Mill (also referred to as Old Mill or Millbay) or Forton (Fortune) prisons during the period 1777–83. These rebel captives, serving various periods of detention, experienced the trials and tribulations common to prisoners in most wars. Several of them, including Cutler and Connor, wrote revealing and compelling accounts of their detentions. Together these Yankee prisoners, despite their ominous plight, played a small, though notable, part in the eventual outcome of the American Revolution.

I

These Americans were not the first prisoners of war in Britain nor were they the first held within the confines of Forton and Mill. An examination of British administrative practices and their implementation prior to 1775 offers a background understanding of the treatment these rebels encountered.

Long before the rebellion in its American colonies, Britain had to accommodate war prisoners—mostly naval personnel—within its island bounds. However, prior to the War of the League of Augsburg (1689–97) and the establishment of a Commission for Sick and Hurt Seamen and the Exchange of Prisoners of War as a subordinate body to the Lords Commissioners of the Admiralty, no formal administrative agency was given responsibility in this matter.[11] Even then, the Commission functioned only on a temporary basis. Its duties (such as overseeing the care of sick and wounded royal seamen and of captured seamen) were not yet formalized. The commission was reestablished during the War of the Spanish Succession (1702–13), but again on a temporary basis, with unclear procedures. Adding to the lack of consistency was the sporadic, sometimes conflicting, intrusion in these matters by one of the secretaries of state of the Privy Council. The secretaries' duties, though, were usually not in the realm of specific prisoner supervision but rather in the formulation of exchange procedures for those captives whose national homelands lay within their respective areas of concern.[12]

The shortcomings of this overlapping and indistinct system of superintending prisoners of war in Britain are apparent. It also became evident, as the eighteenth century progressed, that England's political and imperial interests would involve the nation in further, more extensive conflicts with its European rivals. Perhaps in acknowledgment, the Commission for Sick and Hurt Seamen and the Exchange of Prisoners of War was made a permanent body in 1740, a year after the onset of the war with Spain. The makeup of the commission afterward varied between two and five individuals: one was a physician and the others were nonmedical civilians.[13]

The action making the commission a permanent group still subordinate to the Lords Commissioners of the Admiralty proved fortuitous. Within four years, the "Jenkins Ear" hostilities with Spain expanded into the War of the Austrian Succession (1744–48) in which France and several German states were added to Britain's adversaries. The Treaty of Aix-la-Chapelle (1748) did not end the conflict for long. Hostilities that began in America in 1754 brought Britain into an expanded war less than two years later. This new conflict, usually called the Seven Years' War, saw England again battling France, Spain (after 1761), Austria, and several German principalities. The War of the Austrian Succession and, especially, the Seven Years' War resulted in significant increases in the number of captives sent to the British Isles for detention. It was calculated, for example, that by the end of 1756 there were 7,261 prisoners of war in Great Britain and that this figure had increased more than fivefold by the end of hostilities in 1763.[14] Such figures indicated the need for permanency in the Admiralty's Commission for Sick and Hurt Seamen.

Most of the prisoners in Britain during the Austrian Succession and Seven Years' wars were naval personnel, and they were primarily French or Spanish along with a sprinkling of other Europeans. Controlling large numbers of prisoners produced additional expenses for belligerents, particularly in the more lengthy conflicts. Consequently, the combatants usually sought to arrange expeditious, orderly prisoner exchanges, commonly referred to as "cartels." Although Britain's ambassadors, respective secretaries of state from the Privy Council, Commissioners of the Admiralty, and at times members of Parliament normally participated in making the formal exchange agreements with England's adversaries, it devolved upon the Commission for Sick and Hurt Seamen to oversee actual exchanges.[15]

The matter of establishing detention locales for the prisoners was essential. During the Seven Years' War, a system of parole was used whereby captured officers of a certain rank, who gave their word to abide by specific provisions (i.e., not to escape), were permitted to reside in selected communities. But these paroles were available to only a small percentage of the total number of prisoners.[16]

Two more permanent methods were used to house the great majority of the captives until their exchanges: prison ships (hulks) and land-based prisons. (Warships that were out of commission, called guardships, also were used occasionally to hold prisoners—though primarily on a temporary basis.) The employment of large, usually unseaworthy vessels for incarceration was a long-established practice in Britain. The ships themselves were anchored in scattered English seaport towns such as Portsmouth, Yarmouth, Plymouth, and Chatham. Obviously these ships only could hold a limited number of detainees, but their offshore locations made supervision easier and escape more difficult compared to land-based prisons. They were also more unhealthy than the prisons on shore, though the death rate on board the ships, except for epidemics, was reportedly only slightly higher than for the land-based prisons. Undoubtedly, however, prisoners sent to these forbidding hulks experienced long days of tedious, frustrating, and unbroken suffering.[17]

A wide variety of sites served as detention centers in Britain itself. In London, Liverpool, and Yarmouth, enemy prisoners were placed in local prisons. At Edinburgh and at Portchester Castle, Hampshire (said to be England's oldest regular war prison), they were confined in existing castles. At Winchester they were sent to converted barracks; at Kergilliack (in Cornwall), to a farm adapted for the purpose; at Sissinghurst, in Kent, to a former mansion; and at Knowle, outside Bristol, to an abandoned pottery works.[18]

The sudden upsurge of captives in Britain during the Seven Years' War caused serious supervision problems for the Admiralty and its subordinate Commission for Sick and Hurt Seamen. Although these agencies tried to solve the problems of overcrowding, their success was negligible. Prison ships were limited in number, as was their capacity to hold prisoners, most of whom had been taken from French merchantmen, privateers, or regular navy vessels. Consequently, royal officials relied more and more on larger land-based detention centers to confine the prisoners while exchanges could be worked out.

Besides the previously cited internment centers, two other sites were adapted for this purpose: Forton, in Hampshire, and Mill, in Devon. Both prisons had facilities for such large numbers of captives that, during the Seven Years' War, prisoners from other overcrowded detention locales were frequently transferred there. Thus, in April 1761, almost two thousand prisoners were reportedly sent from Portchester Castle to the more spacious confines of Forton Gaol seven miles to the south.[19]

But whether alien captives were confined in prisons ashore or on the prison ship hulks, the Admiralty and the Commission for Sick and Hurt Seamen were ultimately responsible for supervising them until their exchange or release. For the most part, the treatment proffered by these higher level British officials during the mideighteenth-century conflicts was not unduly harsh. This situation remained even after allegations during the Seven Years' War that French officials were dealing with English prisoners in an arbitrary and unwarranted manner.[20] It was also true that after the financially strapped French court in 1759 stopped monetary support for its servicemen held in Great Britain, the English government gave assistance to these alien captives, as well as to their own detainees in France. In addition, British civil servants made no deliberate attempts to maltreat or starve their captives. In 1757, French officials even admitted that, whenever possible, their cross-channel foes had provided better bedding materials for the prisoners than they themselves had. Two years later, a writer in a Brussels newspaper offered broader endorsement of British prisoner-of-war care. The author claimed that "the English feel for their captives as men and cannot but pity enemies in distress who are not in a capacity to hurt them."[21] The British also had broadened their rather liberal parole system for certain officers, and, in addition, they sometimes gave enlisted-rank captives in prisons ashore opportunities to work outside the prison or to make handicrafts for sale to civilians.

These, then, were the principal features of British policies regarding prisoners of war prior to 1763. The detainees were usually in the hands of the Lords Commissioners of the Admiralty and its subordinate body, the Commission for Sick and Hurt Seamen and the Exchange of Prisoners. In the formulation of prisoner policies such as repatriation, an appropriate secretary of state had input, as did British ambassadors abroad. The general objective of these royal officials was to provide the most satisfactory treatment possible for the prisoners until expeditious exchanges could take place. In doing so, they normally sought to follow contemporary humanitarian precepts regarding the treatment of captives presented by theorists such as Baron Montesquieu and Emmerich de Vattel. Yet, despite the well-meaning efforts of these high government officials and of some sympathetic civilians who offered relief, the prisoner-of-war system had significant shortcomings. Some of these shortcomings resulted from unexpected circumstances, such as overcrowding or monetary and supply shortages. Some of the imperfections, however, stemmed from inappropriate or unwarranted actions by prison personnel. Captives held in the various detention centers and even a few officers on parole complained about faults in the system, but little was done by way of rectification. And for many of the prisoners, particularly those in land-based prisons or those on parole, escape attempts were the obvious solution to their discomforting situation.[22]

II

Several of these practices and their effects would see considerable repetition in the years that followed the April 1775 outbreak of hostilities in Massachusetts. However, the American Revolution also produced some distinctly different circumstances for American captives in the British Isles. Such men were not nationals of a sovereign, recognized government, as were French and Spanish prisoners. Indeed, to most royal officials, beginning with the British troops who confronted the minutemen on Lexington Green, the colonials were regarded as rebels against His Majesty's legitimate government.[23]

Prisoners were captured by both sides in the wake of the Lexington-Concord skirmishes. General Thomas Gage, commanding British forces then bottled up in Boston, mentioned this circumstance in a letter of 13 May 1775 to the earl of Dartmouth, colonial secretary for America: "Five officers have been taken prisoner. . . . We have taken six or seven prisoners who are on shipboard." By the end of the following month, when General George Washington had officially assumed command of the newly created Continental Army, the opposing forces held even more captives. Gage's troops seized Americans at Breed's (Bunker) Hill on 17 June, while earlier, on 9 May, their adversaries, in a daring raid led by Colonel Ethan Allen, had captured the entire garrison at Fort Ticonderoga, New York.[24]

In the first disordered months of warfare, there was little concerted thought given to formulating policies for treatment of prisoners by either the British commanders or the newly gathered Continental Congress. Several states accordingly assigned the matter to revolutionary committees or to particular individuals. And a note of concern about rebel intentions was expressed by one royal official on 29 May: "They [the rebels] wish to take as many prisoners as possible. . . . They say that [then] whenever any of their people are mistreated by General Gage, they will use the people in their power in the same way, life for life." The following August an acrimonious exchange of words did occur between Generals Washington and Gage over the Continental commander's charges of abuse allegedly inflicted on American officers held in Boston jails. Gage rejected the accusations, refusing even to recognize these captured Yankees as legitimate prisoners of war. Nevertheless, during this early period of hostilities, opposing commanders did agree to several exchanges of captives.[25]

By the end of 1776, policies on captured combatants in America had become more defined. On the American side, the Continental Congress, with the recommendation of General Washington, appointed Major David Franks to be commissary for all British prisoners. Franks' brother was an army contractor in London who had influential friends, but this relationship did not produce any signed agreements with the British government regarding either prisoner supervision or exchanges. The treatment of British captives improved with the appointment of Elias Boudinot as the next prisoner commissary. Paroles and exchanges of available detainees became more orderly, even though they were sometimes delayed.[26]

However British commanders in America during this period confronted the greater problem in this matter because they held many more captives than their adversaries. Despite several exchanges and prisoner paroles, General Sir William Howe reported on 3 December 1776 that he still held almost forty-five hundred prisoners, most of them soldiers from his recent New York campaign. Even with the release of two thousand enlisted militiamen, the general was left with the vexing task of finding new confinement facilities in addition to New York City's existing jails. Waterfront warehouses, churches, college buildings, and even the city hall were converted into prisons at one time or another. In October 1776, *Whitby,* a transport vessel moored at Wallabout Bay near Brooklyn, was to serve as the first prison ship anchored around New York. Eventually the death rate on prison hulks during most of the remainder of the Revolution, especially on the infamous *Jersey,* greatly exceeded the previously cited prison ship mortality in Britain.[27]

III

Aside from the problem of finding sites in America to incarcerate the multitude of captured soldiers, at the end of 1776 the British ministry faced the problem of locating detention centers for rebel sailors closer to home. To the surprise of many in England, hostilities were not confined to land warfare in the distant New World. American defiance of royal rule steadily expanded to challenge British sea lanes in the vast North Atlantic.

The array of brigs, brigantines, sloops, schooners, and other vessels fitted out by the Americans for their maritime forays fell into three groupings: privateers, state naval vessels, and ships of the Continental Navy. Privateers, such as those in which seamen Timothy Connor and Samuel Cutler served, were usually speedy, lightly armed vessels authorized by Congress or a state government to seize or destroy enemy ships and generally disrupt enemy shipping. Although deprecated as "legalized piracy" by one contemporary naval historian, privateering, in fact, was recognized in the law of nations. Furthermore, unlike pirates, privateersmen were bound by internationally recognized laws and practices of war. American seamen had been attracted to these unconventional, risky, yet potentially quite lucrative enterprises in previous wars. During the American Revolution, even more men signed on to the privateers' often far-ranging cruises. Massachusetts itself gave out

1,524 privateering commissions. Marblehead, one of the state's main seaports, was said to have long practiced privateering, even passing it down from father to son. And the U.S. government itself issued almost two thousand of these authorizations for marauding.[28]

Eleven of the thirteen original states established and supported their own state navies aside from privateering. The number and type of ships varied, as did their scope of operations; often their activities were not much different from those of privateers. However, some of them accomplished particularly effective services for the patriot cause. The Connecticut State Navy, established in July 1775, emerged as one of the more notable fleets in this category; most of the other state flotillas performed a more limited role during the Revolution.[29]

The formal beginning of the Continental Navy came in October 1775, when the Congress, on the recommendation of its Naval Committee, appropriated $100,000 in Continental currency to fit out four vessels to intercept British shipping off New England. It also named Rhode Island's Esek Hopkins commander of this new fleet, though subsequent delays hindered its early activities. By March 1776, Hopkins finally acted, taking an eight-ship flotilla on an expedition that captured Nassau in the Bahama Islands. Offensive actions by the Continental Navy continued throughout the remainder of that year. These undertakings included John Paul Jones's seizure of prizes off Nova Scotia and raiding in Britain's home waters by means of the small brig *Reprisal,* under Captain Lambert Wickes.[30]

Regardless of the category of ships involved, American operations in 1776 produced trade-offs. Rebel raiders took British prizes, and in turn, many raiders were seized by royal warships. On 2 May of that year, Lord George Germain, colonial secretary, issued formal instructions to the Royal Navy "for taking [any] ships of the rebellious colonies," but such directives already had been implemented. One particular example was the poorly manned Continental Army brigantine *Washington.* She had been taken near Boston by HMS *Fowey* in December 1775, and her crew sent to England. Once there, most of them abandoned the rebel cause for service in the Royal Navy or on East India Company ships. (Officers from *Washington* were ordered sent back to America, as were several rebel soldiers who had been captured earlier in Canada.) During the year following *Washington*'s seizure, other rebel vessels, including Samuel Cutler's *Dalton,* likewise were taken. This fact was reflected in increasing reports to London from such widely

Capture of Continental Navy Brig *Lexington* by H M Cutter *Alert* September 1777. Courtesy National Maritime Museum. Greenwich, London.

scattered outposts as Gibraltar and the West Indies, listing detained American naval personnel. Included in the accounts were queries to the government concerning the disposition of the captives.[31]

Britain's ministry under Lord North was well aware of the increasing and perplexing problem of these particular prisoners and the consequent need to make some disposition of the men. Legally such American naval captives could not be considered prisoners of war, the Declaration of Independence notwithstanding. At the same time, however, a legitimately sanctioned system would have to be established to deal with them. It was not simply their growing numbers, but also that American and Canadian detention centers were too overcrowded. Furthermore the captured mariners were increasingly reluctant to abandon their revolutionary principles.

Action to resolve the issue of rebel seamen captured on the high seas emerged during the latter part of 1776. On 6 August Lord George Germain, seeking to satisfy Admiralty inquiries, wrote to Chief Justice Lord William Mansfield for his private opinion concerning four American naval prisoners in London who had repeatedly declined to enter royal service. Two days later, Mansfield replied to Germain. It was the justice's opinion that the Americans should be sent to guardships or prison ships, because if they were placed in prisons ashore they "might be [so] wickedly advised as to claim to be considered as subjects and apply for *habeas corpus,*" thereby obtaining their release.[32]

Mansfield's advice, while logical, was nonetheless impractical. There were only a limited number of guardships or prison ships available in Britain, and for the most part these were unprepared. Consequently, with no sign of imminent suppression of the American rebellion, despite General Howe's victories, the ministry concluded there was but one solution to the problem—a suspension of *habeas corpus* for those naval prisoners brought to Britain.

Lord North initiated action to this end in the House of Commons. On 6 February 1777, the artful prime minister announced to a lightly attended session that a bill was to be introduced for debate which would deal firmly but fairly with those rebels captured in the commission "of the crime of high treason . . . or the act of piracy on the high seas." North noted that new sanctions were needed to keep these men interned because existing *habeas corpus* laws covered only internal rebellion or a threatened invasion and thus did not apply to these captives. Evidently, he also believed that a law passed two months before prohibiting American trade was insufficient, because it failed to mention specifically imprisonment for captured sailors. And North pointed out that confining apprehended seamen in existing detention centers such as "common gaols" was too impractical. He therefore requested and received permission from the House to propose a bill that would resolve the matter.[33] The day after North's address, Lord Germain formally introduced the portentous bill.

A Bill to empower his Majesty to secure and detain Persons charged with, or suspected of, the Crime of High Treason committed in North America, or on the High Seas, or the Crime of Piracy.

Whereas a rebellion and war have been openly and traitorously levied and carried on in certain of his Majesty's colonies and plantations in America, and acts of treason and piracy have been committed upon the ships and goods of his Majesty's subjects; and many persons have been seized and taken, who are expressly charged or strongly suspected of such treasons and felonies, and many more such persons may be hereafter so seized and taken:

And whereas such persons have been or may be brought into this kingdom, and into other parts of his Majesty's dominions; and it may be inconvenient in many such cases to proceed forthwith to the trial of such criminals, and at the same time of evil example to suffer them to go at large:

Be it therefore enacted by the King's most excellent Majesty, by and with the advice and consent of the Lords spiritual and temporal, and Commons, in this present Parliament assembled, and by the authority of the same, that all and every person or persons, who have been or shall hereafter be seized or taken in the act of high treason, committed in any of the colonies, or on the high seas, or in the act of piracy, or who are or shall be charged with, or suspected of the said crimes, and who have been or shall be committed for the said crimes, or either of them, or for suspicion of them, or either of them, in any part of his Majesty's dominions, to the common gaol, or any other place of confinement specially appointed for that purpose, by warrant under his Majesty's sign manual, by any magistrate having competent authority in that behalf (who is hereby authorised to commit such persons to the place so to be appointed) all and every such person and persons shall and may be thereupon secured and detained in safe custody without bail or mainprize, until the ——— and that no judge or justice of peace shall bail or try any such person or persons, without order from his Majesty's most honorable privy council, signed by ——— of the said privy council, until the said ——— any law, statute, or usage, to the contrary in any wise notwithstanding.

And be it further enacted by the authority aforesaid, that this Act shall continue and be in force until the said ——— and no longer.[34]

The ministry's bill caused lengthy and acrimonious debate in Parliament. Prominent opponents of the American war and of the king's ministers, including John Wilkes, Charles James Fox, Isaac Barré, and Lord Abingdon, vociferously attacked the proposed legislation. Wilkes, long a Crown antagonist, emphatically declared that the intended legislation, which he called a "cruel, persecuting bill," would bring "oppression and tyranny through every part of the realm." He added; "I will not arm ministers with an unconstitutional power." Fox, eloquently defending the precept of *habeas corpus,* denounced the measure and, implying a deeper government intent, warned that the bill's wording revealed "strides not only to destroy the liberty of America, but this country likewise." Barré repudiated the pending statute dealing with the rebellion as the "worst of all, and would be productive of massacre and retaliation if not of more alarming consequences nearer home—America must be reclaimed, not conquered or subdued." He also criticized the bill as "hasty, ill advised, and intemperate."[35] In the House of Lords, Abingdon, like Barré, Wilkes, and Fox, saw the bill as a violation of fundamental constitutional principles. He rejected it as "shocking to humanity" and "averse from that now exploded virtue of universal benevolence."[36]

Lord North, himself an able debater, was prepared for these

challenges. He defended his bill as a necessity for strengthening the government during this critical period. He noted that, in his opinion, Britain was in a "fair way of subduing America," and he did not anticipate extending the act beyond the end of the year. Meanwhile England's maritime commerce must be protected. Finally the prime minister emphatically denied that his government had the intent of introducing "any unconstitutional precedents or designating any power to the crown or them [the ministry], which could be employed to oppressive or bad purposes."[37]

In the end the king's ministry had its way. Parliament adopted the bill, known as North's Act, with negligible changes, on 3 March 1777. (It had passed its third reading in the House of Commons by the very comfortable margin of 112 to 33.) The act would remain in effect for five years.[38] Enactment of this legislation meant success for Lord North's efforts to obtain legal authorization for imprisoning captured rebel seamen who preyed on Britain's sea lanes, but the statute had a distinctly different meaning for the American sailors affected by it. For these men indeterminately confined in a distant land, the act tested their integrity, morality, patience, cohesiveness, courage, and perhaps most importantly, their adherence to a rather singular cause.

2

The Prisons and the Prisoners

During the five years following the passage of Lord North's Act, prisons at several locales scattered throughout Great Britain were opened, primarily on a temporary basis, to hold captured American seamen. The proximity of royal naval facilities and British trade routes were usually prime considerations in choosing such sites. In Ireland, a few hundred men were detained at Kinsale, a small seaport in County Cork. Edinburgh again served as an internment site, though only a small number of Americans were incarcerated in the Scottish city. Pembroke, at the western edge of Wales, held a total of forty Americans in June 1779; all but three "herded together in an old house."[1]

In England the Norfolk fishing port of Yarmouth was used to imprison a limited number of Americans, as was Deal on the English Channel. London housed a small batch of the captives, almost invariably on a transient basis. On the Irish Sea, Liverpool, England's second largest port, also held some rebel prisoners, and, occasionally, a few were listed by the Admiralty in such scattered sites as Bristol, Falmouth, Shrewsbury, Weymouth, and Chatham. The total number of American prisoners kept in all these detention locales, including prison ships, amounted to only a fraction of the total number of Americans held in Britain during the war. The royal government had intended early on that the great majority of them were to be concentrated at a specific locale. Shortly after North's Act was promulgated, Forton and Mill prisons were prepared as the primary internment centers.[2]

I

These two English detention compounds do not, in contemporary histories, carry the intense negative connotations of confinement sites such as the notorious North American prison ships of the Revolution. They also do not rank with the worst prisons of post-Revolutionary wars where American servicemen endured inhumane treatment. For example, conditions at neither of these English prisons equaled those suffered by Union soldiers at Andersonville, Georgia, in the Civil War. Similarly, neither English gaol came close to imposing the terrible brutality, privation, and degradation incurred by Americans in secluded Japanese prison camps during World War II, the wretched cold of North Korean compounds, or the cruel, sweltering heat of North Vietnamese detention. The English prisons were located in regions with the best climates in the country and did not have the extreme, unsanitary, pestilence-ridden features of prison ships.[3]

Forton, in the late eighteenth century, existed as a tiny crossroads hamlet within the district (liberty) of Alverstoke, in Hampshire. Located on part of a peninsula lying between Southampton and Portsmouth, its place name was derived from a combination of "tun" (i.e., a settlement) and "ford" (as in "to ford a body of water"). Forton hamlet itself was adjacent to a fordable stream (Forton Lake) which flowed into Portsmouth Harbor. A small country tavern, along with two or three other structures, comprised the original settlement that lay astride the twisting road to Fareham, four miles to the northwest. This same country road also ran downward from Forton in a slightly southeastward direction a little over one mile into Gosport. A smaller country lane or path extended south and then westward through Forton to a nearby farmstead.[4]

Gosport was the closest significant settlement to Forton crossroads. It probably contained about one to two thousand inhabitants living within its fortifications. By 1775 it was becoming more and more prominent as a victualling port for the Royal Navy. A guidebook from that year described it as "a very neat town with an elegant trade in it, the buildings are mostly good and the inhabitants genteel." The same author added that the community also boasted "paved roads," a chapel, and a good inn for travelers.[5]

Portsmouth was the largest urban center in the immediate vicinity. By the time of the American Revolution, it contained almost twenty-thousand inhabitants and was most easily accessible to Gosport by numerous small ferries that crossed the narrow part of Portsmouth Harbor.[6] The seaport had been the main base of the Royal Navy since the time of Henry VIII, and in 1775, almost all of the town's landmarks were related to maritime pursuits. They included not only the Royal Naval dockyards, arsenals, barracks,

Portion of 1782 map showing Portsmouth, Gosport and Forton. Forton is shown just to the west-northwest of Gosport. By permission of the British Library, Add 1553 F 57.

ropehouses, gun wharfs, and harbor facilities but also the King's Mill, warehouses, breweries, inns, taverns, and shops. The elegant main thoroughfare, High Street, reflected Portsmouth's prominence in social and cultural affairs. The imposing St. Thomas of Canterbury 'parish' Church, (later Cathedral), located astride the street, and the presence of so many military and naval personnel, seemed to add to the town's Crown connections.[7]

Forton Gaol had developed from these Hampshire surroundings well before the American War for Independence. However, when construction began at the crossroads hamlet in 1713, the buildings were intended for a hospital, not a prison. This fact was clearly evident in part of a legal statement involving the merchant and land speculator Nathaniel Jackson: "Mr. Jackson was before his marriage and at the time of his death possessed of a hospital called Forton Hospital near Gosport which he imployed in Entertaining of sick and wounded Seamen of the Royal navy, by contract with the Commissioners for Sick and Wounded Seamen, and which for that purpose was furnished with men near 700 beds and other furniture for such a service and not for private use." With the passage of time and recurrent medical shortcomings at this facility,

a new, better-situated hospital for royal seamen, called Haslar, was built immediately south of Gosport. After its opening in 1753, Haslar was used more frequently for ailing British mariners, so that with the large influx of prisoners during the Seven Years War, Forton found itself converted into a detention center.[8]

Extant maps and personal accounts offer good descriptions of Forton's physical features about the time it was reopened as a prison in June 1777. The main entrance to the facility lay at the end of a pathway off the Gosport-Fareham Road. The prison grounds comprised a total of about three and one-half acres surrounded mainly by farm fields and private estates. The structures, aside from administrative quarters, consisted principally of two spacious buildings which reportedly could hold up to two thousand inmates.[9] During the war in America, one building was used for lower rank captives and one for higher officers. (No parole opportunities within Britain were provided, in contrast to the practice adopted for officers of recognized foreign powers. As a result, these men at first were kept in the same prison area as their crewmen.) There was one airing ground situated between Forton's two main buildings and another nearby, reportedly "on three quarters of an acre of level ground." In December 1777, the Admiralty approved the construction of a shed on this airing ground; it was open on all sides, and seats were placed under it to sit on during hot or sultry weather.[10]

Eight-foot-high iron pickets driven into the ground about eight inches apart surrounded the entire area. Soon after the prison was reopened, the Commissioners for Sick and Hurt Seamen wrote the Admiralty recommending that *chevaux-de-frize* (iron spikes) be placed on the walls of Forton's confinement buildings, but evidently this escape deterrent was not added. Sanitation requirements were not a problem; drainage and disposal were expedited by the proximity of Forton Lake about two hundred feet away, on the opposite side of Fareham Road.[11]

The picturesque, rural, coastal county of Devon in southwestern England became the site of Britain's other major detention center for American seamen. It was at various times called Old Mill, Mill, or in later years, Millbay. The prison was located on a windswept tidal headland (once occupied by several windmills) which lay about one quarter of a mile from the coastal centers of Plymouth Town and Plymouth Dock (Devonport). Its name apparently was derived from a tidal mill that existed at the head of the bay from early Norman times until about 1600. When the prison reopened in May 1777, these two Devon communities were separate entities;

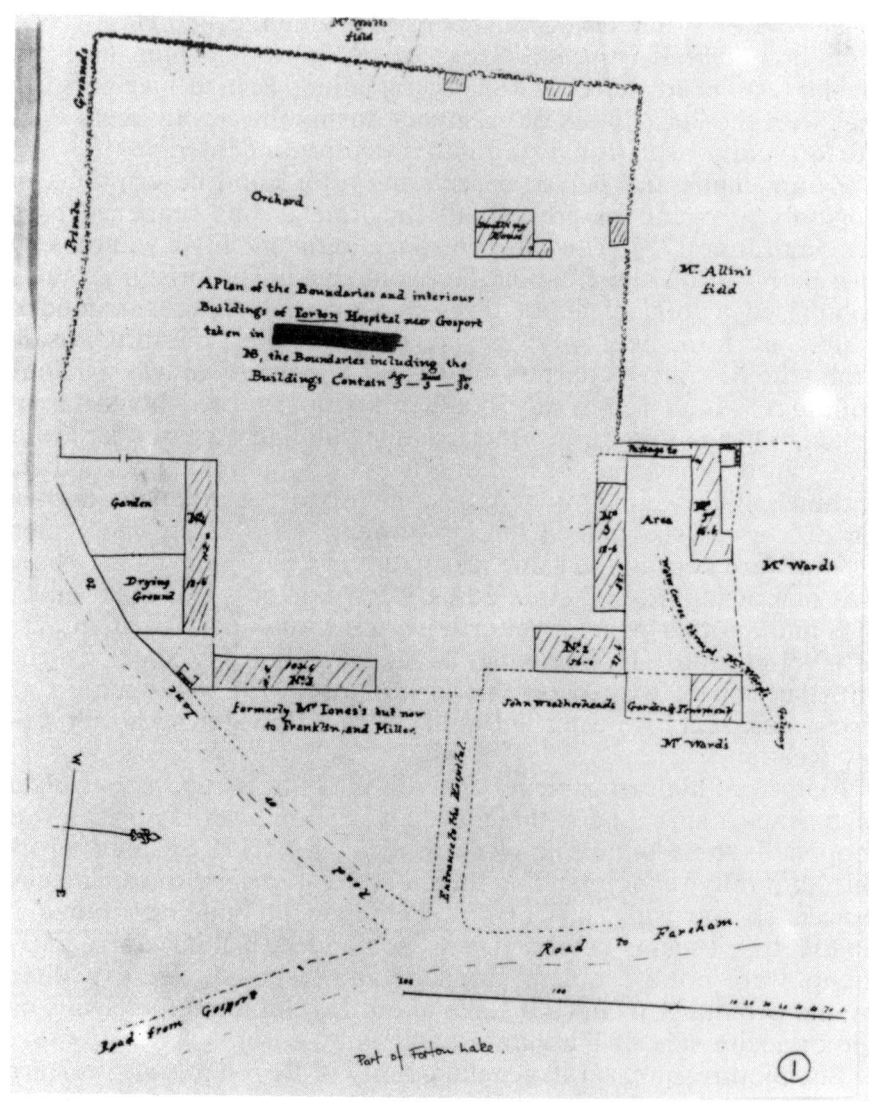

Plan of Forton Hospital, 1755. Copied by Richard Howlett in 1860. Public Record Office, Kew. Reproduced with permission of Her Majesty's Stationery Office.

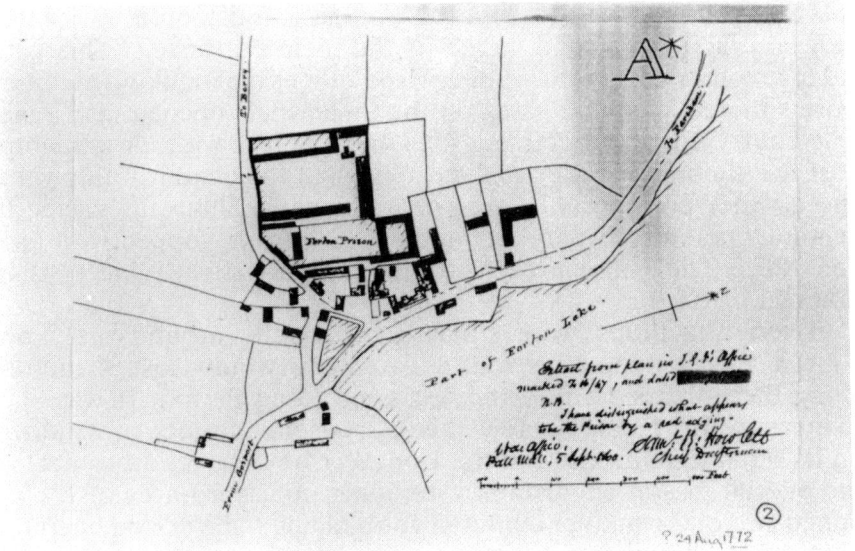

Plan of Forton Prison, 1772. Copied by Samuel Howlett in 1860. Public Record Office Kew. Reproduced with permission of Her Majesty's Stationery Office.

Plymouth Dock was still the common title for the westernmost of the two towns.[12]

By the end of the seventeenth century, the original windmills had become less used or profitable. Consequently, when the need for new prisoner-of-war facilities arose during the War of the League of Augsburg, the Commissioners for Sick and Hurt Seamen and the Exchange of Prisoners, in 1695, had overseen the replacement of the old windmills with an internment site for about three hundred men. Larger, permanent prison structures were built during the War of the Austrian Succession. These new facilities made it possible to hold many more captives, so that by 1762, when almost seven thousand prisoners were reportedly under guard in Devon, Old Mill or Mill controlled the largest single number of such detainees.[13]

A map survey of the Plymouth area, composed in 1778, along with prisoners' descriptions offer reasonably clear pictures of the appearance of Mill Gaol. A curving road leading from Plymouth Town westward to Plymouth Dock ran by the front of the prison. Across the road were several smaller buildings, most evidently placed there to service the gaol. A small woodland or orchard lay near these structures. High double stone walls about twenty feet apart surrounded Mill Prison. An iron gate, located on the center wall and facing the road, acted as the main entrance.[14] This gate led to an outer courtyard where prison offices and cooking facilities were situated. Wooden gates on the inner walls opened into a sizable courtyard, about 250 feet long and 158 feet wide. A tall lamppost for illuminating the area was placed at the center of this yard, and a water pump was located near the gate. The walls varied in height from ten to twenty feet and were all frieze-topped with broken glass. The entire area of the prison was slightly larger than that of Forton.[15]

Prisoner facilities were situated principally around the inner courtyard. Most notable was a two-story windowless structure along the north side, referred to as the Long Prison. It was said to measure 132 feet by 20 feet. The purposeful absence of windows on its outside walls allowed the Long Prison to function as part of the overall prison enclosures. The inner courtyard area also contained two other smaller confinement buildings, the prison hospital, plus other administrative structures. A path, evidently used for disposal purposes, led downhill a few hundred feet to Mill Bay itself. Taken together, these features reveal that Mill, which was built specifically as a prison, was a much more secure confinement site than the converted Forton Hospital. Manpower augmented this structural security. Thus, one prisoner observed that, when he entered Mill in January 1782, its inner gate was "guarded with soldiers with fixed bayonets."[16]

The adjacent communities of Plymouth Town and Plymouth Dock were considerably larger and more prominent than Forton's nearby Gosport hamlet. When Mill Prison reopened in 1777, Plymouth probably counted about thirteen thousand residents and Plymouth Dock, a few more. They were the largest communities in Devon, and both possessed attributes giving them particular recognition in that corner of England. Plymouth Town, with its excellent harbor and protective citadel, was known especially for its considerable overseas commerce.[17] Eighteenth-century Plymouth Dock had augmented its neighbor's seaborne activities with impressive naval yards, victualling establishments, and its status as the district's military and naval headquarters.[18]

Other conspicuous details accented this West Country region. A good road system connecting the region to the British capital lessened the towns' isolation. Politically, the two Devon towns gave adherence to the king's ministry, most noticeably through Lord Barrington, who represented the constituency in Parliament. The Church of England was still strong in the region though recent

Portion of a 1778 map of Plymouth by Richard Cowl. Mill Prison can be seen immediately west of the town. By permission of the British Library, K Top XI 83.

religious revivals had produced an upsurge in the adherence to Methodism and other dissenter sects.[19]

II

Beyond the external settings and physical features of Forton and Mill, there is the relevant matter of the prisons' internal administration. The staffing of both prisons was ultimately the responsibility of the Admiralty. The secretaries of state for the Southern and Northern departments were informed of, but generally excluded themselves from, these details. In actual practice the Admiralty itself performed only a limited role in regard to Revolutionary War captives. As in earlier wars, it generally accepted and confirmed recommendations from the Commissioners for Sick and Hurt Seamen and the Exchange of Prisoners and left this subordinate body to implement the decisions.[20] Accordingly, each prison was directed by a keeper or agent who was directly answerable to the

Commission for Sick and Hurt Seamen. At Forton, the Commissioner chose John Newsham for the post, and at Mill, William Cowdry (Cowdray), (Cawdry) was selected. Ranking below the keeper were a secretary, a turnkey, deputies, clerks, stewards, cooks, laborers, and a per diem physician. Local militia units or companies of invalids usually served as guards at both prisons. Salaries for these prison officials ranged from £100 per annum for the keeper to 5 shillings a week for the laborers.[21]

We have few details about the resident staffs who managed day-to-day activities at the two English prisons. Much more information is understandably available concerning the Lords of Admiralty. Three members of this governmental body were particularly noteworthy. The earl of Sandwich had been on the Admiralty and was first lord during the late 1740s. He was appointed first lord once again in January 1771, with the support of Lord North. Sir Hugh Palliser had begun his naval career as a midshipman in 1735. After forty-years of service (and partly because of his known Tory sentiments), he was promoted to rear admiral and to a seat on the Admiralty itself. Sir Philip Stephens, Admiralty secretary since 1763, eventually served in this capacity for thirty years. Stephens was the main link between the Admiralty and the Commission for Sick and Hurt Seamen.[22]

Members of the Commission for Sick and Hurt Seamen and the Exchange of Prisoners lacked the prominence, titles, and wealth of the Admiralty members. Instead they typically were undistinguished bureaucrats like the agents Cowdry and Newsham. The commissioners, also referred to as the Sick and Hurt Board, consisted of a two-man panel in 1777, but by the beginning of 1783, it had increased to five members. A total of seven individuals served on the Commission during this six-year period. Individual commissioners made periodic inspections of both Forton and Mill after their openings, though commissioner John Bell was the primary representative cited by name in prisoner accounts, following his initial visitation in 1777.[23]

Following the adoption of North's Act in March 1777, the commissioners assumed major responsibility for reopening the two detention centers as quickly as practicable. On 27 May of that year, Mill received its first American prisoners. Its companion prison was not opened for another three weeks; bureaucratic mismanagement was the ostensible reason.[24] Another unstated motive may have been the Admiralty's apprehensions over security following an incident of attempted sabotage in Portsmouth.

On 7 December 1776, James Aitken, a roguish Scot, had attempted to burn Portsmouth's Royal Naval Dockyard. Aitken, also known as Jack the Painter, had recently returned to Britain from several years' stay in the American colonies, where he had given his ardent support to the Revolutionary cause. Aitken later gave an unsubstantiated confession, in which he claimed that he had received support in Paris for his actions. His support, he asserted, had come not only from French officials but also from Silas Deane of Congress's Secret Committee of Correspondence. Aitken's confession, made after his arrest in February 1777, was unavailing. He was convicted of treason and publicly executed the following month in Portsmouth.[25] It is likely that the commissioners, obviously concerned about the protection of Britain's vital naval base and the limited security at Forton, wished to take every precaution before reopening the nearby prison to American rebel seamen.

III

These, then, are details relating to the two large English naval prisons, their administration, and their reopening in 1777. But what had prompted the approximately three thousand American seamen who came to be confined in them to challenge presumptuously the world's then mightiest naval power? "We dare oppose them," boasted one Connecticut naval captain as he took his ship into battle against a larger British warship. Still, what had led him and his crew to attempt such a hazardous venture in their often outgunned, usually poorly equipped vessels?[26] Mention has been made of the disparate authorizations under which these colonial mariners went to sea. But who were they in fact, both as a group and as individuals? The answers reveal much about their subsequent conduct within their distant captivity.

The Americans at Forton and Mill had behind them a maritime heritage stretching back to the first colonial settlements. In fact the first ship constructed in English North America, a thirty-ton pinnace named *Virginia,* was built during the winter of 1607–8 at George Popham's ill-fated Kennebec River community in New England. Almost two decades later, the Pilgrim colonists in Plymouth Colony were taking advantage of plentiful lumber resources to assemble small vessels for trade and fishing. The launching of the bark *Blessing of the Bay* in 1631, less than a year after the Puritan Great Migration to Massachusetts Bay, is a further example of early shipbuilding. Although New Englanders were the first colonists to react strongly to the lure of the seas, other English colonists in America followed suit.[27] The passage of the Navigation Acts in the seventeenth century sparked a large increase in ship-building throughout all the colonies. Thus, Philadelphians were constructing vessels by 1683, and New York reportedly had three active shipyards at the beginning of the eighteenth century. By that time, the southern colonies, despite their scattered plantations and labor limitations, had constructed some small draft vessels for use in their economy.[28]

By the onset of the American Revolution, the colonists had expanded both shipbuilding and overseas commerce. The fact that ships could be built more cheaply in America than in England increased the tonnage of vessels built in the colonies seven and one-half times during the period 1700–1774. By 1774, it was even estimated that one third of Britain's commercial fleet was of American construction. Most of these craft were less than fifty tons burden, but ships were built for overseas trade ranging between one and three hundred tons. As the shipbuilding industry burgeoned, colonial commercial ventures also broadened from an earlier focus on the coastal or fishing trades. By 1775 the colonial merchant marine had expanded to more distant ports, not only in Great Britain and the West Indies, but also in Africa and elsewhere.[29]

Most of the estimated thirty thousand mariners who served on American fishing or commercial vessels were not born to the sea. Primarily, they were land men, mostly from Northern homes, attracted to nautical employment from diverse colonial backgrounds and circumstances. Some were farmers' sons with limited inclination or opportunity for an agrarian life; others were the offspring of artisans, small traders, or merchants, who also lacked desire or opportunity to follow their fathers' occupations. Others were indigent or transient laborers, servants, errant husbands, petty criminals, deserters, or runaway or freed slaves. Still others were men or boys who had been beguiled or impressed into service on board ocean-going merchant vessels.[30] Regardless of background, the majority of those individuals filling the ranks of their colonial merchant marine were inexperienced sailors, as Professor Samuel Eliot Morison has noted, and most of them viewed sea service, rightly or wrongly, as a pathway to new lifetime opportunities. Only a fraction of those embarking on this pathway achieved success, but all of them soon became aware of the risks of the sea and the consequent need for shipboard cohesiveness.[31]

Veteran seamen who had survived the vagaries of wind and wave had given especially clear indications of where their sympathies lay, even before the outbreak of the American Revolution. Many of them had been victims of the arbitrary, unwarranted Royal Navy press gangs that had run amok through American seaports seeking replacements for depleted crews. One such group of rampaging British conscriptors in 1758 reportedly impressed seventy-three men for a frigate, during three days of foraging in New York. Thirteen years later, a press gang from another royal warship shanghaied thirty-one during two days of activity in Virginia.[32] Reaction to such capricious conduct was particularly evident in the violent press-gang riots of the 1760s which erupted in several colonial ports. American sailors, an integral part of the colonial working class, played a fundamental role in these demonstrations. The riots were directed not only at preventing the actions of men from the pursuing vessel but also at the indifference of Crown officials who allowed the persistence of such wanton license.[33]

Economic factors also stoked the politicization of colonial mariners during the pre-Revolutionary decade. British trade regulations after the Seven Years' War had caused considerable hardships for American seamen. Boycotts, nonimportation agreements, and protests that followed restrictive legislation like the 1765 Stamp Act put the crewmen of most colonial vessels out of work. This circumstance, added to the preexisting abhorrence of royal customs collectors, helped radicalize these American "jack tars." Their contentious political beliefs were revealed by the parts they played in provoking and defying British authorities up to the eve, and beyond the outbreak, of hostilities in April 1775. In fact, some historians recently have contended that the numerous protest activities involving these colonial mariners were essential components in shaping "the revolutionary process."[34]

Such, then, are some general background characteristics of the thousands of seamen who entered naval service against Great Britain for reasons of political conviction, personal gain, or a combination of disparate motives. From this basic mold emerged the varied lot of rebel mariners who would be sent under guard to Forton or Mill prisons. In a few instances, men who were taken off unarmed merchantmen found themselves briefly incarcerated in these prisons. But all the other rebel seamen interned in them had come from ships whose cannon provided ample evidence of the violation of the "North's Act."

A few other descriptive comments can be added to this portrait of the Americans confined at Forton and Mill prisons. As a group, they ranged in age from boys of nine to aging men of about sixty. They were mostly white, though a small, indeterminate number of black seamen could be found in their ranks. Similarly, there is mention of at least two Native American detainees in these prisons, but again, complete figures for this nonwhite group are not available. The Americans doubtlessly were aware of these minorities within their midst, but, at least in the capives' writings, there is an absence of racial prejudice.

IV

Obviously it is impossible to illuminate the personal backgrounds of all of these prisoners of whom a significant number were born in European locales, including Ireland, Sweden, Scotland, Holland, and England. However, extant records do make it possible to portray the earlier lives of several of the captives at Forton and Mill. Many of these particular rebel mariners also wrote accounts of their incarceration or related details to their families. The reliability of their accounts is assessed in a postscript to this work, but the following facts are certain about their experiences prior to committal.[35]

Timothy Connor wrote the most detailed account of any inmate at Forton Gaol, yet only some facts are known about his life before his confinement. According to his printed diary, he was born in Massachusetts on 27 August 1751 and he had a married brother named William living in Boston. Unfortunately, these statements fail to clarify his personal background though his surname indicates Irish origins for his family. The *DAR Patriot Index* lists a Timothy Connor born in 1751, but a further check cites him only as a private in a Pennsylvania regiment. *Massachusetts Soldiers and Sailors of the Revolutionary War* includes a Timothy Connor, though his limited listing has him born in 1759 and gives no mention of any service on the privateer *Rising States*.[36]

Jonathan Carpenter arrived at Forton a year after seaman Connor, and there he kept a shorter account of his dreary captivity. More details of Carpenter's life prior to captivity are known than about Connor's. He was born on 19 June 1757, in Rehoboth, Massachusetts, one of eight children of Jonathan and Abigail Carpenter. (The name Carpenter was one of the oldest in the tiny community.) He later wrote that he had received a "common education," followed by work for an uncle in the "farm trade." About nine months after news of Lexington and Concord reached Rehoboth, Jonathan Carpenter enlisted in a local militia company commanded by his uncle Nathaniel. He spent much of the next twenty-six months in military service in Massachusetts, New York, and Rhode Island. Adventure, patriotism, financial opportunity, or perhaps a combination of all these motives, impelled him to sign aboard the privateer brig *Reprisal,* fitted out in Boston in December 1776. The outgunned privateer was captured on 19 February 1778, by HMS *Unicorn,* which Carpenter derisively described as "a 20 gun ship in ye service of the Tyrant King of Great Britain." Four months of prison-ship close confinement followed until 19 June of that year, when Carpenter found himself within the gates of Forton.[37]

Two other prisoners from the Bay State, Caleb Foot and George Thompson, also kept significant records of their Forton incarceration. Foot, born in 1750, was a married seaman from Salem. According to his grandson, Foot, an ardent patriot, entered the Continental Army soon after the onset of fighting. He served under General Washington at Cambridge and then at the siege of Boston. Later, he turned to maritime enterprises as an officer on different rebel vessels. It was as prizemaster of the privateer sloop *Gates* that he was captured by the British frigate *Triton* in July 1778. Following a short stay at Quebec, Foot and several crewmen were sent to Forton.[38] George Thompson (née Thamston) was a Swedish-born resident of Newburyport at the beginning of revolutionary hostilities. He, too, had joined the rebel cause early, and by late 1777, he was engaged in privateering as prizemaster of the Massachusetts brig *Expedition.* Thompson's ship was captured by a better-armed British privateer on 5 November 1777. Like Foot, he was not sent directly to England but first was interned on different prison ships in North American waters. Thompson's eventual commitment to Forton occurred on 19 June 1778.[39]

Dr. Nathaniel Harrington, also from Massachusetts, was one of at least two college graduates held at Forton. Born in Watertown on 1 August 1750, Harrington had graduated from Harvard College in 1769. After a brief school-teaching stint in Westborough, he had been educated in "Surgery and Physics" by an established physician. Following the outbreak of the Revolution, Dr. Harrington served as surgeon's mate in Colonel John Glover's famed 21st Massachusetts Regiment and then joined the 14th Continental Regiment. By the beginning of 1777, he had left the army for duty as a surgeon on a privateer. Harrington's ship was seized while on a cruise from Marblehead. By early 1780, the doctor had joined other Massachusetts seamen in England's Hampshire naval prison.[40]

Men from other New England states also wrote of their experiences in Forton. Nathaniel Fanning, Charles Bulkeley, and Elisha

Hinman were from Connecticut. Fanning, from New London, reminisced about his feelings at the beginning of the war: "I imbibed the idea that the struggle between Great Britain and the colonies would eventually progress to the advantage of the latter. In full belief of the same, I took an active and decided part in favor of my country." His "active and decided part" was as prizemaster on board a privateer, but after two successful cruises, his outmatched brigantine *Angelica* was seized by HMS *Andromeda* on 31 May 1778. *Andromeda* was then transporting General Sir William Howe back to England from his recent command in Philadelphia. The warship's arrival in Portsmouth allowed Fanning and the other harassed Yankee captives to be removed, and in early July they were formally sent to Forton.[41]

Charles Bulkeley from Wethersfield had considerable pre-Revolutionary sailing experience in the West India trade. After war broke out, he served in the Connecticut State Navy and then as a lieutenant aboard the Continental frigate *Alfred.* This warship, previously commanded by John Paul Jones, was outmaneuvered by two British armed sloops near Barbados on 9 March 1778. Bulkeley recorded the immediate aftermath, for both his ship and himself: "After a running fight of two hours we were captured and were carried into Barbados and here I lost my trunk." From this West Indian island, Bulkeley, minus his trunk, but along with five other ship's officers, was sent to another island, St. Christopher. Here they were put aboard the sixty-four-gun ship of the line *Yarmouth,* which soon transported them to Portsmouth.[42]

Captain Elisha Hinman was the highest ranking, most experienced of these three Connecticut prisoners. He was from New London, and prior to the Revolution he had commanded numerous cargo vessels sailing from that port on West Indian commercial ventures. After the outbreak of fighting, he was made first lieutenant, then given command of *Cabot,* one of four armed naval vessels authorized in November 1776 by the Naval Committee of the Continental Congress. *Cabot* took part in Commodore Esek Hopkins's expedition to the Bahamas the following year.[43] Hinman's hard work and early successes earned him command of *Alfred,* considered the fastest ship in the Continental Navy. Unfortunately for Hinman and his crew, including Lieutenant Bulkeley, his triumphs did not continue during his new command. It was due in part to his errors in seamanship that *Alfred* was forced to surrender in March 1778. Captain Hinman then joined Bulkeley and the other ship's officers dispatched to Forton.[44]

Seamen from the mid-Atlantic states, such as Captain John Nicholson and Ralph Moore from Pennsylvania and Lieutenant Luke Matthewman from New York, were also present among Forton's American inmates.

Matthewman, who left an account of his wartime services, was perhaps the most daring, as well as the most interesting of these three naval officers. He wrote that he initially entered the "service of my country" in March 1776 as a lieutenant on board the Continental Navy brig *Lexington,* commanded by Captain John Barry. Early the following year, he was captured by a British frigate, but he escaped after only a month's captivity. He then performed duty on board a Pennsylvania state naval vessel during the unsuccessful defense of the Delaware River. Taken again by the British, he suffered an unpleasant period of imprisonment before making a second successful escape. Afterward Matthewman claimed to have been involved in several daring escapades. These included delivering important congressional dispatches to and from the French West Indies in a tiny, twenty-ton vessel with an unreliable crew; rescuing a supply-laden Virginia naval vessel from capture near Portsmouth, Virginia; and then leading an audacious raid against some British shipping in that seaport's harbor. His reckless triumphs ceased on his subsequent voyage as second-in-command of the Carolina privateer brig *Fair American.* On 7 October 1780 Lieutenant Matthewman's ship was taken after an encounter with HMS *Vestal,* a frigate convoying cargo ships from Newfoundland to Portugal. After *Vestal* reached Lisbon, he made another, but this time unsuccessful, attempt to escape. By mid-November, Matthewman and all the remaining crew of *Fair American* were ensconced in Forton.[45]

Rebel mariners from southern states also were remanded to Forton. Perhaps the most notable of them were Captain John Harris and Captain Alexander Dick of Virginia and Captain Benjamin Chew of Maryland. Harris was an experienced ship captain living in Hampton with his wife Mary and an infant daughter at the start of the American Revolution. In 1776, he was mentioned for service as a lieutenant on board *Manley,* a galley protecting the state's eastern shore. Shortly afterward he fitted out the privateer brig *Mosquito (Musqetto)* for the Virginia State Navy. *Mosquito* sailed from Portsmouth on 6 February 1777, capturing at least one prize afterward. However, the following 4 June shortly after departing Martinique, the Virginia brig was intercepted and captured by HMS *Ariadne.*[46] Harris soon was dispatched to England with all his ship's officers, including Alexander Dick, captain of *Mosquito's* marines. Dick, from a merchant-planter family in Fredericksburg,

Captain John Harris, Virginia State Navy. Reproduced from the *Virginia Magazine of History and Biography* (April 1914). Courtesy Virginia Historical Society.

had received his orders to join the ship only two days before she sailed. His only previous service had been in the state's military units.[47] Captain Benjamin Chew, born in 1756, was from Cecil County in upper Maryland. His great-great grandfather had moved to the colony from Virginia about a century before, and the family had achieved considerable respectability during succeeding generations. The Cecil County Chews apparently had some nautical tradition, because both Benjamin and his older brother Nathan selected the naval service after hostilities broke out. Benjamin's nautical knowledge helped get him assignment in August 1777 as prizemaster aboard a Maryland privateer brig belligerently named *Sturdy Beggar* [viz., "a beggar that rather demands than asks"]. The ship had some initial successes at privateering, but these triumphs did not continue. Captain Chew was captured while trying to guide one of her prizes to port late in 1777. Before the end of the next January, he was listed among those committed to Forton.[48]

V

The overall characteristics of the American captives at Mill were comparable to the captives held in Forton as far as rank, age range, and racial composition are concerned. The number of seamen interned in both prisons also fluctuated during the Revolution. One minor distinction emerging from a review of the captives held in both prisons is the fact that Mill served as a detention center slightly longer than Forton. Similarly, a slightly larger number of prisoners (1,200–1,296) were kept at Mill into the latter part of 1782, and the Devon naval prison appeared to have more New Englanders within its confines. As at Forton, most of these Yankees hailed from Massachusetts.[49]

Samuel Cutler, already mentioned as one of Mill's first inmates, was born in Boston in October 1757, the youngest of eleven children. His father's occupation is listed in the Cutler genealogy as "brazier," and his family's ancestry reached back to the Puritan Great Migration. He is not listed in the multivolume *Massachusetts Soldiers and Sailors of the Revolutionary War* for any service prior to his privateering, but this extensive compilation is not definitive. Although Cutler did not record his personal motivations for signing on the ill-fated cruise of the brig *Dalton* in November 1776, it can be surmised that, like many others, he entered this risky enterprise for a combination of reasons.[50]

Charles Herbert, five years younger than Cutler and a fellow crewman on board *Dalton,* hailed from Newburyport. Charles's mother died when he was only two months old, and Richard Livesey, editor of his memoir, states that he was raised by an aunt named Lydia Pierce. Livesey also identifies Charles as a "true Patriot who cannot betray the cause of his country." His initial efforts for the American cause, from 9 July to 16 November 1775, were as a private in Captain Moses Norvell's Newburyport Company, stationed on Plum Island south of the town. He followed up his brief militia stint by signing aboard *Dalton.* Herbert's patriotism would be sorely tested during long, tedious months following his capture at sea and his incarceration in Mill. The Yankee seaman's apprehensions were clearly evident prior to his formal sentencing in a Plymouth court. On 30 March 1777, having learned that Parliament regarded American privateersmen as "treasonous pirates," he wrote in his journal that *Dalton*'s crewmen were then pessimistically wondering "how soon the gallows may be our fate."[51]

William Wigder was another of the many seamen from Massachusetts coastal communities who engaged in privateering. He was born in Marblehead on 18 September 1748, the third child of William and Mary (Stevens) Wigder. The younger Wigder was married to Mary Dodd (Dobs) less than two months before the outbreak of the Revolution. When fighting did begin, he immediately joined the 21st Massachusetts Regiment, in which Doctor Nathaniel Harrington also served. Like Harrington, Wigder later turned to privateering, though on a different vessel, the Massachusetts schooner *Phoenix* commanded by Captain Joseph Cunningham. It was on board *Phoenix* that Wigder was captured on 12 February 1779. Within three months, he was committed to Mill.[52]

Captain John Manley and William Russell were two other Bay State men who were sent together to the Devon prison and who wrote about their experiences. Russell, once an usher in a Boston school, had displayed his patriotic sentiments even before the war when he participated in the Boston Tea Party. Once the fighting started, he enlisted as a sergeant in the Massachusetts State Train of Artillery. Later he was appointed adjutant of the regiment during the unsuccessful Rhode Island campaign. By early 1779, Russell had left the army, and like many other veterans, he switched to privateer ventures. In June of that year, he signed on as clerk to Captain John Manley on the newly fitted-out, eighteen-gun ship *Jason.* Russell was on board this privateer the following 30 September when, after a brief skirmish, she was forced to surrender to the frigate HMS *Surprise.* The ship's clerk, her captain, and the surviving crewmen were sent to a guardship at St. John's, New-foundland. Following three weeks of detention there, the American rebels were dispatched to England, and in mid-December 1779, they were within the gates of Mill.[53]

John Manley, *Jason*'s skipper, was one of Mill's most noteworthy captives based upon his past service in the rebel cause. He was born in England on 18 August 1732, in the tiny village of St. Mary Church, outside Torquay in Devon. During his youth, Manley had gone to sea, serving in both the merchant marine and later in the Royal Navy. By the early 1760s, he was living in Marblehead, where he was heavily involved in the West Indian trade. Colonial hostilities brought distinctly different activities for Manley when in October 1775, General Washington appointed him commander of the armed schooner *Lee*.[54] One month after his selection, Captain Manley captured a valuable British ordnance brig off Cape Anne. The next year, following other seizures, Congress appointed him a captain in the Continental Navy and then commander of the new frigate *Hancock*. Congress's Marine Committee added to these honors by naming him second in rank of its several appointees. However, the captain's good fortune did not last. In June 1777, a few weeks after capturing an enemy frigate, *Hancock* and her prizes were taken by a much larger British warship near Halifax, and Manley found himself in confinement for nine months. Follow-ing his exchange in March 1778, he was court-martialed, but ac-quitted, for the loss of his ship. He then turned his talents to privateering, commanding several different vessels until he was captured once again, in the West Indies. However, he soon after-ward made a successful escape from Barbados, and after only two months of freedom, he assumed command of the ill-starred *Jason*. Ironically Manley's subsequent detention in Mill returned him to a locale less than thirty miles from his birthplace.[55]

Dr. Jonathan Haskins, who also may have used the names Hotchkiss, Hodgeare, or Hogeease, was one of the two New En-glanders from outside Massachusetts who provided significant ac-counts of their incarceration at Mill. Haskins, originally from Connecticut, had enlisted as a junior surgeon on board the priva-teer sloop *Charming Sally*. This ten-gun vessel sailed from Mar-tha's Vineyard on 27 November 1776. She was able to take one prize off Newfoundland, but the next January, *Charming Sally*'s venture ended when the ship surrendered to the sixty-gun ship *Nonesuch*. Almost five months in custody on board British war-ships followed, until 28 May 1777 when Dr. Haskins recorded that he and eight fellow crewmen were ordered committed to Mill.[56]

The other New England detainee from outside Massachusetts, who wrote more personal and evidently more accurate details of his captivity at Mill, was Andrew Sherburne. Sherburne was among the younger Americans held in the Devon prison. He wrote in his memoirs that he was born on 30 September 1765 in Rye, New Hampshire, into a family that numbered five sons and seven daughters. Not surprisingly, Andrew also wrote that at the age of seven, he was sent to live with an aunt in Londonderry. There he recalled that he was imbued with a mixture of strong religious and patriotic precepts. Perhaps both were influential when, at the age of fourteen, he joined a cruise on board the continental frigate *Ranger* under Captain Abraham Whipple. He later signed on board some privateers and had the misfortune of being stranded in Charleston, South Carolina in May 1780 when the besieged town fell to British forces.[57] Released from imprisonment, he returned to his native New Hampshire. Sherburne was unable to find work at home, and he admitted to being beguiled by promises of pecuniary gain into serving aboard the newly commissioned privateer *Alexander*. The ship, which sailed from Portsmouth, was captured in early 1781 off Newfoundland. Young Andrew was confined on the island from May until the following September. After repeatedly refusing to enter royal service, he was dispatched to England. There, after several weeks' custody aboard the prison ship *Dunkirk* in Plymouth harbor, he was (December 1781) formally sent to Mill. One of the vivid memories Sherburne kept of his arrival was of "the prisoners rushing to the gate from all directions to see if any of their acquaintances were to be found among the newcomers."[58]

Elaborate biographical sketches are less available for those Mill captives from the mid-Atlantic states than for those from New England. If there was one conspicuous detainee from the region, it undoubtedly was Captain Gustavus Conyngham. He was born in County Donegal, Ireland, about 1744, to middle-class parents who had some landholdings. He had emigrated to Philadelphia in 1763, working as an apprentice and subsequently commanding trading vessels in a firm operated by a cousin.[59]

Five months after the Revolution began, Conyngham was sent by Congress to Europe to obtain needed war supplies. His ship, which bore the name *Charming Peggy,* was taken by the British, then retaken by the Pennsylvania captain, and he sailed her to Holland. After a period of uncertainty about his status, Conyngham received an appointment in the Continental Navy from the American commissioners in Paris. Shortly thereafter the newly appointed officer took command in Dunkirk harbor of a secretly purchased ten-gun cutter named *Surprise.* He used the vessel to seize British shipping in the English Channel. British protests to the French government followed, but Conyngham soon obtained an even larger cutter, *Revenge,* and returned to his former activities. By February 1779, when Conyngham returned to Philadelphia, on orders of the Marine Committee, he had captured or destroyed sixty British ships during cruises that had extended from the North Sea to the West Indies. Questions about some of *Revenge*'s dubious doings while on her forays resulted in the ship's sale by Congressional authorization. She was then fitted out as a privateer, with none other than Gustavus Conyngham as her skipper. Privateering forays, however, did not work for *Revenge.* She was captured off New York in April 1779. The following July, Conyngham, once dubbed "the Dunkirk Pirate" was on his way to Mill Prison.[60]

Captain John Green, another Pennsylvanian, was considerably less prominent than Gustavus Conyngham prior to his confinement. Green, also from Ireland, was born in 1736 and had gone to sea at an early age. Like Conyngham, he also had left home to pursue mercantile endeavors. Green's marriage in Philadelphia in June 1765 to Alice Kollock, daughter of a wealthy family in nearby Delaware, definitely aided his aspirations. From 1766 to the Revolution, he was master of four different trading vessels, including the two-hundred ton *Pomona,* of which he was also part owner. In July 1777 he left *Pomona* in Nantes and sought command of an armed ship from the American commissioners in Paris. The following February he was commissioned a captain in the Continental Navy and commanded the warship *La Brune* on a cruise to Boston. By early 1781 he was master of a larger eighteen-gun ship, *Lion,* which he loaded with goods in Haiti for a voyage to Nantes. Unfortunately for Green, his mission was aborted off the French coast. His vessel was taken, "after a chase of 14 hours" by the forty-gun British frigate *La Prudente.* Afterward the American captain and part of his crew were detained "on a man of War for 30 days" before their commitment to Mill, a date cited by Green as 3 September 1781.[61]

One of the few Mill prisoners from the South who left an account of his incarceration was Virginia's Captain George Ralls. Relatively little is known about Ralls's career prior to his capture. He was apparently from Hampton, in Elizabeth City County, and had some maritime experience. Inserts in the *Virginia Gazette* in 1772 and 1776 indicate that he had made trading voyages to Dumfries in Scotland. By the beginning of 1777, Ralls had been given command

Captain Gustavus Conyngham. Original miniature by Luc Sicardi. Photograph of a book illustration in Robert W. Neeser, ed. *Letters and Papers Relating to the Cruises of Gustavus Conyngham,* **(New York, 1915). Collections of the New-York Historical Society. Courtesy New-York Historical Society.**

of the armed schooner *Jenny,* one of the ships in the Virginia State Navy. In March of that year, he sailed to the then neutral Dutch West Indian island of St. Eustatius seeking contraband goods. There he evidently agreed with another American ship captain to cruise together to the Carolinas. Ralls, described by the other patriot commander as "a damned rascal," instead of keeping his word decided to venture into privateering. This proved to be a disastrous decision; *Jenny* was captured on 24 May 1777 by HMS *Seaford.* This event allegedly was followed by Ralls getting "ingloriously drunk." The charge was apparently believed by a committee of Virginia's legislature that shortly afterward characterized him as "a man of very indifferent character and much addicted to drinking." Irrespective of alcoholic tendencies, Ralls was soon sent to Mill on board a prison ship and was incarcerated there in August 1777.[62]

Captain Joshua Barney, younger than but certainly as flamboyant as Pennsylvania's Captain Gustavus Conyngham, stands out among the southern prisoners at Mill for his audacity. Barney was born in Baltimore, 6 July 1759, one of fourteen children of William and Frances (Holland) Barney. At the age of ten he was sent to work in a "retail store" in the community. (Mary Barney later wrote in a memoir of her father that this action was taken, "if only to keep him out of mischief.") Soon, however, Joshua's maritime yearnings caused his father to transfer his son's instruction to a Baltimore ship pilot. A year later, the boy was apprenticed to his brother-in-law Thomas Drysdale, captain of a European trading brig. Young Barney displayed his mettle for seamanship in early 1775 when on a voyage to Nice his brother-in-law died, and with no first mate aboard, the fifteen-year-old took command and successfully brought the leaking ship to her destination. After several subsequent adversities, he eventually returned the vessel to America.[63]

Once home, Joshua Barney entered the ongoing Revolution as sailing master of the Maryland ship *Hornet.* By June 1776, he had earned enough notice to be commissioned a lieutenant in the Continental Navy. Barney, described in contemporary manuscript records as "5 feet 8 inches, black hair and dark complexion," thereafter served on board two continental warships. One of these vessels, the fourteen-gun brig *Andrew Doria,* achieved notoriety on 16 November 1776, when she received a salute from the Dutch governor of St. Eustatius. A few months later, Lieutenant Barney, commanding one of *Andrew Doria's* prizes, was captured at sea, but he was soon exchanged. His next assignment, on board the frigate *Virginia,* resulted in the seizure of two prizes before his recapture by the Royal Navy. Released once more, he temporarily commanded armed merchantmen before an assignment as first lieutenant aboard the sixteen-gun ship *Saratoga*. Barney's voyage on the vessel, shortly after his marriage in March 1780, ended in failure. *Saratoga* was captured by a British frigate, and by the following December, Barney was on his way to incarceration at Mill.[64]

The preceding pages have detailed the settings of Forton and Mill prisons, the hierarchy of royal administration and administrators, and the background stories of several American seamen who were confined in both detention centers. There were obviously both disparities and similarities in their individual backgrounds. Most of the previously cited captives were officers and the only lower ranking sailors mentioned were from New England, but, despite these and other atypical characteristics, each of the aforementioned rebel mariners would experience varying periods of confinement in these two English prisons. How they and their comrades responded to this custody formed an intriguing, though neglected, episode in the War of American Independence.

3

The Time of Settling In,
May 1777–January 1778

Almost all of the Americans entering the bounds of Forton and Mill prisons after they opened in the spring of 1777 had at least one consolation in common: they and the others following them were finally rid of the miseries of shipboard confinement. Some of these rebel seamen had remained crammed on board their captors' vessels for only a few weeks before reaching England, but many others had spent several lengthy and distressful months, often transferred from ship to ship, until they were committed to the British prisons. In a few cases, the captives were sent directly to Britain from detention in America. Regardless of the circumstances, few of these mariners had any pleasant memories of prison ship detention. The mistreatment endured by Timothy Connor and Samuel Cutler was far from unique. Other Americans experienced threats, intimidation, robbery, and petty punishments from royal seamen. Many of the rebels also suffered from cold, hunger, inadequate clothing, and contagious diseases, including smallpox and dysentery. For these men, joy at any landfall seemed to overshadow any forthcoming dangers. Seaman Jonathan Carpenter, who had spent several wretched months in seaborne detention, recalled how in May 1778 he had "rejoiced greatly" at the prospect of leaving his guardship for Forton. And for Caleb Foot the following December, it was like "coming out of Hell and going into Paradise."[1]

But neither Forton nor Mill was intended to be a paradise. The seriousness of the prisoners' plight was made fully evident to them by the magistrates who committed them on charges of high treason until their time of trial. Their predicament was also made clear as they were escorted to their respective prisons under guard, often past crowds of sullen, hostile bystanders. Seaman Charles Herbert, one of Mill's first detainees, apparently comprehended his insecure status and recorded misgivings, which were no doubt shared by his fellow inmates. On 5 June 1777 he said, "Alas, I have entered the gates, but the Lord only knows when I shall get out of them again."[2]

I

One of the first matters that confronted seaman Herbert and other Americans confined at both the English prisons was administrative discipline. The Commissioners for Sick and Hurt Seamen had drawn up a list of regulations that had been sanctioned by the Admiralty. These regulations were read almost immediately to the discomfited, uncertain rebels by the keepers or agents, John Newsham at Forton and William Cowdry at Mill. Although Newsham and Cowdry had considerable latitude for maintaining order in their respective compounds, they were expected to operate within the scope of the following twelve fundamental directives for prisoner supervision:[3]

REGULATIONS which are to be observed by the PRISONERS

I

Good Order in all Respects is to be observed by them, and the Directions of the Keeper and Agent are to be obeyed without Murmuring or endeavouring to raise any Discontent or Mutiny among the Prisoners; much less is any Prisoner to offer any Menace or Insult by Word or Action, to the Keeper and Agent, or any acting under him, upon Pain of being put into Closer Confinement, and upon half Allowance of Provision, or such other Punishment as the Case may deserve; and they are hereby informed, that no Person has a Right to beat or in any manner ill-treat them, or will be suffered to do it with Impunity.

II

If Orders are given for their being regularly mustered, it is expected that each Prisoner shall readily answer to his Name as often as required. If any one should willfully Neglect doing it, the Agent has Orders to put him upon half Allowance of Provisions for three Days.

III

If the Prison is damaged by the Prisoners, the Expence of repairing it will be made good to the Crown, by stopping half the accustomed Allowance of Provisions from all the Prisoners, if they refuse to declare the Names of the particular Persons who did the Damage; but upon their giving in names of those Persons to the Agent, the Delinquent alone will then be subsisted with half Allowance, 'till the said Expence is made good; and such Prisoners will also be put into closer Confinement than usual.

IV

If any Prisoner should be taken in attempting to Escape, or after having escaped from the Prison, he will be put into stricter Confinement on half Allowance of Provisions for forty Days or as the Case may deserve.

V

As Water and Tubs for washing their Linen and Cloaths, will be allowed, the Prisoners are advised to keep their Persons as clean as possible, it being very conducive to good Health.

VI

The Prisoners are not to Fight or Quarrel among themselves, or to raise any Disturbance in the Prison, on Pain of being put into close Confinement and upon half Allowance of Provisions for so long as it be judged, upon Representation to Us, their Offences may deserve.

VII

The Prisoners are expected by Turns to sweep and clean the Prison, and the Prison Yard; for which Purpose brooms and Scrapers will be provided and delivered to them by the Turnkey; those who refuse will be put upon half Allowance for three days, and 'till they submit to assist their fellow Prisoners in what is so necessary for the good of the whole.

VIII

The Prisoners will be indulged between the Hours of Nine and Two o' Clock in the Day-time, to purchase at an open Market at the Gate such Articles of Fruit, or other Refreshments as they may chuse, or any Articles of Cloathing they may be able to purchase with ready Money, or they May Inform the Keeper and Agent of Such Articles of Cloathing as they May Stand in need of, and have Money to pay for, and he will take Measures for their being Supplied with them, and for their not being imposed upon, but whosoever Shall by this Means attempt to procure Spiritous Liquors, or other things Improper for Prisoners to have, or to deliver or receive any Letter unexamined by the Agent will be put upon half Allowance, and punished by Confinement likewise as the Abuse of the Indulgence May deserve.

IX

The Prisoners are ordered to be Victualled according to the Subjoined Scheme.

X

For the better Satisfaction of the Prisoners, and as a Means to prevent groundless Clamours, the Prisoners are to be permitted to Chuse two of their body, and to Change them as they like, to attend every Day at the Receipt and weighing, and to continue in the Cook Room during the Dressing and issuing of the Provisions, to see that they are good in quality, and they [are] provided according to the Scheme of Diet, and if any just Cause of Complaint of any Sort arises, they are, in a becoming Manner, to make it known to the Keeper and Agent, whose Duty it is to redress it as soon as possible; and if it is Neglected, the Prisoners may write to Us; but whoever under this Pretext shall make unjust Complaints will be punished by being put upon half Allowance, and in Closer Confinement, as the Case may deserve.

XI

As the Prisoners are ordered to be Victualing in Messes, if it shall at any Time appear, that, notwithstanding one or More of any particular Mess shall have escaped, the Remainder has received the full Allowance for the whole, by which Means the Escape may be concealed, and an undue issue of Provisions made; the Offenders, upon Discovery, will be put upon half Allowance for Forty days.

XII

If any of the Prisoners should purloin or willfully destroy their Hammocks, Bedding, Hospital Dresses, or any Cloathing furnished those in want will, upon discovery, be put upon half Allowance, 'till the first cost of such Articles is Made good to the Crown.[4]

In addition to these twelve regulations, the Commissioners also published a "Table of Victualing" with cooking instructions for both prisons. The table was based largely upon allowances for feeding rebel prisoners taken during the uprising of Bonnie Prince Charles in 1745. The Commission's member physician performed the work of finalizing this table and of adding to the earlier schedule. Victualling practices for captives held at English prisons during previous wars also may have served as models. In any case, this program for weekly food staple allotments appears adequate for individual nourishment:

TABLE OF VICTUALING

	Beer	Bread	Beef	Butter	Cheese	Pease
	Quarts	Pounds	Pounds	Ounces	Ounces	Pints
Sunday	1	1	¾			½
Monday	1	1	¾			
Tuesday	1	1	¾			½
Wednesday	1	1	¾			
Thursday	1	1	¾			½
Friday	1	1	¾			
Saturday	1	1		4 or	6	½
	7	7	4½	4	or 6	2 or Greens in lieu

The Meat to be boiled into Broth, and the Broth to be served with it to the Prisoners[5]

There was, however, a considerable disparity between this well-ordered food scheme and the reality faced by the first Americans committed to Forton and Mill. By constraining these captives for several weeks on guardships off Portsmouth and Plymouth, the Commissioners for Sick and Hurt Seamen and the prison staffs certainly had enough time to initiate their victualling schedule. But ever-present bureaucratic bungling, inefficiency, and corruption were not taken into account. The resultant shortcomings of the provisions given to the prisoners during these early months would probably sound familiar to captured servicemen in World War I, World War II, Korea, and Vietnam who also endured substandard prison rations. Thus, one veteran of a German prisoner-of-war compound, who recalled subsisting for several months only on soup made from potato skins and moldy bread slices, might easily empathize with Mill and Forton prisoners who told of the bleak inadequacies of their first food allotments.[6]

Internees at both English prisons gloomily recorded examples of dietary deficiencies. At Forton, Timothy Connor reported in his journal (14 June 1777) that "for twenty four hours after we got to prison, we had nothing to eat but boiled cabbage which was part of the officer's allowance. We had a little bread our captain bought for us."[7] Rations improved only slightly in the following months at the Hampshire prison. At Mill that same month, Samuel Cutler also expressed his discontent about food shortages. He noted that, although he and his fellow seamen were scheduled for a daily allow-

ance of three-quarter pounds of beef, one pound of bread, one
quart of beer, and a few greens, in actuality, the beef "when boiled"
weighed only about six ounces, the bread was moldy, and the beer
"ordinary." He also claimed that only one-half pint of salt was
allotted per week for four men, while their small weekly cheese
ration was sometimes inedible.[8] But perhaps the most poignant
allegations of food deficiencies during these first months of prison
operation were rendered by Charles Herbert at Mill. Seaman Herbert, who recalled having "a continual gnawing at my stomach" on
10 June 1777, still wrote two-and-a-half months later about all of
his comrades' hunger:

> We have trouble enough here without hearing bad news; for it is
> enough to break the heart of a stone to see so many strong hearty men
> almost starved to death for want of provisions. A great part of those
> in prison, eat at one meal what they draw for twenty long hours, and
> then go without until the next day. Many are strongly tempted to pick
> up the grass in the yard, and eat it, and some pick up old bones in the
> yard, that have been laying in the dirt a week or ten days, and pound
> them to pieces and suck them. Some will pick up snails out of the
> holes in the wall, and from among the grass and weeds in the yard, boil
> them and eat them, and drink the broth. Often the cooks, after they
> have picked over our cabbage, will cut off some of the butt-ends of the
> stalks and throw them over the gate into the yard, and I have often
> seen, after a rain, when the mud would be over shoes, as these stumps
> were thrown over the gate, the men running from all parts of the yard,
> regardless of the mud, to catch at them, and nearly trample one another
> under feet to get a piece. These same cabbage stumps, hogs in America
> would scarcely eat if they had them; and as to our broth, I know very
> well hogs in America would scarcely put their noses in it. Our meat is
> very poor in general; we scarcely see a good piece once in a month.
> Many are driven to such necessity by want of provisions, that they
> have sold most of the clothes off their backs for the sake of getting a
> little money to buy them some bread.[9]

Officials in London were aware of the shortcomings of prison
rations. While the keepers at the prisons seem to have been doing
little to rectify the situation, the protests of the detainees were
reaching higher authorities. On 29 August 1777 the Commissioners
for Sick and Hurt Seamen were apprised of the deplorable conditions at Mill Prison by a remonstrance that was from the American
captives signed "Humanitas." Their grievances, directed against
Keeper William Cowdry, centered primarily on alleged abuses in
his handling of provisions. Many of these complaints cited the
shortages in the expected rations, which the prisoners laid to the

keeper's avarice. Many other complaints, however, listed the extremely unpalatable quality of what they were actually served, such as "Necks of Beef with Maggots."[10] Apparently moved by such charges, Commission member John Bell made a firsthand inspection. Charles Herbert, who cited Bell's visits to Mill in mid-September 1777, wrote that Bell listened to their complaints and was present when the prisoners received their meager allotments. According to the Massachusetts seaman, the commissioner subsequently promised to rectify this distressing situation. He also allowed the inmates to have an "open market at the gate three hours a day," and he permitted them to send their grievances directly to the commissioners without Keeper Cowdry inspecting the messages. Despite Bell's assurances, however, it took several months to begin to remedy the victualling shortcomings at Mill and Forton.[11]

Food was not the only deficiency facing the first American prisoners. Almost all of them entered Mill and Forton with little more than the clothes on their backs. Many captives had had their extra garments or shoes taken from them by greedy royal sailors while they were en route to England. Lieutenant Nathaniel Fanning later recalled a British seaman justifying such thievery by self-righteously proclaiming, "You are a set of rebels, and it is more probable that you will all be hanged on our arrival in Portsmouth." "That is right lads," added a midshipman, "strip the damned rebels!"[12] The clothing shortages were cited by the prisoners themselves. The journals of Samuel Cutler and Dr. Jonathan Haskins for 22 June 1777 both complain of being "badly cloathed" as well as badly fed. At Forton some of the first rebel detainees reportedly arrived half-naked, though Timothy Connor noted that some of the seamen on board *Rising States* had purposely sold "what trifle of cloathes we had" in exchange for food. Even afterward many fortunate internees at either prison with extra clothing were often obliged to sell them for additional rations.[13]

Luckily for the first ill-clad prisoners, the pleasant late spring and summer months in Hampshire and Devon were bearable even with their limited attire. These initial rebel captives were at least provided with satisfactory bedding, bathing, and privy facilities. They had had little of these during their prison ship detention. Still, as autumn approached, with winter chills not far behind, royal officials realized that some action would have to be taken about prisoner clothing. Consequently, the Commissioners for Sick and Hurt Seamen petitioned the Admiralty and received permission in December 1777 to provide the American prisoners with "a jacket, waistcoat, a pair of breeches, shoes, a cap, two shirts, and two pairs of stockings." The Crown was to underwrite the resultant expenses until reimbursement was somehow made by the American representatives then in Paris. That same month the Admiralty rejected as "unnecessary" an offer from the residents of Plymouth to initiate a subscription for these items.[14]

Illness was another difficulty confronting the first rebel inmates at Forton and Mill. Many of the prisoners had been unwell even before being sent to English prisons. As a result of having been crammed into close, ill-ventilated quarters on ships, with unhealthy sanitary facilities, it could be expected that various diseases would strike the captives well before they reached England. The accounts of Timothy Connor, Dr. Jonathan Haskins, Samuel Cutler, and Charles Herbert all cite ailments affecting the patriot crewmen. Herbert's list is the most extensive. From his capture aboard *Dalton* on 24 December 1776 until his entry into Mill Prison the following June, this Yankee seaman reported several maladies among his shipmates, including colds, fevers, bronchitis, "the itch" (mange), dysentery, and the most dreaded affliction, smallpox. During his shipboard detention, Herbert periodically referred to these illnesses and the sufferings and deaths that resulted from them. He was himself afflicted with smallpox in early April 1777, after which he spent five weeks recovering in Plymouth's Royal Naval Hospital. From there he was sent to his confinement at Mill Prison.[15]

Sickness persisted among the seamen after their internment in land-based prisons. This was true at both Forton and Mill despite the presence of a physician, daily sick calls, and in April 1777 the inclusion of a staff pharmacist who could dispense medicine. Both detention centers, as prison regulations stipulated, also had washtubs for the inmates' use. Efforts were instituted for personal tidiness, the detention areas underwent repeated cleaning, and the Commissioners for Sick and Hurt Seamen made their periodic inspections. Nevertheless, as late as 1782, unhealthy conditions were still cited at both prisons.[16]

Mill prisoners suffered the most from illness during the rebels' first seven months of captivity. The accounts of Samuel Cutler, Dr. Jonathan Haskins, and Charles Herbert note repeated and diverse maladies afflicting their comrades. Some ailments, as on shipboard, were minor, such as colds, headaches, diarrhea, and general aches and pains. They were treated with common remedies, including the popularly ballyhooed "Dr. Ball's Infallible Cure," used for all sorts of ailments. This and other nostrums contained combinations of salt solutions, mustards, balsam, powdered roots, and herbs. Mill's lightly regarded physician, Dr. Manheir or Manheim, evidently prescribed these concoctions on a routine basis for the detainees. Fortunately, in cases of trivial indispositions, they usually had little adverse effect, and the prisoners recovered on their own.[17]

But it was another story for the Americans suffering from more serious illnesses such as the itch or the feared smallpox. The itch, more formally known as mange, was carried by a parasitic mite, and the constant, vexatious irritation it produced was severe enough to send many newly interned rebels to a special section of Mill's interconnected hospital buildings. Charles Herbert referred to this space as the "itch apartments." Jonathan Haskins described them as the "itch wards." Whatever terminology was used, the infected rebels experienced considerable discomfort from this affliction, which was often only increased by the applied remedies commonly given to sufferers. None of the troubled American patients was listed as dying from this disorder, though many of them may have wished they had.[18]

Smallpox, however, was a dreaded scourge that often resulted in death and always resulted in suffering and disfiguration. It was to account for most of the deaths at both English prisons, and it proved especially dangerous when the prisons were overcrowded. This long-frightening virus, marked by high fevers and severe skin lesions, had caused devastating epidemics in seventeenth- and eighteenth-century Europe and America. Colonial cities had been particularly wracked by this plague. Boston, for example, which had a listed population of 10,670 people at the time of its pestilence in 1721, reported that 5,980 of its inhabitants had become infected and that 844 had subsequently died.[19] Because smallpox could spread quite easily where individuals lived in close proximity and were in contact with contaminated articles, sailors—and especially imprisoned sailors—were quite susceptible to the contagion. Physicians at Forton and Mill offered inoculations and made efforts to separate the stricken detainees from other inmates. But journal entries from the early commitment days of Charles Herbert reveal that these measures often failed to avert the personal tragedies of the illness:

[June] 19. [1777] There is one of the prisoners who has been unwell for several days, and is now broke out with the small-pox.

[June] 27. Today another broke out with small-pox.

[July] 17. Several in prison have broken out with the small-pox, all of whom inoculated themselves from the first that they were attacked with it.

[July] 19. The remainder of the prisoners who have not had the small-pox have an offer from the doctor to be inoculated.

[August] 1. To-day six more of our people came on shore from the ship; the occasion of their not being brought to prison sooner was that they were detained with smallpox in Royal Hospital. One of these is very unwell, and has been put in the prison hospital.

[August] 25. Yesterday Daniel Cottle died in the prison hospital; he is the sixth of our company that has died [of smallpox] since we have been in England.[20]

The plague of smallpox produced agony, disfiguration, and fright, yet it simultaneously elicited acts of selflessness by the prisoners. One such prisoner was Daniel Cottle, whose death Charles Herbert recorded on 25 August 1777. On the 26th of the previous month, Dr. Jonathan Haskins had noted that Cottle, "(a black) nurse," had gone to assist the growing numbers of Americans stricken by the smallpox virus. In the hospital wards, Cottle cared diligently for the bedridden sailors, with their telltale pustules and high fevers. Perhaps he was unaware of the dangers of contagion, or he may have had little self-concern. Cottle was soon infected and became still another casualty of the dread disease.

We know only a little about Daniel Cottle's personal background. Herbert listed him among the prisoners aboard *Dalton* from Newburyport, but the only mention of him in the town's vital records states that he was a servant, who in 1774 filed an intention of marriage with Mimbo Giddens, a servant from Exeter, New Hampshire. His magnanimous actions during captivity were an early example of courage and self-sacrifice of a kind that would be repeated often at both Mill and Forton.[21]

There was far less mention of serious sickness at Forton Prison during the summer and autumn of 1777. Timothy Connor made little note of prisoner illness at this time, and neither the Admiralty entries nor the records of the Commission for Sick and Hurt Seamen includes mention of any significant outbreak of smallpox at the Hampshire prison. Obviously there were individual cases of smallpox, along with the itch, at Forton. And although the American prisoners were not supposed to be sent to the Haslar Royal Hospital, outside Gosport, captives were occasionally treated there, as well as at the Royal Naval Hospital in Plymouth. Reasons for the better health of the Americans incarcerated at Forton are a matter of supposition. Perhaps the medical staff there were more competent than the apparently inferior physician at Mill. Perhaps sanitary facilities were better at the Hampshire prison, or perhaps the inmates there took better care of themselves. In any case, the complaints of the Americans at Forton, aside from food and clothing, dealt largely with prison administration and discipline.[22]

II

Whether at Mill or Forton, the American seamen at this time had little respect for prison officials. This was especially true of keepers John Newsham and William Cowdry, who held direct authority over the captives. While the backgrounds of both men are obscure, their actions demonstrated the petty officiousness that marked the lower echelons of the eighteenth-century British bureaucracy. One historian has accurately defined the experience of these men as falling in the realm of "small tradesmen; some were local men who had connections with the commissioners, while a few had formerly held dockyard appointments or overseas posts under the Admiralty."[23]

Both John Newsham and William Cowdry were under the direct authority of the Lords of the Admiralty, and below them were the Commissioners for Sick and Hurt Seamen. They were expected to administer their respective prisons under the directives promulgated by these bodies, most especially those from the commissioners. The keepers, as previously noted, were subject to periodic inspections, usually by a member of the Commission, and they were also expected to remain in close communication with the commissioners. For their part the prisoners were permitted to petition the commissioners and other London officials involved with their care. Despite these limitations the keepers were not under daily scrutiny, and both Newsham and Cowdry had considerable personal power over their charges. Similarly, in financial matters, while each keeper's powers had restraints, the American captives often accused them of corruption, greed, or malfeasance. But the prisoners' disdain was matched by both keepers, who displayed little sympathy for the rebels during their tenure.[24]

John Newsham was evidently less detested by the captives than his counterpart at Mill. Still the American prisoners at Forton showed that they had little regard for Newsham. Timothy Connor, for example, alleged in his journal that the Forton keeper "made it his business to make them [the prisoners] deliver up their money by the point of a bayonet. There is no such thing as refusing." Later Jonathan Carpenter reported that when the keeper once was heckled by the prisoners, he declared threateningly, "It is Tiburn [tree] or Execution Dock which you deserve." Seaman George Thompson cited one occasion when a commissioner arrived "to Right our Grievances, none of us could speak to him on account of the Agent, the Doctor, and the Clerk kept Close by his Side."[25]

Yet, though Newsham occasionally interfered with the prisoners' communications and personal movements, he did permit several of their complaints to government officials. One such remonstrance to the commissioners, dated 17 September 1777 charged the keeper with "arbitrary & unwarranted conduct" and requested an official investigation. Perhaps the most notable negative personal description of Newsham came from Lieutenant Nathaniel Fanning who characterized the keeper as "very old and ugly, and used to creep over the ground not unlike a large crab." Fanning added that the keeper dealt in "cruelty and revenge" and was "ill natured toward all of us."[26]

Keeper William Cowdry at Mill Prison had a far worse reputation among the first Americans under his control. It may have been his highly arbitrary personality and his early confidence in a British triumph; it may have been the fact that Mill's restrictive features provided a better environment for rigid control; or it may have been the greater distance from the prying eyes of London officials. Whatever the reasons, William Cowdry emerges in the writings of Mill's detainees as a far more devious and reviled individual than John Newsham. Long after their release the Mill prisoners retained their contemptuous feelings toward their jailor.

The captives' strong antagonism toward the imperious rule of William Cowdry was discernible during their first months of incarceration. On 3 June 1777, his first day at Mill, Samuel Cutler offered this very negative picture of the keeper: "Mr. Cowdry is as great a tyrant as any in England, and uses us with the greatest severity." On 9 July Cutler stated that Cowdry had arbitrarily ordered that "no person, turnkey excepted, is allowed to speak to us," and during the next three and a half months, Cutler cited several prisoners who were placed on half rations, allegedly without proper reason. Cutler also claimed, on 28 September 1777, that "the agent took Capt. J[ohnson]'s money from him." Dr. Jonathan Haskins added to the grievances against the keeper by declaring that Cowdry permitted his staff subordinates to steal from the prisoners.[27] Haskins and Charles Herbert also noted that on a pleasant Sunday in July 1777, the keeper capriciously refused to allow several English visitors inside the gates, "so they could not speak to us or give us anything." Herbert later testified that on 8 August an elderly prisoner was put in solitary confinement for "complaining that our meat was no good." Two months earlier, an American ship captain had reported from France that he was informed that Cowdry had denied the captives candles, pens, ink, and paper.[28]

The journals of Samuel Cutler, Charles Herbert, and Jonathan Haskins all give the strong impression that keeper Cowdry was lining his pockets with funds allocated to feed the prisoners. These three rebel prisoners each cited a list of complaints given to John Bell, one of the Commissioners for Sick and Hurt Seamen, on 13 September 1777. The list was evidently a copy of a petition of 29 August to the Admiralty, titled "Humanitas," that, as Cutler claimed, focused primarily on "the very ill-usage recd., from the Keeper and Turnkeys." "Humanitas" specifically accused William Cowdry of corruption, and the petition was the reason Bell had traveled to Mill.[29]

The Commissioners for Sick and Hurt Seamen redressed some, but not all, of the Mill prisoners' grievances. Jonathan Haskins and Charles Herbert subsequently noted that food supplies had improved and that even a few of Keeper Cowdry's harsh restrictions had been removed.[30] Cowdry remained as Mill's director, however, and allegedly continued to torment the American detainees.

Like the two prison keepers, the guards did not receive much respect from the American inmates. There were, of course, examples of benevolence. Samuel Cutler, for example, wrote on 8 June 1777 that "an officer of the guard gave me a shilling, and four others a shilling each." However, most comments from the prisoners about their jailors throughout 1777 were quite negative and with good reason. Prison officials and army or local militia sentries were often bribable. Also few of them had much sympathy for their rebel charges. Many of the warders seemed to delight in harassing or defrauding the inmates whenever the occasion presented itself. There were numerous incidents of such victimization. Perhaps Charles Herbert offered the best example of such an episode (also mentioned by Samuel Cutler):

[June] 22. [1777] Sunday, there have been great numbers of people to see us, and the prison guard confederating with the turnkey, have got a box put up at the gate, and they will let no one look in to see us without paying a certain amount. Today we are told they got fifteen shillings in their box which they divided among themselves; but the people who put it in thought it was for the prisoners. We therefore took in our box, and are resolved to put it out no more.[31]

The daily routines prescribed by the keepers at both English prisons were generally, though not completely, similar. In June 1777 Timothy Connor at Forton described part of the regimen he encountered: "We were only allowed the forenoon to walk the yard, and were locked up at two o'clock, but for what reason we knew not; and of weekdays [not to enter the yard] till the sun was an half an hour high." Forton prison regulations also allowed the inmates to gather with outsiders at "an open market near the gate." A contemporary historian offers an assumption that in "good weather, the prisoners spent most of the day in the yard." At Mill, in June 1777, Samuel Cutler portrayed part of his day's activities: "We are allowed every day to walk in the airing ground from 10 to 12, then locked in till 3 o'clock; then we are let out again till 7 o'clock, then taken in and locked up for the night."[32] Unlike Forton, however, Mill in these first months did not allow indiscriminate contact on Sundays with the local populace. Notwithstanding minor distinctions, the American detainees at both prisons were always well aware of their captive status. It was revealed quite clearly during their regular prison checks as well as their daily regimentation.

Discipline concerns also plagued the Americans at both English prisons throughout their years of incarceration. Although the implementation of punishments seems to have been more rigid at Mill than at Forton, both detention centers often invoked the same two authorized penalties for violation of prison regulations. For less severe offenses, such as minor damage to prison facilities, inmates could be put on half rations, individually or as a group. Timothy Connor at Forton and Cutler, Haskins, and Herbert at Mill all cited examples of prisoners placed on half rations.[33]

A much more serious punishment, for offenses such as attempted escapes or insubordination against prison personnel, was being sent to the "black hole." The infamous black hole, as previously noted, had been used as punishment in earlier wars. Timothy Connor described Forton's black hole as "a very small room with neither bed nor bedding to lie on but the soft side of a good plank." In Mill's black hole it was claimed "the water lies upon the floor like a Hogstie." At both Forton and Mill, the black hole was located underneath the prison buildings. Here captives were sent by the keeper to languish for as much as six weeks. The black hole was used at the two prisons, both on an individual and group basis, soon after they opened. This penalty helped break the spirit of several rebels who pined away there. At Mill, according to prisoner complaints, Keeper Cowdry allegedly allowed "the prisoners in the Black hole, but one hour in the day to take fresh Air."[34]

Besides the ever-present threat of punishment, pressures to abandon the rebel cause were experienced by the first American prisoners. Several of the captives already had switched allegiances when they were held on royal ships. (This fact was evident, for example, in letters from Admiralty Secretary Philip Stephens to an admiral on 31 May 1777, in which Stephens directed which rebel captives on certain vessels, who had volunteered to join the British navy, should be permitted to do so.) Those prisoners on ships, whom Stephens declared ineligible for royal service, and those who had not volunteered, were ordered sent directly to Britain.[35]

Once the captives arrived on English soil and were judicially ordered to their gaols, their susceptibility toward defection increased. Most captives were far from home; they had already experienced rough treatment on enemy ships; and they all were well aware of the ominous possibility of a death sentence. It is not surprising therefore that some prison inmates petitioned British officials, singly or in groups, to enter royal service.

These petitions were more successful, in these early months, for captives applying on an individual basis. For example, Thomas Haley at Mill prevailed in his appeal of 21 September 1777, to be "plac'd on board one of his Majestys Ships of War." The English-born Haley declared that he had been compelled "totally against his inclination" into the American service. Earlier, Samuel Cutler noted that one seaman on his ship, William Horner, from Ireland, had successfully switched loyalties.[36] The result was different for sixteen Forton prisoners who petitioned Admiral Sir Thomas Pye in September 1777 "to have liberty to enter the Service of His Majesty" on board a Royal Navy frigate. That same month, the Admiralty refused to grant their request because "the Prisoners are committed by a Magistrate for treason or Piracies." At Mill, also in September, Charles Herbert wrote that "about twenty old countrymen [captives born in England] petitioned the Board [of Admiralty] for permission to go on board His Majestys ships." The request of these inmates, if it existed, never reached the Admiralty in London, and Herbert noted on 2 November 1777 his concern about a possible change in British policy on this matter: "We are informed that there is as hot a press [impressment] now going on as ever was known in England; and that fifteen hundred seamen are wanted immediately, to fit out a fleet."[37]

All these disconcerting features at both prisons were compounded psychologically for the inmates as bad war news arrived from America. The news was not always accurate, any more than it often would be in future conflicts for U.S. servicemen incarcerated in overseas detention centers. (An excellent example of enemy obfuscation was recalled by an American army colonel who wrote how he was informed by his Japanese captors in 1942 that "the Battle of Midway was a glorious victory for the Japanese . . . in which the American Fleet was wiped off the Ocean.") However, in the Revolutionary War months from June until early December 1777, word of rebel reverses pouring into England was quite accurate indeed. The captives learned of these distressing events primarily through the guards or from newspapers, even though such publications were officially denied to them. They were also quite cognizant of the build-up of British forces in Canada and America, because both prisons were in close proximity to naval bases.[38]

Rumors and confirmations of patriot defeats were reported in the captives' writings. At Forton, Timothy Connor read the *Town and Country Magazine*'s prominiterial commentary in August 1777: "General Howe's success against the Rebels. . . . was only the fore-runner of that very capital stroke of General Burgoyne, the taking of the important post of Ticonderoga; an event that has sealed the fate of this campaign entirely to our advantage. . . . Mr Washington may now be said literally to be situated between two fires." Mill prisoner diaries at this time also contained the grim tidings from abroad. On 22 August Jonathan Haskins wrote, "We have the disagreeable news of Ticonderoga being taken by the British troops"; and the following on 2 December, "By Capt. Reaves we learn that Philadelphia is actually taken."[39] Reports also circulated that Washington had been killed. Once again it was Charles Herbert who was the most thorough in reporting the grim war accounts. On 22 and 31 August he cited reports of the capture of Philadelphia and Ticonderoga. (The former was taken on 5 July, the latter not until 25 September.) Herbert continued to report persistent rumors of the capture of the congressional capital, but it was not until 2 December (the same day as Haskins's parallel entry) that he was willing to accept a confirmation of the city's fall. It took another ten days before the prisoners' spirits were at last buoyed by definitive news of General Burgoyne's surrender.[40]

But until the confirmation of this momentous patriot triumph, the captives' apprehensive feelings were evident in their writings.

The men held at Forton and Mill were three thousand miles from home without any apparent chance of exchange. Charles Herbert's diary entries indicate the resulting pessimistic sentiments. On 31 August 1777 he mentioned a general consensus that if the British should "conquer the country, or even get the upper hand of it, we are positive the gallows or the East Indies will be our destiny." Two days later he entered the disquieting rumor that the inmates were all "to be distributed on board his Majesty's ships."[41]

Charles Herbert apparently became more disconsolate as new captives entered Mill while the war dragged on without any apparent resolution. Thus the Massachusetts seaman recorded his twentieth birthday on 17 November 1777, adding, "Alas! little did I think that at the age of twenty years I should have spent a twelve month of my time as a prisoner." Ten days later he heard that King George III's speech to Parliament was in the newspapers and that the monarch "is resolved to carry the war with America at all hazards." On 7 December Herbert admitted to dejection over spiritual shortcomings during his first six months of detention: "It is a great grievance to be shut up in prison, and debarred from hearing the Gospel preached on the Lord's day, though I did not make much improvement of it when I had the opportunity."[42]

Most of those rebels, who had survived the first half-year of confinement, had reacted like Charles Herbert. They had been bent by their many discomforts and harsh treatment, yet most of them somehow had not been broken or divided. A majority of the men of Forton and Mill had shown a surprising amount of unity and resiliency. They had already defied their jailors in various ways, and they had even garnered some surprising encouragement from sources outside their prison confines. Such patterns, formed during these initial seven months of incarceration, would persist and broaden during the remaining period that the two English prisons held American seamen.

There were several factors underlying the prisoners' cohesion and their recalcitrance toward their jailors. One probably was the presence of the ships' officers, at least in the early months, within the same confinement areas. Not recognizing the legality of their ranks, Britain had refused to grant any separate parole accommodations for the rebel naval officers. This circumstance resulted in maintenance of a shipboard chain of authority on land; the lower grades could continue to look to their officers and morale could be sustained. Furthermore, the Americans, unlike most of the prisoners from Britain's previous overseas conflicts, spoke their captors' language. Accordingly, the captives' protests were communicated more efficiently, their acts of insubordination were less subtle, and they especially had greater opportunity to initiate escape attempts.

Other circumstances also influenced rebel brashness and cohesiveness. One was the New World backgrounds of most of the detainees. They had not been raised in the aristocratic, rigidly stratified societies familiar to seamen serving in the navies of European monarchs. The comparatively liberal environment of colonial America had formed in many of the captives a greater sense of initiative and self-reliance. Historians have noted that such attributes appeared among the American crewmen aboard Continental and state naval vessels, as well as those aboard privateers. These ships had disciplinary rules and regulations, as was necessary for often green, sometimes unruly crewmen. Yet the seamen, particularly aboard privateers, also had a degree of autonomy unknown among the ships of the British navy. Seaman George Hewes served on a wartime privateer cruise in which the captain even allowed his crew to decide whether to give chase to sighted enemy brigs.[43]

There was one other essential reason for prisoner fortitude during the first distressful months of confinement. It was rooted in the confidence most of them felt about the rebel cause. Undoubtedly opportunity for financial gain had been one motivating force to many of those men who had served aboard rebel ships. Still many of them also may have felt a vigorous attachment to the principles for which the Revolution was being waged: natural rights and what George Washington termed "the blessings of Liberty."[44]

These rebel sentiments, clearly evident among the captives at both English prisons, were revealed most particularly by the inmates at Mill. Thus Samuel Cutler and Dr. Jonathan Haskins on 4 July 1777 took special note of the first anniversary of the Declaration of Independence. Cutler added his hope, "May they ever continue to maintain it," while Haskins commented, "God send they ever May!" The following month, Charles Herbert wrote that, despite all the newspaper reports of rebel catastrophes, he did not believe Americans would let themselves be conquered. The following 12 December he wrote of earning enough funds to purchase "a book called *The American Crisis* on purpose to lend it to a friend without." The work was by Thomas Paine, whose stirring words beginning, "These are the Times that try men's souls," inspired resounding faith in the American cause.[45] For many rebel captives in English prisons, *The American Crisis* helped buttress their adherence to the struggle for freedom.

Manifestations of this steadfastness were clearly evident among the first internees at Forton and Mill. The previously mentioned complaints they had earlier lodged with the Admiralty and the Commissioners for Sick and Hurt Seamen were not the only remonstrances that the prisoners initiated. They also communicated their discontent over the alleged glaring inadequacies in food, clothing, and health care to the "old crab," Keeper Newsham, and the "tyrant," Keeper Cowdry. Threats of being placed on half allowance failed to deter their complaints, and when Keeper Cowdry occasionally tried to limit their access to the outside world during the summer of 1777, the Mill inmates made their grievances known through other available channels. The prisoners proved quite adept at passing on their complaints directly to visitors or through written messages smuggled from the gates.

The enterprise that the Americans displayed in protesting prison conditions was also evident in personal actions to improve their uncomfortable lot. The eighth regulation promulgated by the Commissioners for Sick and Hurt Seamen allowed the detainees at both prisons the opportunity to purchase goods by cash or barter at a daily market. Keeper Newsham apparently permitted the market to operate on a daily basis following Forton's opening, but Cowdry, as noted, was more restrictive regarding this privilege. Nonetheless, the captives in both prisons took quick advantage of this opportunity. Having almost no cash, they made use of their particular skills to make salable items. Charles Herbert's diary points out his early application of Yankee ingenuity:

[June] 11. [1777] I have finished the box for the Carpenter, and he likes it so well that he wants more made, and he brought me some more wood for that purpose, some for him and some for myself.

[June] 12. I have been busy all day making boxes, and some of the prisoners are making punch ladles, spoons, chairs and the like; for which they now and then get a shilling.

[June] 17. I have been employed for several days past making boxes and carving them. To-day I sold two, one for a shilling, the other for ninepence.

[June] 21. I now have got into such a way of making boxes and selling them, that I can afford to buy myself breakfast every morning; commonly bread and milk, which is brought to prison every morning for sale.

[September] 15. For nearly a month past, the carpenter, of whom I have had my wood, has not been here, so that I have been working a chest up into boxes, on shares [consignment]. When finished and sold, it brought nearly thirty-two shillings; but I have had a partner to work with me, and one third of the avails [sale price] we paid for the chest, so that only one third belonged to myself.[46]

Along with this individual work ethic at both prisons, there remained a broad cohesive spirit among the inmates. They did not divide into separate, antagonistic groups battling each other for leadership in their respective gaols. Instead, prisoner journals for this period at both Forton and Mill reveal a definite lack of rancor, along with a strong sense of common purpose and unified challenge to authority. This feature was shown in the early and recurrent escape attempts of the rebels at both prisons.

III

Americans at Forton and Mill were far more active in trying to flee their respective prisons than were captive Frenchmen or Spaniards during previous eighteenth-century conflicts. Some of the rebels undertook to make their getaways even before their entry into one of the two gaols. Robert Burgoyne of *Dalton,* for example, was reported to have attempted his escape on the evening of 17 June 1777 by swimming from the warship *Blenheim* while she was docked in Plymouth harbor. Dr. Jonathan Haskins, already in Mill, reported that he could not be sure of seaman Burgoyne's success. There were a few other instances of such precommittal escape tries. Most such enterprises, however, were undertaken after the rebels had been locked up in their detention centers.[47]

London officials felt no obligation to respond to individual offshore escapes, but it became another matter when groups of rebels began to break out of the land-based prisons almost immediately after they opened. As early as 25 June 1777, the Admiralty, having noted the escape five days before of eleven Forton confinees, initiated a probe of means to deter escapes and improve security. On 10 July the Board instructed the Commissioners for Sick and Hurt Seamen to offer a £5 reward for the recapture of any fugitive American because "the offenses for which [these] rebel prisoners are confined are of a *Capital* Nature." The reward was payable to individuals apprehending the captives outside the prisons. Two days later, Philip Stephens, Admiralty secretary, noted that he had received word from Commissioner John Bell that the growing number of escape attempts, especially at Forton, were due to material flaws, as well as to the "negligence or connivance" of the guards. Stephens' solution was direct: to strengthen the necessary physical features at both compounds and initiate a more "proper disposition and Vigilance of the Guard." But actions implementing these measures were insufficient. Reports of escape attempts at both prisons increased, and after one Plymouth resident was caught attempting to bribe Mill guards, the Admiralty accepted the commissioner's recommendation to replace all of the sentinels. No steps were undertaken, however, to transfer the American prisoners to shipboard confinement.[48]

Escapes were more easily initiated at Forton than at Mill and were more successful there during the first months of captivity. In fact Captain James Thompson of *Rising States,* who had broken out of Forton on 19 to 20 June 1777, was twelve days later reported to be in Paris by the British ambassador.[49] Back at the Hampshire prison, Timothy Connor recorded eleven such flight attempts from mid-June through December 1777. These are some of them:

June the 23 [1777] the 19th at night, our people made a large hole through the wall of the prison and eleven made their escape. Two were three days afterwards retaken, and brought back again—which were the gunner [James] Woodward, and [Benjamin] Lambert. The next day at ten o' clock they found out where they got away, and soon after searched all our hammocks and beds; took all our chests from us, and put them in another apartment under lock and key; and threatened to put us in irons if we did the like again.

July the 30th four more broke out at twelve o' clock in the day. One got off clear, and the three were retaken and brought back and put into the Black Hole, viz. Christopher Clark, William Tryon and John Cockran, boatswain of the *Yankee* from Boston. There they were kept for forty days half starved; allowed neither bed nor bedding to lie on, but the soft side of a good plank.

October 31st this night seven of the prisoners made a bold push, and broke open the door, and made their escape. Six got clear and one was retaken and brought back the next day, and sentenced [to] the Black Hole for forty days.

December 11th this morning three prisoners broke out of the hospital and made their escape; but by reason of so many five pounders about, they were retaken and brought back before night, and confined in the damned Hole.[50]

At Mill, escape attempts also began shortly after the prison's opening in May 1777. Thus, on 4 June, Josiah Smith, a Massachusetts resident stranded in London, wrote to Benjamin Franklin in Paris that Captain Francis Brown of the sloop *Charming Sally* had successfully broken out of Mill. Attempts to flee the Devon prison continued throughout the remainder of the year. On 30 June Dr. Jonathan Haskins wrote that "12 Lamp Posts [were] Erected round Our walls In Order to Illuminate the Jail lest some shou'd Indeavour to Elope by night."[51] This measure had little effect on limiting flights, which at Mill were then usually initiated as a group undertaking. Charles Herbert, who listed thirteen such tries, offers some good examples:

[July] 12 [1777] Last night four of the prisoners that were in the hospital, one that was in the Black-hole, and one from a prison where there are a number using applications for the itch, made their escape through a drain that leads to the river edge.

[July] 20. Last night we made a breech in the prison wall, and began to dig out, which we expect will take near a fortnight to accomplish, as we have near eighteen feet to dig under ground to get into a field on the other side of the wall.

[July] 22. The hole that is now in hand is only just large enough for a man to crowd himself out. The men that dig it have made great progress since they have been at work; we put all the dirt into our chests, as we have several of them in prison, and when they leave work, they stop up the hole with the same stones that came out, and daub it over with lime, so that it appears like the other wall.

[September] 21. Last evening about nine o' clock, it being very dark, a number attempted to get over the wall by the help of a line, but as the sixth man was going over, they were discovered, and three of the number immediately taken.

[November] 30. Last evening, it being very dark and stormy, we were in general resolved to put in execution a plan proposed—to dig out at the back side of the prison, seize the sentry, confine him, and carry him out of call, but not to hurt him. Upon breaking ground, they unexpectedly saw a lamp placed near the hole, which gave light all round, so that they thought it impracticable to put their design into execution. I think if it had been otherwise, nearly two thirds in prison would have gone out.

[December] 3. This morning the guard discovered another hole which we begun to dig yesterday. I think we have been very diligent and careful to improve every opportunity to make our escape, but the guard is very strict with us, that I think it almost impossible to succeed, and we have reason to think there are some traitors amongst us, who give information of every thing of the kind which we undertake.[52]

These repeated prison breakouts were perhaps the best examples of the fortitude and resistance displayed by the first American inmates of these two English detention centers. The men who attempted these ventures did not face a language barrier, but they nevertheless confronted other serious obstacles. They were often subjected to recurrent, unannounced searches of their persons and quarters. Also, as Charles Herbert noted, there was the ever-present possibility of informers.[53]

Once outside the compounds, there were other difficulties facing those fugitives who were seeking freedom. Few of them had significant sums of British currency, and they had to elude avaricious five-pounder bounty hunters. If recaptured, they were subject to beatings and, worst of all, to forty days in the infamous black hole. Still prisoners frequently took the risk and in doing so they discovered a greater sympathy for their cause among the English populace than they had known existed.

IV

The first rebel prisoners had not experienced much concern for their welfare from Britons. Almost all of the captives had experienced harsh shipboard treatment, and debarking in Plymouth or Portsmouth, they were subjected to bitter castigation from many of the magistrates who sent them to prison. Once inside the bleak, forbidding atmosphere of Forton or Mill, they had to contend with the edicts of keeper Newsham or Cowdry. Even those inmates who had heard of support for America from Englishmen such as parliamentarians John Wilkes and Edmund Burke, must have doubted if any such encouragement could reach them amidst their hostile surroundings.

Despite all this, the detainees at Forton and Mill prisons soon became aware that not all Englishmen regarded them with hostility. At first, many of the local citizenry came to the gates of both prisons merely to gaze with curiosity on these trans-Atlantic captives. One American inmate, who was present as the country folk gathered at the Forton market, overheard a revealing conversation: "Why Lard, neighbor, these be white paple [people]; they tauk just as us do, by my troth; thare's a paity [pity] such good looking paple shou'd troused up [hung] by our grate [great] men." Local residents continued to visit both gaols whenever permitted. They brought in and carried out various communications; they bartered for articles produced by the internees; and they made donations in the charity boxes put out by the prisoners.[54] For these nearby inhabitants, charges of treason and piracy outstanding against the inmates appeared inconsequential.

Visitors from outside the immediate vicinity, not including prison officials, also came to show their concern. On 5 July 1777, for example, Charles Herbert wrote of the appearance of "several American gentlemen," who had settled back in England before the war. These colonial transplants generously contributed to some Mill inmates they had known before. Herbert later made references in his diary to British ship captains coming to the prison and volunteering to carry the inmates' mail to America. The Massachusetts seaman also cited relatives of at least two captives in Britain who journeyed to Mill to offer comfort. At Forton, Timothy Connor's less detailed entries do not cover unofficial visitors from beyond Hampshire during this early period, but such outsiders nonetheless did travel there.[55]

Of all the Englishmen who showed a direct personal concern at this time for these downtrodden strangers in their midst, two men emerge most prominently; the Reverend Thomas Wren of Portsmouth and Deacon Robert Heath of Plymouth Dock. They are relatively unremembered today, but they left grateful and indelible memories for the prisoners they served. Their emergence in this capacity is most intriguing.

The Reverend Thomas Wren's roots were not in Portsmouth or even in Hampshire. He was born about 1725 far to the north in Grange, a tiny hamlet near Keswick in the picturesque Lake District of Cumberland. His parents evidently had some means, because Thomas received a grammar school education in Whitehaven, followed by higher studies at a prominent dissenters' academy in London. Upon completion of his studies there in 1753, Wren was admitted to the Presbyterian ministry.[56]

Thomas Wren filled several temporary posts before obtaining his permanent settlement. Then, in June 1755, he was hired "for a tryal period" as assistant to the Reverend John Norman, minister of the Presbyterian Chapel in Portsmouth. Soon after Wren's confirmation as assistant pastor, the ailing and elderly Norman died. On 9 January 1757 Thomas Wren was installed as minister of the Presbyterian Chapel. This impressive brick structure, built in the "Dutch style of Architecture," had been completed near the upper end of the High Street in 1718.[57]

During the next two decades Thomas Wren remained rather uninspiring as a preacher, perhaps because of his northern-England speech patterns. However, his knowledge and personal piety earned him considerable respect within the community. The minister's spirituality was later extolled by a friend: "Few can be mentioned who have been more distinguished by piety and virtue, by purity of mind and able behavior."[58]

Wren, who was a lifelong bachelor, also performed numerous kindhearted acts within the town of Portsmouth, often personally delivering beneficences to the indigent. His charitable acts outside the seaport included church grants to needy individuals and institutions in other parts of Britain and even a small donation to the fledgling College of New Jersey (later Princeton University). Wren's political views were definitely of a liberal bent; he supported Whig precepts, including opposition to the war in America. He shared those sentiments with his prime parishioner, the former mayor of Portsmouth, Sir John Carter.[59]

Almost from the opening of Forton, in June 1777 to year's end, Thomas Wren unhesitatingly sought to assist the colonial rebel captives. His solicitous actions took various forms. He got to be a helpful observer at confinement hearings. He became acquainted with officers of *Rising States,* who were among Forton's first detainees, and he gave them English currency in exchange for their unusable Continental notes. This was apparently the first financial assistance that Keeper Newsham permitted the inmates. Later Wren was allowed to make small donations of his own money to the captives, and, through local friends and organizations, he sought gifts of clothing and other personal necessities. Wren, along with a Mr. Duckett, an almoner from Gosport, also visited the prisoners regularly. It was through their efforts that a letter of complaint was delivered to the Admiralty in September. The Portsmouth cleric also sent word of the captives' plight to others in Britain whom he regarded as sympathetic. By the close of the year, he was allegedly even aiding inmates in attempts to flee the prison. Wren, in effect, had become the Forton rebels' foremost advocate.[60]

Deacon Robert Heath, the captives' main supporter at Mill, emerged from a somewhat different background. Heath was born in 1741 at Totnes in Devon, about twenty miles east of Plymouth. His parents apparently were not prosperous, for at about the age of fourteen Robert was apprenticed to a tinsmith. When his master failed in business, Heath left for Plymouth, where he was bound

The Reverend Thomas Wren, c. 1725–1787. Courtesy Dr. Williams's Library, London.

The Reverend Robert Heath, 1741–1800. *The Theological Magazine* **(May 1800).**

to a "Clock and Watch maker" and afterward to a silversmith. When the silversmith also went bankrupt, young Heath's indenture ended, and he moved to nearby Plymouth Dock where he began his own successful business venture.[61]

During his indenture to the Plymouth silversmith, Heath, who had been brought up in the Church of England, evidently underwent the spiritual conversion that determined the future course of his life. Influenced by the devotions of his master's son, he began

attending evangelical prayer meetings held at Plymouth Tabernacle. Heath's actions apparently earned the displeasure of his
father, "who was mortified at his son having turned Whitefieldite."
But Robert remained committed to the Calvinist Methodist beliefs,
which he zealously pursued along with his mercantile concerns.
He became a deacon in the Plymouth Tabernacle, and he also
spread his evangelical zeal to smaller communities in the West
Devon and Cornwall regions.[62] His fervor for sermonizing soon
brought him to the attention of the famed English revivalist George
Whitefield. According to his biography, Heath subsequently traveled to London where "Mr. Whitefield introduced him to the Tabernacle Pulpit, and on his retiring, required him temporarily to
supply the Tabernacle at Bristol." In all of this, Heath must have
appeared divinely inspired, for it was also said that he found time
to "visit the sick and distressed areas of the poor" in his Devon
neighborhood.[63]

Opportunities arose to move to other locales and spread the
Calvinist Methodist teachings, but Heath remained in his Plymouth
Dock residence until after the American Revolution. One opening
occurred in 1773 to become minister of the Independent (moderate
Calvinist) Church at Jewin Street in London. Robert Heath's biog-
rapher states that the congregation wanted him to be a candidate
for their pastoral office, but Heath allegedly declined the offer,
because it would have severed his "long standing ties" to the Plymouth Tabernacle. Perhaps there was another reason for rejecting
this possibility. In 1764 Heath had married a Plymouth woman;
their ten children, born in the next twenty years, were enough to
keep the lay minister anchored to his Devon business.[64]

By the autumn of 1777, Robert Heath had assumed a role of
prisoner benefactor at Mill Prison similar to that of Thomas Wren
at Forton. Whether or not Heath appeared at confinement hearings
in Plymouth has not been specified, but he was a regular visitor to
the prison. There the deacon dispensed Christian comfort, gentle
admonishments, sermons, news, clothing, and even some financial
assistance. Samuel Cutler cited this last benefit when he noted, on
21 October, that he and a fellow inmate had received £77 from
various sources, including £20 from Heath. Five days later, Cutler
and his companion used this substantial sum to finance their escape
from Mill, reportedly "by bribing one or more sentries, and pressing themselves through the prison bars." (The two men, disguised
as Quakers, journeyed to London, where, protected by pro-
American patrons, they enjoyed the sights of the city for nine days
before traveling to Harwich and sailing to freedom in Holland.)

Probably Deacon Heath was well aware of how these two Americans intended to use his £20, but there is no proof that he had arranged for the guardians on the fugitives' escape route. Nonetheless, it is true that, like Thomas Wren, Robert Heath had informed individuals in the vicinity and in other parts of England about the rebel captives' plight.[65]

Deacon Robert Heath, the Reverend Thomas Wren, and other charitable residents near Mill and Forton were obviously limited in the financial or material aid they could provide to the growing number of inmates at prisons. The captives' needs increased as the winter of 1777–78 approached. Personal suffering and want was evident at both prisons while bureaucratic inefficiencies showed no sign of receding. The truth of this worsening situation could not remain a secret. The communications of firsthand sympathetic observers like Thomas Wren and Robert Heath affected many concerned individuals and private relief efforts throughout England.

Probably the key concerned individual in the British capital, who sparked benevolent moves there to aid the prisoners, was Thomas Digges. Digges, even today a controversial figure, was born in Maryland to an old, respected Chesapeake family. He was educated at Oxford, returned briefly to the family estate, and some time prior to hostilities in America came to live in England. There he settled in London, where he became a mercantile agent. Thomas, along with his younger brother George, who joined him in the summer of 1775, carried on surreptitious trading ventures with America despite the hostilities. Simultaneously, the elder Digges undertook covert contacts with several prominent patriots in America. One such important rebel was Arthur Lee, a Virginian, who, in 1777, was a member of the American Commissioners in Paris. Consequently, when Thomas Digges was informed by the Reverend Thomas Wren and others of the deplorable conditions existing at the two naval prisons, he passed on the information to Lee. From Paris, the American commissioners authorized Digges, in early December 1777, to spend £50 for the needs of Forton's inmates. About the same time, the Maryland expatriate encouraged many sympathetic Whig gentlemen in their feelings for the imprisoned rebels.[66]

By the end of December 1777, private moves to assist the prisoners had commenced in London. On the eleventh of that month, Lord Abingdon, who had argued so eloquently against North's Act, announced to the House of Commons that he intended to promote a subscription on behalf of the American captives in England. Simultaneously, the Rockingham Whigs dispatched a repre-

sentative to visit and give on-the-spot relief to the inmates at
Forton and Mill. Lord Abingdon's initiative was strongly endorsed
by opponents. A publicized meeting resulted; it was held on 24
December at the King's Arms Tavern in Cornhill "for the purpose
of relieving the DISTRESS of the AMERICAN PRISONERS."[67]

The Christmas Eve meeting proved successful. Over one hundred men attended, including several members of Parliament, four
London aldermen, and many other opponents of the war in
America. The gathering was chaired by Robert Macky, a pro-
American member of the London Common Council. With their
antiministerial sentiments buoyed by recent news of the Saratoga
debacle, the participants commenced a relief subscription that almost immediately obtained pledges of £1300. A committee of
twenty was then appointed to administer and continue the fund.
Its members included London aldermen, prominent merchant-
dissenters Benjamin Vaughan and William Hodgson (a friend of
Benjamin Franklin), and former Marylanders Thomas Digges and
Matthew Ridley. By the time the subscription temporarily closed
on 9 January 1778, about £3700 had been raised from donors that
included Lord Abingdon, Lord Shelburne, and Sir George Saville.
Concurrent with the London efforts, a similar drive in Bristol produced about £200.[68]

V

Aside from individual or group assistance in England, the needs
of the prisoners in England were also given attention by American
officials. These men, as well as relatives and friends of the captives,
were aware of the detainees' incarceration in Great Britain. The
Continental Congress could do little directly for the seamen who
were interned so far away. General George Washington regarded
the captured privateersmen, who were the largest group in the
English prisons, as civilians and showed little concern about the
exchange of naval prisoners in general. Consequently the problem
of overseas prisoners was handled by three American commissioners who, in early 1777, were resident in Paris. One of them
was Arthur Lee, the Virginia aristocrat and friend of Thomas
Digges in London. Another was Silas Deane, a Connecticut law-
yer and former member of Congress. The most prominent of the
trio undoubtedly was the illustrious Dr. Benjamin Franklin of
Pennsylvania.[69]

The American commissioners in Paris soon became the main

recipients of information concerning the inmates at Forton and Mill. On 4 June 1777, Josiah Smith of Massachusetts wrote to Benjamin Franklin from London that the Mill prisoners had begged him to write Franklin that "they were being kept in close confinement on short allowance!" Smith, a passenger on a captured merchant ship, had been detained for two months in Plymouth prior to his release. Another source of intelligence in the months following the opening of the two detention centers was knowledgeable American naval officers who were then in France. Thus, Captain John Porter, who only recently had escaped from Mill, wrote from St. Malo on 6 June 1777, with allegations of bleak, onerous conditions at the prison. Porter charged that the British treatment of the captured Americans was "More Cruel than Turkish Enemies." On 6 September Continental Navy Captains Lambert Wickes and Samuel Nicholson wrote to the commissioners imploring them to send the prisoners "a trifle of Money in order to Relieve their present Necessity's." They added their apprehension that failure to send the captive seamen any financial aid might lead to their defection from the rebel cause.[70]

In fact the American commissioners had acted on the issue of prisoners of war in Europe even before the opening of the two English gaols. In late February 1777, they had proposed to Lord Stormont, Britain's ambassador to France, that an exchange be made for about one hundred captured British seamen that Captain Lambert Wickes of the Continental Navy brig *Reprisal* had brought to France. Some prisoner exchanges using ships, commonly called cartels, had already been successfully concluded in America. The commissioners therefore had hoped to trade the royal seamen for an equivalent number of Americans then being held in England on prison ships. Lord Stormont, however, rejected this overture, knowing that France, then a neutral nation, could not detain the seamen; they were soon released. Later that year, Franklin took a new tack on prisoner swaps by ordering a system of so-called "sea paroles" for captured British seamen. These paroles, to be signed by seized Britons, were to provide for freeing American seamen in trade for their own release. However, the Admiralty refused to even consider this approach, so that by November 1777 none of the more than three hundred rebels in the two English prisons had been exchanged.[71]

Thwarted in their efforts for a prisoner exchange, the commissioners in Paris sought to improve the captives' treatment in England. Franklin's initial appeal for leniency in April 1777 received a curt reply from Lord Stormont: "The King's ambassador receives no application from Rebels, unless they come to implore His Majesty's mercy." Despite this apparent British intransigence, the commissioners decided to send an emissary to England the following autumn. This representative would be instructed to visit the naval prisons, to report on the conditions there, to compile a list of incarcerated Americans, and to dispense financial assistance to them. On 11 December, the commissioners formally appointed a little-known American, Major John Thornton, for the task.[72] Two months before Franklin had written to David Hartley, an old friend and prominent propeace member of Parliament, requesting that he receive Thornton. In a later postscript he also requested Hartley to assist the major's endeavors. In the same vein Franklin, promising reimbursement, authorized his English friend to spend several hundred pounds for prisoner relief, and he closed his letter with an appeal to humanitarianism and conciliation:

> This wish of mine [i.e., for peace], ineffective as it may be induces me to mention to you, that between Nations long exasperated against each other in War, some Act of Generosity and Kindness towards Prisoners on one side, has softened Resentment and abated Animosity on the other, so as to bring an Accommodation. You in England if you wish for Peace, have at Present the Opportunity of trying this Means, with Regard to the Prisoners now in your Gaols. They complain of very severe Treatment. They are far from their Friends and Families, and a Winter is coming on, in which they must suffer extremely, if continued in their present Situation, fed Scantily, on bad Provisions, without Lodging, Clothing or Fire; and not suffer'd to write or receive visits from their Friends, or even from the humane and charitable of their Enemies.[73]

Dr. Franklin, already irritated over reports of alleged British mistreatment of American prisoners, did not receive an immediate response to his somewhat exaggerated appeal to David Hartley. On 11 December, therefore, he sent another copy to his old friend, and he also noted that the bearer of this copy, Major Thornton, had been directed to visit and report on conditions in English prisons. By this time, the commissioners had received word of the Saratoga victory, and Franklin especially believed that their emissary would receive a governmental audience. For that purpose the major was also given letters to Lord North and Secretary of the Treasury Sir Guy Cooper, formerly a friend of Franklin's, who was now a confidant of the prime minister. Both letters requested that Thornton be allowed to visit the prisons, inspect conditions there, and allot what assistance he could to the inmates. Major Thornton was also instructed to seek advice, if possible, from David Hartley before leaving London to visit the prisons.[74]

Major Thornton arrived in London on 16 December 1777. Lord North received him three days later, but nothing resulted from their discussions. Thornton also met David Hartley, and it was perhaps with his advice that the major departed for Portsmouth, arriving there on 28 December. From the seaport he went immediately to Forton. At first, he could only speak to the captives through the gates, with prison officials present. Later he was able to bribe some of the guards in order to talk with several of the prisoners through the gate without supervision. Evidently Thornton's persistence paid off, for the next day Keeper Newsham permitted him a brief, supervised visit inside the prison itself. There the major assured the inmates that the American commissioners in Paris were concerned about their welfare. He also offered them other points for encouragement: the attempts to arrange a prisoner exchange, the recent subscription drives on their behalf, and the news that the Reverend Mr. Wren and the prison cook would act immediately to improve their food supplies.[75]

One week after his visit to Forton, Thornton began a report of his findings for the American commissioners in Paris. Basically, it was a gloomy assessment of the prisoners' situation. Thornton wrote that the 119 Americans he found incarcerated at the Forton gaol were clearly enduring a rigorous captivity and that they were officially forbidden to speak to visitors without a prison official present. Part of their misery, he claimed, stemmed from the strict prison regulations and the corruption and petty cruelties of the prison staff. A second reason for the inmates' discomfort, he stated, was inadequate supplies of food and clothing, augmented by the prisoners' lack of funds to pay for these items. Perhaps the greatest resentment of the Forton men that Thornton cited was that prisoners, tempted to escape by the prison's limited security, were cast into the black hole when they were recaptured. The major did not visit the more distant Mill Prison, but his account implied that many of the same unpleasant conditions prevailed for the 289 Americans who were detained there.[76]

Thornton's memorandum to the commissioners did contain positive findings. He noted that recent subscription drives in London and Bristol should offer some relief to the Americans in English prisons, and he cited concern throughout that nation for the captives' welfare. The major also reported that the December 1777 speeches in Parliament on behalf of the prisoners had caused some relaxation in the severe discipline at Forton. Thornton most par-

ticularly praised the humanitarian efforts of the Reverend Thomas
Wren to assist the inmates in that prison. The major spelled out
some of Wren's activities: he had regularly attended commitment
hearings; he had successfully appealed to Keeper Newsham so that
he was able to deliver small amounts of cash and clothing to the
prisoners; and he was working with Mrs. Elizabeth Harrison, the
chief cook, to improve the meat allowance. In this confidential
account the major also advised the commissioners that Wren was
clandestinely providing some captives "with the means of making
their Escapes."[77]

In Paris the commissioners receipt, in early January 1778, of
Thornton's report could be considered one of the events marking
an end to the first phase in the story of American detention at
Forton and Mill. For more than four hundred downtrodden rebel
captives at the prisons, contact, albeit limited, had finally been
made directly with the rebel representatives in France. True, it was
only a slight opening, but for imprisoned seamen like Virginia's
Captain John Harris, anxious for word from his family, Thornton's
visit had been especially welcome. (Thornton had mentioned Harris as one of the eager prisoners converging on Forton's gate during
his call.) Furthermore, though deficiencies persisted in food and
clothing supplies, the distressing austerity of the first months had
ended. Relief contributions were assembled from London and
other parts of Britain. At Mill, Robert Heath had raised the inmates' spirits on New Year's Day 1778 with news of the London
subscription and gifts of plum pudding. Eleven days later Charles
Herbert noted the receipt of the cash donation from Bristol by
the captives. Shortly thereafter the London relief funds arrived.
Seaman Herbert recorded on 22 January that the prisoners had
agreed on dispersal of the funds according to rank: captains and
lieutenants were to receive five shillings a week, down the ranks
to common sailors, who were to receive only two.[78]

Another feature signifying the close of this initial period of confinement was reflected in Timothy Connor's journal entry on
Christmas Day 1777: "Since the defeat of Burgoyne, things wear
another face. . . . They begin to treat us better." Effects of the
Saratoga surrender became evident at Mill where the quality and
quantity of food improved, and issues of new clothing were made
during the final days of December and the first days of January.
These developments were corroborated by several New Hampshire seamen who wrote to a gentleman in Kittery (28 April 1778)
that, "Since the beginning of the year, we have lived very well
and want nothing but Liberty." In another salutory gesture, the

Admiralty, in December 1777, approved the construction of an open shed on the airing ground at Forton for the inmates' use during summer months. These more indulgent administrative actions probably were in part the consequence of the speeches in Parliament that castigated the ministry for Burgoyne's surrender and simultaneously urged more favorable treatment for the American detainees.[79]

In January 1778 new forces were about to emerge in the relationship between the American commissioners and the naval captives in England. When Major Thornton's report was received in Paris, Franklin probably discerned a turning point in contacts with the prisoners. Thornton not only gave the commissioners a firsthand account of the status of at least some of the captives, but he also supplied the groundwork for further communication with sympathetic Englishmen.[80] Additionally the foundation laid by the major could offer the basis for more direct dealings with the prisoners themselves. By the close of 1777, the commissioners in Paris were already giving monetary assistance to escaped seamen in France, and word of such aid could encourage other inmate flights. More importantly the commissioners likely sensed that the effects of the Saratoga victory might bring an alteration in the adamant British opposition to a prisoner exchange. Almost six thousand British troops detained in America certainly gave the ministry cause for concern. Consequently the arrival of letters from David Hartley in early 1778, which constituted a belated attempt to undermine any Franco-American alliance, seemed to offer such a change, because Hartley was known to be an advocate of prisoner repatriation.[81]

The initial difficult days for the inmates of Forton and Mill, a time of "settling in," had concluded by early January 1778. For the rebel prisoners, whose numbers were to increase significantly at both prisons, external events would continue to affect their captivity—a captivity that already seemed interminable to most of them. Their reaction to this ongoing and often nerve-wracking situation is part of the story of the next phase of their detention.

4

First Fruits of Perseverance, January 1778–March 1779

Several significant developments happened beyond the gates of Forton and Mill in the fourteen months after mid-January 1778. These occurrences—diplomatic, political, military, and naval in nature—were not always in the forefront of the prisoners' minds. Still, even as the growing number of inmates within these two prisons grudgingly coped with the daily difficulties of confinement, external events were having determinative effects just as they had done in the seven months prior to this mid-January date.

I

Diplomatic incidents were one prime component affecting the future of the rebel prisoners in England. In a letter of 3 February 1778 to Benjamin Franklin in Paris, David Hartley implored his American friend to avoid any affiliation whatsoever with France: "Let nothing ever persuade America to throw themselves into the arms of France. Times may mend; I hope they will."[1] Hartley's efforts came too late. Three days after his message was written, the American commissioners had signed two agreements with the French government: the Treaty of Amity and Commerce and the Treaty of Military and Political Alliance. One month after these pacts were secretly concluded, the comte de Vergennes, the French foreign minister, acknowledged to Britain the existence of the Treaty of Amity and Commerce. Shortly thereafter each nation recalled its ambassador, though hostilities did not formally begin until mid-June. Six weeks before this official start of Anglo-French fighting, the Continental Congress had ratified these compacts with the Bourbon monarchy on 4 May 1778.[2]

The formal French entry into the maritime and colonial conflict had a momentous impact on the struggle. France, for its own imperial aims, had become the first European nation to recognize American independence. French action set a precedent for other continental nations envious of British wealth and power, and French participation meant that the war automatically would be expanded overseas. Britain, therefore, would be forced to expend much more of its resources protecting its far-flung empire, particularly in the Western Hemisphere. Closer to home, the North ministry would be obligated to bolster the nation's deficient Royal naval forces to protect against a possible invasion from across the Channel. For France's new American allies, the widening of the conflict also had implications. The straitened rebel government could now anticipate new financial and material aid. This prospect must have seemed imminent with the arrival of a French naval flotilla off Virginia in July 1778. And back in Europe the new alliance meant that American ships would have a legal right to utilize French ports for their belligerent operations and to detain captured British mariners there.[3]

Political developments during this second phase of the Forton and Mill story center primarily on British governmental moves to resolve the increasing antiwar sentiments within their nation. Highlighted by the news of General Burgoyne's surrender, serious complaints had emerged in November and December 1777 over the conduct of the war. The public's desire for peace was reflected in a motion on 2 February 1778 by Charles James Fox, an opposition member in the House of Commons. During an eloquent speech, Fox proposed that no more troops be sent out of Britain for America and that moves be initiated for reconciliation with the rebellious colonies, even at the price of granting independence.[4]

Charles James Fox's straightforward resolution was rejected in the House of Commons, but a similar move by the duke of Richmond in the House of Lords did produce a plan for reconciliation with America, formulated by Lord North. A three-man commission led by the earl of Carlisle was subsequently established to take the government's proposal to America. This Carlisle Commission was not empowered to offer independence, something that even the dying Lord Chatham vehemently opposed when he made his final speech to Parliament on 7 April 1778. Consequently the Continental Congress, which had already ratified the French alliances with their acknowledgment of American freedom, rejected the British overtures for reunion. And though these compacts with France, their traditional adversary, had lessened sympathy among the English for the patriot struggle, the Americans still maintained their supporters within and outside Parliament.[5]

Lord North, who had contemplated resigning after the Saratoga disaster, remained at his post through the urgings of the king. But the pressures on his ministry persisted despite the royal endorsement, the maintenance of his ministry's majority control in Parliament, and the benefit the Tory government received from anti-French patriotic sentiments within Britain. The parliamentary session that convened in November 1778 and lasted into the following summer reflected growing discontent over the government's handling of the conflict. This increased disillusionment was apparent not only in London but also in other parts of Britain. Critical comments from merchants, religious officials, and other dissidents continued to appear in print.[6]

Military events were also affected by the Saratoga defeat, as well as by the British failure to take advantage of the capture of Philadelphia. General Sir William Howe, who had occupied the rebel capital but was unable to gain Washington's surrender, was recalled to England in May 1778. By that time, the ministry had concluded that the necessities of a now-expanding conflict required them to follow a revised military strategy in America. The new plan of action called for evacuating Philadelphia and concentrating available British forces in defensible strongholds.[7]

General Sir Henry Clinton, Howe's successor, acted to implement this adjusted military policy in America. Following an intense engagement at Monmouth Court House in New Jersey (28 June 1778), he was able to bring his forces to stronger fortifications around New York City. In August 1778 a joint Franco-American effort to retake Newport failed badly, but Clinton later decided to abandon this Rhode Island base.[8] However the British general did deviate from the overall strategy of concentration by dispatching an expedition to the South; Savannah was captured and most of Georgia was occupied by the end of January 1779. This success was partially offset the following month in the Northwest when the rebel frontiersman Colonel George Rogers Clark recaptured Fort Vincennes.[9]

Royal naval strategy also underwent changes in the year after the American commissioners concluded the French alliance. Although Britain possessed more fighting ships than France, Lord North's ministry was restricted in the number of frigates it could concentrate in America without leaving the home islands vulnerable. The need for these vessels near Britain appeared more evident following a fierce and controversial battle on 23 July 1778, in which a naval fleet under Admiral Augustus Keppel and the Admiralty's Sir Hugh Palliser fought a French flotilla indecisively off Ushant, near

Brest. Afterward Lord Sandwich, head of the Admiralty, insisted on keeping large numbers of fighting ships in home waters. The operations of the Royal Navy in America thereupon centered on supporting General Clinton's military endeavors and on attacking French possessions and shipping in the West Indies.[10]

American fighting ships quickly took advantage of the openings offered by the changes in British naval planning. In the year after the signing of the French treaties, armed vessels of the Continental and state navies and individually financed privateers became even more active in the Western Hemisphere and near Britain itself. A good example of the intrepid seamen who commanded these ships is the famed Captain John Paul Jones, who had brought the sloop-of-war *Ranger* to France in late 1777. The following spring, Jones, sailing for the Continental Navy, caused considerable consternation in Britain with a daring raid into the Irish Sea.[11] Ships of state navies, such as those of Connecticut and Massachusetts, also were more active in European waters. Privateering surged, too, so much so that some Americans deserted the Continental Navy to join these possibly more lucrative ventures. Although all these rebel ships now had the sanctuary of French ports, increased naval activity produced more chance for capture. This fact was reflected in the growing number of rebels incarcerated at Forton and Mill during 1778 and the first months of 1779. The preceding chapter has examined various aspects of the initial "time of settling in" for the captives: supervision, food and clothing supplies, health care, prisoner exchange overtures, prisoner organizations and prisoner protests, escape attempts, external contacts and assistance from within Britain, and the first contacts with the American commissioners in Paris. The continuation of these features would form a fundamental part of this next phase of confinement.[12]

II

Word of many external developments came to the American inmates at both English prisons through a variety of sources: recently captured seamen, outside visitors, friendly guards, and newspapers or journals. Whatever the origin of the information, the writings of prisoners at Mill and Forton during this fourteen-month interval illuminate reactions to these events.

Diplomatic and political incidents were given careful, though not always accurate, mention by the captives. Thus, on 28 February 1778, Charles Herbert at Mill Prison made the earliest journal entry concerning the Franco-American Alliance: "We are credibly informed that America has formed an alliance with France, for the space of twenty-one years; but whether it is anything more than an alliance for trade, we have not yet learned. We heard that it took place the 26th of this month." Dr. Jonathan Haskins, also at Mill, reported similar, though more bona fide, word of the event later, on 24 March 1778. At Forton, three days before Haskins's notation, Timothy Connor cited the treaties along with his own belief in Britain's apprehension and its unpreparedness for war.[13]

Seamen Herbert, Haskins, and Connor also took note of wartime discontent in Great Britain. By mid-January 1778 all three men had languished in their respective prisons for over seven months so such tidings seemed to buoy their spirits. Within Forton, Timothy Connor referred to the reported dissension on 7 June 1778, when he reported that the "newspapers give us an account of great riots and mobs throughout England." Other press readings also led Connor to conclude that sentiment in the kingdom "runs in our favor." That November he could easily empathize with another prisoner who mentioned his pleasure in reading a copy of the London *Evening Post* "in which is a burlesque of the Ministry, very severe." David Hartley also conveyed a sense of the antiwar sentiment in the country when he visited the Hampshire prison.[14] At Mill, the diary entries of Jonathan Haskins and especially Charles Herbert reveal the captives' knowledge of external political tensions. Herbert cited several newspaper and other accounts of dovish feelings in Parliament, the circulation of peace petitions, the departure of the Carlisle Commission, and the renewal of the North Act for their detention. Some of his assessments of these events were accurate. However, Herbert's declaration on 11 March 1778 that England was then "little short of civil war" was exaggerated. In fact, the *Gentleman's Magazine* and the *Annual Register for 1778* each lists relatively few instances of civil disturbances in Britain.[15]

The Mill journals of Charles Herbert and Jonathan Haskins offer the best picture of how much the prisoners knew concerning external military and naval developments. Both detainees provided accounts of details or rumors they had heard about such occurrences in America or nearer their own confines. Again Herbert's entries are more complete than those of Dr. Haskins, and it also appears that the Massachusetts seaman was able to obtain more information on episodes closer to Britain. Although several significant military engagements were not included in his notations, Herbert, on 3 May 1778, did cite with pleasure a newspaper account of Captain John Paul Jones's raid on Whitehaven. This report, also mentioned by Haskins, was that Jones's men had "spiked up the cannon, and set fire to a ship, and had it not been for a man that deserted the boat and alarmed the town, the boat's crew would have set fire to all the shipping in the harbor."[16]

At Forton the American inmates had access to similar sources for news of military and naval events, but the journals of Timothy Connor and Jonathan Carpenter (sent to the prison in May 1778) offer less comment on these incidents. Their notations also contain more inaccuracies. Connor, for example, reported on separate occasions during this period that the French had seized Halifax and that General Sir William Howe had been captured.[17]

One particular affair that captives at both prisons mentioned was the bloody but unresolved naval engagement off Ushant. Jonathan Carpenter's journal notes of this battle do not ascribe a victory to either side, but Connor, Haskins, and Herbert list it as an outright French triumph. The 1 August diary entry of Charles Herbert, which is almost a facsimile of Jonathan Haskins's (and, as Professor John Alexander notes, is an example of plagiarism by one of them), offers an erroneous and sarcastic evaluation made by the inmates:

> August 1 [1778]. We have seen a vast number of men come in from the ships, in boats, whom we suppose to be wounded, as we are informed that there are between seven and eight hundred wounded in the royal hospital who were taken out of the fleet. This was the fleet which they have been raising for two years past, concerning which they have boasted so much, and which they have called the terror of France. This was England's pride—the fleet that was to sweep the seas, and accomplish such wonders. Alas! many of them are disappointed of their expectations, for in their first engagement, they were worsted.[18]

III

The American prisoners digested the various reports of happenings outside their confines. Most of them were emboldened by news of the French alliance, while perhaps their morale was further inspired by the propeace activities in England and by the British evacuation of Philadelphia. But for the average rebel captive in either Forton or Mill, there were more immediate matters of concern: absorbing the continuous arrival of new detainees; resisting arbitrary or harsh discipline; maintaining proper food, clothing, and shelter; sustaining communication and comfort from outside sources; planning and effecting escapes; preserving Revolutionary loyalties; and anxiously anticipating a general prisoner exchange. Beyond all these considerations were the mundane, often onerous, challenges of daily confinement.

The steady influx of new rebel captives throughout 1778 and into the beginning of the next year was obvious to those inmates still confined in Forton and Mill. At the former prison, the new detainees included Continental Navy officers Elisha Hinman and Charles Bulkeley and privateer prizemasters Nathaniel Fanning and Caleb Foot.[19] Among the new arrivals at Mill were Massachusetts privateer captains John Revell, William Lucran, and Faunel Jones. These men had been taken either in the West Indies or at a considerable distance from the American coast. Groups of French prisoners also began to be crammed into separate sections of both gaols at this time, though their officers (as had been the custom in previous wars) were usually granted paroles outside the prisons.[20]

Until he was exchanged in the spring of 1779, Timothy Connor, one of Forton's first American inmates, kept an accounting of the increasing number of rebel captives. The Massachusetts seaman rattled off the various rebel commitments to his prison in a rather dispassionate manner, citing only the officers by name.[21] To the west, at Mill Prison, Charles Herbert briefly noted the detention of rebel and French seamen, but, except for Captain John Revell of Salem, Massachusetts, he did not list the rebels by name. Jonathan Haskins's shorter entries, which were often very similar to Herbert's, also make slight reference to the new arrivals. Both Herbert and Haskins mentioned a curious episode at the beginning of November 1778, when two Americans appeared at Mill's outer gate, but were then mysteriously moved elsewhere.[22]

The growing number of detainees resulted in overcrowding at both prisons. British authorities solved part of this problem when they sent many of the French prisoners to prison ships until their expected exchange. These guardships were also still used in England for some American seamen though usually on a temporary basis prior to incarceration in a land-based gaol.[23] On 29 June 1778 Jonathan Carpenter noted "24 French Prisoners brought to this place & put into another prison prepared for that purpose—." Carpenter wrote that more French captives were put in this separate compound until December when their numbers became so large that many of them were "marched away" in "small parties" to Winchester Castle. At Mill the preparations for French internees had begun in August of the previous year when the Admiralty, perhaps sensing impending hostilities, moved to prepare space there "for at least 1400" more inmates.[24]

By early 1778 the American prisoners had undergone a segregation of their ranks. At Forton, Timothy Connor wrote that this division had occurred on 20 January 1778, when the common seamen and "under officers" were separated from higher ranks. It was a rearrangement evidently made at the request of the interned officers. The officers' petition reflected their continued adherence to principles of subordination while they were simultaneously promoting the cause of liberty. A similar change, illustrating this paradox, was made at Mill five weeks later as described by Charles Herbert: "[February] 26. The officers in this prison [have] moved into another, which has been preparing for them, so that all the officers who were committed to prison as such, are in a prison by themselves."[25]

Meanwhile there had not been much change at the higher levels of prison supervision. As a result of the expanded hostilities, membership on the Admiralty's Commission for Sick and Hurt Seamen and the Exchange of Prisoners had increased by one in early 1779. Yet even with the influx of new detainees, William Cowdry remained the sole director at Mill, as did John Newsham at Forton. Complaints against them, justified or unjustified, continued to be lodged by the prisoners and others, but both keepers nonetheless retained the support of their bureaucratic superiors in London.[26]

An interestingly different picture of the two keepers emerges from prisoner accounts during this period. Newsham appears as a blustering, fumbling, somewhat indecisive administrator and Cowdry as an overbearing, officious bully. Newsham still made his presence known accompanying outside inspectors and other visitors to his compound. He scrutinized prisoner mail, including a suspicious letter in August 1778 between the Mill and Forton detainees.[27] Nevertheless the Forton keeper continued to allow the Americans to send correspondence to their families and friends and to their compatriots at Mill. Furthermore he permitted the rebels to post complaints to officials in London or to pass them on to sympathetic visitors such as Thomas Wren, David Hartley, or Sir John Carter. Newsham's alleged swaggering and petty peculation persisted, though his invoking of arbitrary punishments appear to have been more restrained. His letters to his superiors reveal considerable indecisiveness. Thus in February 1779 he rather pleadingly asked the Commissioners for Sick and Hurt Seamen for advice on handling the "refractory behavior of the prisoners."[28]

Some of Newsham's increased circumspection may have been induced by an earlier warning from a Portsmouth barrister that the keeper could be indicted for any unwarranted death of a rebel prisoner. Perhaps an even greater reason for the increased caution of the "old crab" was a reprimand he received from the Admiralty and the commissioners in October 1778 for allowing a letter from Benjamin Franklin, dealing with a prisoner exchange, to be read to the Americans.[29]

William Cowdry received no similar reprimand from government officials. Throughout this fourteen-month phase, he offered little forbearance to the growing number of rebel internees. He frequently interrupted the inmates' outside contacts through unannounced lockouts and personal searches. The often partisan statements of patriots George Ralls, Charles Herbert, and Jonathan Haskins offer testimony to these facts. Captain Ralls claimed that while some conditions improved after word arrived of General Burgoyne's defeat, the keeper in 1778 still continued "carrying arbitrary and inhumane orders into execution." Ralls cited the case of a prisoner whom the keeper supposedly committed to the black hole for merely complaining about ill treatment. No corroboration exists to this specific charge, though Captain Ralls's more general accusations against Cowdry for continued indifference to the inmates' suffering were reflected in other captive writings. Charles Herbert, prior to his exchange, listed several allegations against the keeper. Cowdry, who, he claimed, withheld rations in an attempt to compel prisoners to eat spoiled meat and capriciously placed a prisoner in the black hole "for little or nothing." Herbert also charged that the keeper refused to grant needed new shoes to men on half allowance. To this list of accusations, Dr. Haskins added Cowdry's practice of threatening to impose half allowance on all inmates in attempts to obtain information.[30]

IV

Threats or actual punishments meted out by either keeper were largely ineffective in changing the behavior of the American detainees. Throughout this phase of their confinement, they displayed an increase in disobedience and defiance toward their jailers. Such contentiousness was directed not only to the keepers at each prison but at all levels of manifested authority. Inmate misconduct, however, could be selective. For example Charles Herbert reported that prisoner disorder at Mill was greater when the local, less stringent militia, rather than regular army units, served as guards; this circumstance was repeated at Forton.[31]

Several descriptions from Forton during this period illustrate what Keeper John Newsham called the American prisoners' "re-fractory" nature. Thus Nathaniel Fanning offered one example of the repeated vexations that his fellow rebel officers inflicted on their captors. According to Fanning, the captives, often during the dead of night, would make so much noise that the turnkey would have to be summoned, along with guards, to their prison building. Upon entering, the jailers discovered "every man in his hammock, the bays all secured, and all quiet." But after the bleary-eyed warders departed, "threatening us in the most abusive language," Fanning claimed that the captives would maliciously "repeat our common exercise."[32]

The enlisted ranks at the Hampshire prison also demonstrated unruliness. Jonathan Carpenter cited instances of his rebel comrades' verbal insolence to the guards, and once, 8 September 1778, they broke the guards' door locks to protest an allegedly unwarranted imposition of close confinement. Seaman Timothy Connor reported several acts of insubordination by his compatriots. On 16 May 1778 an inebriated Edward Leger "struck the doctor and cook." On 13 June, Connor mentioned a significant protest of officers and enlisted men over the failure of the guards to deliver their purchased beer. On 17 August, he reported that a prisoner was sent to the black hole for "exchanging a few blows with a turnkey." However, neither Connor nor the other imprisoned Americans listed the most serious incident of rebel recalcitrance: in January 1779 several of them broke into the prison hospital, threatened the doctor, and beat John Rogers, a turncoat seaman.[33]

At Mill there were also acts of insubordination by the rebel captives. Dr. Jonathan Haskins and Charles Herbert recorded many of them during this fourteen-month interval. Haskins and Herbert both cited a minor disturbance in the prison on 10 August 1778, which stemmed from an alleged lockout of the prisoners following a protest they had made to a visiting commissioner. A more serious incident of disobedience was reported three months later when three intoxicated inmates broke "windows in Cawdry's office [by throwing stones] because he would not suffer more strong liquor to come in; this afternoon they were all committed to the B[lack] hole." This incident was also entered in Charles Herbert's journal, along with the August episode. Unlike Haskins's account, Herbert's does not include the names of the drunken sailors involved in the November affair. Nonetheless, the Massachusetts seaman does augment his account by claiming that after stoning Cowdry's windows the inebriated sailors also assaulted a guard. There were certainly other examples at Mill of drunk or sober inmates defying their jailers, but fewer incidents were reported there than at Forton.[34]

Reactions of staff members and sentinels toward this inmate unruliness varied and depended in part on whether prison guards were from the stricter regular army regiments or were more easygoing local militiamen, whom Timothy Connor aptly dubbed "old fogues" [invalided soldiers]. In June 1778 Connor mentioned a militia officer of the guard who was kindhearted enough to release Benjamin Chew from close confinement so that he could meet a visitor. He also referred to a benevolent turnkey who occasionally supplied the inmates with news. At Mill, Charles Herbert cited assistance, including abetting escapes, from sympathetic militiamen, and he pointed to a few congenial prison officials who provided news about current affairs. He also noted that a relatively tolerant militia captain of the guard was on duty at the time Keeper Cowdry's windows were broken and he prevented his men from firing on the drunken perpetrators. In this affair, Herbert claimed the home guardsmen "behaved very well toward us, and very much like gentlemen."[35]

But it was another story with sentinels drawn from regular army units. There were repeated instances in which they allegedly harassed, insulted, cheated, robbed, or assaulted prisoners. It was also claimed that sometimes these guards deceived inmates into believing they would aid escape attempts and then betrayed the plans. The most severe case of hostility reported toward these jailers occurred on 25 March 1779. According to Nathaniel Fanning the incident erupted when a malevolent captain of the guard took a red hot poker and began applying it to the inmates' shirts drying on the prison fence. Fanning wrote that the prisoners thereupon rushed to save their clothing, "which so enraged this son of old beelzebub that he ordered the sentinel to fire his musket in among us, who instantly obeyed and killed one man [Bartholomew White] and wounded several."[36] The corporal of the guard subsequently was brought before a jury meeting in Keeper Newsham's residence, but the killing was ruled accidental. Other, similarly partisan, descriptions of the episode by inmates Caleb Foot, George Thompson, and Jonathan Carpenter testify to heightened prisoner bitterness in the aftermath.[37]

V

Intermittent food deficiencies also caused inmate discontent at both English prisons. Shortages of other personal needs, such as clothing, shoes, or bedding were also reported but on a lesser scale. The causes of these inadequacies during this period included corruption, indifference, the rapid diminution of the prisoner relief fund, and several of the captives' own intemperate habits. There were occasions at both prisons when the rebel detainees experienced a serious want of basic necessities that was reminiscent of the first harsh months of confinement.[38]

At Forton, Timothy Connor, one of the first inmates, wrote in May 1778 that the prisoners had had nothing to eat for two days "but stinking beef," which they had thrown back through the cookhouse window in protest. A month later Connor was still citing the bad provisions provided to them despite the subscription funds gathered on their behalf. Nathaniel Fanning recalled "going part of the time half starved, and often picked up bones in the yard, and begged [from] others without the walls of the prison of people who lived near there." Fanning also made a fabricated accusation that British officials had deliberately put ground glass in the prisoners' food. The Connecticut officer even asserted, perhaps with considerable exaggeration, that he had been obliged to eat the marrow from bones in order to at least "partly satisfy the cravings of a hungry appetite." Seaman Jonathan Carpenter, another later inmate at the compound, also refers to victualling shortages, though in much less detail.[39]

Charles Herbert and Jonathan Haskins cited similar food deficiencies along with other shortages at Mill. Among Herbert's descriptions (corresponding to, but more than Haskins) was the seaman's entry of 12 April 1778, concerning discontent over substitutions in the prison's dietary offerings. On 30 June, Herbert noted that after finding maggots once again in their meat, the captives resolved to live off donations. Two weeks later he alleged that the French prisoners had a half-pound greater bread ration per day. In September, he reported receiving only one shirt since his imprisonment. Probably the most serious result of prisoner food deprivation during these months that was mentioned by Herbert (but, noticeably, not by Haskins) occurred in early January 1779. Herbert asserted at the time that in response to the imposition of half allowance the hungry seamen had killed and eaten a stray dog.[40]

The effects of seaman Herbert's negative accounts are, however, mitigated by other factors. The food shortages at this time were for brief periods and were relatively few in number. The French captives apparently did receive a larger bread ration than the Americans, but Herbert admitted that "the other allowance of the French is the same as ours." Furthermore the outside financial

subscription that lasted until 13 December 1778 enabled the inmates to buy provisions at the ongoing prison market. Lastly the
seaman's entry for 27 March 1778, reveals how much of the rebel
captives' deprivation was of their own doing: "There are many in
prison who have sold all their clothes that were given them
by subscription, to get a little money to gamble with, and buy
strong beer."[41]

The American inmates continued their irritation over inadequacies in health care, albeit on a comparatively less intense basis.
The dissatisfaction was more pronounced at Mill than at Forton.
Thus, while Timothy Connor made note at this time that some of
his comrades had died in the prison hospital, he did not criticize
its care or facilities. Connor also mentioned a few captured rebels
who had received special attention at nearby Haslar Hospital.
Jonathan Carpenter, another Massachusetts seaman, reported with
satisfaction in March 1779 that he had left the prison infirmary
"cleansed of ye Small pox."[42]

But at Mill the inferior quality of medical treatment persisted;
smallpox claimed several more victims, including John Lott, a Native American inmate. The penologist John Howard, after an unannounced visit there in January 1779, found the prison hospital
badly serviced, badly maintained, and poorly ventilated. Afterward
he recommended quarterly inspections and reports on the condition of the wards.[43] The accounts of the American inmates amplify
Howard's findings. Captain George Ralls charged that sick prisoners were being cared for by "neglectful, ignorant, and unskilled
persons," so that "when a Man becomes Sick, he absolutely lan-
guishes to death for want of proper necessaries and relief." Jonathan Haskins and Charles Herbert endorsed Ralls's accusations.
They both charged, after the death of a prisoner on 14 May 1778,
that ailing rebel inmates were being denied necessary nourishment
for recovery. Six months later Herbert spelled out the infirmary's
deficiencies, including structural leaks and the lack of a fireplace.
Herbert had earlier singled out Mill's physician, Dr. Manheir (Manheim), as the prime cause of patient mistreatment. When the doctor
suddenly died in June 1778, Herbert and Haskins declared in similar fashion that there was little sadness among the captives. Subsequently Herbert wrote that there had been a few improvements at
the infirmary, at least in patient care.[44]

VI

Discontent about matters involving food, clothing, and medical
care seems to have been overshadowed by the prisoners' concern

and resentment over emergent British efforts to entice rebel inmates to defect. By the beginning of 1778, the royal government anticipated imminent war with France. This fact, along with a depletion of naval personnel in ongoing American hostilities, impelled the Admiralty to solicit new recruits in the prisons from among the captured rebel seamen; they were already following this practice on the high seas. A full royal pardon for those prisoners who would enter His Majesty's service, plus promises of protection, were included in the offer. The British search for new recruits was clearly embodied at this time in the numerous visits of military, and especially naval, officials to the prisons. Joined by the Mill and Forton keepers, these officials did their best to entice or pressure rebel inmates to desert the rebel cause. Word of such alleged high-handed actions eventually reached Benjamin Franklin, who conveyed his displeasure over it in a letter to David Hartley in March 1779:

> For we learn from those who have escaped, that there are Persons continually employed in cajoling & menacing them, representing to them that we neglect them, that your Government is willing to exchange them, and that it is our fault it is not done: That all the News from America is bad on their Side; we shall be conquer'd and they will be hang'd, if they do not accept the gracious Offer of being Pardon'd on Condition of serving the King, &c [45]

The captives at Forton seemed more attentive toward the efforts to sway their allegiance. Timothy Connor noted on 13 November 1778 that recently "several of the captains and lieutenants of the navy have been here to enter as many men as they could get, telling them there will be no exchange so as to get more." He added that these Royal Navy recruiters had gotten about twenty men to switch sides. A month later, Connor declared that another effort by naval officials garnered fifteen defectors from various ranks. Jonathan Carpenter reported, with evident disdain, the departure of these turncoats on 17 December.[46] Prizemaster George Thompson, who also recorded this incident, cited the desertion of three other inmates a month later. But Thompson added that the rebel detainees did not passively accept the actions of the changelings. He asserted that loyal officers and enlisted men at Forton had agreed that anyone announcing his intention to defect after 24 January 1779 "Showld Sofer the punishment of 39 Strips and to heave one of his Ears cut of." It was evidently this agreement that had caused the band of patriot prisoners shortly thereafter to storm the prison hospital and beat the renegade seaman John Rogers.[47]

Meanwhile, at Mill Prison, similar efforts occurred to encourage defections from the ranks of rebel inmates. Charles Herbert offered the best portrayal of these actions. On 15 August 1778 Herbert wrote that officers from Admiral Keppel's ships, along with an American renegade, had come to the prison to offer pardons for inmates willing to enlist in the Royal Navy. He added that thirty prisoners, "chiefly old countrymen," (those born in Britain), had volunteered. But three days later, he noted different circumstances in the case of five Americans recently sent to the prison directly from shipboard captivity. According to Herbert, these five seamen, despite squalid confinement below deck, had repeatedly rejected bounty offers, as well as a royal pardon to enter royal service. On 6 October Herbert listed a total of thirty-two detainees, including a dozen American-born captives, "chiefly inconsiderate youths," who had accepted the promised pardons and had left the prison to board British warships. Seaman Herbert, who reported little vindictiveness toward these backsliding comrades, nonetheless affirmed his own continued allegiance: "For my own part, to enter on board a [British] ship of war is the last thing I would do. I would undergo every thing but death before I would think of such a thing."[48]

Charles Herbert maintained his own loyalty to America, but as the autumn of 1778 stretched into winter, his journal entries reveal that other rebels were not so steadfast. On 20 October he told of pardons arriving for fourteen of the defectors. Two days later, he noted that forty-five detainees by then had changed sides, but added hopefully, "those who remain, I believe are true sons of America." This statement, however, proved too optimistic. On 15 January 1779 Herbert increased the total number of renegades to forty-nine, a number that he claimed surprised him despite the allegedly harsh treatment the prisoners had received.[49]

A statistical list of Mill prisoners compiled by Charles Herbert after his exchange in March 1779 discloses much about those who deserted the American cause. According to Herbert's count, a total of 380 rebels had been committed to the Devon prison up to the date of his departure for France. Of this number he cited sixty-two fellow detainees (16.3 percent) who had left aboard British ships. The sixty-two turncoats included thirty of the sixty-one inmates whom he reported as British-born. Removing the "old countrymen" and also excluding twenty-six other non-American captives from the count results in a defection rate of only 7.1 percent. At Forton, without giving a breakdown like seaman Herbert's, Timothy Connor figured the defection rate among all the rebels at only 5.7 percent; the Admiralty figure for this gaol is a slightly higher 7.8 percent.[50]

The fact that over 90 percent of American-born captives committed to these gaols at this time did not defect can be explained in part by concerns about negative reaction or personal ties at home. But an even more fundamental reason can be discerned from pronouncements of the captives themselves—their staunch devotion to the rebel cause. At Forton, this sentiment was repeatedly expressed by inmates including Timothy Connor, Jonathan Carpenter, and Nathaniel Fanning. Connor, in October 1778, clearly reflected these sentiments in a bit of doggerel: "The Americans There'r [ever] Loyal and always very true; Unto some other country what would you have them do?"[51] That same month, at Mill, Charles Herbert expressed his loyalty while rejecting the offer of a pardon for entering British service: "This prison has been a little hell upon earth, but I would prefer it as much before a man of war, as I would a palace before a dungeon." Earlier that year, Herbert had written of his comrades' manifestations of patriotism and defiance toward their captors on the anniversary of the Declaration of Independence:

> [July] 3. As it is two years to-morrow since the Declaration in America, we are resolved, although we are prisoners to hear it in remembrance; and for that end, several of us have employed ourselves to-day in making cockades. They were drawn on pieces of paper, cut in the form of a half-moon, with the thirteen stripes, a Union, and thirteen stars, painted out and upon the top is printed in large capital letters, "Independence," and at the bottom, "Liberty or Death," or some appeal to Heaven.

> [July] 4. This morning when we were all let out, we all hoisted the American flag upon our hats, except about five or six who did not choose to wear them The agent [keeper] seeing us all with those papers on our hats, asked for one to look at, which was sent to him, and it happened to be one which had "Independence" written on the top, and at the bottom, "Liberty or Death." He, not knowing the meaning of it, and thinking we were going to force the guard, directly ordered a double sentry at the gate. Nothing happened till one o' clock; we then drew up in thirteen divisions, and each division gave three cheers, till it came to the last, when we all cheered together, all of which was conducted with the greatest regularity. We kept our colors hoisted till sunset, and then took them down.[52]

VII

Above all else, the fidelity, perseverance, resourcefulness, and intractability of American prisoners was illustrated by their many escape attempts. During the period from mid-January 1778 to the spring of the following year, the rebel detainees at Forton and Mill attempted to flee at a slightly greater rate, in proportion to their numbers, than they had in the initial phase of incarceration. During the earlier, eight-month stage of confinement (mid-May 1777 to mid-January 1778), Charles Herbert and Timothy Connor together reported twenty-four separate escape attempts from their respective prisons, whereas for the next fourteen-month period they listed forty-nine. The increase during the second period might seem to be explained by the fact that both detention centers held more prisoners than before. But there were also offsetting circumstances, such as improved security at both prisons, lengthier escape preparation, increased rewards for recaptures, and the definite word in early January 1779 of an impending prisoner exchange—all of these served to deter intended breakouts.[53]

There were several characteristic features to escape attempts, individual or group, during the second phase of captivity. They were generally better organized and more carefully planned, especially as their jailors became more watchful. Larger numbers of inmates were involved in the group endeavors to flee. There was definitely greater encouragement and assistance from outside sources who had become more familiar with the rebel prisoners and their plight. Lastly, the officers, whether off privateers or from Continental Navy ships, undertook and were more often successful in these breakout ventures than were lower-ranked seamen. (Studies of American prisoners in Germany during World War II also reveal that officers were most often in the forefront of escape attempts.[54]) Seaman Charles Herbert was particularly perceptive concerning the reasons officers' flights predominated. He credited "good friends and their [more substantial subscription] money." Behind these general features are actual stories of Forton and Mill inmates who risked serious punishment or worse in attempts to cast off their disheartening confinement.[55]

The attempted and the successful escapes initiated at Forton prison provide fascinating examples of individual or group daring, determination, and shrewdness. The journal of Timothy Connor, the irregularly kept diary of Jonathan Carpenter, and the highly partisan narrative of Nathaniel Fanning list various means employed to flee the prison, or as Carpenter facetiously called these efforts, to make "leg bail."[56]

The endeavors to "make leg bail" took various forms at Forton. Seaman Thomas Manning, who was afterward sent to the black hole, hid out in the prison for a day, then got over the compound gate at night before being retaken. On 27 May 1778 John Crow was successful in reaching freedom by way of the prison privy, but the following September Daniel Steward failed in trying the same means. Captain Elisha Hinman of *Alfred* effected a less arduous and more uncomplicated escape only five days after his incarceration on 18 July 1778; the Connecticut captain merely bribed a guard. However, five months later, the same stratagem failed for another captive.[57]

Other means used to break clear of Forton were said to include stealing a guard's keys, taking advantage of the lighter security of the prison hospital, donning disguises at the prison market, and for large-scale breakouts, tunneling out of the prison. The majority of these burrowing forays were abortive, but one, on 23 July, resulted in the successful flight of Captain Benjamin Chew, and another, on 6 September, freed Captain Alexander Dick. An intriguing confederate of Captain Chew in the July escape was Rene-Etienne-Henry de Vic Gaiault Boisbertrand, a former French infantry officer who had gone to America seeking a colonelcy in the Continental Army. He had been captured with General Charles Lee in December 1776 and thereafter had been sent to Forton, where he was confined with the American inmates. After he and his fellow fugitives reached safety in France, Boisbertrand petitioned the American commissioners, seeking a commission for himself in the patriot army, this time as a general.[58]

Because tunneling proved to be the single most successful means employed by Forton inmates to make unsanctioned group departures, a description of these schemes offers considerable insight into the fortitude and ingenuity of the imprisoned Americans. The writings of Timothy Connor and Jonathan Carpenter regarding digging schemes are generally superficial, but Lieutenant Nathaniel Fanning's narrative provides an engrossing glimpse into the organization, deception, and arduous labor involved:

> It will not, perhaps, be here amiss to mention what was done with so much dirt and stones, taken out of the great number of holes dug by the prisoners; which I will inform the reader, so far has any relation to those under the prison where the officers were confined, and where I was. The dirt was partly lodged in an old stack of chimneys nearly in the centre of our prison; the fire-places below having been for years before stopped up, and we were lodged upon the second and third floors. The chimney aforesaid being white-washed, we used when our work was finished for the night, to paste a piece of white paper over the hole where we emptied the dirt into the hollow of the chimney. The dirt, &c. was put into small canvas bags, by those who were employed

in digging under ground, and from thence passed from one to the other until it was at the place of deposit, where it was emptied, and then passed back to be filled again, where the diggers were at work. This kind of work began generally about 11 o' clock at night, when all was still excepting the sentinel, who would from time to time cry, "All's well," and last till about 3 o' clock in the morning; at which time the hole in the chimney was closed as before related, and all of us would retire to rest. After a while the chimney was filled with dirt and stones; however, we soon found another place to deposit what we took out of the holes: this was in the garret of the prison, underneath the floor. It was lathed and plastered, through which we made a hole large enough for a man to get through into the garret; here we put several cartloads of dirt and stones, and the hole was secured in the same manner as the one before mentioned in the chimney.[59]

VIII

Many obstacles faced the American fugitives once they were outside the prison's gates. Although the guards at Forton, as well as at Mill, had no orders to fire on escaping prisoners, there were instances in which pursuing sentinels took pot shots at runaways. A greater threat, as described by Nathaniel Fanning, was the numerous bounty-hunting five-pounders who lurked about the area "followed by their great dogs, and armed with great clubs," searching for inmates who were observed beyond Forton's confines. The five-pound reward was a strong incentive for many of Hampshire's poor country people.[60]

For the intrepid rebel seamen who got free of the county, there were other threats to the success of their flight. Edward Manning, a shipmate of Timothy Connor on board *Rising States,* was one escapee whose luck ran out in London. According to a 7 March 1778 entry by Connor, Manning had the misfortune of encountering a press gang that forcibly took him on board a royal warship. Two other patriot fugitives, John Watson and John Swain, met with similar unexpected problems. In a letter to Benjamin Franklin and Arthur Lee on 17 January 1779, they informed the two American commissioners that after breaking out of Forton the previous month, they had boarded an English ship bound for Holland that was blown off course and came ashore near Calais. There French officials, believing all those on board to be their British adversaries, had committed them to a nearby prison. The commissioners soon intervened to provide freedom at last for the two jail-weary captives.[61]

Seamen Watson and Swain were among the Forton escapees during this period who achieved freedom with little funds of their own and with little outside assistance. But many other American fugitives, including Benjamin Chew, Alexander Dick, and Elisha Hinman, benefited very much from considerable covert help given by sympathetic Englishmen. There was, in fact, something of an eighteenth-century "underground railroad" to shepherd them to freedom in France. It operated in both Portsmouth and London. The chief conductor on the journey was Thomas Wren, the diminutive Presbyterian minister of the High Street chapel in Portsmouth.

Many details are now evident concerning these abetted flights to liberty. Once the runaway rebels were beyond Forton, they had two alternative routes to follow. They could proceed a mile by road to temporary shelter with Duckett in Gosport; he then spirited them across the narrow harbor to Portsmouth. Otherwise they might take advantage of natural cover and select a more circuitous route around the harbor to reach the royal seaport. Regardless of the route selected, the first destination was the Presbyterian chapel on Portsmouth's High Street. The chapel was unobtrusively set back from the street. (Thomas Digges gave it the covert title "a certain house in Amster[da]m.") Adding to its security was the fact that the Reverend Wren boarded almost behind the chapel on St. Thomas's Street. Once the escapees were inside the structure, Wren and his confederates offered a helping hand. Nathaniel Fanning later described this sanctuary: "His house [the chapel] was an asylum for the Americans who made their escape from confinement; and every one of these, if they could once reach his abode, was sure to find a hiding place, a change of wearing apparel and money, if they were in want of it, and a safe conveyance to London."[62]

London was the next obvious station on the escape route. Portsmouth's harbor was closely guarded, especially after Jack the Painter's sabotage actions. There were, however, several less well-scrutinized stage coaches and other conveyances leaving daily on the city's main road for London. Supplied with money, identification papers, disguises, addresses, and other helpful aids from their Portsmouth sympathizers, the fugitives set off for the British capital. Once they reached London with its burgeoning, polyglot, overcrowded population of more than seven hundred thousand people, the escapees could almost, as Nathaniel Fanning wrote, "consider themselves in perfect safety." The security was not absolute though, as the previously cited Edward Manning of Forton and at

High Street Unitarian Chapel, Portsmouth, 1840. From William Gates, *Illustrated History of Portsmouth* **(Portsmouth, 1900) Courtesy Portsmouth City Council.**

least two Mill fugitives could testify after they fell victim to the city's ever-present press gangs.[63]

The initial destination for Forton's escapees upon arrival in the bustling city was usually the home of Thomas Digges, who lived at Number 23 Villars Street, Strand. Alexander Dick, who broke out of Forton in September 1778 and reached London, along with other rebels, told of Digges's assistance. The Virginia captain of marines and his fellow American fugitives had little money left from their Portsmouth benefactors, but Digges willingly provided £25 in exchange for a note that Dick gave him drawn on Benjamin Franklin. From the care of Thomas Digges, many of the runaways were transferred to the guardianship of Dr. Griffith Williams, a Welsh surgeon and apothecary who lived adjacent to London's docks in Wapping.[64]

It appears that the fugitives took different paths from their London sanctuaries to leave Britain. Until hostilities with France formally opened in May 1778, it was not too difficult to obtain passage to that nation's ports directly from London. Dr. Williams' residence near the city's docks served well for this purpose. Throughout that year and the next, escapees could also board ships taking them to Dutch ports or to Ostend, which were then considered neutral. According to Nathaniel Fanning, some runaways traveled to Dover and from there easily made the short Channel crossing to the continent. (The English port had at least one sympathizer, in the Reverend Thomas Denward.) Elisha Hinman, who had been sheltered near Portman Square by another sympathetic Londoner, was escorted to Deal, given false papers, and put aboard an outbound vessel.[65]

Fleeing prisoners who got to Ostend could receive assistance from Francis Coffyn, a Flemish resident of nearby Dunkirk who, by late January 1778, was working for the American commissioners. These commissioners were the men whom most of the fugitives called after reaching the continent. In Paris, their countrymen usually provided maintenance and assisted their return to America, or for those who desired it, facilitated a return to action in the rebel cause. There Dr. Franklin also made good on many of the notes given by escapees to their benefactors in England.[66]

Two other uncorroborated, though intriguing stories relating to the abetting of rebel escapes from Forton were told to the author by a retired minister of Portsmouth's High Street (now Unitarian) chapel. One anecdote was that Sir John Carter, who had obtained his wealth from breweries, had the escaped inmates hidden in beer kegs and then loaded onto his company's ships bound for the continent. The other tale was that the Reverend Wren on occasion disguised himself and accompanied the fugitives to London. The latter narrative would seem to contain the greatest possible element of truth. There was a theater located on Portsmouth's High Street opposite and a little north of the chapel; the playhouse could have been used by Wren and his associates as a source of new, innocuous garb for the Forton runaways, though there is no definite proof of it.[67]

A final matter to consider is why those assisting the Forton escapees were not interrupted by local authorities. This point is particularly intriguing because Major John Thornton, who knew many of the details of the operation, was allegedly a spy for Britain. Two reasons emerge: if Thornton was a double agent, he might not have wished to reveal this fact over what seemed a trifling matter; or British intelligence, if aware of the ring, might have deemed it too unimportant to act against. Regardless of the reasons, the American sympathizers in Portsmouth and London continued their covert aid to the fugitives.

To the west, at Mill, there was no similar organized operation for steering rebel runaways to the continent. There were, of course, sympathetic Englishmen in Devon; Charles Herbert, without citing names, briefly mentioned their collusion. Other sources reveal that at least one of them, Philip Hancock of Plymouth Dock, did abet a prisoner's flight. On 20 May 1778 Hancock personally assisted the escape from Mill of David Welsh, a Continental Navy lieutenant who had been captured aboard the brig *Lexington*. Hancock even accompanied Welsh to Holland. In other cases, however, the evidence of such outside help is inconclusive. Thus, although Deacon Robert Heath provided Samuel Cutler with £20 that the Massachusetts seaman used to finance his successful escape, there is no positive evidence that the deacon knew the purpose for which the grant would be used.[68] There is also no extant proof that Heath was part of an operation to spirit Mill fugitives out of the country. In the last analysis, therefore, rebel fugitives from the Devon prison appear to have relied more on individual initiative in making successful getaways.

Charles Herbert's journal indicates that the various escape attempts undertaken at Mill during this period were similar to those at the less-secure Forton gaol. Herbert's entries show that there were instances in which prisoners bribed guards (not always successfully) to assist their flight. The Americans, also on occasion, assumed disguises to facilitate their breakouts. There were times when rebel inmates attempted to scale the prison walls or to swim an adjoining inlet, and there was at least one instance when the prison hospital was employed as a springboard to freedom. Mill's drainage and sewerage vaults were also used, though with limited success.[69] As at Forton digging was the primary means chosen for group escapes. In late December 1778 the Devon prison experienced its largest rebel breakout attempt, involving 108 inmates. Herbert, one of them, was recaptured nearby within a day, and most of the other fugitives soon joined him back at Mill. His description of the captives' secret labors to prepare for the escape is reminiscent of Nathaniel Fanning's account of similar rebel efforts in the Hampshire prison:

[December] 27 [1778]. Sunday. At this time, we have a hole in hand, which we began a month ago. This hole is dug down by the side of the prison, about nine feet perpendicular, and from thence it is dug about fifteen feet under ground, across a road; and our intention is to dig into a garden on the other side of the way. A great quantity of dirt has already come out of this hole, and we have much trouble in concealing it. We have filled every hole and corner in the prison where we can with safety hide it, and a great many large stones are laid fore and aft the prison, in piles, under our hammocks, with old garments laid over them.—There has been so many holes discovered of late, in this prison, that we are very cautious how we proceed with this. We work only when the militia are on guard, which is every other day, because they are not so suspicious and exact in searching, as the 13th regiment.[70]

By the spring of 1779, several other sympathizers in London, besides Thomas Digges and Dr. Griffith Williams, were assisting the rebel fugitives. One was Captain Tristram Barnard, a former Nantucket whaler. Barnard helped Lieutenant John Channing after his breakout, and Channing subsequently wrote to Franklin that Barnard had "distinguished himself by his generosity toward the unhappy Prisoners" who had reached the British capital. Captain Barnard came to Paris in October 1778, offering his services to the American cause. A second expatriate, Nantucket whaler Shubael Gardner, wrote to Franklin that a Londoner named John Blyth had "hidden as many as forty escapees at his own house at his own expense." Ultimately, a feeling emerged that the American commissioners could act more directly to coordinate the secret succor to rebel fugitives. Thus, on 29 December 1778, George Seegar, a Forton escapee, wrote to Franklin from Nantes that "an Agent should be appointed in London, who should advance small sums to such prisoners, who break out of Prison to bear their Passage to France."[71]

IX

The fact that the prisoners organized group escape attempts as well as partisan celebrations of the Fourth of July at Forton and Mill only partly illustrates their solidarity and ability to regulate many of their affairs. These abilities were particularly evident at both English prisons despite the separation of officers from the lower ranks. Moreover, American-born captives, perhaps reflecting their own national traits of resourcefulness, obstinacy, and courage, were the leaders of these refractory groups.[72]

Such organized prisoner groups at Forton had boldly submitted remonstrances to Keeper Newsham or his superiors, and they pressured would-be defectors to abandon their intention to enter royal service. Prisoner governing bodies also sought out suspected informers in their midst; arbitrated disputes among fellow inmates;

and attempted to regulate personal conduct, hygiene, and sobriety while instituting their own regulatory codes. Perhaps most important they endorsed various means to maintain inmate morale during seemingly endless captivity. Leaders of American detainees at Forton encouraged the production of salable handicraft items and especially promoted education. Nathaniel Fanning wrote that regular schools were kept in which "the masters taught reading, writing, arithmetic, and navigation." Fanning, who improved his knowledge of French, declared that the learning gained by the inmates was "a most fortunate circumstance" in the whole course of their lives.[73]

At Mill, Charles Herbert's extensive coverage of this period reveals a similar situation of captive self-assertiveness. For example, Herbert recorded (17 July 1778) that the Americans had drawn up a list of their own regulations, including a ban on "gambling and blackguarding," which was read to all the prisoners. A week later he noted that three captives who had violated these articles were seized by inmate enforcers who tied them to a post and "poured cold water down their arms and neck for the space of half an hour." Herbert cites other assertive actions by his fellow crewmen: freeing and protecting an inmate who had been arbitrarily committed to the black hole, instituting their own punishments for alleged informers or thieves, and determining food purchases from their monetary allotments. The captives also compiled protests about their treatment; they celebrated the first anniversary of the Saratoga victory; and, on 24 December 1778 one hundred of them (including Charles Herbert) signed a petition affirming their loyalty to America and their refusal to enter British service. Although Mill apparently lacked Forton's formal schooling endeavors, seaman Herbert noted prisoner self-education in reading, writing, "cyphering," and navigation. Herbert himself sent out for books to improve his knowledge.[74]

X

Sympathetic Britons continued to demonstrate their concern for the incarcerated rebels. During this fourteen-month period, David Hartley occasionally journeyed from his London home to visit American captives in Forton. Sir John Carter, from nearby Portsmouth, crossed the harbor at least once to visit the detainees. At Mill both Charles Herbert and Dr. Jonathan Haskins mentioned several individuals who came to offer comfort as well as information. And even after the sizable subscription collected throughout England in December 1777 and January 1778 was expended, individual donations continued. Charles Herbert mentioned, for example, that on 7 January 1779, two weeks after the subscription money ran out, "a gentleman came to the gate and gave in a crown" for the Americans. But the greatest direct comfort and assistance to prisoner morale was supplied by two pious Englishmen, Thomas Wren and Robert Heath.[75]

The Reverend Thomas Wren's illegal help to rebel fugitives from Forton, which qualified as treason, has already been noted. But the Portsmouth cleric aided the captives in several other ways. It was through Thomas Wren's strong encouragement and involvement that prison instruction began. It was also Thomas Wren who helped bring the prisoners mail and the latest news or rumors from London and the continent. Usually Keeper Newsham allowed such items to pass. However, in early November 1778, when Newsham, citing orders from the Commissioners for Sick and Hurt Seamen, attempted to stop a letter from the American commissioners, Wren protested so vociferously that he was allowed to read it to the inmates. Not all news brought by the Portsmouth minister was good. John Harris was given word of his beloved wife's death; it was Thomas Wren who consoled the Virginia naval officer and probably offered spiritual assurance.[76]

The Reverend Mr. Wren also sustained American morale in the realm of temporal needs. On 12 February 1778 Benjamin Franklin sent a draft for £100 in response to an appeal from David Hartley requesting funds for a supplemental program. Franklin added that he approved of "Mr. Wren's prudent as well as benevolent conduct in the Disposition of the Money." The minister, who had already expended £50 of his own money after Forton's cook had run out of funds, quickly put the commissioner's funds to use. On 25 March, Wren wrote directly to Franklin explaining how, with the officers' approval, he had devised a scheme of monetary distribution that would provide the needed supplemental food allowance.

He added that he was offering the services of Duckett, his associate, to supervise the fair distribution of purchased meat. By the beginning of April, Wren had instituted his plan of cash distribution, though, as he noted in letters to David Hartley, financial problems persisted. Before summer, the minister was again obliged to use his own resources, plus contributions from friends in Hampshire and beyond, to keep this program going longer.[77]

But the charitable efforts soon bore fruit. Other prisoner assistance arrived through the work of Wren and Duckett. These two men were given the responsibility of receiving and distributing Forton's share of the almost £4000 donation raised in England for prisoner relief. These sums were allotted until completely expended in June 1779, on an average basis of about 1s 3d per week for common sailors and, in recognition of their higher rank, double that amount for officers. (This was less than the weekly payments of 2s for common sailors and 5s for officers that Wren had anticipated in January 1778.) At times, however, the London donations were delayed, and in other cases, many of the Americans drank or gambled the money away. Consequently, they sometimes lacked the funds to purchase personal items such as tobacco, extra clothing, books, tea, and writing supplies. It was then that the genial Portsmouth parson was said by one inmate "to beg clothing and money for us."[78]

The benevolent deeds, availability, and selflessness of Thomas Wren were recognized by the American commissioners in Paris with whom he was now in contact. But the greatest accolades for his work came from the Forton inmates themselves. Thus, with deep gratitude Timothy Connor mentioned the regular visits made through all seasons by Wren, in which the cleric dispensed money, goods, comfort, and any promising news. Jonathan Carpenter and George Thompson referred to his exemplary concern for them while twelve inmates lauded him with the simple, well-chosen title, "good Mr. Wren." Perhaps the most descriptive recollection of the benevolent parson during these months was offered by Lieutenant Nathaniel Fanning:

> He made it a part of his duty to visit us once a week during my continuance here, and was in the habit of calling us "my children." Often have I experienced the good man's bounty. Frequently some bad characters among the Americans, would accost him with abusive and insulting language, if he did not supply all their wants: his only reply would be, "have a little patience my children," and I will endeavour to bring you the next time I come whatever you are most in need of.[79]

To the west on the Devon coast, Deacon Robert Heath was earning similar plaudits for his work on behalf of the Americans interned at Mill. Heath, like Wren, had an assistant for his humanitarian work. The helper's name was Miles Saurey; he was listed in the Plymouth town records as a linen draper. It is probable that Saurey was also a Calvinist Methodist and, for this reason, shared Deacon Heath's charitable zeal.[80]

Regardless of their sectarian ties, both Devon men were in the forefront of the relief provided to the Mill inmates. The diaries of Charles Herbert and Dr. Jonathan Haskins contain several entries, from late January 1778 until spring of the following year, in which Heath and Saurey presented a variety of welcome gifts to the interned rebels. Included were clothing, tea, handkerchiefs, books, sugar, tobacco, and loaves of white bread. The kindly deacon and his linen draper friend also brought newspapers, mail, and information, sometimes with religious strictures mixed in. Thomas Wren, of course, had performed similar acts of generosity at Forton, but the deeds of Robert Heath were performed within a distinctly spiritual motif. Thus, on 14 June 1778, Herbert and Haskins stated (in almost the same words) that while distributing books to the captives, Deacon Heath added the strong admonition that "many of us pay no regard to the Sabbath." Six months later, Herbert noted that the deacon had made a special trip to the prison to pray for two "dangerously ill" seamen, "which is the only public prayer that has been made in this yard since we came to prison."[81]

Perhaps the single most appreciated presentation from Robert Heath and Miles Saurey (as from Wren and Duckett at Forton) was cash distributed from the London-initiated subscription fund. (But for the Devon men, the distance to the capital was almost three times as great as it was for the Hampshire men.) Mill prisoner accounts at this time relate the comings of these two benefactors and the dispensing of varying sums until the donations dried up in December 1778. Following the exhaustion of these funds, there was a brief period of restricted rations, and some captives allegedly took to eating dog meat. The temporary ration deficiency, however, was interrupted two days after the new year, when Deacon Heath provided some welcome relief with a gift of fresh bread loaves. It is little wonder that Herbert said of this man, we "love the ground he treads upon."[82]

The American inmates at Mill gave adulation and thanks to Heath and Saurey, as their counterparts at Forton did for Wren and Duckett. One example of the captives' gratitude occurred on 14 November 1778, when they presented both Devon men with a "letter of thanks for the many favors we have received at their hands." The prisoners' great respect for the two men seems to have reached paternal veneration. Accordingly, Charles Herbert wrote in his entry for 12 March 1778:

> Today our two fathers came to see us, as they commonly do once or twice a week. They are Mr. Heath and Mr. Sorry, the former is a Presbyterian minister in [Plymouth] Dock; the latter a merchant in Plymouth. These are the two agents appointed by the committee in London to supply us with necessaries. A smile from them seems like a smile from a father.[83]

XI

While all these activities were taking place in England, concern for the prisoners continued, indeed increased, across the Channel. In Paris the American commissioners made repayments to individuals, including Thomas Digges and David Hartley, who had made small advances on behalf of the detainees. The emissaries were also kept informed of expenditures from the subscription fund. Furthermore, Benjamin Franklin, on his own initiative, made attempts to get additional relief funds to prisoners through contacts in England. American seamen such as Benjamin Chew, George Ralls, Elisha Hinman, Charles Bulkeley, and Alexander Dick, who had successfully escaped to France, were given monetary aid, carefully recorded on a list kept by Franklin. Some also received help from the commissioners in returning to America or signing aboard rebel ships in French ports. Not all the escapees traveled to Paris, so the commissioners often had to send monetary aid through representatives in other continental towns. Among these agents were Francis Coffyn at Dunkirk, Jonathan Williams, Jr., at Nantes (temporarily), and John Bondfield at Bordeaux.[84]

The American commissioners also sought to maintain direct communication with the prisoners in England. On 19 September and again on 20 October 1778, the three representatives sent letters to the captives that included praise for their steadfastness and empathy for their situation. The former letter also requested that the prisoners keep the commissioners informed of "the precise conditions of your captivity so that we may enforce the same provisions here." This statement was an undisguised warning to British officials. Earlier that year complaints of maltreatment from escaped rebels and from agent Jonathan Williams at Nantes had caused

David Hartley M.P. 1743–1814. Courtesy Hull City Council and Robin Hartley Russell.

Franklin to broach the matter of prisoner supervision with David Hartley.[85]

But the single most important effort of the representatives in Paris at this time was working toward a prison exchange. British officials had imperiously rejected the Americans' initial offer for a cartel agreement. That, however, was in 1777. A much more favorable atmosphere for such an accord had emerged by the first months of the following year.

The American commissioners found several reasons in 1778 to anticipate movement on this issue. Among them were increasing antiwar sentiment in Britain, the many royal captives still in America, the negative political reaction to newspaper reports of deplorable conditions in the prisons, growing criticism over Lord Stormont's inflexible repudiation of Franklin's overture for an exchange, and the considerable support given to the prisoner-relief subscription. Major John Thornton's prison visits and Lord North's Conciliatory Commission also marked a change in conditions. Even more influential was the entry of France into the conflict and the fact that the expanded conflict would put captured British seamen under belligerent control on French soil. Finally there was Major Thornton's return to Paris carrying a note from Lord North stating that the British government, with David Hartley as its authorized mediator, at last was willing to discuss prisoner affairs.[86]

Nevertheless, effecting an exchange was another matter. In May 1778 Captain John Paul Jones, fresh from his forays on the Irish Sea, deposited almost two hundred prisoners in France. The commissioners almost immediately surmised that this fact would impel the British to conclude a prisoner exchange. Their supposition appeared correct on 29 May when Hartley wrote to Franklin that he would "apply for the exchange of prisoners without delay" but added cautiously, "official departments move slow here." A week later the English mediator wrote to Franklin proposing that if the Americans forwarded a complete list of prisoners they were willing to send to Calais, the royal government was prepared to do the same. Already irritated over an unsubstantiated rumor that Britain planned to send some captives to "hard labor in Senegal," the American commissioners sought to make the most of the situation. They replied to Hartley, declaring that Captain Jones held "at least two hundred men," and they in turn proposed that a distinction be made between captives from the Continental or state navies and those from merchant-sponsored privateers or trading vessels. The commissioners also made the rather presumptuous offer that if all the American detainees were released and if there were more of them than of British seamen in France, the difference would be made up by freeing Britons held in America.[87]

David Hartley presented a distinctly pessimistic outlook on a prisoner exchange when he wrote to Benjamin Franklin on 14 July 1778. He informed Franklin that the Admiralty adamantly refused to make any distinction between Continental Navy and merchantmen-privateer captives and that the Lords also wanted safe passage assurances from French officials for any cartel vessel to Calais. Hartley also made known to his American friend that the commissioners' request for a total release of imprisoned rebels was premature.[88] The emissaries in Paris now realized that further exertions would be needed to achieve their goal.

Negotiations moved forward slowly during the remainder of the summer and the autumn of 1778. Much of the bargaining, by necessity, had to include France and Antoine de Sartine, France's naval minister; it was, of course, French ports that would be used in the final cartel agreement. After either Nantes or Lorient had been settled on as the most suitable exchange site, the commissioners dispatched letters on 18 or 19 September and 20 October to the American prisoners, informing them of the imminence of an exchange with priority given to those "in captivity the longest." These messages, one of which Keeper Newsham tried to keep Thomas Wren from delivering, also urged the prisoners to refrain from escape attempts. Dr. Walter Farquharson, of the Commission for Sick and Hurt Seamen, and Newsham gave a similar warning directly to the Forton inmates, bluntly informing them that anyone caught attempting to flee "should positively be put on the Back [bottom] of the List." But despite the new, albeit tempered, optimism, disputes now flared up between the Admiralty and the commissioners over an accurate count of available British prisoners in France. By the end of November, the matter appeared to be at an impasse, and Franklin wrote to Hartley pointedly asking if he had abandoned exchange plans.[89]

Meanwhile these drawn-out maneuverings were having effects on the prisoners. The long-standing interchange of correspondence between Forton and Mill now centered primarily on cartel negotiations. On 2 October 1778, two American seamen at Forton, along with Antoine-Felix Wybert, a French army engineer captured at Fort Washington, wrote to Franklin about their frustration over not being released. They also informed the commissioners that British officials were blaming the American negotiators for the delay, and they cited "great Anxieties in us as the ensuing Winter approaches." At Forton, Jonathan Carpenter and Timothy Connor noted concerns in their journals. Connor had mentioned hearing news of an exchange agreement from Duckett on 28 March 1778, but as time passed without definite confirmation, the inmates of the Hampshire prison had become more disillusioned and had abandoned what Thomas Wren had described as their "tollerable patience." Contravening this gloom, however, were reports of the optimistic pronouncements of Thomas Wren's visits. They climaxed in early October, when the Portsmouth cleric read to the inmates the contents of the American commissioners' letter of the previous month which announced an imminent cartel.[90]

Prisoners at Mill experienced similar mood swings during this period. Seaman Charles Herbert reported the possibility of an impending release in January 1778, while at the same time he cautioned himself not "to put so much dependence on getting out as to be disappointed of it." On 17 April 1778 he referred to his fellow inmates' increased hopes for exchange after receipt of a letter from Captain John Harris in which the Forton prisoner told of an expected cartel within a month. When this did not occur, disillusionment prevailed at the Devon prison. By August, Seaman Herbert's disillusionment was obvious, and not even the coaxing of the "fathers," Robert Heath and Miles Saurey, could dispel the malaise. The feeling of despondency continued through September. On the 25th of that month, Jonathan Archer, who had been committed to Mill the previous spring, expressed this somberness in a letter to his father in Salem, Massachusetts: "I can give you no encouragement of our being exchanged at present, and how long it will be first, God only knows. But I expect a long confinement." Then, in early October, news arrived from Forton of Thomas Wren's reading the news of an imminent cartel. This word buoyed the hopes of Charles Herbert, along with his patriotic sentiments. But not all rebel inmates withstood the pressures on their loyalties. As noted both Herbert at Mill and Timothy Connor at Forton cited several prisoners who entered royal service from September 1778 onward.[91]

On 10 December 1778 David Hartley happily wrote to Benjamin Franklin that the American commissioners' most recent proposals had been accepted by the Admiralty and the king. Eight days later Hartley sent a follow-up letter, noting the royal government's stipulation that the captives were to be exchanged by seniority in groups of one hundred alternately from Mill and Forton. Because the Devon prison had been in operation longer, the first cartel ship would sail from Plymouth. The exchanges of Americans would continue as long as equivalent batches of British captives were sent to England on cartel vessels. And while royal officials had earlier warned that inmates apprehended in escape attempts would be remanded to the bottom of the exchange list, they did not always carry out the threat. Thus a relieved Charles Herbert wrote on 10 January 1779, that although he had been involved in the previous month's large-scale breakout, the Admiralty had informed Keeper Cowdry that those men were to be forgiven if it was "discovered through what corruption, or negligence, we effected our escape." Twelve days later, Herbert joyously reported that his name was "about fortieth upon the agent's list."[92]

Benjamin Franklin replied to David Hartley's 10 December letter on New Year's Day 1779. He informed his English friend that Jean-Daniel Schweighauser, an American agent at Nantes, was ready to receive the American prisoners there or at a nearby port. In February, Franklin followed up these preparations with a proposal to send his controversial secretary (who was a secret British agent), Edward Bancroft, to England to expedite prisoner exchanges. This proposed mission, opposed by fellow commissioner Arthur Lee and discouraged by David Hartley, was abandoned the following month. Although Franklin questioned British sincerity in promulgating the existing cartel arrangement, it was the vagaries of the weather rather than duplicity that delayed the arrival of the exchange ship in Plymouth until 5 March.[93]

It took another three weeks until the cartel vessel weighed anchor from England. On Saturday, 13 March 1779, Charles Herbert wrote that Keeper Cowdry had announced that those prisoners scheduled for release would embark the following Monday. That day, ninety-seven rebel detainees, who had earlier received their requisite royal pardons, were marched under guard to the exchange ship docked in Plymouth Harbor. (Herbert reported that from the list of one hundred, two seamen had died and one was too ill to travel.) Once on board the American sailors were given good accommodations, food, and welcome freedom of movement on the ship. Contrary winds, however, prevented them from shoving off for France until almost month's end.

In the meantime several of the chosen parolees were treated to a final display of local benevolence. On Thursday, 18 March, a week before the actual departure of the cartel ship, Herbert described how Robert Heath had come on board, "and brought some wine, tea, and sugar, and other necessities, for those who are sick." It was a noble parting gesture from the captives' "father," one who had done so much to assist, comfort, encourage, pacify, and also evangelize Mill's rebel detainees.[94] Long afterward Deacon Heath was remembered with adoration by these men in their distant nation.

The departure of the exchange ship, sailing southward to France, climaxed another stage of the rebels' British captivity. The Mill cartel in March 1779 was followed soon by a similar transfer from Forton. Together, these exchanges had shown that the expanding and protracted course of the war, along with the determined efforts of the commissioners in Paris had softened Britain's initial refusal to negotiate this issue. However, many Americans still remained at both prisons, and others would be committed or transfered to them in coming years. For some of these rebels, the time of incarceration would be brief; for others, like seaman Samuel Harris from Ipswich, Massachusetts, confinement was to last for over four long years—a period of overseas detention longer than for prisoners in any other American conflict prior to Vietnam.

5

The Inconstant Waves of Dame Fortune,
March 1779–December 1780

The departure of the first cartel vessel from Plymouth harbor in the spring of 1779 symbolized the opening of a new phase in the story of the American inmates at Forton and Mill prisons. It was a period whose bounds could be said to extend from that ship's setting sail until the onset of winter the following year. For the rebel detainees still held within the gates of the two detention centers, this twenty-one month time span would, in one respect, be marked by a continuation of previous internment features—loneliness, frustration, despair, and failed hopes. It also included further administrative pettiness, pressures to defect, deficiencies in food and medical care, and organized inmate defiance and politicization, combined with various forms of external assistance.

This interval produced some new aspects of the tale of American mariners imprisoned abroad. Among them were an unforeseen and unfortunate collapse of prisoner-exchange agreements, expanded escape incentives, and a broadened base of external communication and support. These months, in short, brought a series of developments to the incarcerated rebels that must have seemed as inconstant as the ocean waves. And, as in the earlier periods of this detention, political, diplomatic, military, and naval developments many miles beyond the confinement perimeters had their effects on both prisons.

I

Politically Lord North's ministry was buffeted by several threats. Vigorous protests, both in Parliament and the press, persisted against the government's apparently ineffective wartime policies. North's handling of administrative and financial matters received severe denunciations from prominent politicians including

Charles James Fox, Edmund Burke, and John Wilkes. Together with them an increasing number of country gentlemen were joining London aldermen seeking the prime minister's downfall. Another peril came from Yorkshire, where, in late 1779, the Reverend Christopher Wyvill directed the Yorkshire Association's reform movement which sought to reduce executive powers and to achieve financial reforms in government. Wyvill, who capitalized on increased public discontent over the conduct and expenses of the war in America, soon had the support of several of North's opponents including Fox, Wilkes, David Hartley, and William Pitt the younger. And in Ireland, commercial dissatisfactions became so serious that the ministry in 1780 was obligated to make concessions by lifting a number of the island's trade restrictions.[1]

Yet despite these and other challenges, the government managed to survive through 1780. In April of that year, Lord North had been so hard pressed that he was even making overtures to the peace-minded Lord Rockingham for a coalition government. Rockingham, however, overplayed his hand with demands that included the authority to negotiate a peace agreement granting freedom to America and reducing executive influence in Parliament. Consequently the possibility of a coalition collapsed, while royal support for the existing ministry became more firm. The chaotic Lord Gordon riots in June of that year restored North's standing among those politicians fearful over possible social disruption. Finally the arrival of more encouraging war news from America also strengthened the ministry enough to survive the September elections.[2]

Diplomatically this interval was marked by Britain's increasing isolation. In April 1779 Spain concluded an alliance with France, and two months later, it officially entered the war. Together the two Bourbon governments sought to reduce England's power, not only in Europe but throughout the reaches of its empire. Then, in March 1780, other anti-British antagonisms surfaced when Russia, joined initially by Sweden and Denmark, organized a League of Armed Neutrality. The League, which was later expanded to include other European nations, sought to limit British naval depredations by supporting a strong declaration of neutral shipping rights. In December 1780 the North ministry, informed of Dutch intentions to join the League, acted to undermine this action with a declaration of war against Holland. Despite its outward stance of nonalignment in the conflict, Holland had previously shown a sympathy toward the colonial rebels by allowing American ships to sail into Dutch ports in Europe and the West Indies. Holland had also permitted sanctuary for several escaped seamen from

English prisons. But despite Britain's actions to contravene these partisan moves by Holland and other continental nations, its status in Europe had become increasingly isolated.[3]

Militarily the months between the spring of 1779 and the beginning of winter in 1780 found Britain even more constrained in deploying its available troop strength. Spain's entry into the conflict increased the threat of an invasion attempt and thereby necessitated Britain's keeping several regiments at home. In November 1779 the ministry used this manifest danger to obtain adoption of a measure for raising more soldiers, seamen, and supplies, but other areas of peril to the Empire also needed to be addressed. The existence of such external threats in Ireland, India, Gibraltar, and widening hostilities in the West Indies, all served to restrict the operations of British forces.[4]

In spite of these restrictive factors, however, the actions of British forces in America did bring England more favorable war news, at least until the autumn of 1780. Probably the most heartening development for the government, though obviously not for the imprisoned patriot seamen, resulted from initially successful operations in the southern states. There British units beat off a Franco-American attempt to retake Savannah in the autumn of 1779. General Sir Henry Clinton afterward launched a counteroffensive against rebel forces in neighboring South Carolina that soon brought victories. In May 1780 over five thousand American combatants surrendered the stronghold of Charleston. Two months later, Lord Cornwallis routed Continental forces at Camden, and most of the state soon fell under royal control. It was not until their defeat at King's Mountain on 6 October 1780 that British forces suffered their first significant setback in the campaign, and word of this reversal did not reach London until after parliamentary elections.[5]

The largest naval engagements that occurred during this period proved indecisive. This was particularly true of the bloody, though inconclusive, battles fought between British and French squadrons in the West Indies, though in January 1780 Admiral Sir George Rodney inflicted a convincing defeat on a Spanish flotilla off Cape St. Vincent while bringing relief supplies to Gibraltar. Otherwise the fears of an imminent invasion attempt that gripped the residents of southern English seaports were unconsummated, even though the available Bourbon ships outnumbered the British. As in earlier months the greatest number of sea clashes involved fights between fewer than five or six ships. This was particularly true for American privateers, state naval vessels, and Continental Navy frigates.[6]

The activities of these three categories of armed patriot vessels at this time were generally inglorious. After 29 October 1779 those Continental Navy ships that previously had operated under the direction of the Marine Committee were placed under the superintendency of another congressionally initiated body called the Board of Admiralty. This new organization dispatched the ten frigates under its command on several cruises to the West Indies, Europe, and along the Atlantic coast. The overall record of these missions was unsatisfactory, and four of the Board's ships were abandoned to the British in May 1780 with the surrender of Charleston. State naval vessels also suffered serious losses during 1779–80. Privateer ventures were marked most notably by a few armed cutters fitted out in France and, starting in May 1779, commissioned by Benjamin Franklin with the express purpose of capturing British ships for prisoner exchanges. Franklin's armed vessels, manned by multinational crews, took some prizes off the British Isles, though by January 1781 most of them had been lost. Similarly, in the Western Hemisphere, rebel privateering often proved haphazard. All these engagements resulted in an increasing number of rebel seamen finding themselves incarcerated in prisons both in America and Britain.[7]

If there was one conspicuous naval engagement involving American seamen during this period (or, for that matter, during a longer period encompassing the later naval history of the United States), it was the memorable battle between *Serapis* and *Bonhomme Richard* on the evening of 23 September 1779. The renowned John Paul Jones captained the converted French merchantman; Captain Richard Pearson commanded the forty-four gun British warship. The battle began off Flamborough Head on the Yorkshire coast. The ensuing struggle between these two warships involved bluster, courage, and carnage on both sides. It climaxed with the surrender of Captain Pearson, though two days later *Bonhomme Richard* had to be abandoned.[8] This notable engagement also had tie-ins with the English prisons, for mixed in with Jones's multinational crew were former Mill and Forton inmates, including Nathaniel Fanning, Henry Gardner, John Burbank, Samuel Stacy, and Antoine Wybert. The American victory also was to produce a genuine, though fleeting, opportunity for a further exchange of captives.[9]

II

News of this particular sea battle, like other external wartime events, reached the Americans confined at Mill and Forton. As in the months before, newspapers from London and other English communities usually were available for prisoner reading. Opportunities also existed for receiving information via amicable guards, sympathetic visitors, letters from home, or newly arrived captives. Regardless of their source, wildly exaggerated rumors of non-existent British reverses continued to be cited in prisoner journals. Thus George Thompson, on 18 July 1779, reported learning of "General Provosts [Augustine Prevost] armia being defiated in South Carolina by General Lincone [Benjamin Lincoln] 1400 being kiled and wounded and 700 Tacken prissoners."[10] But these accounts are not so detailed as those rendered by seamen Timothy Connor and Charles Herbert, and fewer comments appear in them about the sources of such reports.

The actual knowledge and attitudes of the captives concerning external events is difficult to ascertain, but there was definitely no lessening in the number of Americans incarcerated in the two main English detention centers. The earlier departures of inmates, such as Charles Herbert, Samuel Cutler, Alexander Dick, Benjamin Chew, and George Ralls, were offset by the imprisonment of the likes of William Wigder, Caleb Foot, John Manley, Luke Matthewman, and Gustavus Conyngham. The arrival of these Yankee seamen, along with other detained naval personnel, maintained rebel rosters at both Forton and Mill. Still, drop-offs in the size of the inmate population during the months from March 1779 through December 1780 did occur, stemming primarily from escapes or exchange accords.[11]

Just as the implementation of the first prisoner-exchange agreement, which brought freedom to almost one hundred Mill inmates in March 1779, could be said to have concluded one phase of the prisoner story, so, too, could the culmination of a cartel agreement from Forton qualify as the opening event in a new stage. The Americans in Forton had been well aware of the liberation of their fellow patriots in Devon. Prizemaster George Thompson already had recorded on 15 March that "a letter came from plemouth which Give an account that the prissoners was ordered to bee Imbarct on bord of the Cartell Ship Milford and to proced for France with the first faire wind." The following 5 April seaman Jonathan Carpenter noted that the transfer had indeed commenced: "We received a letter from Plymouth which tells us that the Cartiel ship sail'd from there 25 of March with 100 men for Nantz [Nantes]." The next day, Timothy Connor added his own sentiments, in jottings separate from his personal journal: "The 6th [of April] we are received the News of the Cartel Ship Been Sail'd the 25th of march for Nants [Nantes] with 97 amaricens on Board; God sand them quick pass [passage]."[12]

Expectations of their own immediate release increased among the Forton inmates, but it took another three months before some of them benefited from another exchange. Although the wait was frustrating, captives like Timothy Connor had become somewhat inured to unrealized dreams of leaving Forton with a royal pardon, which was to be followed by boarding a ship bound for freedom in France. Inevitably, bureaucratic quibbling delayed fulfillment of the inmates' yearnings.

Benjamin Franklin, laboring diligently to complete this second exchange, probably did not anticipate such a lengthy delay. Several days after receiving word from Nantes of the Mill prisoners' arrival, the American commissioner wrote to David Hartley offering considerable "Thanks for your unwearied Pains" in that agreement. He also asked his English friend if he knew "whether it is intended to send another hundred immediately?" Hoping to speed the process, Franklin then assured Hartley that he could easily assemble one hundred British prisoners in France ready for exchange. British officials therefore would not be "obliged to wait for them." Another incentive for furthering future exchanges was also raised when the American commissioner added, "We have still a greater Number [of British captives] in Spain."[13]

David Hartley's reply to Franklin's letter came on 11 May 1779. He stated that he had spoken the previous evening to John Bell, one of the Commissioners for Sick and Hurt Seamen, about a further prisoner exchange. According to Hartley, Commissioner Bell was well disposed to implement an exchange but suggested "that it be made at the French port of Morlaix," in Brittany, which was much closer to England than Nantes. Hartley began to act upon the commissioner's proposal, but ten days after his letter, Thomas Digges, who was then working closely with the parliamentarian, wrote to Franklin that the cartel ship *Milford* had not yet returned to England. Her absence, Hartley had told Digges, was causing considerable concern and threatened a new accord.[14] On 26 May Franklin wrote to the Committee for Foreign Affairs in America citing the success of the first exchange and, without mentioning specific progress, declared that he anticipated "receiving a second Number from the Prison at Portsmouth." Five days later, however, he wrote Thomas Digges that there was significant opposition in the French government to using Morlaix as the exchange port. Digges's return letter of 11 June told the American commissioner that now the British government had brought up its own obstacles to an agreement. The expatriate Maryland merchant stated that the Admiralty still had no word of the arrival of their cartel ship from Europe and that no further exchanges would occur until its return.[15]

Ten days after Digges's letter, *Milford* arrived back in England with its British prisoners, thereby resurrecting the delayed transfers. On 24 June 1779 David Hartley joyfully wrote to Franklin that the next group of American captives "is either sailed or under orders from Portsmouth, viz. Forton prison to Nantes." Hartley added he had overcome the the opposition of the Commissioners for Sick and Hurt Seamen to using Nantes as the exchange port, and he suggested that the commissioners might in future be willing "to sweep away greater numbers than 100 at a time." That same day George Thompson noted from within Forton that Keeper John Newsham had reportedly received orders to "Deliver 120 prissoners to the Captn on bord Cartell as Soon as She should bee redy to Receive them on bord ."[16]

The actual departure from Forton of those Americans chosen for repatriation did not occur for several more days. On 25 June seaman Jonathan Carpenter wrote in his journal that the captain of *Milford* would need another five or six days to take them on board. This fact was also relayed the next day in a letter from twelve captives to David Hartley.[17] But even this added delay was overshadowed by the evident exhilaration of those fortunate prisoners chosen for exchange. Nathaniel Fanning, many years afterward, recalled his feelings when Keeper Newsham's clerk called his name from among the one hundred twenty selected: "Never I believe was joy equal to what I now Experienced." Fanning, Carpenter, and the other selected Americans were told to keep themselves "in readyness to go on bord ye carteel" and were then separated from their remaining fellow captives. Fanning was mistaken by a month in recalling the actual date that the chosen inmates left Forton, but his brief description of that 2 July 1779 event remains quite fascinating: "We began our march which began in company, or rather escorted by about forty British soldiers, and a number of black drummers and musicians who beat up the tune Yankee doodle, which they continued playing, till we arrived at the place of emarkation."[18]

Nathaniel Fanning paused in his recollection of this glorious day of liberation to regret the fact that "we left behind several poor fellows who had been prisoners for three years and upwards." The lieutenant from Connecticut thought his remaining comrades had been humbled by the fact that he and others incarcerated for lesser periods were being freed, but he surmised that these men might have been consoled by their ardent patriotism. Most likely this was an exaggerated assumption, as was his claim that several of the captives had been prisoners for three or more years.[19]

Thomas Digges, who had recently returned from a trip to Paris and a meeting with Franklin, may or may not have directly observed the exchange proceedings at Gosport. However, shortly after this episode, he wrote to Franklin telling him that the transfer had gone off with good will on all sides: "There were 17 officers & 102 men. . . . They behaved very quietly & properly as they passed to the Ship. . . . The general language of the Lower class of People as the American Prisoners past to embark was they are fine fellows, God Bless them, & send them safe home."[20]

Jonathan Carpenter and Timothy Connor, also among the Americans receiving pardons, offer more matter-of-fact, and quite similar, accounts of this moment in Gosport. Seaman Connor's entry for Friday, 2 July, states simply: "This morning we were called to be ready; and in the afternoon we marched off through Gosport and went on bord the Milford at Spithead." Carpenter's notation for this date, while very comparable, did include some demonstrative and reflective sentiments: "This morning we were called to be in readiness, and in the afternoon march'd off through Gosport, and went on bord the Milford carteel Ship laying at Spit-head &c. The day long wished for is come at last, Huzza—I having ben in Fortin prison one year & 12 Days."[21]

III

Timothy Connor's description of his release was equally dispassionate. Aside from it and his earlier daily accounts of captivity, he left one other intriguing item of prison memorabilia. This rewarding document is a manuscript containing fifty-seven songs, which were evidently written during the course of Connor's twenty-five month internment at Forton. Professor George Carey, who transcribed these ballads into an excellent edited volume, has noted that it is a matter of "conjective uncertainty" how seaman Connor obtained or wrote them or even if they were actually sung by the captives. Nonetheless the contents of this songbook offer some of the most telling insights into the personalities, the expectations, the concerns, and the beliefs of the thousands of Americans in these distant British prisons.[22]

Many of Connor's ballads focus on feminine companionship and love, from which the seamen clearly had been divorced since their incarceration. They were nevertheless subjects on which the captives brooded as the frustrating days of detention dragged endlessly on. Several of Connor's compositions, with subtitles such as "A Love Song," or "A New Song," contain words that reflect the inmates' longing for wives or sweethearts in far-off America. Verses from one such ballad, "Molly's Lamentation for the Loss of her William," while conjecturing about an absent loved one's thoughts, in fact reflect those of the imprisoned American:

> He has crost the raging seas his Molly for to teze
> And that is the cause of my grief
> I sigh, lament and mourn waiting for my love's return
> Of whom shall I seek for relief
>
> I grive lament and weep which wakes me from my sleep
> And in dreams I do see my true love
> O cursed be the day that from me he went away
> Over the raging seas for to rove. . . . [23]

The songbook contains a lesser number of ballads devoted to the category of the sea. In these songs Connor wrote of dashing, successful privateering enterprises; the courage and fortitude of American seamen who faced the dangers of the seas; and the monotony of shipboard life. One prominent such chanty employed nautical allegories with obvious sexual connotations. Its opening lines are quite reminiscent of the venerable sailor's ditty "Blow the Man Down."

> As I was walking through Francis Street
> A lovly Frigate I change [chanced] for to meet
> She was well fitted for the Sea
> And all she wanted was company
>   foldrol etc
>
> I asked where was her place of abode
> She told me in black Squirs road
> And that night she'd send me word
> That I was welcome to come on board
>   foldrol etc. . . . [24]

Several songs contain political lyrics designed to perpetuate the inmates' loyalty to the Revolutionary cause. Their verses were usually framed to recount alleged British violations of American rights, not unlike the grievances listed in the Declaration of Independence. They also stressed the necessity of unity to attain the goal of freedom, even in the face of great adversity. Such themes are reflected in these lines from another of Timothy Connor's ballads:

Americans did flourish in unity and bliss
Till that grand Villain Bute invaded our happiness
By sending of the stamp Act into America
For to enslave, enslave the Sons of Liberty. . . .

Come all you Brother Soldiers let us united be
And follow our officers to the groves of Liberty
Where we and our commanders may agree in unity
We will show them Bunkers-hill play like Sons of Liberty.

In ending my ditty come fill us up to a bowl
Here is a health unto America that scorns to be control'd
Likewise to George Washington, Adams, Hancock and Lee
In ending my ditty Success to Liberty
Finis[25]

A final and perhaps overriding theme that can be discerned from this songbook is the loneliness, frustration, and melancholy of the American captives. The thousands of miles separating them from home and hearth, their longing to return to loved ones, the mixture of rumors and uncertainties about their future—these sentiments clearly superseded the immediate concerns of the patriot inmates. Verses penned by Timothy Connor in August 1778 illustrate such plaintive feelings:

O now the cold winter comes on
And Forton runs hard by my side
For work at my trade I have none
And the best of my friends I have tried
O he thats a friend to himself
Will provide for a cold winters day
That will serve him in time of his need
When the best of his friends are all floon. . . .

By this experience I've learnt
And Forton runs hard by my side
For want of an industrious Wife
That something for me will provide
O then I will tumble and toss
Till dinnertime lie in my bed

If the girl would but serve me so
I would not care how soon I was Wed. . . . [26]

IV

For Timothy Connor, the sentiments expressed in the prison ballads may have been only memories following his exchange in July 1779, but for many other Americans the distress of imprisonment continued at both Forton and Mill. Veteran inmates not selected for the exchange, such as Forton's George Thompson and seaman Samuel Harris at Mill, were still acclimating new detainees, like Caleb Foot or William Wigder, to the confinement surroundings. Internment continued in separate confinement areas at both gaols for French naval personnel of lower ranks. Unlike the Americans, however, the French mariners were moved during the invasion threat in 1779 to inland confinement locales. Several Spanish sailors were also committed to Forton and Mill after their nation formally entered the hostilities but in considerably smaller numbers than their French counterparts. A small but significant number of Dutch sailors were added to this polyglot mixture of detainees, again in their own section of the prison. Their presence was noted by William Russell at Mill, who wrote in his diary on 31 December 1780, "We have now 122 Dutch prisoners."[27] The remark was made only eleven days after Britain's declaration of war on the Netherlands.

Regardless of the increasing national diversity seen among the inmates during this interval, the American captives, as a group, remained under much the same administrative control. The membership of the Commission for Sick and Hurt Seamen increased to four in 1780 with the addition of Robert Lulman.[28] This move was evidently related to the growing number of captives in Britain. There was, however, no concurrent change in the top administration at Forton and Mill, where John Newsham and William Cowdry supervised the growing number of detainees, American and otherwise.

At Forton, the extant accounts continue to portray John Newsham as a blustering, overbearing bureaucrat. Perhaps the best example of these character traits is in an incident recorded in the diary of Jonathan Carpenter on 29 May 1779. Carpenter described the scene when Keeper Newsham announced to the prisoners that he had sent the names of inmates designated for release to London for the requisite pardons. According to the Massachusetts seaman, the inmates responded to the keeper's announcement by shouting indignantly, "Damn his Majesty & his pardons too; who wants any of his pardons? What murder and treason have we done?"[29] This defiant cry of the captives allegedly was met with the following retort from Newsham:

> Why you impudent rogues, don't you know that you are Rebels and were committed to prison as pirates for Murdering and plundering his Majesties subjects? (& if we should subdue America) The Law of Nations would swing every dog of ye, and without his Majesties most gracious Pardon, you would never step a foot from this place except it was to Tiburn [Tiburn gallows] or Execution Dock, which you deserve other than an exchange.[30]

Keeper Newsham did not report this confrontation to his superiors. There were undoubtedly other similar instances when he rebuked defiance by his American charges. Instead his letters to the Commissioners for Sick and Hurt Seamen and the Admiralty deal in a rather mundane manner with such topics as commitments, prisoner exchanges, escape attempts, health care, financial expenditures, and prisoner requests to enter royal service. Perhaps concern about further inquiries resulting from the March 1779 shooting death of Bartholomew White caused the keeper to minimize mention of disciplinary matters to his superiors.

The journals and correspondence of Forton prisoners from the spring of 1779 to the close of the following year became less numerous after the departure of the likes of Timothy Connor, Jonathan Carpenter, and Nathaniel Fanning. Those seamen who remained and kept diaries or wrote letters from Forton, including George Thompson and Caleb Foot, offer little direct mention of John Newsham. Thompson noted on 26 June 1779 that the prisoners had written a grievance leter to "Mr Nasham, but wee could knot get anay Redress from him; he told us he hade his orders from the bord of Commissioners." In a letter of 21 August 1780, Caleb Foot dismissed all his jailors, Newsham included, as "bloody tyrants." In short, it appears that there continued to be little respect for the Forton keeper from the American inmates.[31]

Because of the exchange or escape of prisoners at Mill such as Jonathan Haskins, George Ralls, Samuel Cutler, and, most prominently, Charles Herbert, regular and revealing inmate accounts are less available for this period. William Russell's journal entries are enlightening but sporadic in appearance. Captain Gustavus Conyngham's interesting comments cover only a very brief time span; Captain John Manley was incarcerated for a much longer time, but most sources covering him during this interval are secondary. And, unfortunately, the surviving portion of William Wigder's fascinating diary begins only after January 1781.[32] American attitudes about Keeper William Cowdry for this time span nonetheless can be surmised from the writings that deal with Mill's rebel captives or, in some cases, from the keeper's correspondence with his superiors in London. Thus the fact that William Russell's published journal excerpts and the letters of Gustavus Conyngham make only passing mention of Cowdry during these months may indicate that his autocratic behavior was mollified somewhat, at least compared to the earlier years. Nine days after his committal (30 December 1780), Russell made the general observation that "The Agent is pretty good-natured."[33] Seaman Russell's comment might have indicated a change in the keeper's demeanor; it also could have been an initial impression, or perhaps it indicated that the inmates had learned to adjust their own particular counteractions to Cowdry's supervisory actions.

Other sources pertaining to this period offer no definite portrayal of Keeper Cowdry's handling of his rebel detainees. In one instance however, Thomas Digges in London alleged (12 October 1779) that the Mill prisoners' "scanty allowance" stemmed from their having "a more griping Agent than at Portso [Portsmouth]." Also several of the Americans who escaped or were exchanged from Mill did provide comments about their former lives in detention. Their remarks are almost entirely negative, but their criticisms are surprisingly general regarding the prison administration and do not single out the keeper for particular scorn. As for William Cowdry's reports to his superiors, they, like Newsham's communications, deal with matters other than inmate discipline.[34] The overall impression that both keepers seemed eager to convey to their overlords in London, while not directly stated, was that they were maintaining order in their respective prisons, at least as far as discipline was concerned. The American inmates incarcerated at Mill or Forton held a differing perspective of the manner in which they were responding to prison authority.

V

Most Americans interned at either Mill or Forton displayed through repeated actions that they were neither complaisant nor subservient toward prison authority. The prisoner organizations, which had emerged soon after the detentions began, continued to operate during this period. These regulatory, self-governing, but covert bodies existed in the officers' and lower-rank sections of both prisons; they were able to replenish their numbers from among new arrivals when veteran inmates departed. Furthermore the rules that these inmate organizations instituted to regulate the conduct of the detainees were passed along to subsequent arrivals. Not surprisingly these unauthorized groups usually directed the various forms of organized defiance against prison officials.[35]

Ultimately it was the keeper who found himself the object of prisoner discontent. An excellent example of Yankee recalcitrance came in response to Keeper John Newsham's blustering to the prisoners on 29 May 1779, as reported by Jonathan Carpenter. A group of inmates vocally and vociferously dismissed any chance of royal success: "Overpower & Subdue America. . . . You have not done it yet nor won't till the D[evi]l's blind & his eyes aren't sore." Following this derisive and colorfully colloquial rejoinder, Carpenter claimed that John Newsham left the scene, leaving the hapless turnkey to try to restore order.[36]

Perhaps because of the limited firsthand accounts from this phase of internment at Mill, there is no similarly recorded instance of insubordination toward Keeper Cowdry personally. However, on 26 July 1780, seaman William Russell recorded one sharp incident of recalcitrance toward the prison staff. Russell described the contentious affair as follows:

> When we were turning in at sunset some high words arose between the soldiers and our people. An officer and two men came to the window and asked if we were English, and began to use uncivil language. Upon which [James] Pike said he was an Englishman and was taken by the Americans in the first of the war, and would fight for them as long as they had a vessel afloat. They called him a rascal and threatened to put him in the Black Hole. We laughed at them and told them there were more rascals outside than in. They went out of the yard and soon returned with six or seven more soldiers to put Pike into the Black Hole, but not knowing him they seized on several and let them go. They searched the prison, and we told them that if they confined one they should confine all. Whereupon they went out again and we clapped our hands at them and gave them three Cheers.[37]

The keepers had to cope simultaneously with other ongoing problems associated with supervising the restive rebel detainees. It mattered not to the captives that they were far better off at Forton or Mill than aboard prison ships or in shipboard confinement; they knew quite well that they had lost their personal liberty,

Old Inn at Forton. Forton Barracks in Background. The Inn was said to be in operation at the time of the American Revolution. Courtesy Gosport Historical Society.

and they were quick to seize upon real or imagined inequities. Their doubtlessly partisan list of alleged injustices focused on conditions such as health care, rations, personal supplies, proper heat and ventilation, and contacts with outside visitors. The prisoners also had to contend with increasing attempts to entice or pressure them into defecting from the patriot cause. Not surprisingly, Newsham and Cowdry faced recurrent reaction in the form of captive dissidence and numerous escape attempts.

The shortcomings of the prisons during this interval are evident in testimonies from both gaols. At Forton, Caleb Foot provided limited, though significant, information on this topic. On 30 June 1779, five months after his committal, Foot glumly wrote to his wife that while he was not in "great suffering on account of provisions," he nonetheless "felt the want of clothing." Eight months later, however, in another fretful message, he told her that the limited rations for those sent to the black hole consisted of "only two pounds of beef and one pint of peas for one week to live upon."[38]

The portions of George Thompson's Forton journal that cover his confinement until his escape on 1 November 1779 do not directly mention food or clothing deficiencies. But there were letters from the Hampshire gaol that do mention them. One such letter sent by Robert Birrell to Benjamin Franklin (3 February 1780), cites particularly the alleged inadequacies of the inmates' clothing:

"We are in a great Measure destitute of Cloathing, in want of a great Many Articles for which we suffer, such as shoes Stockings, fuel and articles etc." Four days later, another letter on behalf of 280 inmates declared that the interned seamen "lacked stockings & had no jackets." And even though the London merchant-physican William Hodgson corroborated the prisoners' account, immediate relief was slow to arrive. This fact was indicated in a letter to Franklin from Thomas Mehaney of Forton, on 13 August, in which he begged the American commissioners to advance money to the Reverend Mr. Wren for purchasing needed clothing.[39]

The American captives at Mill, like those at Forton, experienced shortages of clothing, provisions, and personal supplies, especially after the early prisoner subscriptions dried up. Thus, Gustavus Conyngham declared on 31 August 1779, shortly after he was committed to the Devon gaol, that after the prisoners had had nothing to eat for forty-four hours, they "protested so loudly that the guard had to be called out to disperse them." On 28 October, shortly before his escape, Captain Conyngham wrote, "provisions very bad & little of it." Afterward, from his sanctuary in Holland, he wrote two letters to Benjamin Franklin in which he included insufficient rations in a damning list of complaints against his Mill gaolers. At about the same time, thirteen imprisoned Mill seamen also wrote to Paris citing hunger as a major part of their "most disagreeable State of Confinement," and they implored Franklin for "a little money from our Prize money or money due." Captain John Manley's prison letters to Franklin are less specific in this regard, but William Russell in December 1779 gave brief mention of what he regarded as deficiencies in victualling: "Our diet is short, only 3/4 pounds of beef, 1 lb of bread, 1 qt. of beer per day per man."[40] In fact, except for any mention of cheese, butter, and peas or greens, these rations cited by Russell conformed to the table of victualling prescribed by the Commissioners for Sick and Hurt Seamen in 1777.

Clothing shortages did exist at Mill though they appear to have been less serious than at Forton. James Adams, prizemaster from a continental sloop of war, wrote to Franklin (3 November 1779) citing pointedly "my present necessity for Clothes" and added that the garments given by his captors were insufficient. By the following May, however, Adams was writing to Paris that royal authorities had satisfied his needs, at least in this regard.[41]

Mortality rates at both prisons remained at a similar low level. Thus, in a report from the Commissioners for Sick and Hurt Seamen covering the period from 30 May 1777 to 7 November 1780, only seventeen deaths were listed among 503 Americans committed to Mill. The Forton figures from 15 June 1777 to 7 November 1780 were cited as twenty-three deaths for 707 committals.[42] The majority of these deaths had occurred during the early months of confinement. Although these statistics reflected the fact that health care had improved at both prisons, there were still some significant instances of dissatisfaction. At Mill, the prior inadequacies in medical attention were rectified somewhat as Dr. Walter Farquharson, the medical member of the Commissioners for Sick and Hurt Seamen, made more regular visits to the prison. Perhaps these visits were made in response to John Howard's criticisms after his inspection in early 1779. Howard had then declared that he found the prison hospital "dirty and offensive." And while official British records for this period mention no unusual outbreak of disease, real and imagined illnesses undoubtedly persisted. Most likely, the perception continued that the prison staff was indifferent to complaints from the prisoners. James Adams claimed that the staff regarded the prisoners as being in the same category as "poor indigents" or "criminals."[43]

At Forton Prison, which Dr. Farquharson also visited, there was almost no mention of medical matters during this period in the accounts of Caleb Foot or George Thompson. On 13 October 1779 Thompson did mention rather off-handedly that he had become ill and been sent to the hospital, but he added no further details. Nonetheless, the following February, several American inmates sent a letter to Benjamin Franklin alleging that the British were deliberately taking the most seriously ill seamen, stricken with "all kinds of Distemper," through the American confinement areas. As a result, they added, "We are growing Very Sickly amongst us, Scarce a day but [several] more is taken down with the Fever." And John Howard, who had visited the prison in March 1779, commented on unfavorable sanitary conditions, which also must have been disturbing: "The Floors of the bed-rooms and hospital could not but be dirty and offensive. . . . The straw, by long use, was turned to dust in the mattresses, and many of them here and other places, had to be emptied to rid them of vermin."[44]

The American captives also continued to grumble over their physical environment. They made occasional mention of dampness, cold, stuffiness, or poor lighting. Similarly John Howard, after his inspection of both prisons, referred to poor construction methods at Forton and a lack of glass-enclosed windows at Mill. But he also praised the "healthy, airy" situation at the Devon prison and declared that "the Americans had more spacious apartments than the French."[45] Certainly the comparative superiority of land-based detention over shipboard or prison ship confinement as described in Caleb Foot's journal helped lessen rebel complaints about their surroundings.

There were similar limitations on the complaints of prisoners regarding external contacts. Mail from home had not reached the captives during their confinement on the high seas, and its arrival was often sporadic on prison ships. Likewise, supportive outside contacts were rare for those held in shipboard captivity, and they were carefully scrutinized for those on prison ships. The Mill and Forton inmates, on the other hand, generally had easier access to communication with each other, with rebel officials in France and America, and most importantly, with friends and family at home. They usually had less trouble meeting with sympathetic Britons and with American merchant-ship captains temporarily detained in England. They continued to mix with local citizens at the prison markets where they could also sell or barter their handmade crafts and other possessions. Nevertheless, restrictions on outside contacts were evident at the land-based detention centers. John Howard did report one inmate's complaint that Keeper Newsham was still examining mail. And at both gaols, prison officials normally kept tabs on prison visitors. But, though prisoners like Caleb Foot and Gustavus Conyngham complained about the mail delays, it was not a major factor in their discontent.[46]

If there was a single most bothersome element for most of the rebel inmates at this time, it was the increased and ongoing effort to get them to defect. The causes for the growing exertions of the British were obvious. Their war had not only continued but had expanded. With Spain now officially in the conflict, more soldiers, sailors, and naval vessels were needed to protect strategic outposts such as Gibraltar and Barbados and to compensate for the ongoing wartime depletions in personnel. Closer to home, there were ever-present needs to maintain garrisons in Ireland, to counter at least one army mutiny in Scotland (April 1779), and to preserve the civil order that seemed to be threatened by the Lord Gordon riots which raged in London during June of the following year.[47] All these pressures made it only natural that royal officials would intensify their efforts to inveigle American seamen to abandon their rebel loyalties and enter His Majesty's service.

Indications that the British were determined to cajole or entice their captives to abandon their American allegiance was illustrated by the increased appearance of various recruiters at both prisons. Their ongoing presence was mentioned by Captain John Manley in a letter of 16 July 1780 to Benjamin Franklin: "Our People are solicited daily to enter the English service." Most of the mustering agents represented Royal Navy units, but there were some who sought defectors for the army or merchant marine. Some recruiters in the latter category were seeking men for the fishing or whaling fleets in America, which could prove to be a more certain and less oppressive route for a prisoner to return to home and hearth.[48] Regardless of who the enlistment officers were, there were reports that the British were using unethical means to obtain American turncoats. Benjamin Franklin referred to such alleged methods when he wrote to David Hartley in the spring of 1779, charging that the British government was deliberately delaying exchanges in order to give "more opportunity of seducing the Men by promises and Hardships to seek their Liberty in engaging against their Country." The following December, Gustavus Conyngham alluded to these supposed maneuverings when he urged Franklin to send more aid to the Mill prisoners in order to thwart attempted subversion efforts. Perhaps the most blatant endeavor to obtain renegades, as alleged by Forton prisoners, was their gaolers' provocative practice of transporting corpses from their own hospitals "through the Midst of us, sometimes nine or ten a day." To this charge, which may well have been overstated, Franklin could only advise the captives that every inmate who defected gave additional incentive to the enlistment agents and consequently endangered further cartels.[49]

The great majority of imprisoned Americans resisted the British attempts to obtain their defection as they had in previous months. However, as before, some among them succumbed to the blandishments of their captors and entered royal service. Their names are recorded in the records of the Commission for Sick and Hurt Seamen or the Admiralty, or, to a lesser extent, in prisoner journals. Thus Caleb Foot mentioned no such renegades, while George Thompson, in the seven months prior to his escape on 1 November 1779, reported only three instances in which a total of eight inmates defected. At Mill, on 4 July 1780, William Russell "regretted" that, following a defiantly spirited Independence rally, "Mr. Patten and one John Adams should have chosen this day to turn traitor and enlist on board the British sixty-four gun ship *Dunkirk*." The Admiralty and the Commission for Sick and Hurt Seamen, which had to obtain the requisite pardons to complete applications for those entering British service, kept a far more thorough count of rebel inmates offering to change sides. Admiralty records for this twenty-one month period list twenty-three applications for pardon, including seven on 11 December 1780.[50] While the exact background of these twenty-three detained seamen was not stated, there are indications that a majority were old countrymen (i.e., were originally from the British Isles).

VI

Prisoner committees endeavored to dissuade other prisoners from defecting, but the principal means of undermining recruitment efforts and at the same time putting an end to confinement continued to be escape efforts. By now, however, a new factor was definitely facing those captives attempting to "make leg bail." With the successful completion of the first cartel in the spring of 1779, prisoners who attempted to flee knew full well that recapture meant not only being punished in the black hole but probably being sent to the bottom of any future cartel list. More ominously, Caleb Foot asserted in August 1780 that retaken escapees were being impressed onto Royal Navy vessels. (The Admiralty's sharply increased need for more seamen seems to give considerable credence to Foot's claim.) Despite all these impediments, American seamen rarely hesitated to take advantage of an opportunity for unsanctioned departures. This fact was evident in a pronouncement from the Admiralty (23 November 1780) calling for greater alertness and additional security measures. It stated that since December 1778, a total of 213 American prisoners had escaped from Mill and Forton prisons, and 110 of that number had broken out since the previous January. The declaration also suggested collusion between the guards and inmates in these flights. Twelve days later, a new directive from the Lords ordering more security measures cited the high cost that had been involved in retaking the fugitives. Once again rebel officers, with their greater skills and means, had been most conspicuous in the various attempts to flee these two prisons.[51]

At Forton, the less secure detention center, both the American officers and lower ranks kept the ever-eager five-pounder bounty hunters quite busy because of their many attempted escapes. Official records, as well as the prisoners themselves, cited such recurrent endeavors at the Hampshire prison. The success rate of these undertakings was far greater at Forton than at Mill. Thus a report of the Commission for Sick and Hurt Seamen on 14 November 1780 declared that 42 percent of the Forton prisoners who had tried to escape since 15 June 1777 were successful, while the breakout rate at Mill for almost the same time span was only

16.5 percent. The commissioners' records are not so illuminating concerning the several flights as the prisoners' themselves. George Thompson, prior to his escape, cited a total of sixty-two rebel inmates who were involved in separate attempts. It should be noted, however, that some of the flights he reported were made at Mill Prison.[52]

The largest breakout scheme from Forton during this period had not yet been successfully implemented. Planning for it began in late November 1780, when about seventy American inmates, led by Lieutenant Luke Matthewman and Captain John Smith, first gathered to formulate their enterprise. Matthewman, who had been committed to the prison earlier that month, wrote a rather explicit description of the effort. According to his account, a tunnel was dug under the officers' quarters to a secluded area outside the prison gates. One major problem, as Nathaniel Fanning had earlier noted, was how to conceal the excavated dirt. In this case, a space above the ceiling of the tunnel and below the building itself was used. But the first tunnel was discovered just as it was nearing completion, so in late December the undaunted inmates were obliged to begin work on a second one.[53]

George Thompson and Caleb Foot, two other successful Forton escapees, also described their flights from confinement. Thompson, who fled on the evening of 1 November 1779 with another inmate, did not describe the actual means to break out. He merely stated that he and a fellow captive made it to the Gosport home of a sympathetic Thomas Francis, who had them transported across Portsmouth Harbor to the care of Thomas Wren.[54]

Foot and three comrades achieved their escape the following October. The Salem seaman, like George Thompson, did not detail the means of escape, but he did invoke some theological allegories in recounting the event:

> Saturday October 14th, 1780
>
> At 8 A.M. I left my country seat in company with Mr. [George] Dissmore [Dismore], Mr. [Samuel] Rice, and Mr. Atwood. We fled from the Valley of Destruction to the City of Refuge, [Gosport] where we spent but little time, and then we crossed the Gulf of Despair [Portsmouth Harbor] and arrived safely at the Promised Land [Portsmouth] where we dined and spent the remainder of the day very agreeably to think that we had passed thus far on our pilgrimage. On the 15th, at five o' clock in the morning, Mr. Dissmore took stage with me, and we arrived at the New Jerusalam [London] at eight P.M., where we were received with joy, and happy we were to arrive safely at our port. We spent some days in the most agreeable manner. But there being some-

thing more than all this happiness to call our wandering minds, we must leave this new abode, and cross the water once more, for which we embarked on the 26th of October, on board a small ship commanded by John Handy.[55]

At Mill, American prisoners also attempted to escape during this period. However, as at Forton, records of the Admiralty and the Commission for Sick and Hurt Seamen do not give a complete picture of the endeavors to break free. In addition, fewer accounts exist for this time period for the Devon prison describing rebel attempts to flee detention.

Nevertheless there are two tales that do offer intriguing portraits of successful flights from confinement. William Russell wrote that on 28 December 1780, Captain Samuel Gerrish, with the help of a barber, disguised himself as a French officer. Shortly afterward some paroled French officers visited their interned seamen in the prison, and "when they retired, Captain Gerrish placed himself among them, and went out bowing to the Agent [Keeper] who did not know him." Another personal, albeit anglophobic account of a successful escape from Mill's confines was offered by Captain Gustavus Conyngham, the so-called "Dunkirk Pirate." Conyngham, prominent for his depredations against British shipping in the English Channel, had experienced some harsh treatment from his captors even before he was sent to Mill during the summer of 1779. The rough handling evidently persisted in the Devon prison, as Conyngham noted his recurrent commitment to the black hole. On the evening of 3 November, the captain broke out of Mill along with over forty other inmates, and he was fortunate enough to make a successful dash to freedom in Holland. The particular escape method was tunneling, and the captain rather symbolically described it in a letter to Benjamin Franklin the following month. Because he and his fellow Americans had been confined in Mill "on suspicion of high treason on his majesties high seas," it was therefore only proper, he declared, that "we committed treason as well through his majesties earth and made our escape." Conyngham's freedom, however, proved temporary: on 17 March of the following year, the Dunkirk Pirate was recaptured from a ship bound for America and shortly afterward was again behind the gates of Mill Prison.[56]

Some of the Americans who fled from Mill at this time did not even share Captain Conyngham's transitory good fortune. Seaman William Russell recorded two separate unsuccessful attempts to tunnel out of the prison in January 1780. Captain John Manley reported from Mill (16 July 1780) that his recent attempted escape had ended when he "unluckily wa[s] retaken and severly punished by being con[fined] to the black hole and kept 40 Days on half allowance." Many of the fugitives were recaptured near the prison or in other parts of Devon. (Manley and his companions were recaptured while hiding in the Plymouth Guildhall.) Six rebel seamen who made it out of England, found, as did some other escapees, that even getting to the continent might not mean freedom. Eight days after their flight from Mill, these Americans wrote to Benjamin Franklin (11 November 1779) from Cudant in France, telling him that they had been put in the town jail "upon Suspicion of being Englishmen." They implored the commissioner to get them released, grant them monetary support, and provide them with passes for nearby Brest where they might board a ship for home.[57]

Altogether a majority of the alleged number of escape attempts from both prisons still ended in failure. Some attempts were uncovered by the guards or prison staff; others were divulged by informers among the inmates; and others were thwarted by avaricious five-pounders. Sometimes these local bounty hunters succeeded by deceiving an escapee. They would assist in a getaway, entertain the escapee with a night of drinking or general carousing, then return the hungover fugitive to authorities and pocket the reward. Several justices of the peace at Fareham in Hampshire directly alleged such fraud in a letter (29 September 1779) to the Commissioners for Sick and Hurt Seamen and recommended a reduction in reward payments. Fourteen months later, the Admiralty also took note of such deceptions, while simultaneously lamenting the growing number of escape attempts. The Lords' solution was to order increased security at the gaols, but, simultaneously, they only considered reducing the recapture bounty to 10s, the amount paid for the recapture of French or Spanish prisoners.[58]

VII

For the Americans who achieved authentic and successful breakouts, several sympathizers in England were still there to spirit them to freedom. In Devon it appears likely that Gustavus Conyngham received some form of assistance from a mysterious "Mr. Cummings," who met the captain by a prison gate four days before his flight and offered the captive naval officer his services. Keeper Cowdry's report of the subsequent escape appears to verify the external connivance.[59] Outside collaboration also was alluded to by the Fareham justices in their September 1779 letter to the Commissioners for Sick and Hurt Seamen. The justices, who called the American fugitives "more dangerous than the French or Spanish," added that "when they escape from Prison, they are not to be distinguished from Englishmen and are known to have many friends in their Neighbourhoods who take every occasion of giving them protection and assistance." Perhaps one nearby resident who might have influenced the justices' statement was a publican in Hampshire named Mason. According to an Admiralty report on 6 June 1779, Mason, "for two guineas," had attempted to help several American fugitives get to a ship near Stokes Bay. Mason's intentions were discovered, however, and the hapless publican was thereafter impressed "and put aboard one of the King's ships."[60]

Unlike Mason, the Reverend Thomas Wren was not interrupted in his continuing surreptitious endeavors on behalf of American fugitives. George Thompson noted the parson's assistance in early November 1779, when he and another Forton escapee reached the High Street chapel. Wren, after hiding the seamen in his church, acted to find them a "safe house" in Portsmouth. After some initial difficulties, the parson arranged temporary refuge in the town and visited the fugitives with reassurances of continuing aid. Wren proved as good as his word. On 6 November he and other local sympathizers (possibly including Sir John Carter) secured passage for them aboard the merchant ship *Polly*. Ten days later *Polly* sailed from Portsmouth; before her departure, Thompson noted that Wren had sent the two Americans a supply of clothing.[61]

These and other covert actions by Thomas Wren and his associates to abet rebel escapes persisted without apparent disclosure. But had British intelligence officials intercepted a letter from Thomas Digges to Benjamin Franklin on 13 November 1780, the illicit activities of the Portsmouth parson might have been speedily ended. In his letter Digges asserted that the "exemplary exertions of a very worthy little agent" in Hampshire had resulted in many Forton inmates crossing Portsmouth Harbor "to a certain *House* [the High Street chapel] in Amsterdam [Portsmouth]."[62]

Although some escapees were guided to liberty by ship directly from Portsmouth, the primary route to freedom remained by way of London. Several other men in or near the British capital also provided sanctuary for escaped American prisoners during this period. One of these individuals not previously mentioned in this study was Thomas Viny, a carriage-maker, of Tenterden in Kent. In June 1779, Jeremiah Pierce, a fugitive from Forton, informed

Franklin that the commissioner's former London friend, Thomas Viny, had eagerly hidden him during his flight. Another English benefactor to the escapees was the Reverend William Clark. Dr. Nathaniel Harrington wrote that when he had reached London, following his breakout from Forton in April 1780, he accidentally met Clark in a safe house. The nonconformist minister, evidently a kinsman of Harrington, hid him for several days, after which the doctor claimed, "As I had no Money he generously paid my board, & lent me five Guineas to defray my Expenses to France."[63]

But merchant Thomas Digges still served as the most prominent source of aid to the runaways who reached the vicinity of London. In fact, when Digges visited Benjamin Franklin at Passy in April 1779, the former Marylander was told of the commissioner's continued willingness to help underwrite his illicit activities. Many seamen who successfully fled Mill, Forton, or other confinement locales had been told of the security and assistance that reportedly awaited them at Digges's Villars Street residence. Among these fugitives was Gustavus Conyngham and four comrades, who reached this rendezvous on 8 November 1779, a week after their breakout. Conyngham wrote that after their arrival, "Mr. Digges did everything in his power to save me and all my Countrymen that chance to fall his way. . . . Happy we have such a man Among that set of tyrants the[y] have in that Country." Two things that Digges did for these American fugitives, perhaps with the help of Dr. Griffith Williams in nearby Wapping, was to advance them money and to arrange to smuggle them on board a ship bound for still-neutral Holland. The Dutch vessel sailed on 10 November for Rotterdam. Within a month, Digges was concealing nine more escapees.[64]

Thomas Digges had fewer American runaways to handle during this phase of the conflict, perhaps because of the ongoing cartel negotiations. However, the Maryland merchant still incurred significant expenses for his work. He was able to receive a little help from sympathetic Englishmen, but the greatest part of his reimbursement had to come from the rebel commissioners in Paris. Digges therefore sent accountings for his outlays during these months to Benjamin Franklin in Paris, who usually supplied the requested remuneration. This matter apparently was included in the discussions that Digges had with the American commissioner at Passy in late April 1779. There the Marylander obtained a reaffirmation of Franklin's financial commitment to abetting prisoner escapes, though the primary purpose of his mission—to explore possible Anglo-American reconciliation—ended in failure.[65]

VIII

The uppermost thoughts were of home for most of the Americans who obtained freedom either through escape or exchange. Such feelings repeatedly had been expressed in the writings of seamen such as Charles Herbert and Jonathan Haskins at Mill and Timothy Connor and Jonathan Carpenter at Forton. For these men the strange new sights in France briefly whetted their curiosity, but they soon sought out ways, either through resident American agents or direct appeals to Benjamin Franklin, to return to home and hearth.

Not all of the former prisoners looked for quick passage across the Atlantic. For a considerable number who were in France in mid-1779, a new rebel venture was emerging. Continental Navy Captain John Paul Jones was seeking new enlistees for his warships *Bonhomme Richard* and *Alliance*. Benjamin Franklin had authorized Jones to commence his recruiting efforts in April. The following month Franklin wrote to Congress's Committee on Foreign Affairs about the initial success of this endeavor, particularly among recently released Mill inmates.[66] After the arrival of the cartel ship from Forton in early July, more freed captives volunteered, including Lieutenant Nathaniel Fanning and seaman Henry Gardner. There were at least forty-three former American captives serving on board Captain Jones's aging warship *Bonhomme Richard* when she engaged HMS *Serapis* in their memorable battle that September. Fanning survived the clash relatively unscathed, but Gardner was wounded. Nathaniel Bailey, Stephen Loley, and Joshua Carvell were among the ex-prisoners who died in the fight.[67]

Obviously the former detainees from Mill and Forton were aware of the danger that accompanied service under John Paul Jones. Besides the risks of combat, there was the risk that, as former prisoners whose paroles technically forbade them from reentering rebel service, they would receive serious punishment if they were recaptured.

What then were the reasons that impelled these courageous seamen to return to the perils of active service? For Nathaniel Fanning, who was only a midshipman aboard *Bonhomme Richard*, service meant merely "a short cruise in the English Channel" before sailing for America. Probably other recently released mariners also regarded enlistment merely as a brief stint of adventure and perhaps personal gain from prize money. But, more important, they may have considered the benefit that their service would have, both for the Revolutionary cause and for their still-incarcerated comrades in England. They probably knew that Captain Jones had already brought back scores of British seamen from his earlier forays. Because these royal prisoners had been used in the already completed cartels, it seemed logical that any new British captives taken by Jones could easily be employed for similar purposes. Benjamin Franklin, in fact, suggested as much in a letter (24 April 1780) to a French naval officer.[68]

IX

The loyal American seamen, recently released or still enduring incarceration, remembered and respected many Britons who gave them support. Although some were esteemed for their assistance to escapees, most were highly regarded for offering succor to the captive rebels in their midst. In either case, the prisoners' loved ones in faraway America also must have been somewhat relieved to learn of such benignly disposed Englishmen.

In Hampshire the principal advocate for the American captives during this period remained the Reverend Thomas Wren. Aside from abetting escapes, the Portsmouth parson continued to benefit the prisoners in familiar ways. He made regular trips from his High Street chapel to the prison outside Gosport, all the while displaying an undiminished sympathy for the rebel detainees. Within the prison confines he oversaw the schooling that was offered to responsive inmates; he dispensed donated clothing and other personal items; he helped distribute mail; he intervened with prison officials on behalf of the prisoners; and he endeavored to maintain the inmates' morale with optimistic talk of impending exchanges. Evidently his efforts in this area became widely recognized for in February 1780, Benjamin Franklin wrote to the parson specifically requesting that he try to dissuade Americans from entering royal service.[69]

Perhaps most important, Thomas Wren continued to distribute monies from Paris and from a new, albeit less bountiful subcription fund when the initial fund was exhausted. Letters from Thomas Digges to Benjamin Franklin during 1780 mention "our Good friend Mr. W[ren]" traveling to London at his own expense to receive these contributions and then returning to Portsmouth. For their part, the American commissioners continued to send gratitude and thanks to the Presbyterian cleric for his many humanitarian endeavors.[70]

In late 1779, Duckett the almoner, Thomas Wren's associate in prisoner relief efforts, left Hampshire for an inherited farmstead near London. Others in the county took his place. Sir John Carter and his coterie of antiministerial Whigs in Portsmouth augmented the various benefactions from around the seaport community. In addition Wren apparently found charitable contributions in other parts of the county. One Mary Walters wrote from Gosport to David Hartley sometime during 1780: "When it is known what is done in London, there are many here who will be willing to contribute to the relief of their fellow creatures in distress, small sums have already been given to many now at nearby Forton."[71]

At Mill Prison to the west, the leader of humanitarian efforts on behalf of the interned Americans remained Deacon Robert Heath. The assistance he provided apparently was similar to that offered by the Reverend Thomas Wren, though in the deacon's case, again there is no definite proof that he actually abetted escape attempts. Heath, joined by Plymouth linen draper Miles Saurey, continued collecting clothing, shoes, and other items from Devon residents for use by the prisoners. (Heath received particular praise from Thomas Digges for the material assistance given to Captain Gustavus Conyngham who reportedly had arrived "nearly naked" at Mill.) He also brought mail, books, and news to the captives, and, like Wren, he sometimes intervened with prison officials on behalf of the inmates. Additionally, Heath continued to offer personal and spiritual consolation to the jailed Americans, including predictions about future cartel agreements. Probably most important, Heath and Saurey conveyed and apportioned what financial donations were gathered in London. Deacon Heath, at the request of Thomas Digges, covertly advanced £51. 7s 6d to Gustavus Conyngham during his incarceration at Mill. After Conyngham's daring escape, Digges forwarded Heath's claim for compensation to Franklin.[72] The privateer captain, however, never mentioned that the deacon had had any part in his breakout though the American commissioner in Paris perhaps had.

The endeavors of Robert Heath and Miles Saurey received distinct recognition outside Devon. Appreciation was expressed in a letter of 10 March 1780 sent to Benjamin Franklin from Doctor William Hodgson. Hodgson was a Londoner who had been active twenty-seven months before in the original prisoner relief subscription. His letter stated approvingly, "The Agents for our Fund at

Plymouth are Messrs. Heath and Saurey, both very zealous Friends." David Hartley, for his part, made only general references to these two men for their undertakings on behalf of the prisoners. As for Heath himself, letters dispatched by Thomas Digges to Benjamin Franklin in 1779–80 offer the most glowing accolades. In these letters the Maryland-born London merchant repeatedly lauded Heath for various charitable acts the deacon bestowed on the American captives. Digges, referring to Heath as a "very worthy man of Plymouth," also described him on 10 March 1780 as "a second Wren to those people [i.e., the prisoners]." Five months later the merchant wrote to the American commissioner that, while the deacon may have lacked Thomas Wren's "cleverness," nonetheless his "intentions are equally good."[73] The fact that Robert Heath did not badger the commissioners in Paris with letters for reimbursement may have added to their respect for his endeavors.

Throughout 1779 and 1780, Thomas Digges continued as the principal coordinator of relief efforts for the American inmates. In fact, on 3 May 1779, while on his fruitless mission to Paris for Anglo-American reconciliation, Digges, in Benjamin Franklin's presence, even took an oath of allegiance to the new United States. That same month the Maryland expatriate returned to London, where he soon appeared to display his fealty by performing several missions for the American commissioners, perhaps the most important of which was promoting the best interests of the prisoners.[74]

It was in this matter of supervising the captives' welfare that Thomas Digges sent the American commissioners in Paris letters under various pseudonyms including William Singleton Church, V. J. Drouillard, Donald Forbes, and Arthur Hamilton. Using these aliases, Digges conveyed reports on the means by which various inmate needs were being met and on the inmates' overall condition. He also forwarded inmate complaints to the Admiralty or the Commission for Sick and Hurt Seamen, seeking improved prisoner treatment from these bodies and from prison officials themselves. The Maryland merchant acted on behalf of the American detainees in other direct ways. He worked with sympathetic Britons to implement further prisoner cartels. He conveyed special financial aid to individual inmates upon Franklin's request and supervised the cash donations doled out to Thomas Wren and Robert Heath or Miles Saurey from the prisoner relief fund. In this last capacity it was Digges who informed Franklin in October 1779 that the subscription fund was down to £50. The following January when this was gone, the merchant initiated a new fund in London. While he performed all of these beneficial functions, however, Digges was quite zealous about sending Franklin bills for his claimed out-of-pocket expenses.[75]

Several Whig politicians in London, including John Wilkes and David Hartley, continued to show their support for the American prisoners' welfare. They contributed to the newly established prisoner relief fund (John Wilkes donated £50) and spoke on the captives' behalf in Parliament or to relevant government officials. The most prominent of these political benefactors continued to be Franklin's friend David Hartley. It was Hartley who, at Thomas Digges's request, had successfully intervened with the Commissioners for Sick and Hurt Seamen in 1779 to have Gustavus Conyngham transferred from close confinement in Falmouth to Mill Prison.[76]

One other Englishman, William Hodgson, formally emerged during this stage of the confinement story as a prominent benefactor of the American prisoners. Hodgson, who had studied and briefly practiced medicine, had switched to commerce and was living on Coleman Street in London after the American Revolution broke out. He adopted particularly strong pro-American attitudes during the conflict and, as noted, was one of the contributors to the original prisoner relief fund. When Thomas Digges's American birth precluded his lobbying the Commissioners for Sick and Hurt Seamen or the Admiralty for a new cartel during the autumn of 1779, Digges was able to recruit Hodgson for the endeavor.[77] The London merchant-physican, who claimed to have had earlier dealings with the commissioners, willingly accepted the task and thereafter became particularly active in prisoner affairs. Besides urging and being directly involved in further captive exchanges, Hodgson participated in distributing monies from the prisoner relief fund. Like Thomas Digges he corresponded with Benjamin Franklin about the prisoners' status. Together with Digges, he worked on ways to ameliorate the disadvantages of the American inmates. However, by the beginning of 1781, there were ominous indications that a split between the two men was brewing.[78]

X

In Paris, Benjamin Franklin still supervised matters relating to the Americans incarcerated in Britain. Occasionally, imprisoned seamen hailing from New England wrote to fellow commissioner

John Adams, but ultimate decisions on the detainees were in Franklin's hands. Franklin continued his various activities to mitigate prisoner discontent. He wrote letters to the captives offering advice and encouragement; he acted to replenish monetary assistance to the prisoners after Thomas Digges initiated a new fund drive in early 1780; he gave money and administrative help to sometimes demanding or unfortunate American escapees who reached the continent; he expanded his network of sympathetic French merchants and bankers; and he even provided aid to some captured British seamen and Frenchmen who had volunteered for the rebel cause. Additionally Franklin maintained his contacts with supportive Britons and with government officials in order to obtain better treatment for the rebel internees. He also kept American officials apprised of his activities. Throughout this period, however, the Pennsylvania diplomat's main prisoner-related undertaking involved negotiating exchanges of captives.[79]

Although the cartel from Forton was completed only three months after the Mill exchange, agreements on further transfers encountered considerable bureaucratic obstacles. The American commissioners, who had rejoiced at the achievement of the captive trade in July 1779, initially found themselves at a disadvantage in trying to follow up this agreement. The terms for exchange that were accepted had called for the captives to be transferred in groups of no less than one hundred each. However, one month after the Forton cartel, Jean-Daniel Schweighauser, agent for American affairs in Nantes, reported that he had only ninety-two British captives available for repatriation, over two hundred fewer than the number of Americans then interned at Mill and Forton. Franklin, as noted previously, attempted to compensate for this imbalance by commissioning French privateers to seize any vulnerable British ships and, in effect, hold the crews as hostages. But this risky scheme collapsed, with negative effects reverberating on the commissioner's reputation. Franklin also briefly considered, then abandoned, reviving his earlier plan of using sea paroles for captured enemy seamen in order to free American seamen in Britain. In October 1779 Thomas Digges sent the commissioner in Paris other pessimistic tidings. According to Digges, "As yet there is no cartel [exchange agreement]," and the merchant added that he "was very much plagued with their [the prisoners] solicitations & keeping them quiet."[80]

Shortly before Digges's pessimistic pronouncements, however, Franklin received news that he hoped would rectify the situation. The previous April the American commissioner had instructed

Captain John Paul Jones that as one part of his upcoming cruise he was to "bring to France all the English Seamen you may happen to take Prisoners" to use in future cartel negotiations. Later, following his victory over HMS *Serapis,* Captain Jones had sailed into Texel Harbor in then-neutral Holland with 504 captured seamen. On 11 October 1779, Jones wrote to Franklin proposing that all the captured sailors except the captain of *Serapis,* Richard Pearson, should be released if British officials would "give Liberty to all the Americans that have so long languished for it in British prisons."[81] The elated Franklin endorsed Captain Jones's proposal and, believing that the negotiating cards were now in his favor, he wrote to David Hartley on 19 October declaring that "we now have more English Prisoners than you have American." He added that he was ready to take "every step that may soften the Rigours of War," and he asked his friend to urge British functionaries to agree to an exchange for "the poor Prisoners on both sides before the severity of Winter comes on." The situation appeared even brighter a week later when David Hartley wrote that prospects for the exchange were good and that he was "anxious for word of M. de Sartine's consent to the passport to Morlaix that we may get our Cartel Ship on float again." On 30 October Thomas Digges also assured Franklin that the French passport was the only impediment to effecting an exchange.[82]

Nevertheless British officials had no intention of acceding quickly to this American proposition, which could pave the way for freed seamen to rejoin rebel naval forces. Thus the Commissioners for Sick and Hurt Seamen informed William Hodgson in November 1779 that the suggested exchange was disapproved and that they confidently expected to force Captain Jones to leave Holland so that he could be seized. The British ambassador was already putting pressure on the Dutch government to expel Jones or face retaliation. The confrontation was avoided when John Paul Jones accepted the urgings of the French ambassador, the Duc de la Vauguyon, to leave the British prisoners in his custody in exchange for what the American captain believed was the ambassador's promise to exchange these captives only for Americans held in England.[83] Using his frigate *Alliance,* Jones then slipped by the British naval net to safety in France. But Vauguyon, by February 1780, had begun to exchange the captured seamen for French prisoners. Franklin's anger over this duplicitous action was probably compounded by his frustration and concern about the prisoners after he received a letter sent from William Hodgson on 28 January 1780. In it, Hodgson reported that the American captives were "suffering exceedingly," and they did not understand why nothing had been done to forward the cartel, because the Commissioners for Sick and Hurt Seamen had already told the London merchant that they were very "desirous of an Exchange."[84]

Almost simultaneously with the scheme to use the British prisoners in Holland for effecting a third prisoner cartel, Thomas Digges failed with a different approach. In December 1779, two ships under flags of truce arrived in England. Together they carried about 120 Britons who had signed parole documents in America, under which they had agreed that their release was tied to the British government's liberation of an equal number of captives in England. Digges even forwarded one of the parole agreements to Franklin in Paris to substantiate his case. Unfortunately nothing of direct benefit for the American captives emerged from this stratagem. The following February, Digges wrote dejectedly to Franklin that the Admiralty had concluded that the paroles were invalid, because the signers should not have arranged such compacts with rebels and furthermore that the individuals involved "are not on a footing with the Rebel Prisoners here who can only be released by a formal Act of Pardon."[85] Digges's letter gave the clear impression that the Admiralty was attempting to take advantage of this and earlier failures by blaming the cartel deadlock on Franklin, in the hope of increasing defections from among the disgruntled seamen. Petitions to the American commissioners in Paris, including those from several Mill prisoners (2 November 1779) pleading for relief, had shown no sign of success. An appeal from nine rebel officers at Mill (5 November 1779) to Admiral Lord Shuldham seeking parole status was rejected almost out of hand. Consequently, by the beginning of the next year, English recruiters had considerable opportunities to capitalize on the inmates' disillusionment.[86]

A third cartel was finally promulgated in early 1780. By then Benjamin Franklin believed that he had an agreement with Antoine de Sartine, the French naval minister, under which up to five hundred British prisoners in France would be provided for a trade for Americans held in England. The commissioner's resultant confidence was reflected in a letter to Thomas Wren on 26 February 1780, in which he declared, "I hope their [Britain's] confinement of our People is now nearly at an end." It seems that Franklin felt that Sartine had made his gesture to compensate for the recent duplicity of the French ambassador in Holland. For its part, the Admiralty was affected by the entreaties of imprisoned British mariners in France, so that it, too, was amenable to a new cartel.[87]

Benjamin Franklin 1706–1790. Reproduced by courtesy of the Franklin Collection, Yale University Library.

On 28 February 1780, John Bell, one of the Commissioners for Sick and Hurt Seamen, wrote to David Hartley that an exchange vessel was about to depart from England. The next day Hartley transmitted the glad tidings to Franklin, along with apologies for the bureaucratic delays. About a week later the cartel ship, with 119 Americans from Mill Prison, sailed southward from Plymouth Harbor. Soon afterward it docked in Morlaix, the approved transfer point that the Admiralty had insisted upon since the previous autumn.[88]

There followed a grand, embarrassing slipup. It had been Benjamin Franklin's understanding that Sartine would send one hundred British captives to Morlaix for this exchange. To show his good faith, in early 1780 Franklin had turned over eighty-six British prisoners recently taken by the privateer *Black Prince* and held by the Americans at Brest and Lorient to Sartine so that the minister could fill the complement from a previous cartel. However no British prisoners were delivered at the beginning of March when the new transfer vessel arrived at the French port loaded with American prisoners. The captives were set free after the cartel ship docked, and almost all of them sought out the nearest American agent for assistance. Meanwhile the exchange ship returned to England carrying only a receipt for those prisoners who had been transported to Morlaix. Informed of this disastrous circumstance, Franklin immediately sought, but failed to receive, an acceptable explanation from Sartine.[89]

The Morlaix fiasco marked the effective end of the Anglo-American cartel arrangements. On 27 March 1780, several days following the return of the empty cartel vessel to England, David Hartley wrote his friend in Paris of his hope that the recent bungled episode would not delay further exchanges. A more realistic assessment was offered the next day when William Hodgson declared to Franklin that "the Board of Sick and Hurt is disgusted at such an outcome of this business." In May, Hodgson added that the Admiralty had decided not to accept any British prisoners held by France in trade for Americans. In the same month Thomas Digges informed the American commissioner that "nothing is expected, nor even is another cartel talked of here." The following August, Digges and Hodgson both reported that the Admiralty refused to exchange American prisoners except on a "man to man" basis and furthermore that they would accept only those captives taken by American ships in European waters.[90]

This new, hardened British stance on exchanges following the shortchanging at Morlaix was understandable, but it left the American captives quite dispirited. In August 1780 prizemaster Caleb Foot wrote his family, "I am sorry to inform you that I have no prospect of getting my liberty till the wars are over, if we do then." These disconsolate sentiments were echoed by Captain John Manley that same month when he wrote to Benjamin Franklin, "The French and Spanish are both to be exchanged, and we lay foresaken by everybody."[91]

The year 1780 concluded with American hopes of cartels being further dashed. Earlier, the Admiralty had agreed to count within their stipulations several British seamen who had been returned to England. It was in this regard that William Hodgson had written to Benjamin Franklin (20 September 1780) that although the Americans had been credited with sixty-seven British captives recently sent from French ports, there remained "52 due to England on Ballance." The following 4 December, the London merchant-physician wrote to Franklin that "the Board [Commission] of Sick and Hurt Seamen" still claimed that there were "forty one [British] prisoners due and no more exchanges until that debt is paid." For Franklin, these words seemed to signal the collapse of yet another way of ending the impasse.[92]

XI

This interval in the confinement saga of Americans in England included a personal facet. This feature, varyingly to be repeated in future conflicts, comprised letters written by the inmates' families and conversely, prisoners' letters to their loved ones across the Atlantic. From these messages, often laced with faulty spelling and grammar, contemporary readers can obtain insights into the disruptive, heart-rending effects of such distant incarceration. The Americans held on prison ships in locales like New York harbor, in extremely constrained and oppressive conditions, nevertheless could sense their relative proximity to family, friends, and fellow patriots in contrast to those interred so far abroad.[93]

Among the most compelling letters penned by prisoners' kin was that sent by Ann Conyngham (1756–1811) from Philadelphia on 22 September 1779 to Benjamin Franklin in Paris. Ann had married the famed "Dunkirk Pirate" in 1773, and the union apparently had blossomed into a deeply tender relationship. She was living in Philadelphia when her husband was captured in the West Indies and subsequently sent in close confinement to England. Ann had already written to the president of the Continental Congress, enclosing a letter from her husband that alleged abusive treatment by his captors.[94] She had originally expected some form of assistance from the Congress, which met in Philadelphia, but now that her "Gusty" was in England, she turned to the illustrious Paris commissioner. Her plaintive but polemic words speak for themselves:

Honoured Sir;

In what manner shall I apologize for the liberty I now take, but sertain I am you will excuse me when you now that I am the Wife of the unfortunate Capt. Conyngham, one who I beleve you are not unacquanted with. In what language shall I address you Sir to endeavour to save the life of the best and tenderest of Husbands. To you Sir, I look up for redress in hopes it may be in your power in sum measure to appeas the wrath of his enimies, If Thay would one moment think of the distress of an afflicted wife, if they had not lost every feeling of that humanity, which once characterized Britons: thay seartainly could not be so cruell as to part us for ever: Oh! what must be his feelings at this moment, to be confined in a strange place, where he has not one friend, to whom he can realy on, waisting his health and spirits in hopeless grief—and at last Compleating the measure of his sufferings by an ignominious death—Good God, my hart shudders at the thought. Forbid it Heaven—Is it posable no means can be procured for his safty, and my only hope, my only support, under every affliction and distress—

Pardon me Sir, if I request the favour of your forwarding the inclosed as directed: as they will be the means of affording some relief to my dear Gusty—

Your distinguished character for benevolence and humanity has imbolden'd me to take this liberty—

I must inform you Sir, that Capt. Conyngham was Commander of the Cutter Revenge, who was taken in April, carried into New York, from thence sent to England, to have his tryal—

"This, I presume, will be a sufficient motive with you to procure justice for him, and to afford some consolation, so Hond. Sir, your most obedient and most devoted—

Ann Conyngham[95]

One of the best examples of an inmate's perturbed and forlorn communications home was written by Caleb Foot from Forton Prison. On 10 July 1778, Caleb had signed aboard the privateer sloop *Gates,* thus commencing a lengthy absence from his wife Mary and, at that time, an infant daughter. In a subsequent memorandum, Foot recalled that two days after enlisting he took leave of Mary, who was in the late stages of another pregnancy. On the afternoon of 13 July, *Gates* weighed anchor from Cape Anne, only two days before Mary bore a son who was named for his father.[96]

Caleb's capture shortly after sailing and his eventual commitment to Forton in February 1779 brought forth deep feelings about connubial separation, even greater than during earlier service in the Continental Army besieging Boston. Affectionate sentiments, intermixed with feelings of guilt about leaving home during his wife's travail, are clearly evident in the letter that the imprisoned privateersman wrote to her on 30 June 1779:

Most Affectionate Friend—I think it my duty to write [at] all opportunities to let you know my welfare, for I think it must give you some easement of mind to hear from me in my long absence. I am certain it would give me infinite pleasure to hear of your welfare, for it gives me great concern, considering the situation that I left you in when we parted, and have not had the happines to hear from you, nor do I expect to for I am certain that you must labor under great disadvantage in sending to me. But if you send a letter to France and direct it to Forton Prison, near Portsmouth in Great Britain it may get to me if there is nothing in it concerning government. Letters have come here by the way of France from America in six weeks from the date.

" I have sent you a letter on the same by Mr. Marton [Josiah Martin] of Linn [Lynn, Massachusetts], and this I send by favor of Mr. Darmer of Salem, so that if one miscarries I trust the other will arrive safe to your hand and find you and yours in good health as by the blessing of God they leave me at this present writing. There are about six hundred prisoners in England, and there is a cartel appointed to exchange them to France as soon as possible. But I do not expect it will be my turn till late in the fall, for a great many of them have been here between two and three years. So, no more at present, but I remain your loving husband till death.

Caleb Foot.[97]

Neither Caleb Foot nor Gustavus Conyngham were still confined in English prisons when the year 1781 began, but there were many other American seamen who remained incarcerated in Forton or Mill prisons at that time. Some, like Samuel Harris of Ipswich, Massachusetts, had been languishing in detention for over three years. But regardless of how many long months they had spent in either prison, their future status, like the ocean's waves, was indeterminate. They had no certainty either about when or how they would depart from their prisons. For some of them Benjamin Franklin seemed to offer one possible answer, that is, after the collapse of cartel negotiations in 1780. The American commissioner shortly thereafter turned to encouraging escapes, either directly from Paris or through the assistance of a network of agents that he had employed in French and Dutch seaports.[98] Some of the American inmates, especially the lower-ranked seamen with their limited means, were not able to attempt to follow this risky course of action. For them it may have seemed that "Dame Fortune," in the guise of external unfolding events in Europe and North America, would ultimately determine their future.

6

Farewell to All That,
January 1781–April 1783

On 31 December 1780 seaman William Russell took the occasion of the year's end to comment on his personal situation. It had been almost thirteen months since he had begun his confinement in Mill Prison along with Captain John Manley and several crewmen from the privateer *Jason*. Hopes for an early exchange had been dashed the previous spring with the fiasco surrounding the Morlaix cartel. Word of subsequent British unwillingness to engage in further such exchanges had reached the prisoners, adding to their existing woes. Simultaneously the war news from America indicated protracted hostilities with few signs of any imminent resolution. The apparent impasse in diplomatic events added to the inmates' malaise. All of these frustrating developments must have affected Russell, whose brief entry for the day read, "The year closes at midnight, *and we are still in prison.*"[1]

William Russell had good reason for feeling disheartened about his imminent prospects for liberty but not about a lengthy, drawn-out incarceration. Less than eighteen months after his gloomy year-end entry, he and most of his shipmates left the gates of the Devon prison as free men. A significant number of Americans remained incarcerated at both Mill and Forton until early 1783, but even before then, the extensive use of these two prisons was effectively concluding. The seemingly stalemated wartime situation would be broken in consequence of dramatic and decisive military, diplomatic, and political events.

I

The pivotal military event, one that reverberated determinatively in political as well as diplomatic realms, occurred on Virginia's York Peninsula in October 1781. Two months before, Lord Cornwallis had moved his southern forces to this locale, apparently intent on establishing a strongly fortified base for possible military and naval operations. Whatever his ultimate purpose, the British commander had overoptimistically calculated that his movements would receive continuous support from naval units in Chesapeake Bay and from General Sir Henry Clinton at New York. Cornwallis miscalculated badly on both suppositions. Washington and the French general, the comte de Rochambeau, deceived General Clinton into believing that their combined Franco-American forces were about to attack New York City. They then marched their troops speedily to Virginia, where the French admiral, the comte de Grasse, had gained temporary naval superiority on the Chesapeake. Lord Cornwallis soon found himself in a hopeless position; after holding out for almost three weeks against a superior enemy force of about sixteen thousand men, he formally surrendered his own seven thousand man army on 19 October.[2]

Political reverberations in Britain from the humiliating Yorktown debacle meant the inevitable fall of the Lord North ministry. Indeed, when news of the Cornwallis capitulation reached London about five weeks after the event, the British prime minister is reported to have cried out, "O God! It is all over!" Although George III, along with several Tory members of Parliament, attempted to mitigate the momentous reversal in America, the opposition Whigs, led by Charles James Fox, denounced the government for its unsound and unsuccessful prosecution of the conflict. Some radical members of the opposition led by Christopher Wyvill, while opposing the tactical means, nonetheless joined the push to bring down the ministry. During February 1782 spirited debates were held over a bill to "conclude a Peace or Truce, with America," and motions of no confidence in the ministry were barely defeated. The following month Lord North accepted the inevitable and resigned. The new Whig ministry, headed by the marquis of Rockingham, acted quickly on its announced intention of resolving the conflict. One of the government's first peace initiatives directly affected the American naval prisoners; on 25 March the ministers officially recognized the seamen held in British detention centers as prisoners of war.[3]

Diplomatic events during this period were primarily tied in with the official beginnings of peace negotiations. Although Britain's chief negotiator in Paris met with Benjamin Franklin on 12 April 1782, policy disputes, plus the excessive initial demands of other allied powers, delayed swift progress toward a settlement. Bargaining proceeded more rapidly following Rockingham's death on

1 July and Lord Shelburne's succeeding to preeminence in the new ministry. By the end of that month, Shelburne had acquiesced to the advisability of recognizing American independence in order to obtain a beneficial peace compact. A few contentious issues persisted, but on 30 November Great Britain and its former American colonies concluded a conditional agreement for settlement that recognized the independence of the United States. The following 20 January an armistice and preliminary peace accord between Britain and her other adversaries was agreed upon. The final treaty was inscribed on 3 September 1783.[4]

Naval developments during this last phase of the conflict were for the most part indecisive and of limited significance. One prominent exception, however, was Admiral Sir George Rodney's notable victory in the West Indies (12 April 1782) over a French flotilla under Admiral de Grasse. This triumph in "The Battle of the Saints," though not complete, did restore much of Britain's naval pride and allowed it to safeguard imperial possessions outside continental North America.[5]

As for maritime events involving the United States, the twenty-eight month interval examined in this chapter was marked in one respect by administrative squabbling over management of the Continental Navy. This bureaucratic contention was part of an overall decline in the operational utility of the navy. In July 1781 members of the Continental Congress, irritated over the ineffectiveness of the Board of Admiralty, replaced this body with a secretary and an agent of marine. Neither of these new appointments was able to turn around the flagging fortunes of the Yankee fleet, whose operational vessels had been reduced to three commissioned frigates at the time of Yorktown. Actually the largest number of engagements with British ships was undertaken by American privateers. These armed vessels were active primarily in the Western Hemisphere, though *Black Princess,* the last of Benjamin Franklin's small corvettes, took some prizes off the French coast until its own seizure in late 1781. Most of the rebels consigned to British prisons for this period were crewmen from privateers, many of whom had previously served in the Continental Navy.[6]

II

News of many of these external events, though not always accurate, filtered into the two English prisons. The diary of William Wigder at Mill reveals that the primary sources of information concerning military, naval, political, and diplomatic events were newspapers from nearby Plymouth or Exeter and sometimes periodicals arriving from London. The greater proximity to the British capital kept London journals as the main printed source of wartime developments for Forton's American inmates. The *Hampshire Chronicle,* though published close-by in Winchester, is seldom cited in extant prisoner accounts. Guards, visitors, letters, and friendly ship captains passing through also disseminated information. Thus the captives, at least from the standpoint of knowledge of outside incidents, did not find themselves in a rigidly deprived situation.[7]

Nevertheless American detainees at Mill and Forton prisons were always aware of their loss of personal freedom. The familiar routines of captivity persisted, at least until the captives were designated as prisoners of war in March 1782. Extant records of the Admiralty and the Commissioners for Sick and Hurt Seamen appear to substantiate this situation, at least from Britain's outlook. There is a paucity of individual prisoner accounts from Forton for this final stage of confinement. A letter from the incarcerated Benjamin Golden to Benjamin Franklin (2 December 1781) is perhaps the one significant manuscript item from the Hampshire prison.[8] At Mill Prison, however, more inmates wrote accounts of events during these several months. William Russell's journal continues to provide some interesting details; other valuable printed material can be found in the biographical memorial of Andrew Sherburne and most especially in the fascinating, meticulously worded diary of seaman William Wigder.[9]

Taken together these manuscript records, individual printed accounts, and various communications to Benjamin Franklin offer an insightful portrait of the American prisoners at Mill and to a lesser extent Forton during the final phase of captivity. Confinement figures for these two detention centers are a good general starting point.

Although the overall tempo of Anglo-American hostilities, particularly on land, wound down after the Yorktown surrender in October 1781, there was no corresponding decline in the number of Americans sent to Mill and Forton. Rebels continued to be captured aboard armed patriot vessels and dispatched to these and other prisons. The year 1781 was marked by the largest number of captured rebel vessels whose crews were sent to Mill Prison. Similarly some of the incarcerated Americans were taken as part of the crews of ships of allied nations. Keeper John Newsham at Forton cited three such detainees among the complement of a French privateer taken in early 1782.[10] Other rebel prisoners—including several who were not seamen—were transferred to these internment locales from detention centers in Ireland, Canada, the American states, and the West Indies. One effect of the new prisoner consignments was reflected in a complaint by Keeper Cowdry in January 1782 that the expected arrival of 170 more transfers would result in overcrowding at his prison. The keeper's concerns evidently were justified because the following month Captain John Green reported 590 Americans were then crammed into Mill. These developments combined to keep the number of Americans incarcerated at Mill and Forton surprisingly high, even though many internees continued to depart through exchanges, defections, or escapes.[11]

Prisoner accounts and reports by royal officials confirm the continuance of a sizable contingent of Americans in these two gaols. In June 1781 William Wigder claimed that there were still 244 Americans confined at Mill, out of a total of 1,132 prisoners of war held there. By August of the following year, after two sizable exchanges, the number of announced American inmates at Forton and Mill was listed as only 163. However, that October the Commissioners for Sick and Hurt Seamen declared to the Admiralty that this total had grown to 284. And even with the signing of preliminary peace articles the next month, more captives arrived from various locales. In February 1783 the Admiralty was informed that there were still 272 American detainees in both prisons. However, this figure would soon drop precipitously.[12]

III

William Cowdry and John Newsham remained in charge of their respective gaols until the departure of the last of the patriot inmates. They evidently strove to follow their superiors' instructions: no governmental allegations were listed as having been initiated against them for malfeasance or dereliction of duty, and they both appear to have submitted the requisite paperwork on time to the Commissioners for Sick and Hurt Seamen or to the Admiralty. Official satisfaction with the performance of the two keepers in supervising the recalcitrant Yankee inmates was ostensibly shown in April 1782, when the Admiralty recognized their exertions and increased their salaries from £120 to £200 per annum. Eleven months later, Newsham's authority was enlarged when he was named agent for the nearby Haslar Hospital.[13]

If the attitude of royal officials toward the Mill and Forton keepers during this final phase of confinement seems to be one of overall satisfaction, many American inmates still held a different opinion. Perhaps these Yankee detainees, who had already displayed their obstinate temperament, became more emboldened as the conflict turned inexorably in their favor. But whatever the reason, contemporary sources indicate that the dedicated rebel captives faced their British supervisors with increasing brashness, indifference, and disobedience, which continually undermined prison authority.

The availability of individual prisoner accounts from Mill allows for a much better picture of William Cowdry's lessening authority than for that of his counterpart at Forton. William Russell, confined at Mill since December 1779, made a number of comments about this fact in his journal. Most of his remarks are innocuous. However, on 19 June 1782, the seaman claimed that when the visiting duke of Richmond asked the assembled Yankee internees if they had any complaints against Cowdry, one rebel officer allegedly responded "that Cowdry was a dirty fellow." (The duke was said to have replied forthrightly, "Government keeps dirty fellows to do their dirty work.") Four days afterward and one day before his departure on a cartel, Russell cited further disrespect for the jailors: "Cowdry sent a Paper into the Prison to sign that he had used us with marks of Kindness & c. It was immediately torn up." Two months before Russell's account of this incident, Captain John Green wrote his own disparaging opinion of the Mill keeper: "He has been in Every Sense a bad man, whome has been & Continues in Naverey and Insolence."[14]

Andrew Sherburne, who entered the Devon prison thirteen months after Russell, offered his own derisive opinion of Cowdry: "He was a petulant old fellow, and the prisoners, and especially the Marblehead men took pleasure in affronting him."[15]

William Wigder, whose detailed, informative journal begins in January 1781, offered the most references at this time to Cowdry. These references stand out for the generally positive portrait they provide of the keeper during this final stage of confinement. Wigder described the Mill keeper as something of an impartial jailor, perhaps affected by the further expanded, unwinnable war, who was now attempting to conciliate problems in order to make himself more amenable to the American prisoners. For example, on one occasion (15 August 1781), when the keeper permitted the rebel inmates to collect a back allowance, he wrote, "Mr. Cowdry seems very good." Earlier, in March, Wigder related how the keeper offered to expedite a petition to government officials that sought improvements in food supplies. There were also two occasions that year on which Cowdry reprimanded guards for alleged abuses toward the American inmates. All this brought him little respect from his charges. Wigder noted one occasion during the late summer when the keeper was heckled so vociferously for ordering an impromptu search that he was obliged to take refuge in his office. Nevertheless Cowdry retained his basic administrative authority; Wigder mentioned occasions when the keeper strictly punished prisoners for attempting to escape or throwing stones at his windows and one instance when he "allowed no beer to come to the gate."[16]

The Commissioners for Sick and Hurt Seamen sent accounts to the Admiralty alleging unruly behavior of the rebel prisoners at Forton toward John Newsham. Unfortunately there are no extant journals by American inmates at the Hampshire gaol for this time period. Benjamin Golden, writing to Benjamin Franklin from the prison on 2 December 1781 referred to his confinement area as one of "misery and discontent," but he did not single out the keeper or staff for blame. Seaman Golden even implied supervisory restraint in the face of one recent patriot display of partisanship. According to Golden, following news of the Yorktown victory, several of the American inmates organized a "General Illumination" to celebrate the triumph. Although this pageant could not have been missed by Newsham, there is no mention of his repeating his previous fulminations against the Yankee rebels. The following June, William Hodgson told of hearing a rumor that the Forton prisoners had become so "riotous and ungovernable" that they were "meditating to set fire to the prison." Thus, despite the paucity of direct evidence, it would appear that, in Hampshire, Keeper John Newsham was also having difficulty managing his gaol.[17]

Official records and prisoner accounts reveal that the keepers' subordinates and local militia guards at both English detention centers also were involved in controversies during this final phase of the confinement saga. In July 1781, John Allyer, John Grant, and William Sheffield, three turnkeys at Forton, were discharged when the Admiralty received allegations of their complicity in prisoner escapes. They were restored to their posts the next month after receiving exoneration, but suspicions of staff collusion in prisoner flights continued. The following autumn Captain William Fitzwilliam of the Surrey militia stationed at Gosport wrote to both the Admiralty and the Commissioners for Sick and Hurt Seamen alleging complicity between the clerks, the turnkeys, and the American captives at the nearby prison "to let prisoners escape in order to retake them and claim the reward." (This deceptive stratagem, noted in the previous chapter, appears to have been practiced more by the staff at the less secure Forton Gaol than at Mill.) Fitzwilliam also enclosed a deposition from a journeyman carpenter at Forton who specifically accused one clerk and a turnkey of direct involvement in such intrigues. Fitzwilliam sent out follow-up letters requesting a broad inquiry into the allegations. However, Fitzwilliam's regiment was reassigned from the area, and no such investigation was held. Nonetheless several subsequent turnovers in the staff at the Hampshire gaol indicate that there probably was truth in Captain Fitzwilliam's charges.[18]

Admiralty and Commissioner for Sick and Hurt Seamen archives offer no similar charges of collusion against Keeper William Cowdry's staff at Mill Prison. It may have existed nonetheless, but the stronger security features at Mill would have made such chicanery more detectable. Staff turnover did occur at Mill during this period, but there is no mention in governmental records, or for that matter in prisoner journals, that the changes were the result of intrigues with the prisoners. In one instance (24 May 1781), Wigder noted that Cowdry discharged a turnkey for drunkenness, and later (26 September 1781) he reported that the keeper had reprimanded a turnkey for delivering unauthorized beer. In other cases he declared that the turnkeys definitely played a role in thwarting escape attempts. The Massachusetts seaman indicated that there was prisoner collusion with the guards, not the staff. He cited instances in June and November 1781 when these detached soldier-guards were alleged to have taken payoffs from the captives. The following February, Admiralty records reveal that a sergeant and a corporal were in fact court-martialed for taking bribes to abet an escape.[19]

Although some of the guards or staff at the prisons continued to find common ground with the inmates, these last several months of detention also saw many instances of friction. The absence of detailed personal accounts restricts our insight into such events at Forton, but the pattern of previous incidents was probably repeated. So, if Benjamin Golden mentions the captives defiantly celebrating news of the Yorktown victory, it can be surmised that there were similar patriot observances at the prison in 1781 and 1782 on Independence Day. It can also be presumed that there were numerous minor verbal clashes between the prisoners and their jailers. Keeper John Newsham did report one serious case (3 April 1782), when the officer of the guard wounded one inmate "who had irritated and insulted him."[20]

No similarly serious staff-prisoner altercation appears in the relevant governmental records covering Mill for this period, but the inmate records for this concluding phase of confinement provide some portrayals of emerging friction at the Devon prison. Andrew Sherburne and William Russell offered a few recollections of discord between captors and captives at the prison. Writing forty-five years later, Sherburne recalled that upon receiving word of Cornwallis's surrender, the Mill patriots, like those at Forton, staged a boisterous parade in the prison yard. When Keeper Cowdry dispatched guards to the yard to control the demonstration, some of the prisoners reportedly increased the tension by insulting them. The fortuitous intervention of several American officers was said to have averted more serious trouble. The memorial of the New Hampshire seaman also includes one other instance of hostility in which a guard fired upon (and narrowly missed) a prisoner who had inadvertently dropped a discarded meat bone on him.[21]

In his journal William Russell noted two other troublesome incidents during this period. One of them occurred on 6 June 1782 when the Americans defiantly jeered and then threw stones at soldiers called to the yard by the sergeant of the guard. Although these troops twice threatened to fire on the rebels, Russell claimed that they backed down following orders from their officers. Sixteen days later, and two days before his own exchange, the Massachusetts seaman referred to two Americans put into the black hole for throwing stones at Keeper Cowdry's office.[22]

Once again the extensive account of William Wigder offers the most thorough listing of contentious incidents. These occurrences had several causes: Americans' disdain of orders to turn out or to clean their wards, insults exchanged between inmates and prison staff, guards firing at the confinement wards, inmates refusing to extinguish their candles, and, on special occasions such as Independence Day, inmates brazenly parading their revolutionary sentiments in the prison yard. Overall, however, seaman Wigder's journal reveals that at Mill these episodes did not happen frequently and that the American prisoners during 1781 had reached a significant level of tolerance for their jailers, or at least an unspoken compromise with them. Both jailers and the jailed by this time even appear to show a certain degree of respect toward one another. Thus, in August 1781 Wigder noted with satisfaction that the captain of the guard "has ordered his Sentinels to treat us with the Greatest Civility, and gave permission for Each man to have a strong pint of beer."[23]

IV

The Americans continued to be more concerned with clothing, food, and health care than they were with discipline. The correspondence of the prisoners and their English benefactors reflects the persistent problem of providing clothing for the captured rebel seamen. For instance, in January 1781 Thomas Wren wrote to Benjamin Franklin of a desperate need for clothing because "many who come lately are very bare"; the next month Samuel Hubbard, a recent arrival at Mill, stressed to the Paris commissioner, "I am badly of[f] for cloths." Later that year Ipswich seaman Samuel Harris, by now a longtime Mill inmate, claimed that the prisoners had not received new attire for over eight months. Other former captives at Mill, Forton, or other British detention centers reported even lengthier deprivations. In 1781 and 1782 William Hodgson emphasized the evident need to provide replacement clothing, especially for protection against the coming winter.[24]

During this period the problem also appeared in captive accounts. William Russell's earnings from teaching school in the prison apparently enabled him to buy his own clothes and food during most of his detention, but Yankee seamen Andrew Sherburne and William Wigder noted shortcomings. As far as clothing was concerned, Sherburne declared that, like most of his shipmates, he had entered Mill with not a "single article of clothing except what I had upon my back." Despite the prevalent shortages of attire at the prison, however, Sherburne was able to receive some items from fellow New Englanders who felt sympathy for the youth.[25]

Seaman Wigder, whose published diary covers only the year 1781, also mentioned clothing inadequacies, especially among the new inmates. He also cited the fact that gifts from private sources of clothing, as well as other necessities, were occasionally distributed. Wigder further mentioned that inmates, particularly the officers with money, could purchase requisite attire. He did note irregular instances when the royal government provided some articles of clothing.[26]

British administrative records indicate that officials made efforts to meet the captives' clothing needs. For example, the Admiralty ordered an inquiry into a June 1781 petition from two hundred

Mill prisoners complaining about shortages of food and wearing apparel. The Commissioners for Sick and Hurt Seamen answered the detainees' petition by claiming that the "Supply of cloathing has never been discontinued," that the keepers tried to ensure that all inmates were "properly outfitted," that the only evident shortcoming, that of stockings, was being rectified, and that, in fact, some prisoners had sold their clothing supplies.[27] Nevertheless dissatisfactions persisted as more ill-clad American prisoners arrived. In December 1781 William Hodgson, who had already noted these deficiencies to Benjamin Franklin, also cited them to the Commissioners for Sick and Hurt Seamen. The following May this body ordered that Americans about to be exchanged from Forton be immediately provided "with 20s each of Naval Slops [sailors garb]."[28]

Bureaucratic difficulties continued until the end of confinement. At Mill, in April 1782 Captain John Green noted the arrival of seventy-four American prisoners from Ireland, "in want of every species of Cloathing Necessary to make life comfortable." That September, the Commissioners for Sick and Hurt Seamen were still reporting "a want of cloathing." The following January, Jacob Smith, a Mill inmate for over fourteen months, wrote to Franklin that some of his comrades were "Entering Out of Prison [defecting] Averry day for want of Close and Vitels." And in early February 1783, a little more than a month before the last Americans left, the detainees in Forton Prison were said to be "in great want of every Article of Cloathing, particularly Shoes and Stockings."[29]

Shortcomings in the quantity and quality of food also remained a problem for most of the American captives. There were, of course, some exceptions. A prisoner like William Russell was able to use his teaching wages for purchasing extra victuals at the prison market. Officers receiving extra relief donations also obtained further sustenance. And Andrew Sherburne, during his confinement at Mill, mentioned skilled mariners who painstakingly carved and then sold ship models. Sherburne claimed that one of them, John Deadman of Salem, Massachusetts, sold a rigged three-decker that he had labored on for twenty-two months for twenty guineas. The majority of American detainees, however, lacked the wherewithal to procure additional cash and consequently had to endure recurrent inequities in their rations.[30]

Prisoners who wrote to the American commissioners in Paris, such as Jacob Smith at Mill or Benjamin Golden at Forton, generally linked their accusations of inadequacies in clothing to charges of shortcomings in rations. In the petition that the American seamen at Mill sent to the Admiralty in June 1781, the captives alleged that their bread rations were only two thirds of that of the prisoners of other nations; that the quality of food was generally inferior; that they were denied the same privileges as other nationals to supplement their provisions at the prison market; and that unlike the French, Spanish, or Dutch inmates, they lacked their own agent to look after their needs. The subsequent investigative report by the Commissioners for Sick and Hurt Seamen was defensive in tone. The commissioners admitted that the American detainees received a smaller bread allowance than the prisoners of other nations, but they argued that the loaves were better in quality. They also added that the food served at the prisons was "of a more nourishing kind than what is allowed His Majesties troops while on board of Transports." They denied the other charges and concluded with a repudiation of the inmates' allegation that their condition was "miserable and calamitous." Obviously the commissioners were seeking to vindicate their administrative policies, but, similarly, in striving for attention, the rebels quite likely were overstating their particular complaints.[31]

Without doubt the victualling situation was not so bad as it had been when the two detention centers first opened. However noticeable deficiencies remained in the provisions offered the American captives. Evidence of this fact, probably with varying amplification, is presented in prisoner letters, in the correspondence of their British supporters, and most especially, in the journals of the captives. The reminiscences of Andrew Sherburne for 1782, though not always exact, provide a good picture of the food limitations at Mill:

> The provision while I was there, was in general, pretty good, but we had not enough of it. I think we were allowed twelve ounces of bread, and twelve ounces of beef per day. We were divided into messes, four in a mess. At eleven o'clock, we drew a three pound loaf to each mess. The bread was very dark colored, and was supposed to have been composed of rye, oats, barley and peas; the members of each mess would generally convene when the bread was served out. One person would divide the loaf in quarters as exactly as he could; then one of the mess would turn his back, and another, in the presence of the rest, touches a piece of the bread, saying to him who had turned his back, who shall have that? "John," who shall have that? "myself," and who shall have that? "you shall have it;" of course, the fourth quarter must fall to the person not named.[32]

The Commissioners for Sick and Hurt Seamen, in their response to the June 1781 petition, also responded in part that "the Americans have all the appearance of health and Vigour, . . . no people have enjoyed more perfect health than they have done." As proof of the physical soundness of the inmates, they declared that "only 18 have died since confinement began." In actuality, health care had improved considerably by 1781, and the rebel detainees at Mill and Forton were far better off than their comrades on British prison ships. John Howard's findings on mortality at both of these prisons definitely reflect this fact. The British penologist wrote that of twelve hundred Americans confined at Forton from 13 June 1777 to 6 November 1782, sixty-nine had died; of 1,296 Americans interned at Mill from 27 May 1777 to 1 August 1782, only forty-five Americans had perished.[33] Still statistics on Forton offered by John Alexander indicate an increase in the death rate at the Hampshire prison during the last phase of confinement. Furthermore, administrative records themselves indicate some of the limitations in prisoner medical treatment during the final phase of detention. William Hodgson, in communicating a message from Benjamin Franklin to the Commissioners for Sick and Hurt Seamen (4 December 1781) concerning further prisoner relief, briefly noted apprehension about the prisoners' physical well-being during the approaching winter. Already during the previous July, the commissioners had delegated their medical member, Dr. Walter Farquharson, to assist the resident physician at Mill in battling an unspecified illness. The malady may have been smallpox, because William Wigder mentioned on 10 August, "Americans that had the Small pox were removed into the Lower Hospital, where one of them died shortly afterward." Earlier that year, William Russell cited two different occasions on which several prisoners, without administrative approval, "inoculated themselves" against this disease. And during 1781 as well as 1782, the detainees petitioned the Admiralty alleging insufficient preventative care for this scourge.[34]

Forton, too, is represented in these government manuscripts. In June 1782 the Admiralty instructed the Commissioners for Sick and Hurt Seamen to send a qualified surgeon and a medical chest to assist over one hundred Americans who had apparently been stricken with an unspecified malady as they were preparing to leave the prison on a cartel. The following February, William Corbett, the agent at Haslar Hospital outside Gosport, blamed the lack of sufficient shoes and stockings for causing an increasing number of "Fevers and Colds" among the remaining Americans. It could be argued, of course, that similar deficiencies in the Continental Army or on armed patriot ships could have caused as many illnesses; but most of the rebels in those circumstances were there on a purely voluntary basis.[35]

The American inmates often wrote about the level of medical care and their own well-being. (Those captives who avoided any significant illness were clearly a small, fortunate minority.) At this time, prisoner correspondence with the American Commissioners in Paris makes only oblique references to such matters, but accounts by Mill inmates offer a broader, more intimate depiction. William Wigder, for example (10 March 1781), stated that he and several other Yankee captives were "taken Sick," apparently after eating spoiled cheese. As the year progressed, he mentioned, in passing, occasional prisoner bathing and inoculation in order to avoid infection. Unlike Charles Herbert four years before, Wigder cited no large outbreaks of debilitating illnesses. In fact for the year 1781 his journal lists only six deaths, two of which were from smallpox.[36]

The year after Wigder's entries, Captain John Green and William Russell pictured a brief though extensive illness (possibly influenza) that afflicted his countrymen at Mill. Russell's description provides a good insight into the prevailing standard of medical care. On 5 June 1782 he related how most of the Americans, including himself, had been debilitated by an unspecified malady. Russell claimed that the ailment, transitory in nature, had caused him "violent" pains in his "head, back, stomach, and legs with a dry cough." Believing, probably correctly, that prescribed remedies were valueless, the Massachusetts seaman improved simply by allowing nature to take its course. He included in his entry for this day a sample conversation between an inmate and the resident physician expounding on medical offerings.

> "Doctor, I've a violent pain in my head. "
> Reply: "Take some Mixture."
> "Doctor, I've a sour Stomach."
> Reply: "Take some Mixture.'
> "Doctor, I've a violent Fever on me every Night."
> Reply: "Take some Mixture."[37]

Looking back on his own days of imprisonment at Mill, Andrew Sherburne was more positive about the medical treatment that he had received. He recalled that when he was stricken with an apparent infection, the male nurse assigned to his ward was slow in giving him attention, but when he was subsequently transferred to the prison hospital, through the timely intervention of an interned ship's doctor, he received better care. Sherburne's praise is somewhat backhanded: "However tyrannical and inhuman the British government was in other respects, they were to be praised and respected for the suitable provisions they made for the sick in the hospital at Mill Prison." In fact, as Sherburne recalled the event, the encouragement of his comrades and the intercession of the interned New England ship's doctor seemed to do as much for him as the hospital staff. He recollected that the American physician convinced the resident Mill doctor to allow him to depart from the gaol on one of the final cartels. In fact, this action seemed to have the greatest curative effect on Andrew Sherburne.[38]

V

The two most common topics in the records of the Admiralty and of the Commissioners for Sick and Hurt Seamen are defections and escapes. These two aspects of detention also figure quite prominently in the published accounts of American seamen during the final confinement phase.

The need to replenish the supply of crewmen for His Majesty's frigates and commercial ships remained high during the remainder of the conflict. Although the French invasion threat had subsided after 1779, British naval units still had to operate in widely scattered areas of the globe. Holland's entry into the fray added to Royal Navy manpower requirements. Merchant vessels' captains, who often had their crewmen impressed onto the king's warships, also sought ways to fill their ship's complements. Adding to these difficulties in obtaining able-bodied crewmen were recurrent, often successful opposition efforts within Britain to restrain impressment and the dreaded press gangs. Consequently action to entice imprisoned rebels, many of whom had been incarcerated for long periods, was stepped up throughout 1781 and even much of 1782. The growing eagerness, if not desperation, to tap this source of new recruits can be seen in an Admiralty order to the Commissioners for Sick and Hurt Seamen on 5 June 1781. In it, the Lords noted that in response to Admiral Sir Thomas Pye's appeal for more seamen, previous bureaucratic formalities were to be reduced, and henceforth Keeper John Newsham "may have discretion to permit such prisoners to come out of prison the moment they solicit to enter with such Lieutenants as may be sent to Forton from time to time for that purpose." Similar orders were almost simultaneously passed on to Keeper Cowdry.[39]

Many inmates did accept whatever inducements were offered to desert the patriot cause. According to notices sent from the Commissioners for Sick and Hurt Seamen to the Admiralty, 116 rebel detainees requested pardons from January 1781 to March 1783 for the purpose of entering British service.[40]

A larger number of these defectors came from Mill Prison, a fact that perhaps was related to the tighter security at the Devon gaol. Thus seaman John Claypoole wrote on 1 September 1781, shortly after his incarceration, "It seems impossible to get out of this place with out the wretched alternative of entering their Infernal service which however I find many are reduced to the Necessity of doing." Yet, regardless of which prison had the greater number of turncoats, the distinct majority, as in previous confinement periods, were old countrymen. Similarly, as in the earlier phases of detention, almost all the defectors agreed to enter service with the Royal Navy, though one man, Shubal Clark, was released in March 1782 with the stipulation that he serve in the Southern Whale Fisheries.[41]

It is not difficult to comprehend why many Forton and Mill inmates chose to become renegades. Old countrymen often had strong personal ties to Britain, and for them the decision to end an unpleasant incarceration by switching sides was usually not too difficult. For other detainees, born and raised in America, assuming the character of turncoat was ordinarily more difficult. But the deprivations related by Benjamin Golden at Forton and Samuel Harris at Mill in their individual letters to Benjamin Franklin in 1781 produced much of the pressure on individual men to abandon the rebel cause. Golden and Harris, along with William Wigder, Andrew Sherburne, and William Russell, retained their loyalty to the struggle for freedom, though many others did not. Following his second successful escape from Mill in June 1781 Gustavus Conyngham offered his own brief assessment of causes for such defections: "Hunger, Obliges them to do it, Not having that Supply Other Nations, and States, have, Nor their Grieavences heard Only At the Sole And Absolute Will of A Commissary."[42]

Obviously defections of inmates were observed by their comrades. The incomplete published journal of William Russell had scornfully cited some renegade crossovers during 1780, and though he made no further printed remarks on the subject, it would appear that his contemptuous attitudes persisted. Looking back Andrew Sherburne recalled without rancor that "at different times, numbers had deserted, and sometimes shipped on board his majesties ships;" his recollection is corroborated by British manuscript rec-

Seaman William Wigder. Courtesy Peabody & Essex Museum, Salem MA.

ords. Sherburne also mistakenly claimed that men were impressed directly from the black hole onto Royal Navy vessels.[43]

William Wigder's diary offers the most detailed account of defections during the year 1781. He listed without comment several occasions during this time in which rebel seamen, and even officers, ignored their comrades in order to enter royal service. His several entries give the impression of restless captives who were impelled by a variety of factors to desert the cause: the apparent bureaucratic delays in arranging cartels, the absence of word from loved ones, the seeming indecisiveness of the fighting prior to Yorktown, the lack of a strong patriot commitment, and above all, the oppressive features of prison life.

By 22 August 1781 the Massachusetts seaman was writing glumly, "no news of aney Exchange and our people daily Entering the English Service." Throughout the remainder of 1781, Wigder continued to list native-born Americans and old countrymen who switched sides. These defections, however, did not always work to British expectations. Thus on 27 March Wigder's account cites two Mill seamen who changed their minds about becoming turncoats when rumors of a possible cartel were heard. The following October he reported the recapture of another former prisoner who had accepted a pardon only to desert from the Royal Navy.[44] But the fact remained that a considerable number of inmates were abandoning their supposed attachment to the American struggle, and it was a sore point to those rebels who did retain their loyalty to America.

There were many, many more interned rebels who sought a means of release from Forton or Mill prison that was quicker than defection. The Commissioners for Sick and Hurt Seamen counted 214 fugitives who were said to have fled the two prisons from January 1781 through the following sixteen months. The figure includes those who broke out individually and in groups—it does not include abortive escape attempts. As before, the great majority of the breakouts were from the less secure Hampshire prison. Several of the fleeing rebels were involved in more than one escape attempt. Thus the Admiralty noted (16 February 1782) that Thomas Kinsey of Forton had been recaptured for the fifteenth time. Seaman Kinsey's efforts exemplify many of the Yankee captives' undaunted desires to get clear of their incarceration by any available means.[45]

Regardless of staff replacements, stricter instructions to the guards, and efforts to tighten each prison's security, attempts to escape, despite the omnipresent risks, did not conclude until the early spring of 1782. It was then that the new Rockingham administration recognized the Americans' status as prisoners of war. It was also then that peace negotiations were initiated, and, at the end of April 1782, Parliament offered pardons and called for a general prisoner exchange. Earlier that month other governmental bodies had recognized the inevitable. On 12 April several days after the Americans were deemed war prisoners, the Commissioners for Sick and Hurt Seamen, with subsequent Admiralty approval, decreed that because the £5 reward "is attended with enormous Expence" and because the prisoners "expect to be soon released" the bounty "should be reduced to 10s a Man."[46]

No records exist that give an exact number of escape attempts at Forton and Mill during the period of almost four years since these two detention centers had opened. However, based upon documents at the Public Record Office in Kew, the National Maritime Museum, and various narratives of the captives, my own estimate is that there were then over 200 various attempts to flee from these prisons. Also, during this duration, I estimate that at least 25 percent of the American detainees were involved in some sort of breakout enterprise.

Escape from Mill or the less-protected Forton Gaol was still a difficult matter. Official records reveal that Keeper William Cowdry and Keeper John Newsham were both doing their best to maintain security within their respective prisons. Guards were instructed to be ever more vigilant; patrols were added around each detention center; and perhaps because of Captain William Fitzwilliam's allegations regarding collusion, the staff and sentinels' interaction with the detainees was checked more closely. Furthermore both keepers continued to make use of informers to nip planned rebel breakouts in the bud. At Forton, for example, the Commissioners for Sick and Hurt Seamen advised the Admiralty (12 November 1781) that in an upcoming inquiry into prison escapes a certain John Drury should not be interrogated. Drury, the commissioners explained, "has been useful in giving information of Plans laid to escape." It may well have been seaman Drury who provided information in August 1782 that his fellow inmates "have a hole nearly finished & plan to escape into Gosport, seize a ship, & take it to France." In May of that year William Russell at Mill stated that an alleged betrayer named Samuel Owens had had his life threatened by inmates, and several days later, William Wigder mentioned that an unnamed Judas had thwarted an attempted breakout. Despite all this the escape efforts persisted.[47]

Coverage of the American breakout efforts at Forton is limited during the months from January 1781 through early 1782. The *Hampshire Chronicle,* which previously had reported several flights from the nearby detention center, makes no mention of such occurrences during this time period. Those prisoners who successfully fled to Europe and who afterward wrote to Benjamin Franklin usually offered only general information regarding the method of their escape. One exception to this pattern was the four Forton inmates who declared to the American commissioner (24 February 1782) that they had successfully fled the prison by giving "four Guineas a Piece to the Commissary Clerk," who thereupon assigned them the names of French prisoners for an upcoming cartel. The Commissioners for Sick and Hurt Seamen occasionally noted some of the circumstances surrounding the breakouts. Their informative, but impersonal, listing of the means employed by the Yankee inmates includes tunneling out from the prison, bribing guards and very probably prison staff, absconding from the less-scrutinized prison hospital, and somehow getting over the eight-foot gates surrounding this detention center.[48]

Fortunately, Lieutenant Luke Matthewman's account offers a lively contrast to these superficial governmental listings. Matthewman's own unauthorized exit from Forton occurred on the evening of 3 or 4 January 1781, several days after the failure of another attempt by the inmates to dig their way to freedom. Matthewman, whom the Commissioners described as "30 years of age, 5 feet 8 inches tall, stout made, fair complexion, pitted with the Small Pox, Long Brown Hair," related how the Americans' second digging endeavor had only temporary success. According to the privateer officer, the new tunnel came up considerably short of its objective, "breaking up in the cellar of an old woman." Thereafter events moved swiftly. The elderly Englishwoman fell backward in surprise but recovered enough to shout for the guards. Lieutenant Matthewman stated that the fugitives quickly gagged the woman "and about 60 got out of the hole." Despite this alert response the endeavor was an overall failure. Matthewman and his ship's captain, John Smith, got away and reached safety in Europe, but the other fifty-eight escapees were soon retaken and sent back to Forton's confines.[49]

At Mill Prison, the official records list fewer actual escapes than at Forton, though only a fraction of the attempted breakouts are cited. Letters from successful fugitives, as well as British manuscript documents, provide only limited general insights into the several attempts to flee during this period. However, the diaries of William Russell and William Wigder, along with the subsequent recollections of Lieutenant Joshua Barney and Andrew Sherburne, add detail and color to the record of attempted escapes from Mill during the final confinement phase.

The published accounts of seamen Sherburne and Russell provide fewer details concerning breakout endeavors at Mill than does William Wigder's diary. In Sherburne's case, this limitation is more understandable, because he entered the prison at the end of 1781 when American attempts to flee the Devon gaol were declining. Nevertheless he does recall one incident in which a dozen prisoners escaped one dark evening by taking a "long, loose wooden beam," hanging it out a prison window, then lowering themselves to the ground by a series of hammocks tied to the beam. Another breakout method, which seaman Sherburne euphemistically called "a Yankee trick," involved smuggling interned ship's boys through a hole near the inner gate and having the lads stand in for absconded mariners: "Sometimes, the poor fellows have a hard time getting through the hole, and will squall [squeal] a little, but the shouting and laughter of the prisoners in every direction, in the prison and out, prevented the boys being heard." The published portions of William Russell's journal for this period cite only four escape attempts; two of these were successful, one by tunneling out and one by using unspecified disguises to leave through the gate. Russell's complete manuscript work probably would have contained more such enterprises, including a February 1782 incident in which Captain Bennet Neigus was wounded during an unsuccessful breakout attempt.[50]

William Wigder's meticulous printed diary from 3 January through 6 December 1781 gives the most complete rendering of the several breakout endeavors during this period. Seaman Wigder cited thirty-seven escape attempts from Mill, only twelve of which resulted in complete or partial success. Some Yankee inmates, like Captain John Manley, were listed as having been apprehended seeking to flee on at least three different occasions. Most of the methods noted by Wigder, such as bribing the sentinels, have already been mentioned. However, his diary adds a few others, including the ruse of going to the bay to empty laundry tubs, then swimming away before the surprised guards reacted. Another less pleasant means was to navigate through the prison's sewage channels that emptied into Milbay. Perhaps the most ingenious subterfuge was recorded on 2 October. An inmate named Alexander Tindill [Tindale] attempted to replace the body of a recently deceased comrade "& go out in the coffin." Although Tindill's wildly imaginative scheme failed and landed him in the black hole, he was involved in yet another unsuccessful attempt a little over a month later. Yankee persistence finally paid off since it was reported (31 March 1782) that Tindill at last had engineered a successful breakout.[51]

Bribing the guards was still the most common and the most direct means of fleeing confinement at Mill. Seaman Wigder's account cites several instances when gratuities were willingly ac-

Names	Age	Stature	Complexion	Countenance	Hair	What Cloathing
Reuben Palmer	23	5-7	reddish	slight	long brown	Blue Jacket & white Waistcoat
Thomas Norton	17	5-6	dark	middle	short brown	blue Jacket and Waistcoat
Aaron Richardson	23	5-10	fairish	middle	long brown	Blue Jacket and Waistcoat
Thomas Russell	38	5-8	dark	stout	short dark	light coloured Coat and Waistcoat
John Lockhart	20	5-7	fair	slight	short light	light Coloured Jacket and Waistcoat
Thomas Lockhart	18	5-6	fair	slight	short light	Blue Jacket and Waistcoat
William Grant	26	5-10	darkish	middle	long dark	Blue Jacket and Waistcoat
Isaac Allen	30	5-7	dark	stout	short thick	Blue Jacket and Waistcoat
Daniel Edwards	26	5-8	dark	middle	short dark	Blue Jacket & whitish Waistcoat
Rich.d Eggeshall	23	5-7	fair	middle	long light	brown Jacket and Waistcoat
Robert Fulton	40	5-5	dark	stout	short dark	lightish coloured Jacket and Waistcoat
Simon Crandell	22	5-9	fair	middle	long brown	blue Jacket and Red Waistcoat
And.w Lepear	19	5-7	fair	slight	long dark	linen Coat Waistcoat & Breeches

Descriptions of thirteen American prisoners who had escaped from Forton Gaol, March 1782. ADM 98/14, Public Record Office Kew. Courtesy Public Record Office Kew.

cepted by the sentinels. As though underscoring the point, he wrote in his diary on 14 June "A man that has money, has friends." Ten days earlier Wigder provided an excellent example of just how corrupting the lure of cash could be to some of the watchmen. He noted that Captain Gustavus Conyngham, serving his second internment at the prison, and three other American seamen had made a successful flight "by given 20s to the————who was on————[duty?]." Two days afterward, Wigder recorded that a sergeant and several soldiers from the regiment on guard the day of the breakout were arrested as accomplices.[52]

One of the stories of an American escape during this time earned considerable popularity years later. The daring breakout of Lieutenant Joshua Barney from Mill on 18 May 1781 is mentioned in the journals of both William Wigder and William Russell. However the most thorough and vivid portrayal of the event was published in an affectionate biography by Joshua's daughter Mary.[53] Joshua Barney had been formally committed to Mill Prison on 16 January 1781, after a trans-Atlantic crossing from his confinement in New York. He soon demonstrated that he felt no dread of the Mill's administrative hierarchy when he complained vociferously to Keeper Cowdry in April about allegedly arbitrary actions of the captain of the guard. According to his daughter, early in his detention Lieutenant Barney was sent to the black hole for several days on suspicion of plotting an escape. Nevertheless by early May he had laid the groundwork for his unauthorized departure. He deceived the prison staff into believing that his mobility was limited because of a badly sprained ankle. He cultivated the friendship of a prison militia guard whose prior service in America had left him with strong sympathies for its inhabitants.[54]

Once ready Lieutenant Barney effected his scheme. Shortly after noon on 18 May, the Maryland privateersman, still feigning the sprained ankle, hobbled over to the prison's inner gate to converse with the sympathetic guard. Informed by this accomplice that the moment to bolt would be during the approaching one o'clock dinner period, Barney returned to his prison room. There, as Mary Barney continued, he "equipped himself in the undress uniform of an English officer, which he had provided for the occasion." The lieutenant discarded his prison garb, and got several of his patriot comrades to distract the sentinels while others smuggled one of the ship's boys to stand in his place. When another of his inmate friends, "a tall stout man," stationed himself in a strategic locale near the inner prison gate, and when the staff's dining hour had begun, the time for action had come.[55] Mary Barney described the subsequent hectic events with obvious filial adoration:

> Thus prepared at all points, our bold adventurer descended into the court; he reached the gate without challenge; interchanged a wink with the soldier, which satisfied him that now was the accepted time; and springing, with the agility of a cat, upon the shoulders of his tall fellow-prisoner, who stood ready for the purpose, was in a moment over the barrier, and safe upon his feet: he threw his great coat from him as he lighted upon the ground thrust four guineas into the hand of his *blind* friend, the soldier, as he passed him; and walking boldly through the outer gate, without even being seen by its careless guardian, whose back was towards the prison, was in ten minutes safe, in the house of a well known friend to the American cause, in Plymouth![56]

Once outside the confines of Mill or Forton prison, significant dangers still faced a rebel fugitive. For instance William Wigder mentions one occasion (17 March 1781) when a woman at the prison market spotted an American inmate in disguise who had gotten past prison sentinels. She immediately informed the jailors, who tracked down the fugitive and returned the man for punishment. The following June, Wigder told how Captain John Kemp, formerly master of the armed schooner *Greyhound,* broke out of detention but mistaking the address of his contact in Plymouth, appeared at the wrong house. Captain Kemp was soon betrayed, recaptured, and taken before a local magistrate, who quickly dispatched the escapee back to Mill. (Kemp subsequently accompanied Alexander Tindill during a successful escape in March 1782.[57]) Local militia units, alerted by the keepers at both prisons to search for recent runaways, scoured the countryside. The appealing £5 reward, which was in effect until April 1782, provided great incentives to local residents for seeking out the fugitives. Luke Matthewman claimed that in January 1781 almost all the Americans recaptured after an abortive escape were seized through the actions of local five-pounders. Beyond the immediate prison regions, descriptions of individual fugitives sent out by the Commissioners for Sick and Hurt Seamen posed still another impediment to freedom. Perhaps such desciptions played the primary role in the recapture of seven runaway Americans near Chichester on 13 August 1781, nine days after their escape from Forton.[58]

The American escapees still had active sympathizers in the vicinity of both detention centers. These individuals concealed the fugitives until they could be successfully spirited to other advocates in London or else smuggled aboard ships bound for the continent. It was probably with help from Portsmouth supporters in March 1782 that several escaped Forton inmates were secreted on "a small sloop" that took them to France.[59]

From Mill Gaol, Joshua Barney, following his prison breakout, received temporary sanctuary in the home of an advocate in Plymouth. From there, the unnamed supporter guided Barney to his father's residence. Mary Barney described this new refuge only as the house "of a venerable clergyman" of the community. (This clergyman may have been the Reverend Andrew Kinsman of Plymouth's Calvinist Methodist church, in which Robert Heath served as a deacon.) Barney remained hidden there until his local benefactors purchased a boat for him and another American who was stranded in Plymouth. The small craft was supposed to take the two fugitives, masquerading as fishermen, directly to France, but as she approached the Channel Islands, she was stopped and boarded by a British privateer. The captain of the privateer, unaware of the Americans' true identity, nevertheless had them transferred to his vessel on its passage to England. As the ship neared Plymouth Harbor, the Maryland lieutenant was able to slip off the vessel, seize her dinghy, and flee to the Devon village of Causen. From there, Barney reached the safety once more of his Plymouth protector. This time the disguised runaway's escape route, financed by his Devon patrons, took him to London by way of Exeter and Bristol. A six-week stay in the British capital under the hospitable care of a Virginia expatriate concluded when Lieutenant Barney took a packet boat to full liberty at Ostend.[60]

Earlier that year, Lieutenant Luke Matthewman and Captain John Smith had an easier time following their breakout from Forton. They found their way to the Reverend Thomas Wren's High Street chapel immediately after their breakout in January 1781. There they were given sanctuary by the parson until they could be safely moved to London, where more welcome assistance awaited them.[61]

London's environs contained several individuals who hid the American fugitives until they could be guided to safety on the continent. Foremost among them had been Thomas Digges, who in June 1782 claimed to have assisted more than 160 escaped rebels. At the beginning of the previous year and just before a rift fully emerged between him and Benjamin Franklin, Digges had reportedly secured hideaways for Luke Matthewman and John Smith in the capital. The Maryland merchant also was said to have obtained passage to Ostend for the two escapees, along with an Englishman, and, prior to their departure, to have given them let-

Lieutenant Joshua Barney. Courtesy Independence National Historical Park, Eastern National Park and Monument Association.

ters to Franklin. It seems suspicious that subsequently the vessel carrying the three men was boarded by a government official, who took the Franklin letters from the Americans' English companion. British authorities by this time had been apprised of Digges's hiding of American fugitives, and Digges well may have reported Matthewman and Smith in order to conceal his duplicity. The two Americans were able to slip away on another vessel bound for

Ostend. Digges's puzzling absence from London for much of 1781 and his break with Franklin account for the sharp decline in the number of fugitives seeking his aid. Prisoners, hearing of these developments, certainly had reason to question his trustworthiness. Still he was not completely ignored by American captives, as evidenced by an allegation by the Commissioners for Sick and Hurt Seamen in May 1782 that he had failed to deliver up two Americans he had supervised during their testimony at a London trial.[62]

Evidently covert aid to American fugitives by other London-area supporters such as Thomas Viny and Griffith Williams declined after government officials acted to quash such illegal activities. One indication of this apparent crackdown is contained in a letter of 19 October 1781 from John Adams to Franklin. In it the new American minister to Holland cited a Londoner, Thomas Boer (Beer), who was apparently known to Thomas Digges. Boer and his family were then stranded without funds at Ostend. Adams requested that they be given merited relief because Boer had recently been "obliged to fly from England for having assisted American Prisoners to escape."[63]

VI

Breakout attempts were only one of the ways in which the durability of the inmates' cohesion was manifested during this final confinement phase. The rebel captives also showed their unity in remonstrances against substandard conditions in the gaols and alleged arbitrary actions of the guards or staff. Prisoner groups took the lead in allocating subsistence funds and benefactions among themselves. Furthermore, in a mischievous manner, they instigated harassments against their captors. William Wigder's diary for 1781 is replete with examples of cohesiveness among Mill's Yankee detainees. Years later, Andrew Sherburne recalled some of the manifestations of these inmate regulatory bodies. According to the former Mill internee, the prisoner associations established their own particular articles of conduct and held trials for accused transgressors. Sherburne listed two of the penalties for seamen found guilty: tying the offender "up to the lamp post" and "putting a dozen lashes on the bare back."[64]

The interactions among Americans at these two prisons were indeed not completely harmonious during these later months. Under the various stresses that marked close confinement, it was almost inevitable that antagonisms between individual inmates would erupt. Sometimes they were expressed merely as verbal encounters, but occasionally they led to far more serious confrontations. Such an incident occurred on a Sunday in early February 1781. Both William Russell and William Wigder wrote on that day how Captain John Manley, angered over alleged repeated affronts from Captain Daniel Brown, challenged his fellow privateersman to a duel with pistols. Somehow Manley was able to obtain the pistols (perhaps from prison officials who had contempt for them both), but Brown refused the combat. Afterward, Manley had the satisfaction of boasting that his fellow inmate was no more than "a Great Coward." The following month, Captain Brown, evidently a bellicose character, lost a brawl with another prisoner over a card game. Wigder also briefly noted a quarrel between Joshua Barney and a brother officer that occurred only a few days before Barney's escape. The only dispute among the detainees that had the potential to expand into a general melee occurred the following September, when it was recorded that several prisoners had to be parted after a fight broke out between two of their number. That more serious episodes failed to happen within this frustration-ridden environment would seem to be further evidence of the commitment, self-regulation, and resiliency of most of these Americans.[65]

VII

Among all the emotional stresses of confinement, two of the most prominent remained the fear of being forgotten and yearning for loved ones across the Atlantic. Examples of pangs of forced separation have already been discussed with reference to earlier phases of detention. American seamen who reflected these longings included Charles Herbert at Mill and Timothy Connor at Forton. In this final period of incarceration, hankering for home and hearth was especially manifested in the diary of William Wigder.

One prominent feature of William Wigder's eleven-month journal is his irritation over delays in receipt of letters from America. On 10 August 1781 the Massachusetts seaman noted the arrival of a letter from his wife dated the previous 15 May, informing him that "she and my William [Wigder's son] was well." The following 2 November he again mentioned receiving a letter from his devoted Elizabeth that had been dispatched from Newburyport on 2 June.[66]

Wigder also wrote of his gratitude to a recently incarcerated seaman at Forton who had written to him about his family's well-being. He was similarly appreciative of some merchant captains who took the Mill captives' mail on their trans-Atlantic voyages. Sending messages home ordinarily was not a problem, but once Wigder mentions that he had sent a letter "out by Stilth [stealth] because I did Not Want the Agent [Keeper] to See it baring Date 31 the July."[67]

Aside from Wigder's recordings of family news from faraway America were his personal thoughts, frustrations, and other feelings. An entry made on 11 June 1781 offers especially fascinating insights into personal sentiments common to captives in most wars. In twentieth-century American wars thousands of captive American servicemen in distant detention centers must have had dreams of home similar to these described by William Wigder many many years earlier:

> Last night I dreamed I was in Marblehead and see Sylvester Stevens; after discoursing with him about his Giting home, I said to him tis Dam'd hard now I have got so near home and Cant git their; I thout he asked me What the Matter was; I sayes Why you See I am this Side of the weay and the Souldiers Standing Sentry over by Mr. Roundays house; I thout I Left him and Went a Little further & Met George Tucker down by the eand of Bowden's Lain wheir he Stouped and Shock hands with me and Said he was Glad to See me; he Said my Wife was Just Deliver'd a Boy; I thout I Started at that and Said it was a dam'd Lye; it was imposable for I had been Gone tow years and leatter and it was inposable; I thout I Left him in a Great pashan and [as] I was Going Down towards Nickes cove I met my Mother and Stopt and talked with hur; she asked me why I was not a Going home to see my wife; I tould hur no, I was dam'd if ever I desir to See hir a Gain; She said the Child was a honest begotten Child, and it was Got before I went to See, and it was mine; I Said it was inposable for the Child to be Mine for I had been Gone Mour then two years and it was Inpousable; I tould hur I was a dam'd foule to Coum home, but I Could go back in the Brig I came in; I thout She pursuaded upon me to go home, but I thout I was in Such a pashan, I Swore I would Never See hur a Gain; I thout She intreated me to go home, but I Swore I would not, and it was no use to ask me; but before I was don taling With hur a bout it, I awaked.[68]

VIII

There was continued assistance to the American prisoners by benefactors both inside and outside of Britain during the concluding phase of the Forton and Mill confinement saga. Mention has already been made of several Englishmen who assisted rebel escapees. These men, along with other British Samaritans, also took part in legitimate support endeavors on behalf of the trans-Atlantic captives. Even these legal actions were not universally popular, for until the beginning of peace negotiations in the spring of 1782, Americans were belligerent foes. This reality limited any widespread sympathy for the rebel inmates in the country. William Russell noted one good example of such strong antagonism. He wrote in his journal on 28 February 1781 that a member of the House of Commons had declared that the American detainees, "*instead of a Prison, ought to have a halter.*" Later that year, Captain John Green complained to a British official about a recent article in the *Plymouth Gazette* that Green alleged was "Wholly calculated to prejudice the Minds, of the good People of this Country, against us, both as Prisoners and Men."[69]

At Forton, the Reverend Thomas Wren remained the inmates' prime advocate. The Presbyterian cleric maintained his indefatigable endeavors on behalf of the American prisoners until the closing of the prison. This self-styled "visitor to Forton" performed his usual tasks of offering both spiritual and secular instruction to the inmates. Additionally he tried to sustain the captives' morale with optimistic news about possible cartels or with mail from friends or family; he helped keep communication open with the interned Americans at Mill; and, when necessary, he still interceded with prison officials on behalf of the inmates. In December 1782, as the final prisoner exchange from Forton was being arranged, he even volunteered to send a good-conduct certificate to Paris on behalf of at least one detainee.[70]

Most noticeable, of course, was the laborious work performed by the Portsmouth minister in distributing material aid to the captives. Occasionally, the Reverend Mr. Wren was able to obtain assistance from sympathetic residents in Portsmouth for the rebel inmates. In February 1781 he wrote to William Hodgson that a local gentleman had promised to contribute anonymously "something regularly to the relief of the American prisoners." But for more dependable monetary backing of the inmates, Wren had to look to the American commissioners in Paris and their representatives in London. In late December 1780 Thomas Digges had written to Thomas Wren requesting that allotments of one shilling per week be distributed to each captive. However, Digges was mysteriously absent from London for much of 1781, and he failed to stipulate how the funding would be underwritten. The Reverend Mr. Wren consequently turned to William Hodgson for guidance about reimbursement, additional financial grants from Paris, and possibly new subscription funds from London benefactors. The cleric also retained his contact with Benjamin Franklin, principally on the subject of prisoner relief, and even though he was never fully reimbursed by either the Americans or their British agents, he never threatened to abandon his work.[71]

At Mill Prison, both William Russell and William Wigder cited several dissenter clergymen who offered spiritual encouragement to their comrades. But it was still Deacon Robert Heath and Miles Saurey, his linen draper friend, who, despite alleged incidents of administrative harassments, were the nonofficial providers for the inmates' physical needs. Wigder pointed out episodes during 1781 when these two humanitarians delivered soap, clothing, and other welcome benefactions to the prison. On occasion, they also brought mail to the American detainees, along with word of their comrades in Forton Gaol. In September 1781 both men had a role in implementing a forthcoming limited prisoner exchange, and, according to William Russell, it was Miles Saurey, on 14 June 1782, who conveyed a letter from Thomas Wren informing the Americans of the imminent departure of a cartel ship from Portsmouth.[72]

The principal responsibility of Robert Heath and Miles Saurey on behalf of the American inmates, like that of Thomas Wren, was dispersing the small allotments that were provided them by the commissioners in Paris.[73] William Russell and William Wigder both refer to the anxious captives awaiting arrival of the deacon or the linen draper, who ordinarily brought these funds from London. Wigder intermittently lists the amounts apportioned to each man as varying from sixpence to a shilling per week, but even these paltry sums did not always materialize. Thus it was that seaman Wigder noted on 10 February 1781 that Deacon Heath "had no money for us, but was going to write to London, and if he had no answer, he would Supply us with Six pence." Four days later the Massachusetts seaman recorded a rumor that Thomas Digges was about to visit them, apparently with cash, but the undependable London merchant did not appear. The money allotments were resumed in March, though Heath and Saurey at times had to advance their own funds to the prisoners. This development was evident in a letter from Miles Saurey to William Hodgson on 27 February, noting that since Saurey had not heard from Digges, he would be obliged to provide what cash he could. Saurey's out-of-pocket advances apparently became recurrent because he mentions another grant in a message (5 March 1782) to David Hartley. Truly the various humanitarian endeavors of Heath and Saurey continued until the final Americans departed from Mill.[74]

In Parliament, Whig politicians maintained their vocal support for the prisoners even before the March 1782 collapse of the North ministry. David Hartley was not in the House of Commons during part of this final confinement phase, but he nonetheless continued his considerable efforts on behalf of the American captives. He kept up his contacts with those individuals near both prisons who visited the inmates; he worked with benefactors in London, chiefly William Hodgson, who were providing assistance to the inmates; he continued his vocal support, especially with British governmental agencies, for favorable treatment at the prisons; he worked to speed the final cartels following the beginning of peace negotiations; and perhaps most particularly, he kept his friend Benjamin Franklin abreast of his actions in these matters. Thus, on 5 April 1782, Franklin thanked him profusely for his endeavors on behalf of the American internees. In this same correspondence, the Paris commissioner also relayed his personal confidence that Hartley would help expedite the prisoner exchange bill that was to be introduced into Parliament.[75]

Some British public officials even made individual visits to the prisons. Although there is no evidence during this period of David Hartley himself visiting either Forton or Mill, William Wigder did note (16 November 1781) that Winchcombe Hartley, David's half-brother "one of parliment, & a friend to America was in the Yard." The duke of Richmond was another of America's parliamentary friends whose long-standing support of the captives was mentioned by Wigder and was also cited by the Commissioners for Sick and Hurt Seamen. The duke traveled to the Devon gaol in June 1782 to wish the released captives a safe voyage home. He added a personal note of encouragement, reportedly telling the joyful men that "We had gained what we had been fighting for, and we should find it so in America."[76]

IX

Perhaps the most significant development occurring in 1781 within the ranks of the prisoners' London advocates was the fall from leadership of Thomas Digges and his replacement by William Hodgson. On 29 December 1780 Digges wrote to Benjamin Franklin that he had acted to comply with the Paris commissioner's request that the prisoners' allotments should be doubled during the next four months. However, by 20 March 1781 William Hodgson was writing to Franklin that Digges had not advanced any monies to the captives' agents at either Forton or Mill and that the Marylander had not reimbursed these benefactors.[77] An already suspicious Franklin now became even more concerned. He replied to Hodgson on 1 April, declaring in part, "What is he who can break his Trust by robbing a poor man and a Prisoner of eighteen Pence given charitably for his Relief, and repeat that crime as often as there are Weeks in a Winter. . . . If such a Fellow is not damn'd it is not worth while to keep a Devil." But well before this letter was written, Digges was already in hiding and would not formally resurface until the start of the following year. Hodgson quickly took this opportunity to attack his fellow London merchant's alleged "villany" and malfeasance. Franklin, in turn, sent Hodgson (25 April 1781) a power of attorney to recover any missing funds, and he now made the Coleman Street merchant his principal London representative for matters involving the American prisoners. Later that year entries in William Wigder's journal reveal that the captives also had become aware of Thomas Digges's peculations.[78]

Even after Digges's reemergence in the British capital at the beginning of 1782, he was unable to regain the confidence of the American representatives in Europe. He had somehow retained the friendship of David Hartley, and he hoped to use this connection, along with his record of previous assistance to escaped prisoners, to gain acceptance for himself as a mediator of a wartime truce. However, his mission for this purpose, undertaken in late March 1782, proved a failure. In Amsterdam, John Adams received him coolly, despite the sanction he had from the new Shelburne ministry. Benjamin Franklin showed that he had not lost any of the loathing he held for the Maryland expatriate when he wrote to Hartley on 5 April, "As to Digges, I have no Confidence in him or anything he says or may say of his being sent by Ministers."[79]

Apparently undaunted by the collapse of his continental undertaking, Thomas Digges sought to display his adherence to the rebel cause. In early 1782 he was able to get a few Mill inmates transferred to his care in London while they testified on behalf of two Irishmen, Luke Ryan and Edward Macatter. The two Irishmen and their crews had been captured the previous year commanding Dunkirk privateers which had been commissioned by Benjamin Franklin. Although they claimed American and French citizenship, they were sent to Newgate Prison and charged with piracy. Both men were found guilty on 30 March, but Digges's intercession with the Admiralty may have won them a subsequent pardon. The

Maryland merchant's efforts were extolled by Captain John Green, a Mill detainee who had testified for the Irishmen and who had received a £20 loan from Digges.[80] Digges also sent Green a cheery note as the captain was about to be exchanged in June 1782. If these actions were designed to reingratiate himself with rebel representatives, they were unsuccessful. American agents at Dunkirk and Ostend had already added charges of dishonesty against him, and about the time of the Mill cartel, Franklin advised Robert Livingston of the Department of Foreign Affairs, "Beware of him [Digges], for he is artful and has cheated many."[81]

William Hodgson acted with little difficulty in filling the shoes of the Marylander. Hodgson, who concurred with Franklin's assessment of Digges as a scoundrel, worked diligently with the commissioner to make good on outstanding bills totaling at least £300 that were owed to creditors on behalf of the prisoners. Franklin entrusted Hodgson with complete responsibility for dispensing approved financial allotments to the captives' agents at Forton and Mill. Hodgson thereafter kept Franklin informed of the varying disbursements he had made or hoped to make to the captives. He also worked diligently to obtain additional grants from sympathetic Britons living in London. Dr. John Witherspoon, son of the eminent president of the College of New Jersey (Princeton), had reason to be particularly grateful to Hodgson. Witherspoon had been sent to England following his capture on a privateer (February 1781) at St. Eustatius. After his release that summer, Hodgson, with Franklin's support, provided the requisite assistance to enable the young surgeon to travel to Paris.[82]

Besides these activities William Hodgson acted as an intermediary with either the Admiralty or the Commissioners for Sick and Hurt Seamen in matters relating to prisoner complaints or prisoner exchanges. His tireless work in these capacities lasted into the spring of 1783, and it was gratefully recognized by the American internees in Britain. The London merchant received similar accolades personally from Benjamin Franklin when he called on the commissioner in Paris in July 1782.[83]

For all of his humanitarian endeavors, William Hodgson magnanimously requested no compensation. On 13 July 1782 he assured the American peace negotiators in Paris that if further services were required of him, "It will give me the utmost Satisfaction in all Occasions, if I can be of the least use to you, your Friends, and Countrymen." Hodgson at this time displayed his own affection for Benjamin Franklin by offering to pay for the painting of a portrait of the Pennsylvania diplomat, so that "I may with rapture tell my Children I had the Honour on some degree to enjoy the Friendship of a Man of whom the World thought and think so highly."[84]

There were other private citizens in London who volunteered various forms of assistance to the captives. Most of them had some Whig sympathies, though the prisoners were occasionally contacted by individuals with Loyalist ties to America. Andrew Sherburne, for example, mentioned that John Wentworth, former Tory governor of New Hampshire, "allowed some of the Portsmouth people [to] borrow small sums of money of him, and were to refund the money to the governor's mother who lived in Portsmouth." In August 1781 William Wigder wrote that Thomas Danforth, refugee son of the late Loyalist Judge Samuel Danforth of Cambridge, Massachusetts, had visited the detainees and offered "his services to any belonging to Boston, Cambridge, or Charleston that was confined unjustly."[85]

X

On the European continent, the several appointed agents in France and John Adams in Amsterdam assisted former American captives. The agents, including Francis Coffyn at Dunkirk, Jonathan Williams, Jr., at Nantes, and John Bondfield at Bordeaux, were the most immediate representatives with whom the escaped or exchanged captives had contact in Europe. These deputies in France sought passage homeward for the new rebel arrivals or, in several other cases, provided expense money for travel to the commissioners in Paris. To a great extent, these appointed delegates performed quite well during this last confinement phase, though there were a few cases in which escapees complained that they had failed to obtain needed assistance.[86]

Meanwhile, John Adams, who had been appointed minister to Holland on 29 December 1780, was also involved in matters relating to former American captives. On 18 October 1781 he wrote to Franklin that he had already been allowed to send prisoners under his care to Amsterdam. He added that he had become short of funds since assuming his post because he "had relieved considerable numbers who had escaped from England with small sums." Despite lack of cash, Adams worked energetically through the remainder of the conflict to obtain passage homeward for former detainees or to find them service for the patriot cause in Europe.

The Massachusetts delegate also labored in a significant, albeit subordinate, role in executing prisoner cartels.[87]

Benjamin Franklin in Paris remained the principal figure in affairs affecting American captives in Britain. By now in his midseventies, Franklin was already dealing with a host of responsibilities for the struggling United States. With the onset of peace negotiations in early 1782, diplomacy became a major concern. The commissioner nevertheless found the time to address many of the problems associated with the patriot inmates. Thus, when the controversial Thomas Digges disappeared in early 1781 leaving the relief fund nearly bare, it was Franklin, operating through William Hodgson, who was able to restart the subsidy program. He was also able to supply his new London merchant connection with another £400 intended to meet prisoner needs for the coming winter. But because of an unexpected influx of new detainees at Mill and Forton, along with petitions for aid from other confinement locales in Britain, Franklin had to assign allotments on a preferential basis at the two prisons. Individual inmates occasionally wrote to him seeking special grants for themselves. Simultaneously the commissioner was obliged to meet financial needs of former detainees who arrived in Paris nearly destitute. The list of American escapees "furnished with moneys" to return home reveals that 120 former prisoners were allocated such expenses from January 1781 through the summer of 1783.[88]

Other problems involving the American captives also had to be tackled by Franklin. It was necessary for him to work through trusted British intermediaries in order to seek redress of a variety of prisoner complaints about alleged abuses. He also had to rely on Englishmen such as William Hodgson, Thomas Wren, and Robert Heath for general information regarding the inmates' status. (Additionally, there were letters from government officials or concerned family members in America dealing with needs of specific detainees.) In September 1782 the commissioner even received an appeal to assist two prisoners in England, from their wives who were then in Dunkirk. These husbands were recorded as John Kelly and Edward Macatter, who had been pardoned but not released following their conviction earlier that year for piracy. (Macatter had commanded the privateer *Black Princess* prior to her capture during the latter part of 1781 and Kelly was probably a member of her crew.[89] Overall the topic of most concern for Franklin was prisoner exchange, in which he remained the principal American negotiator. Arranging cartels required effort, tact, and especially patience, but the commissioner met the challenge.

As letters to Franklin indicate, once former inmates reached Europe, difficulties still remained. Several escaped prisoners wrote to the commissioner from different places in Europe telling of their straitened circumstances. Eight American seamen who had recently fled from Forton sent a letter from Lorient on 8 April 1782, claiming that there was no American agent present to help them: "And as we are destitute of both Money and Clothing, we have made bold to apply to your Excellency requesting [If you Please] some Asistance."[90] Some fugitives were even less fortunate. Four other escapees wrote to Franklin in February 1782 that they had successfully broken out of Forton and reached Havre de Grace, but upon applying for a passport to Lorient, a magistrate had examined them and without explanation sent them to a local prison. Here, they told the commissioner, "We remain in a Dismal situation, destitute of Money, Cloths and Necessarys of Life." Shortly thereafter, Franklin got them released. Other former American inmates, including the heroic Lieutenant Nathaniel Fanning, also unexpectedly found themselves sent to French gaols during this period.[91]

Not all Frenchmen were inhospitable to these unanticipated strangers in their midst. In fact, in July and August 1781, Hector St. John de Crèvecoeur, author of the noted *Letters from an American Farmer,* who had recently returned to Caen in Normandy from New York, provided special assistance of his own to five patriot fugitives from Forton who had arrived penniless in Caen. Crèvecoeur followed this action by telling Franklin of his willingness to aid other rebels in similar situations, without compensation. Besides Crèvecoeur there were other unappointed individuals in France and Holland who bestowed assistance on these trans-Atlantic allies who appeared in their midst.[92]

XI

Any signs of a resolution of the American War that may have been observable to government officials at the beginning of 1781 were not apparent to the prisoners until late that year. The Mill prisoners' petition to the Admiralty (1 June 1781), complaining of food and clothing deficiencies, was but one example of their seemingly static situation. Three weeks later, following his second successful escape from the Devon prison, Gustavus Conyngham wrote pessimistically to Benjamin Franklin, "We have but few friends in England at Present." In July, William Wigder, still confined at Mill, reflected his ongoing frustration as he found himself exhorting the Almighty to "Extricate us from the Cruel & Tyrannical power of Britain."[93] To add to the gloom, funds for inmate relief seemed tenuous indeed for much of that year. Meanwhile, on the continent representatives such as John Adams and Francis Coffyn were complaining of a lack of cash to aid escapees. For their part British officials, probably with memories of the uncompleted Morlaix exchange in 1780, were balking at undertaking any new general cartel. They were also rejecting any exchange involving Britons not taken by American vessels off Europe.[94]

Despite such early negative indications, tentative steps toward resolving the American prisoner problem were taken even before news of Cornwallis's surrender reached London. British officials, unwilling to accept an extensive captive exchange, did allow for individual exceptions. For example, Benjamin Franklin, apparently with urging from the Committee for Foreign Affairs, negotiated the release of Dr. John Witherspoon, Jr., by early September 1781.[95]

Dr. Witherspoon's liberation was followed that autumn by the successful negotiation of an exchange of a larger number of prisoners. Franklin had already noted that "the Admiralty would not accept any English in Exchange but such as have been taken by Americans" in European waters. Consequently, when the privateer *Black Princess* captured the armed sloop HMS *Snake* off the English coast in the summer of 1781, the Paris commissioners had a bargaining card. Negotiations for a prisoner swap, with William Hodgson as an intermediary, proceeded rapidly, and on 31 October the Commissioners for Sick and Hurt Seamen forwarded a list of fifty-three favored Mill and Forton inmates who were available for an exchange. Thirteen days later the Admiralty noted that pardons had arrived for the selected Americans. Then, in late December, the actual exchange was promulgated. For the British, the transfer included the captain and crew of *Snake,* as well as a major who had been traveling on her. Among the rebels freed from Mill was former Continental Navy Captain John Manley.[96]

A month before this exchange began, Benjamin Franklin, buoyed by news of the Cornwallis capitulation, had sought to expand the basis for cartels. In November 1781 he wrote through Hodgson to Admiralty officials suggesting a complete exchange of captives. Any British prisoners taken by Americans and held in France, along with British prisoners detained in America, would be exchanged for, among others, "the American Prisoners now Confined in England." But as the year concluded, Franklin had not received any favorable response from Britain.[97]

The year 1782 commenced with bright prospects at last for the rebel inmates of Forton and Mill. Part of their optimism came in the person of Henry Laurens, who had been released from the Tower of London on 31 December 1780. Laurens, a wealthy South Carolina planter and the president of the Continental Congress, had been captured on a packet ship off Newfoundland in September 1780 while on a mission to Europe. Recognizing the prominence of their American captive and having retrieved some of his secret papers, British officials soon had the South Carolinian sent to the infamous Tower. Laurens's secretary, Moses Young, was sent to Forton, from which he eventually escaped on 5 February 1782. Laurens' own incarceration was not so long, but it was certainly more strenuous. However, with the help of Edmund Burke in what became an exchange for Lord Cornwallis, he was given his freedom.[98]

After receiving his parole, the ailing planter retired to Bath for recuperation while the Admiralty, in turn, sought to use his prestige to aid his interned countrymen. Thus, on 27 February 1782 the Lords granted Henry Laurens limited "access to the Forton and Mill captives," and they also permitted him "to relieve their [the prisoners'] necessities." After Lord Shelburne became secretary of state, Laurens met with him, in part to seek further action for the relief and exchange of the detainees. He visited the Americans in the prisons; Andrew Sherburne, recalling the occasion, stated that the inmates at Mill "treated him with every mark of respect." Captain John Green, who was also present during this visit, afterward wrote to Laurens that several of the prisoners were reluctant to "spoke with you & thank'd you in person for the honor don them, but for Fear of offending the Keeper, whom watch'd all your mossions [motions]." The South Carolinian was said to have donated £200 for the captives' welfare during his visit. He also made some efforts to facilitate further cartels, but his precarious health prevented him from doing more. In May 1782 he sailed for the continent.[99]

Henry Laurens departure proved no deterrent to the American prisoners' rapidly growing expectations for release. The fall of the North ministry and recognition of the Americans as legitimate prisoners of war in March 1782 were among the reasons for the captives' increased optimism. The following month a bill that had been introduced into Parliament by Edmund Burke calling for a general exchange of captives was adopted, and the Commissioners for Sick and Hurt Seamen compiled lists of all detainees in Great Britain. Benjamin Franklin wrote that he regarded the March act of Parliament as not only a renunciation of Britain's threat to try the rebel seamen for treason but also, in a circuitous way, even an acknowledgment of American independence. The Parliamentary act also occurred almost simultaneously with the previously cited reduction in rewards for recapturing escapees. Finally, in May 1782 arrangements were initiated for transporting the released seamen to Boston, Philadelphia, or the Chesapeake. Lord Shelburne told Franklin of his hopes for a "happy issue of the problem." This message was gratefully received by Franklin, who had earlier written to Robert Livingston in Philadelphia that an exchange would "make so many of our Countrymen happy, add to our Strength, and diminish our Expence."[100]

XII

By midyear the prisoner cartels were well under way. William Hodgson, who had been informed by an undersecretary on 7 April 1782, of George III's willingness to accept a general prisoner exchange, submitted a proposal to Benjamin Franklin four days later by which "eight or nine" ships would convey the estimated eleven hundred American captives still in Britain. Franklin replied to Hodgson on 26 April, making some additional suggestions regarding the transport ships but basically leaving the "whole Transaction" to the London merchant's "Judgement and Equity." Hodgson evidently had no difficulty accepting the "Conditions of the Exchange" that were put forward by royal officials on 8 May. Two days later he was writing to Franklin that "there remains nothing to be settled," and upon the completion of minor formalities, the cartels would commence. That same month, in Mill Prison, Captain John Green was expressing similar optimism about an imminent release. Green, whose letters only recently were expressing repeated complaints about overcrowding and other prison deficiencies, was now writing, "the times are Changed & all things have Changed with them."[101]

A temporary postponement occurred when bureaucratic inefficiency delayed getting adequate clothing supplies to the American inmates scheduled to leave Forton. Nevertheless, on 7 June 1782 Hodgson could inform Franklin with satisfaction that "the Prisoners from Forton to the amount of 330 are gone." The London merchant did note his concern over the aforementioned report that before their embarkation, the rebel prisoners were "riotous, ungovernable" and had even considered burning the Hampshire gaol. This parting Yankee gesture, however, did not postpone the next cartel. On 24 June an even larger exchange took place at Mill, and by the beginning of July about one thousand detainees had been freed.[102]

William Russell offered an excellent description of the departure of the cartel from Mill Prison on 24 June. This large-scale exchange included seventy or eighty prisoners recently transferred from Kinsale in Ireland, as well as William Russell, William Wigder, John Green, and apparently the long-held, long-suffering, Samuel Harris of Ipswich, Massachusetts. Shortly before the exchange date, seaman Russell recorded an example of the strong spiritual sentiments that helped sustain him throughout the long ordeal of confinement: "When I come to reflect on the precarious situation we were in some months gone, in a strange land, not knowing what might happen, and then to comprehend the reality of the Transporting News, of being released from this dismal place of exile and suffering, *I am compelled to cry out, O God, in the midst of Thy Judgments, Thou has remembered Mercy!*" Russell's later account of the day of release reveals the common relief and joy of the freed captives, which doubtlessly was evident among liberated prisoners in subsequent American conflicts:

June 24th [1782] The Escort came and the Agent [Keeper William Cowdry] opened the *Gate of the Castle of Despair,* and 400 Americans marched out to the Water side, where we found four Launches, and a Cutter waiting to receive us; I went on board the Cutter, and in a short time was on board the Good Ship *Lady's Adventure,* a Cartel bound to Boston. We had our complement on board by 6 o' clock. The Agent came off and received a Receipt for 400 Men and wished us a good Voyage.

We immediately hove up anchors, and at 8 o'clock made sail. I was transported with Joy at my deliverance from a loathsome Prison, where I've been confined thirty Months and five days, almost despairing of ever seeing my Native Country, my Loving Wife and Dear Children and my relatives and who are dear to me; but "Glory to God in the Highest" for His goodness unto us. I thank God I've a prospect now before me of seeing *America,* that *Land of Liberty,* and on my arrival of finding all connected with me in health and happiness.

The Rev. Robert Heath and Mr. Saurey took their leave of us. The Ship is 700 Ton with accommodations, and well found, the Captain and crew are very civil, and *now I've taken my departure from Old Mill Prison, and hope never to see it again.*

We have fine Wind, and May God grant us a quick passage, and guide the Ship to her desired Port.[103]

The festive departure from Plymouth Harbor of seaman William Russell and his comrades did not signify an imminent shutdown for either Mill or Forton. William Hodgson had written to Franklin on 13 July 1782, that "the prisoners are all gone except about 120 who remain for some time sick in the Hospital and they I expect will go in a few days."[104]

The London merchant was too optimistic in his pronouncement. In September 1782, five Mill prisoners, whose illnesses had prevented their departure on the June cartel, petitioned Lord Shelburne for redress. They declared that despite healthy recoveries, they were still being denied passage to France. Simultaneously, new committals to both gaols were made through transfers from other British land-based detention sites, from prison ships, or from British privateers. Official records substantiate the resultant realities. The Commissioners for Sick and Hurt Seamen, who reported a total of 157 American captives still held at Mill and Forton on 28 August 1782, noted that the number of such detainees had risen to 214 by the following 23 September and to 284 by 16 October.[105]

This increase in number created significant difficulties for the patriot internees. There was one uncorroborated incident that summer in which four prisoners, recently sent to Mill to await exchange, charged that they had been impressed onto a British frigate. A more general complaint was the lack of clothing and other supplies. On 16 October the commissioners in London acknowledged that the Americans, now formally considered prisoners of war, lacked such outfitting, and they requested immediate assistance from the Admiralty. Evidently the need was not quickly met, for two weeks later, officials at Mill, and subsequently at Forton, cited "riotous behavior" within the prisons over the shortcoming. Almost simultaneously, the Admiralty formally acknowledged the delays in dispatching these men homeward.[106]

It was not until the beginning of 1783 that the bureaucratic logjams hindering implementation of the final cartels were finally broken. Once more success came largely through the efforts of William Hodgson. Hodgson, who had been so confident the previous summer that an end to detention was at hand, had become more circumspect during the following autumn. On 14 October 1782 he had listed the number of captive Americans at "about 120" (less than half the number cited by the Commissioners for Sick and Hurt Seamen) and hinted at unspecified difficulties in arranging another cartel. The next month he had to admit to Franklin that the detainees actually numbered 240 and that significant obstacles in procuring ships, as well as differences over prisoner-exchange details, were obstructing the final cartels. Then, on 12 December he wrote to Paris that Lord Shelburne's office had informed him that the delays were caused by Congress's "absolutely" refusing to comply with the exchange agreement.[107]

Fortunately, William Hodgson could obtain assistance on this matter from influential friends in Parliament, such as David and Winchcombe Hartley and the duke of Richmond, who had already aided prisoner relief. The Hartleys, Richmond, and other sympathetic parliamentarians, desirous of reconciliation with the United States, strongly supported Hodgson's efforts to remove the roadblocks to an exchange. The signing of the Preliminary Articles of Peace on 30 November 1782 in Paris had provided a spur to further conciliation. Consequently, after marshalling support from influential Whig politicians and adding his own undaunted lobbying, Hodgson could be confident in writing to Franklin in January 1783 that, although he did conclude that "Congress" had refused to comply with the original exchange agreement, nevertheless "the Admiralty have now absolutely ordered vessels to depart immediately with all the American prisoners."[108]

Hodgson's letter of 8 January 1783 brought considerable relief to Benjamin Franklin, who reminded the London merchant later in the month that he had been assured more than three months before that the prisoners were about to be exchanged. In this same message Franklin noted that he had earlier assembled several American ships that had stood by to participate in the cartel. The Paris commissioner added that because of the delays he would now have to use hired vessels for this purpose, and he urged Hodgson to send him a passport as quickly as possible.[109]

Benjamin Franklin's strong desire to obtain an immediate and final resolution to the prisoner problem possibly was made even greater by related circumstances. Having anticipated completion of the exchanges by the previous autumn, Franklin had not provided assistance adequate for the total number of American captives which reached 312 by early February 1783, including 272 at Mill and Forton. The result of his miscalculation was evident in some discomforting letters that he received from the rebel inmates, including the previously cited one from Jacob Smith at Mill Prison. Smith wrote that food and clothing shortages were causing daily defections. To illustrate the seriousness of the situation, he added that some of his comrades "that have Been Hear these Aight Months and but Had the Lest Asistance from Any Body."[110]

The redemption of Jacob Smith and his fellow rebel inmates at the two English gaols was not long in coming. On 3 March 1783 the Admiralty issued orders for the immediate and complete exchange of all American prisoners in Great Britain. The captives in Mill sailed for Morlaix about eleven days later. William Hodgson noted their departure in a letter to Franklin on 25 March, in which he also repeated Lord Shelburne's claim that Congress had "broken their faith" in the terms of the cartel. Hodgson nonetheless assured Franklin that the Commissioners for Sick and Hurt Seamen had informed him that Shelburne's irritation would not interfere with the embarkation of the detainees at Forton. Indeed that same day the London commissioners reported to the Admiralty that the American prisoners at the Hampshire prison, only recently charged with "riotous behavior," were all about to sail.[111] These men were apparently the last of the prisoners at Forton, though on 21 April the Commissioners for Sick and Hurt Seamen reported four Americans still at Mill. On the following 10 June, this body asked the Lords about the disposition of five Yankee seamen from the West Indies. They observed that the five men were being detained in Plymouth, though apparently not at Mill, because "all the American Prisoners, who were confined in England, have been released and sent to France."[112]

Benjamin Franklin encountered several important diplomatic and financial matters before he departed Paris for the United States during the summer of 1785. Yet, despite all these other pressing matters, problems relating to the former American prisoners in Great Britain continued to require some of his attention. Such postcaptivity issues varied in nature: furnishing monetary assistance or passage facilities to released seamen still stranded in Europe; extricating former inmates from personal predicaments on the continent; and supplying responses to charges made by these mariners against their former British captors for abusive or unwarranted treatment. The Pennsylvania commissioner was not always successful in meeting these challenges; some of them lingered long after his departure from France. Yet the illustrious Franklin could look back with satisfaction to the bright spring of 1783, when the forbidding gates of Forton, Mill, and smaller British prisons had finally opened to relinquish all of his imprisoned countrymen. For all of his indefatigable efforts on behalf of the American captives in Britain—forwarding relief funds, encouraging escapes, working to effect exchanges or releases—he has aptly been cited by one historian as "the first American POW activist."[113]

7

Epilogue

Forton and Mill prisons had ceased to be used as confinement sites even before the signing of the Paris Peace Treaty in September 1783. The Admiralty's order on 3 March of that year for the immediate and total exchange of all American prisoners was not promptly executed. In addition to the four Americans still being held at Mill on 21 April, the Commissioners for Sick and Hurt Seamen on the following 18 June requested instructions from the Admiralty concerning the disposition of a "small number" of prisoners still incarcerated at Kinsale. A few American seamen also wrote to Benjamin Franklin at this time concerning their temporary detention at other locales in Britain.[1] Captives of allied nations also remained at the two prisons during the spring months of 1783. Thus, the 21 April report concerning the four Americans remaining at Mill also mentioned that the prison still held twenty-three Frenchmen. The same month, the *Hampshire Chronicle,* while reporting that all French, Spanish, and American prisoners had been exchanged, noted that "341 Dutchmen" still detained in various Hampshire detention sites would not be "sent home until specific terms are agreed upon between our Court and the States General." Such obstacles, though irritating, proved temporary. At last, on 20 August 1783, the commissioners forwarded a request for a survey of vacated buildings at Forton and Mill.[2]

The chronicle of American seamen confined at Mill and Forton prisons during the War of Independence had concluded months before these surveys were initiated, but subsequent details may be added to the story. What, for example, eventually became of these detention sites? What did the future hold for some of the Americans incarcerated within the perimeters of these gaols? And what were the later careers of some of the individuals from Britain and the United States who were directly involved with the plight of interned rebel seamen? Answers to such questions are part of history's ongoing process. Together they form an epilogue to this

Portion of a lithograph of Plymouth c. 1820 showing Mill Prison. Courtesy National Maritime Museum Greenwich, London.

study of a little remembered, albeit noteworthy, episode from this nation's beginnings.

I

The Mill (Millbay) buildings continued to serve as a prison site well after 1783. A decade later Anglo-French hostilities led to the prison's reopening. This conflict, which expanded into the protracted Napoleonic Wars, saw a considerable number of Britain's adversaries incarcerated in the Plymouth prison. Although the United States was also engaged in strife with Britain during the late stages (1812–14) of this belligerency, American captives were held primarily in Devon's larger, more isolated, Dartmoor compounds. Only a relatively small number of U.S. seamen, usually sick or special cases, were sent to Mill. An 1820 survey of the Plymouth area reveals a prison still on the site, but twenty-five years later, the St. Andrew Tithe Apportionment shows a barracks there. Evidently the structure served this purpose at least through the Crimean War of the midnineteenth century. Subsequently these buildings were torn down, and the West Devon Record Office now lists the original location of Mill Prison as "near to the Duke of Cornwall Hotel, not far from Brittany Ferries exit into Millbay Road."[3]

Forton Gaol was also reinstituted as a detention center during the Anglo-French and Napoleonic Wars. However, the number of French captives held there was not large, and a fire in the prison's hospital (1807) resulted in all the buildings being torn down. That same year, a spacious barracks was completed close by the prison site. Shops, taverns, and private homes soon were added, and in 1848 the Royal Marine Light Infantry was officially installed in the barracks. From this locale, the marines received training and were sent to partake in several imperial conflicts. In 1923, the Royal

Marines left the complex for new quarters in Eastney. Less prominent than Forton Barracks was a Victorian era prison that was used to hold both military and civilian offenders. Today a visitor making the pleasant uphill walk from Gosport will pass a few small government installations, Forton Field, and the 'parish' church of St. John the Evangelist before reaching the site of the eighteenth-century prison. A housing complex now stands there.[4]

Americans who pass the Forton or Mill sites today are mainly tourists, but this was not the case during the two world wars of this century when the United States was allied with the United Kingdom. Especially in the second of these conflicts, a great many American servicemen were stationed in or near Plymouth and Portsmouth. And at both of these ports in June 1944, Americans then departed, not as former prisoners, but as part of a famed invasion force bound for Normandy.[5]

II

Turning again to questions about the more distant past, what subsequently happened to the Britons who aided Americans incarcerated in their nation's prisons during the Revolution? Political figures are the easiest to trace. David Hartley, foremost among the English benefactors in government, traveled to Paris to sign the peace agreement finally concluding the war in September 1783. The following year he was defeated in a parliamentary election for Hull, and thereafter he retired to Bath. His brother, Winchcombe Hartley, who had once visited the Mill prisoners, was defeated contesting for a seat in Berkshire, and following a later loss for Gloucestershire, he retired from politics. John Wilkes's political fortunes declined after the Revolution; he also withdrew from government after an election defeat in 1790. Edmund Burke, who like Wilkes had spoken on behalf of the American prisoners in the House of Commons, retained a seat in Parliament and continued his opposition to the Crown; but he showed little sympathy toward the revolution that erupted in France.[6] The duke of Richmond, who had personally encouraged the Mill prisoners during their exchange in 1782, was active in the House of Lords for the next twenty-two years. During that time he served in the cabinet of William Pitt the Younger, and among other actions, he proposed a plan for a new system of fortifications for Plymouth and Portsmouth. Lord Abingdon, who had aided prisoner relief in 1777, also

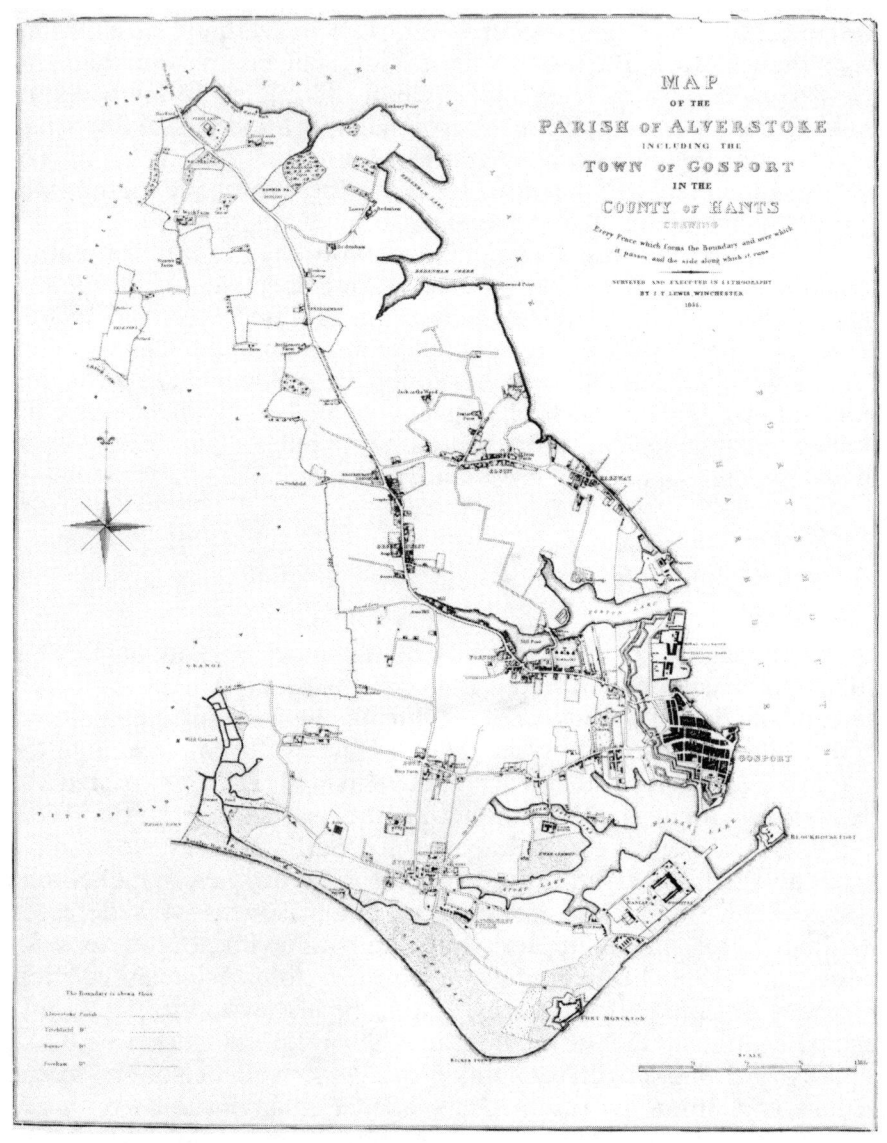

Map of the Parish of Alverstoke including the town of Gosport, 1832. Forton Barracks is shown just east of the town. Courtesy Gosport Museum.

remained in the House of Lords after 1783, but his main interest was in Irish affairs.[7]

Little is known about the later lives of most of the nongovernmental individuals who aided American prisoners. Thus Miles Saurey, Plymouth's kindhearted linen draper, disappears from the personally recorded scene following a brief note concerning his contacts with the prisoners that he sent to Henry Laurens in April 1782. Considerable information, however, does exist about two Londoners, William Hodgson and Thomas Digges. Hodgson continued to be antagonistic to Britain's established order. He was found guilty of "toasting the French Republic" and comparing George III "to a hog butcher." The merchant-physician served a two-year sentence in Newgate Prison for these offenses, and after his release he abandoned radical activism to focus on science and literature. Hodgson died at the age of 106 in 1851.[8] Thomas Digges, who attained the age of seventy-nine, was able to establish a surprising amount of credibility with several Americans following the Revolution. This turnabout occurred despite a stint served in an Irish prison and Benjamin Franklin's continued antipathy. In one incident in 1793, the American consul in England even approached Digges about conducting a search in Yorkshire for heirs of a recently deceased Virginian. Near the end of that same decade, Digges returned to Maryland as the inheritor of his substantial family homestead along the Potomac River, and there he received the honor of several personal receptions at the nearby Mt. Vernon estate of George Washington.[9]

Two men, Robert Heath and Thomas Wren, stand out among Englishmen from Devon and Hampshire who befriended the American captives. During the Revolution their numerous humanitarian exertions on behalf of these prisoners showed them to be aptly described by the scriptural passage reading, "The man who continues in the light is one that loves his brother."[10]

After the war Robert Heath spent an increasing amount of time as an unpaid evangelical, itinerant preacher in England's West Country. In 1789, two years after his wife's death, Deacon Heath abandoned all his business interests for ordination as a Calvinist Methodist minister. Shortly thereafter he accepted a call as pastor of the Rodborough Tabernacle outside Stroud in Gloucestershire where years earlier the famed revivalist George Whitefield had preached. He spent the remainder of his life ministering to his congregation there. The Reverend Robert Heath also continued to travel to nearby religious gatherings, and it was on his return from one such assemblage that he suddenly died on 17 July 1800.[11]

In Hampshire the Reverend Thomas Wren remained in his post as minister of Portsmouth's High Street chapel. There, like his counterpart at Rodborough, he delivered regular spiritual homilies to his congregants, ministered to the infirm and dying, promoted charitable activities for the indigent, and in other ways continued to do good work. Unlike Robert Heath, however, Wren received praise for his prisoner relief efforts from the new American republic. In 1783 the Congress of the United States sent the Reverend Mr. Wren a resolution of thanks for his many benefactions to the Forton captives, and the College of New Jersey (Princeton) rewarded him with a doctoral degree.[12] Later, in April 1787 John Adams, then Minister to Great Britain, visited Portsmouth seeking his assistance in investigating an alleged counterfeiting scheme involving an expatriate North Carolinian. On 30 October of that year, Wren was silenced when he was said to have been "carried off suddenly by an inflammation in his bowels." Eleven days later Richard Price, a liberal dissenting clergyman, offered this touching and appropriate farewell: "Dr. Wren's death has given me great concern; He was one of the best of men, and will be happy in a better world."[13]

III

The Americans most involved in this historical episode also complement the story. These rebels can be divided into two principal groups: those men who worked in Europe to ameliorate the lot of rebel detainees in British gaols and the actual detainees who experienced the Forton and Mill confines.

From his lodgings in Passy, outside Paris, Benjamin Franklin undoubtedly was the key figure in matters relating to the American naval prisoners. His function as one of the commissioners in France expanded when he served as one of the Paris peace negotiators. He returned to a tumultuous Philadelphia welcome in September 1785 and almost immediately afterward was elected to the Supreme Council of Pennsylvania. Despite increasing infirmities Franklin was selected as a state delegate to the Constitutional Convention. He supported ratification of the completed document and lived to see the inauguration of the new national government.[14] John Adams, as another Paris commissioner and as minister to Holland, had labored in a lesser, though still significant, role on behalf of the rebel captives in Britain. He, too, served as a member of the peace delegation, and in February 1785 he was appointed

United States minister to Great Britain. There, in a conciliatory gesture, he assured George III that the two nations "though separated by the ocean, and under different governments, have the same language, a similar religion, and kindred blood." Such sentiments of reconciliation toward his former mother country were evident later when John Adams served as the first vice president and second president of the United States.[15]

Three other men, Jonathan Williams, Jr., Francis Coffyn, and John Bondfield, also proffered assistance to the captives from various locales on the continent. The American-born Jonathan Williams, agent in Nantes, returned to the United States with Benjamin Franklin. He was a merchant in Philadelphia for several years, but the highlight of his later career came in 1801 when he was appointed the first superintendent of the United States Military Academy at West Point. After the war, Francis Coffyn applied for and received the post of American consul in Dunkirk. Franklin, who recommended him for the position in March 1784, emphasized the fact that the Flemish businessman had "for seven years constantly taken care of and relieved the poor prisoners escaping from England, without compensation." Coffyn stayed in Dunkirk handling commercial matters affecting the United States, and prior to his death on 14 May 1795, he was involved in (sometimes questionable) mercantile undertakings with American merchants. John Bondfield, who had been a Canadian merchant prior to his appointment in March 1778 as American agent in Bordeaux, remained in the city after the Revolution. There he used his American contacts and his status as consul for the United States to pursue his own commercial endeavors.[16]

As for the captive American seamen, Joshua Barney, Gustavus Conyngham, and John Manley were perhaps the most prominent among the naval officers who were detained at Mill Prison. Barney, who had effected a daring escape from the Devon prison in June 1781, soon afterward returned to America, where he successfully captained *Hyder Ali* (*Hyder Ally*), a one hundred ton, sixteen-gun warship fitted out and commissioned (2 April 1782) by the state of Pennsylvania. After the Revolution, Barney undertook several commercial ventures. He also served as a captain in the French Navy from 1796 to 1802. His initial involvement in the War of 1812 was as a privateersman, but he subsequently reentered the United States Navy and gallantly commanded a small force of sailors and marines during the American defeat at the Battle of Bladensburg outside Washington. Barney died on 1 December 1818 in Pittsburgh, Pennsylvania.[17] Gustavus Conyngham also returned to maritime mercantile enterprises after 1783 but was unable to enter the regular navy or obtain congressional compensation for his wartime services. Nevertheless his devotion to his country remained undiminished, and during the War of 1812 he helped prepare Philadelphia's defenses against possible British attack. He died in that city in November, 1827. John Manley obtained command of the Continental frigate *Hague* (formerly *Deane*) after his exchange and return to America in 1782. The frigate took several prizes in the West Indies, but in January of the following year, she was forced aground on Guadeloupe by a larger British warship. Although Manley remained in seaborne trade until his death in February 1793, the loss of *Hague* effectively ended his naval career.[18]

Captain John Green, a less distinguished captive than Conyngham, Barney, or Manley, achieved some historical notoriety after his return to America in August 1782. The following November he commanded the twenty-gun warship *Duc de Lauzun* on a voyage from Philadelphia to Havana to obtain gold bullion. His successful return cruise, escorted by Captain John Barry of the frigate *Alliance,* included perhaps the last significant American naval engagement of the Revolution. Green earned even greater prominence during peacetime. In February 1784 he captained the three hundred and sixty-ton *Empress of China* on a voyage that opened trade markets in China with the United States. He subsequently made other journeys to Asia prior to his death at his Bucks County home in September 1796.[19]

Dr. Jonathan Haskins and Captain George Ralls contributed some documentation about their Mill imprisonment, but they are less prominent in historical annals than the three aforementioned naval officers. Haskins married a local woman following his return to Connecticut in 1783. Soon afterward he relocated to eastern Maine, where he practiced medicine until his death in 1801. The postprison career of the flamboyant, though often incompetent and inebriated, George Ralls remains more murky. Despite his protests Ralls was dismissed from Virginia's naval service following his return to America. Later he became a landowner, and in November 1792, he was listed as one of the original trustees for the town of Centerville in Loudon County. His will, revealing a moderate estate, was probated in the Virginia county in February 1799.[20]

Seamen Samuel Cutler and Charles Herbert were rebel mariners from the lower ranks who left the most notable accounts of the early phases of confinement at Mill. Cutler, who successfully escaped detention in October 1777, eventually returned to New England. He settled in Newburyport, Massachusetts, where he married in January 1794, helped raised four children, served as vestryman and warden in the town's Episcopal church, and prospered in commerce and insurance. In June 1832 both Cutler and his wife drowned when the schooner they were aboard capsized.[21] Charles Herbert experienced more far-flung adventures after his exchange in March 1779 and before his return to Newburyport seventeen months later. He reentered patriot service in France on board the Continental Navy frigate *Alliance* and participated in her seizure of several prizes in the North Sea. Prior to his return voyage to America, he even met Benjamin Franklin in Paris. Unlike Samuel Cutler he did not enjoy prosperity in his later years. Seaman Herbert wed a Newburyport woman, sired fourteen children, and worked as a blockmaker in the town until his death in September 1808. His widow was unsuccessful in her attempts to obtain a federal pension or prize money in recognition of his wartime services.[22]

The most prominent firsthand coverage by seamen of occurrences at Mill during later confinement stages was by three New Englanders: William Wigder, William Russell, and Andrew Sherburne. Wigder, who had so poignantly expressed his dreams while in captivity, rejoined his family in Marblehead following the cartel agreements of 1782. He subsequently returned to the sea, serving on several peacetime commercial voyages. Evidently he was an able mariner, for prior to his death at Nantucket in 1823, he captained the merchant brig *Increase*. William Russell, who was exchanged at about the same time as Wigder, spent only a brief time at home before signing aboard a Massachusetts privateer. When this ship was taken, Russell was incarcerated aboard the dreaded prison ship *Jersey* in New York harbor. He was paroled in the spring of 1783, but his health had deteriorated so much that after his return to Cambridge, he was unable to resume schoolteaching and he died the following year.[23] Andrew Sherburne, like Russell, joined a privateer soon after his homecoming, was captured, and experienced a period of confinement aboard *Jersey*. Sherburne came through his imprisonment reasonably well; he returned to New Hampshire, undertook several commercial voyages, married in 1790, settled into farming, and became an ardent Baptist. He later worked as a missionary, traveled to Ohio, and finally settled in western New York, where he died in 1832.[24]

The postconfinement activities of many of the American inmates of Forton can be traced as well. However, records are more readily available for the officers than for the men in the lower ranks.

Caleb Foot, George Thompson, Dr. Nathaniel Harrington, Elisha

Hinman, Nathaniel Fanning, and Charles Bulkeley were all New Englanders from the upper ranks who were incarcerated at Forton. Prizemaster Caleb Foot reached Amsterdam following his escape from the prison in October 1780. There he volunteered to serve on a South Carolina privateer that sailed from the Dutch seaport the following summer. He eventually returned to his wife Mary and their children in Salem, but there he contracted tuberculosis, to which he succumbed in May 1787. George Thompson, the other prizemaster from Massachusetts, escaped from captivity in November 1779. After reaching safety in France, he returned to Newburyport the following spring and soon embarked on other privateering ventures. He returned home from these cruises, married in January 1782, settled into commercial ventures, and raised five children. Ship's doctor Nathaniel Harrington received five guineas from Benjamin Franklin in Paris following his escape and used the money to travel to Nantes, where in May 1780 he enrolled as a surgeon on board *Governor Livingstone,* a Virginia letter of marque. The privateer sailed for the West Indies after several months' delay, and there the Massachusetts physician reportedly died the following January.[25]

Elisha Hinman, Nathaniel Fanning, and Charles Bulkeley were all naval officers from Connecticut. Elisha Hinman, with assistance from Franklin, returned to America following his escape in July 1778. During the remainder of the war, he captained several privateers that seized a number of prizes. His postwar activities were centered in New London, where he operated a mercantile enterprise, occasionally commanded a revenue cutter, and raised four children prior to his death in 1805. Of this group, Nathaniel Fanning rendered perhaps the most conspicuous service for the rebel cause following his escape in June 1779 from Forton. He served with gallantry on board *Bon Homme Richard* in her memorable battle with *Serapis;* he then enrolled as an officer on privateers operating from French seaports. He was twice more captured and released, and he finally returned to America in late 1781. Fanning then settled in Connecticut for an indeterminable period before he moved to Charleston, South Carolina. In this southern seaport he was appointed commander of the United States Naval Station. He was acting in this capacity at the time of his death in September 1805.[26] Charles Bulkeley, who had been captured aboard *Alfred* along with Elisha Hinman, returned to America by way of France following his successful flight in the summer of 1778. During the remainder of the war, he served on privateers and was involved in defending New London during Benedict Arnold's September 1781 raid. Bulkeley entered commerce in the town after the conflict, raised seven children, commanded a privateer during the War of 1812, and lived to the age of ninety-five.[27]

New York Lieutenant Luke Matthewman was the most conspicuous representative from the mid-Atlantic states to record his experiences in captivity at Forton Gaol. After reaching Holland following his successful breakout in January 1781, he joined a privateer that eventually returned him to America. He served aboard *Hyder Ali,* commanded by Joshua Barney, and was captured and exchanged. Shortly before the conclusion of hostilities, he served again on an American privateer. When his reminiscences of wartime experiences were published, he was living in Philadelphia and claimed that he was engaged in transporting freed slaves to their chosen destinations.[28]

Captains Benjamin Chew, Alexander Dick, and John Harris were officers from the southern states who were incarcerated in the Hampshire prison. Chew, who successfully fled detention in July 1778, returned to Maryland thanks to financial assistance from Benjamin Franklin. How long he remained there is unknown, but he was listed as a Georgia resident in 1790, and his death in Savannah was mentioned in a newspaper notice fifteen years later. Captain Dick was another escapee who received money from Benjamin Franklin to help underwrite his return to America. The former marine officer subsequently joined the Continental Army as a major and served under General Washington at the siege of Yorktown. Following his retirement from active service, Alexander Dick settled back into a comfortable planter life in Fredericksburg, Virginia, until his death in 1786. His commanding officer aboard *Mosquito,* John Harris, was less fortunate following his exchange and return to Virginia. An affidavit stating that he died in March 1783 seems to be corroborated by a letter written soon afterward by his sister-in-law in Hampton, which declared, "Poor Harris died in this town after a tedious illness. He has left everything to his daughter by your [late] sister, who is a fine little girl."[29]

Timothy Connor and Jonathan Carpenter were the two detainees from the lower ranks who provided the most detailed accounts of prison life at Forton. Connor wrote the lengthiest of the descriptions, but little is known about his life after his exchange in July 1779. There was a Timothy Connor who registered an intention of marriage in Boston on 26 August 1780 with one Hannah Hulton. In April 1783 a Timothy Connor was chosen hogreeve by the Boston commissioners, and seven years later the city's census revealed someone of that name heading a household of two males under sixteen and two females. Still it remains inconclusive if this was the same Timothy Connor captured with the crew of *Rising States* in 1777. This uncertainty is not the case, however, for Jonathan Carpenter. The Massachusetts mariner continued his diary long after his exchange with seaman Connor. Carpenter noted that quite soon after the cartel ship deposited him in France, he signed aboard an American privateer. That vessel's cruises resulted in the capture of several prizes, and Carpenter returned to his home in Rehoboth with about £150 for his personal share. He tarried only a brief time there before setting out for Vermont to battle loyalists and Indians. He also took a farmstead near the town of Randolph. It was in Randolph that Carpenter married, raised a family, became a Baptist, and died on 14 March 1837, in his eightieth year.[30]

IV

The prime focus of this study has been the experience of the Americans who languished within the walls of Forton and Mill prisons during the American Revolution. It is not one of the more publicized or glamorous events of this momentous conflict, but the story of these few thousand men is a distinct and relevant segment of the complete portrait of all the servicemen who participated in this nation's struggle for freedom.

First it must be reemphasized that a considerable distinction existed between the naval prisoners confined at Mill or Forton gaols and those sent to the extremely squalid prison ships anchored off New York. Obviously the British prisons were situated further away from inmates' homes. But certain aspects of the dreaded offshore prison hulks were found again only in such later American wartime prisons as Andersonville during the Civil War or some Japanese prison camps during World War II. Rebel seamen confined on Revolutionary War detention vessels suffered from inadequate rations, gross overcrowding, improper heating and ventilation, deficient sanitary facilities, inferior medical care, and chronic illnesses. Here the major concern of the captives was simply survival. One historian estimated the death toll at such detention centers at nearly twelve thousand.[31]

The Mill and Forton detention experience provides a far more conventional field for historical examination and assessment. Inmates at these two British prisons saw overcrowding, disease, food shortages, and other shortcomings, especially during the first months of confinement in 1777. Yet a comparative evaluation of the entire confinement period reveals that the two English prisons—particularly in the latter stages of the Revolution—were vastly superior to prison ships. The accounts of William Russell and Andrew Sherburne, who experienced incarceration in both types of prisons, offer clear evidence of the great divergence in treatment.[32]

Many distinctly American attitudes and traits also can be discerned among those patriot seamen who were confined to the far away prisons in Britain. The commonality of these attitudes and traits—evident among American prisoners from the savage Indian wars of the seventeenth century to the controversial Vietnam conflict of recent years—has been noted in Robert C. Doyle's insightful book, *Voices from Captivity: Interpreting the American POW Narrative*. In this volume, published in 1994, Doyle illustrates how the memoirs of captives from these disparate wars, including experiences such as adaptability, boredom, communal interaction, loyalty, resistance, escape attempts, spirituality, release, and postconfinement reflection, have all had distinct connections to the culture and traditions of the prisoner's American homeland. Such circumstances have also been cited in recent historical articles, most notably Professor Jesse Lemisch's "Listening to the Inarticulate." By adding to the specific features that Doyle, Lemisch, and other historians have sketched out, the scholar can amplify even further the contributions that these little-remembered American seamen tendered in the fight for independence.[33]

One characteristic demonstrated by the interned seamen, both at Forton and at Mill, was a surprising degree of unity. Although the captured colonial mariners had been separated into different quarters based on rank, at the officers' insistence, the two groups nevertheless did interact. (According to Francis Abell's *Prisoners of War in Britain, 1756–1815*, this was not the case among the more class-conscious French or Spanish detainees.) Reflecting the participatory heritages of their distant homeland, the Yankee captives in both prisons had acted early on to form their own communities for advancing their special interests. The resulting cooperation between American naval officers and enlisted men had been particularly evident in planning and effecting many escape attempts. It also appeared in the manner in which the prisoners combined to form regulations for self-government within their respective prisons. The previously cited journals of Charles Herbert, William Wigder, and Andrew Sherburne give clear evidence of the diverse ways at Mill Prison that unapproved bodies strove to maintain discipline.[34] They supervised health, sobriety, honesty, and other matters involving personal morality. At Forton accounts from the various ranks of prisoners also allude to such detainee organizations. Communications from Keeper John Newsham and requests from these groups to the Reverend Thomas Wren provide further proof of their presence. Regardless of the extent of the actual authority of such prisoner bodies, they clearly displayed colonial republican governmental concepts.[35]

Another feature that these imprisoned American seamen exhibited was self-reliance. In the "good old colonial days," Benjamin Franklin had been a prime example of self-reliance, and the interned mariners at Forton and Mill likewise demonstrated such personal initiative. At the Devon prison, for example, Charles Herbert and Andrew Sherburne both mentioned their shipmates' whittling various items to be sold at the prison market. Both internees also cited prisoners eagerly reading books or seeking instruction in practical subjects in order to advance their knowledge.[36] Lieutenant Nathaniel Fanning's accounts of the well-attended schooling offered by Thomas Wren and by captured Frenchmen illustrate the Forton inmates' interest in self-improvement. In addition inmates at the Hampshire prison, like their Mill counterparts, were allowed to sell their finished products at the local prison market. The songbook diligently compiled by Timothy Connor is yet another example of the American's ability to adapt to their distant confinement.[37]

Defiance of authority was another trait exhibited by the rebel captives. American resistance activities, manifested especially in the prerevolutionary decade, in fact had antecedents reaching back to the first years of colonial settlement. Many incidents of prisoner unruliness occurred at both Forton and Mill. The American seamen openly challenged prison officials, with seeming disregard for a possible stay in the black hole. Rebel mariners repeatedly disparaged prison guards and staff; they unhesitatingly petitioned government officials in London when their grievances went unredressed; they organized demonstrations to celebrate patriot holidays or triumphs; and they acted in a multitude of ways to make life quite exasperating for the "old crab" (John Newsham) or the "great tyrant" (William Cowdry).[38] The ever-declining respect that both officials received was mentioned in prisoner accounts. Thus Jonathan Carpenter noted the inmates' response one day in May 1779 to Keeper Newsham's admonitions about possible pardons being withheld: "Pardon, D[am]n his Majesty & his Pardon too." At Mill, almost two years later, William Wigder described incidents in which Keeper Cowdry was heckled so vociferously by inmates that he was forced to seek refuge in his office. By 1782 both administrators were clearly attempting to ingratiate them-

selves with their Yankee charges.[39] The subsequent exchanges of
the patriot seamen were perhaps met with considerable relief by
both Newsham and Cowdry.

Ingenuity and courage—two features that had allowed many of
the early colonists to survive and thrive in the rigors of colonial
America—were also in evidence at the two British prisons. These
characteristics were shown especially in the multitude of escape
attempts by rebel seamen who recklessly ignored the omnipresent
dangers of failure. Captain John Green reflected such brashness
when he wrote openly to a British general in October 1781 that
American captives at Mill considered it "our duty, (if possible)
to escape from captivity." And the disparate means employed by
internees trying to flee Forton and Mill strongly attest to Yankee
resourcefulness. Their often well-planned escape methods included
climbing the walls, jumping the pickets, laboriously digging tun-
nels, bribing guards or staff, stealing keys, picking locks, feigning
illness to use the less secure prison hospitals, and assuming an
assortment of disguises. And Alexander Tindall's bizarre, though
ingenious, plan was to leave Mill by displacing a corpse in a coffin.
The undaunted determination of the captives was further shown
by the fact that several of them even made breakout attempts only
hours after being released from the black hole.[40]

The would-be escapees had to exhibit further toughness once
they were outside the confines of the prisons. In many respects,
the obstacles between the fugitive seamen and full freedom on the
European continent were even greater than the problems of flight.
There was certainly a broad spectrum of dangers: five-pounder
bounty hunters and informers, unfamiliarity with exact escape
routes, lack of funds, roving press gangs, suspicious magistrates,
and the necessity to find proper bookings and papers to get aboard
outbound vessels. Dangers existed even for those seamen who
reached the continent. In fact several fugitives arrived in France
penniless or else found themselves temporarily sent to one of that
nation's prisons. Yet the lengthy list of monies donated by Benjamin Franklin to mariners who successfully reached sanctuary in
Paris gives added proof of the adroitness of these patriots.[41]

Perseverance, another attribute of early American settlers, also
was rekindled among many internees in British detention centers.
Those captive seamen who did not defect required such perseverance to cope with the seemingly endless boredom and frustration
of incarceration. They also needed it to endure the letdowns associated with long-distance separation from home. And resolve was
further necessary in order to survive the uncertainties that accom-

panied their captivity, particularly the disappointments following false rumors of cartels. At Mill, Charles Herbert reflected the thoughts of inmates who stoically had to prepare themselves for unfulfilled expectations. In January 1778, over a year before his actual exchange, this New England seaman wrote that he had already cautioned himself "not to put so much dependence on getting out as to be disappointed of it." Similar thoughts in Timothy Connor's Forton journal, as well as his songbook, reveal still another resolute Yankee who was able to gird himself against depression.[42]

V

The one feature that most distinguished these captive seamen who "gave as good as they got" was their devotion to a cause. Adherence to an ideal was also found in varying forms among the earliest American colonists, the religious motivation of New England Puritans being a prime example. For several of their descendents at Forton and Mill, such fidelity had been transposed to a secular sphere—the cause of independence. There were, of course, backsliders among the rebel prisoners: they included informers, turncoats, and others who cooperated with their captors. But the number of such collaborators was surprisingly small considering the ominous uncertainties of incarceration. Furthermore a large percentage of those seamen who did become renegades were old countrymen, born in the British Isles. The great majority of rebel prisoners understood what they were fighting for and keenly sensed what historian Robert Middlekauff has called "The Glorious Cause" of Independence. Many of the seamen, motivated at least in part by nationalistic fervor, returned to the conflict only a brief time after their release from a lengthy detention.[43]

In 1779 Captain John Paul Jones bestowed special praise on the many American seamen recently released from onerous captivity who nevertheless had eagerly signed on to his command. Clearly these men realized the many risks involved in their actions, but they were soon to serve their country valiantly in Jones' upcoming bloody combat with *Serapis*. Other American leaders of the revolutionary era also recognized the contributions made by the prisoners at Mill and Forton. George Washington, who had left the problem of these naval prisoners to others, nonetheless lauded all the mariners who broke free of confinement "as he would have praised brave and loyal soldiers."[44] And in August 1787 the venerable Benjamin Franklin added his own earthy and partial praises for these faithful former internees:

> The revolutionary war is a glorious Testimony in favor of Plebian Virtue—our military and naval men are sensible of this Truth. I myself know that our Seamen who were Prisoners in England refused all the allurements that were made use of, to draw them from their allegiance to their Country—threatened with ignominious Halters, they still refused. This was not the case with the English Seamen, who, on being made Prisoners entered into the American Service and pointed out where other Prisoners could be made—and this arose from a plain cause. The Americans were all free and equal to any of their fellow citizens—the English Seamen were not so.[45]

From a contemporary perspective, this historical episode has been largely overlooked. During the 1960s and 1970s, some notable articles did appear that related to American prisoners at Forton and Mill. More recently one eminent naval history of the American Revolution *(Rebels under Sail)* devoted a few pages to the subject, but most of the recent surveys of the War for Independence contain almost nothing about the two British prisons. Their sites in Devon and Hampshire bear no historical markers. Deacon Robert Heath's Plymouth tabernacle was torn down almost two centuries ago, and the Reverend Thomas Wren's Presbyterian (later Unitarian) chapel was destroyed by German bombers in early January 1941. (It was rebuilt fourteen years later.[46]) In America bicentennial observances of the Revolution ignored this significant incident. But the seamen who suffered incarceration in these two British prisons and the men who helped them in their plight warrant more thorough consideration and recognition. It is hoped that this study will restore some of the respect that they once commanded and deserved—in our nation's distant past.

Appendix

Two points mentioned in the text concerning prisoner writings may need additional elaboration. The first item involves the extent of anglophobia expressed in captive narratives; the second pertains to the amount of plagiarism in four of the detainees' accounts.

In the former matter, it must be remembered that all the Mill and Forton prisoner accounts cited in this study were written by men who were especially loyal to the rebel cause. I was unable to uncover recordings of captives who abandoned patriot precepts and entered British service or announced their support of George III. Similarly there are no existent day-to-day recordings by John Newsham or William Cowdry describing the actions of the prisoners. The personal portrayals of incarceration represented in this work therefore offer a distinctly pro-American and anti-British bias. This circumstance is particularly evident in the often spurious or slanted writings of Nathaniel Fanning at Forton and Gustavus Conyngham at Mill.

Other features of this captivity are also noteworthy. Obviously the captives experienced occasional shortages of food and clothing; medical care was sometimes substandard; the jailors, on occasion, could be arbitrary and short-tempered; and for the initial phase of this confinement story, there was little love between Keepers Cowdry and Newsham and the American rebels. However, consider the fact that the British government looked upon these captives as rebels and did not recognize them as prisoners of war until March 1782. Consequently, until this latter date, the interned patriots could not expect the same level of treatment accorded captives of belligerent nations. Nonetheless on balance the Americans were treated rather humanely, compared, for example, to the unfortunate prisoners taken in the Scottish rebellion of 1745. The later phases of imprisonment even offered several examples of a certain amicability, if not of respect, between captors and captives. William Wigder's Mill diary for 1781 offers perhaps the best examples of this interesting detente.[1]

The matter of plagiarism is centered on four of the American prison journals—those written by Timothy Connor and Jonathan Carpenter at Forton, and Charles Herbert and Dr. Jonathan Haskins at Mill. Professor John Alexander has noted the evident similarities in wordings in five of Connor's entries to those appearing in Carpenter's diary. Because Carpenter's diary is considerably shorter and less detailed than Timothy Connor's lengthy journal, I am inclined to agree with Alexander that Carpenter was somehow privy to Connor's work and borrowed from his jottings.[2] As for the three American seamen at Mill, I also concur with Alexander's assessment that about half of the Dr. Haskins diary was probably plagiarized from the Samuel Cutler or Charles Herbert journals. There are no indications, though, that Haskins appropriated writings from any of the other Mill prisoners.[3] One possible theory on the drafting of the work ascribed to the doctor is that he somehow copied from the daily entries of Cutler and Herbert while all three men were imprisoned, and, following his release, he filled in the remaining entries through memory. There is no positive proof for this supposition and this intriguing mystery may never be solved.

Notes

Chapter 1. Antecedents

1. William Cutter, ed., "A Yankee Privateersman in Prison in England," *New England Historical and Genealogical Register* 30 (1876): 174–75.

2. George G. Carey, ed., *A Sailor's Songbag: An American Rebel in an English Prison, 1777–1779* (Amherst: University of Massachusetts Press, 1976), 13; Cutter, "A Yankee Privateersman," 175–77, 343. The *Hampshire Chronicle* [England] for 12 May 1777, stated that HMS *Terrible* and *Rising States* had entered Portsmouth harbor on 10 May.

3. John Alexander, "Forton Prison during the American Revolution: A Case Study of British Prisoners of War Policy and the American Prisoner Response to That Policy," *Essex Institute Historical Collections* 103 (1967) 367: *The Salisbury and Winchester Journal* (England), 27 October 1777, 7 June 1779; Cutter, "A Yankee Privateersman," 343.

4. Jesse Lemisch, "Listening to the Inarticulate: William Wigder's Dream and the Loyalties of American Revolutionary Seamen in British Prisons," *Journal of Social History* 3 (1969): 8, 13; Alexander, "Forton Prison," 319; Cutter, "A Yankee Privateersman," 343–44.

5. Francis Abell, *Prisoners of War in Britain, 1756–1815* (London: Humphrey Milford, 1914), 215–16; Alexander, "Forton Prison," 369–70; Carey, ed. *A Sailor's Songbag*, 3; Cutter, "A Yankee Privateersman," 344.

6. Reverend Samuel Cutler, ed., "Samuel Cutler's Diary," *New England Historical and Genealogical Register* 32 (1878): 42–43; Abner Morse, *A Genealogical Record of Several Families Bearing the Name Cutler in the United States* (Boston: S. G. Drake, 1867), 38.

7. Cutler, "Samuel Cutler's Diary," 43.

8. *Ibid.*, 43, 184–85.

9. Philip Stephens to Vice Admiral John Amherst, 11 February 1777, in William B. Clark and William J. Morgan, eds., *Naval Documents of the American Revolution,* (Washington, D.C.: Government Printing Office, 1980), vol. 8, 580–81; Olive Anderson, "The Treatment of Prisoners of War in Britain during the American War of Independence," *Bulletin of the Institute of Historical Research* 28 (1955): 63; Cutler, "Samuel Cutler's Diary," 185–86.

10. John K. Alexander, "American Privateersmen in the Mill Prison During 1777–1782, An Evaluation," *Essex Institute Historical Collections* 102 (1966): 329; Howard Applegate, "American Privateersmen in the Mill Prison During 1777–1782," *Essex Institute Historical Collections* 97 (1961): 303–4; Cutler, "Samuel Cutler's Diary," 32, 186. Alexander is critical of several parts of Applegate's article.

11. John Ehrman, *The Navy in the War of William III, 1689–97* (Cambridge, Eng.: Cambridge University Press, 1953), 176; Anderson, "Treatment of Prisoners

of War," 64, 64 n; Olive Anderson, "The Establishment of British Supremacy at Sea and the Exchange of Naval Prisoners of War, 1689–1783," *The English Historical Review* 85 (January 1960): 77–78 n.

12. Mark A. Thomson, *The Secretaries of State, 1681–1782* (Oxford: Clarendon Press, 1932), 14, 82; Anderson, "Treatment of Prisoners of War," 64 n.

13. Herbert W. Richmond, *The Navy in the War, 1739–1748* (Cambridge, Eng.: Cambridge University Press, 1920), vol. 1, 23; Anderson, "Treatment of Prisoners of War," 64n.

14. Walter L. Dorn, *Competition for Empire, 1740–1763* (New York: Harper, 1940), 1–426; Abell, *Prisoners of War in Britain,* 119, 449–50.

15. Catherine M. Prelinger, "Benjamin Franklin and the American Prisoners of War in England during the American Revolution," *William and Mary Quarterly,* 3d ser., 32 (1975): 272–82; Abell, *Prisoners of War in Britain,* 24–27; Anderson, "Treatment of Prisoners of War," 64–65, 65 n, 69–71; Anderson, "Establishment of British Supremacy at Sea," 86–87.

16. Abell, *Prisoners of War in Britain,* 27, 284–85; Anderson, "Treatment of Prisoners of War," 71.

17. Abell, *Prisoners of War in Britain,* 37–114.

18. *Ibid.,* 115–272.

19. *The Gentleman's Magazine and Historical Chronicle for the Year 1761* 31 (1761), 147; Abell, *Prisoners of War in Britain,* 215. At the time of this transfer, there were reportedly over twenty five thousand French prisoners in England (*Gentleman's Magazine* 31 [1761], 187).

20. *Gentleman's Magazine* 28 (1758), 419; 30 (1760), 43; Abell, *Prisoners of War in Britain,* 9–10, 27–28.

21. *Gentleman's Magazine* 29 (1759), 604, 30 and (1760), 101; Abell, *Prisoners of War in Britain,* 7–8, 17–29.

22. William E. S. Flory, *Prisoners of War; A Study in the Development of International Law* (Washington, D.C.: Government Printing Office, 1942), 15–16, 117; Robert C. Doyle, *Voices from Captivity: Interpreting the American POW Narrative* (Lawrence, Kans.: University of Kansas Press, 1944), 39–41; Abell, *Prisoners of War in Britain,* chaps. 3, 10–19.

23. Robert Middlekauff, *The Glorious Cause: The American Revolution, 1763–1789* (New York: Oxford University Press, 1982), 266–70; Stephen Conway, "To Subdue America: British Army Officers and the Conduct of the Revolutionary War," *William and Mary Quarterly,* 3d ser., 42 (July 1986): 381–407; *Salem* (Massachusetts) *Gazette,* April 23 1775.

24. Lt. Gen. Thomas Gage to the Earl of Dartmouth, 13 May 1775, in K. G. Davies, ed., *Documents of the American Revolution, 1770–1783; Colonial Office Series,* vol. 9, *Transcripts,* January–June, 1775 (Dublin: Irish University Press 1976), 132; John Alden, *A History of the American Revolution* (New York: Knopf, 1969), 181–86, 196–97; Doyle, *Voices from Captivity,* 119–20; Middlekauff, *The Glorious Cause,* 276–77, 281–92, 302–3.

25. Hugh Finlay to his brother-in-law Ingram, 29 May 1775, in Davies, *Documents of the American Revolution,* vol. 9, *Transcripts,* 145.

26. Charles H. Metzger, *The Prisoner in the American Revolution* (Chicago: Loyola University Press, 1971), 71–77.

27. Sir William Howe to Lord George Germain, 3 December 1776, in Peter Force, compiler, *American Archives,* 5th ser., vol. 3 (Washington, D.C.: Clarke and Force, 1843), 1054–58; Danske Dandridge, *American Prisoners of the Revolution* (reprint, Baltimore: Genealogical Publishing Company, 1967), chaps. 4–5, 15,

22–41; Davies, *Documents of the American Revolution,* vol. 10, *Calendar,* no. 12392; Bowman, *Captive Americans,* 12–14, 28–29, 42–49; Metzger, *The Prisoner in the American Revolution,* 171–76; Lemisch, "Listening to the Inarticulate," 9–10, 12–14.

28. William M. Fowler, Jr., *Rebels under Sail: The American Navy during the Revolution* (New York: Scribner, 1976), 13–15, 72, 95, 281–82; Gardner W. Allen, *Massachusetts Privateers of the Revolution* (Massachusetts Historical Society), *Collections,* vol. 77 (Boston: Massachusetts Historical Society, 1927): 716–17; Alfred F. Young, "George Robert Twelves Hewes (1742–1840): A Boston Shoemaker and the Memory of the American Revolution," *William and Mary Quarterly,* 3d ser., 38 (1981): 604.

29. Sheldon S. Cohen, "We Dare Oppose Them: The Connecticut State Navy in the American Revolution, 1775–1780," *Connecticut Historical Society Bulletin,* 47, no. 3 (July 1982): 74–95; Fowler, *Rebels under Sail,* 281–82. General descriptions of state navies may be found in Charles O. Paullin, *The Navy in the American Revolution: Its Administration, Its Policy and Its Achievements* (reprint; New York: Haskell House Publishers, 1971), chaps. 11–17.

30. Fowler, *Rebels under Sail,* 56–61, 91–102, 130–36.

31. Instructions by Lord George Germain for Royal Navy Ships, 2 May 1776, in Davies, *Documents of the American Revolution,* vol. 10 *Calendar,* no. 2191; Vice Admiral Samuel Graves to Philip Stephens, 15 December 1775, in Davies, *Documents of the American Revolution,* vol. 10, *Calendar,* no. 768; also no. 656, 764, 824, 827, 885, 900. The vessels carrying these military and naval prisoners from England landed in Halifax, Nova Scotia. Davies, ed., *Documents of the American Revolution,* vol. 10, *Calendar,* nos. 716, 905, 1603. Mention of American naval prisoners held in Gibraltar and the West Indies in October 1776 are cited in volume 10, nos. 2191 and 2202; Fowler, *Rebels under Sail,* 27–28.

32. Lord George Germain to Lord [James] Mansfield, 6 August 1776, Lord [William] Mansfield to Lord George Germain, 8 August 1776, in Davies, *Documents of the American Revolution,* vol. 12, *Transcripts,* nos. 63, 64, pp. 171–180; vol. 10, *Calendar* nos. 1928, 1945.

33. William Cobbett, comp., *The Parliamentary History of England from the Earliest Period to the Year 1803* (London: Longman & Co., 1814), vol. 19, 3–4.

34. *Ibid.,* 4–5.

35. *Ibid.,* 11–12, 14, 27–33.

36. *Ibid.,* 52–53.

37. *Ibid.,* 13, 15–17, 45–47. The contentious debates over this bill were also covered in *The Annual Register . . . for the Year 1777* (London, 1778), 53–65.

38. Sheila Lambert, ed., *House of Commons Sessions Papers of the Eighteenth Century,* vol. 28, *George III Bills 1776–77 and 1777–78* (Wilmington, Del: Scholarly Resources, 1975), 1–2; 17 George III; Cobbett, *The Parliamentary History of England,* 19: 51. The act was renewed until 29 March 1782 when the Americans were declared prisoners of war (22 George III, c10). John Raithby, ed., *The Statutes at Large of England and Great Britain . . . ,* (London: Eyre and Strahan Printers, 1811), vol. 14, 182.

Chapter 2. The Prisons and the Prisoners

1. Ernest J. Moyne, "The Reverend William Hazlitt: A Friend of Liberty in Ireland during the American Revolution," *William and Mary Quarterly,* 3d ser.,

21 (1964): 288–93; John Howard, *The State of the Prisons in England and Wales, with Preliminary Observations and an Account of Some Foreign Prisons, 2d ed.* (Warrington, Eng.: W. Eyres, 1780), 161; (3d ed., 1784), 188, 192, 194; Lemisch, "Listening to the Inarticulate," 7 n; Anderson, "Treatment of Prisoners of War," 76–77, 77 n; Abell, *Prisoners of War in Britain,* 360–64.

2. Lords Commissioners to Commissioners for Sick and Hurt Seamen, 19 April 1777, in Clark and Morgan, *Naval Documents of the American Revolution,* 8: 779–80; Howard, *State of the Prisons,* 3d. ed., 188–91; Lemisch, "Listening to the Inarticulate," 7 n. (Manuscript material concerning the locales in Great Britain that held American prisoners and matters relating to the prisoners themselves can be found in correspondence between the Admiralty and the Commissioners for Sick and Hurt Seamen, 1777–83. Those documents are located in the National Maritime Museum, Greenwich, Adm/M/404/405, and the Public Record Office, Kew, Adm/98/11–14. These documents are hereinafter cited as CSHS and Adm).

3. Charles Bracken, *A History of Plymouth and Her Neighbours* (Plymouth, Eng.: Underhill, 1931), 7–275; William G. Gates, *Illustrated History of Portsmouth* (Portsmouth, Eng.: Charpentier & Co., 1900), vii–734; A. Temple Patterson, *Portsmouth: A History* (Bradford, Eng. Moonraker Press, 1976), 6–147; Frederick M. Williams, *Plymouth as a Tourist and Health Resort* (Plymouth, Eng.: J. H. Keys, 1900), 5–22.

4. Mrs. Sarah Quail, City Records Officer, Portsmouth, to author, 28 September 1988 (Mrs. Quail cites much of her information on Forton from *Victoria County History,* 1908); Map of the Parish of Alverstoke including the Town of Gosport, 1832. H. T. Rogers, "The Inns Outside the Ramparts," *Gosport Records* 7 (September 1973).

5. Leonard F. W. White, *The Story of Gosport* (Southsea, Eng.: SWP Barrell, 1966), 1–195; *The Portsmouth Guide, or A Description of the Ancient and Present State of the Place* (Portsmouth, Eng.: 1775), 46. Gosport apparently was named for a goose market once held near its harbor.

6. Henry and Julian Slight, *Chronicles of Portsmouth* (London: Lupton Relfe, 1828), 90–93; A. Temple Patterson, "Portsmouth, A French Gibraltar," *Portsmouth Papers* 10 (1970), 1–17: Gates, *Illustrated History of Portsmouth,* 281–299. The first official census report of Portsmouth in 1801 listed its population as 33,226. Patterson, *Portsmouth,* 91.

7. G. H. Williams, "The Western Defenses of Portsmouth Harbor, 1400–1800," *Portsmouth Papers* 30 (1979): 1–74; John Webb, "An Early Victorian Street, The High Street, Old Portsmouth," *Portsmouth Papers* 26 (1977); *The Portsmouth Guide,* 1–76; Gates, *Illustrated History of Portsmouth,* 281–99.

8. Diane Venables, "Forton Barracks and the Royal Haslar Hospital," *Gosport Records* 12 (December 1976): 7–24; Samuel Pratt v. Mary Jackson, The Appellant's case to be heard at the bar of the House of Lords on the First Day of February, 1726, p. 2; Mr. [Samuel] Howlett's Report on Lands at Forton near Gosport (5 September 1860), Ms Gosport Museum; A. L. Revell, *Haslar, the Royal Hospital* (Gosport Society, Gosport 1978): 23–24.

9. A Plan of Forton Hospital, 1755, by Richard Howlett; Forton Prison in 1782 as copied by Samuel Howlett, Howlett Report (1860). Original in the British Museum, PCRO 684 A/5/2; Revell, *Haslar,* 24.

10. Alexander, "Forton Prison," 369–70; Eunice H. Turner, "American Prisoners of War in Britain, 1777–1783," *The Mariner's Mirror* 45 (1959): 201–2; CSHS to Adm 10 November 1777, Adm 98/11/137, CSHS to Adm. 6, December 1777, Adm /98/171; Howard, *The State of Prisons,* 4th ed., 185–87.

11. Forton Prison Plan 1782; Alexander, "Forton Prison," 270–71; CSHS to Adm, 12 November 1777, Adm 98/11/140.

12. Bracken, *Plymouth and Her Neighbours*, 96; Llewelleynn Jewitt, *A History of Plymouth* (London: Simpkin, Marshall & Co., 1873), 125; Ms. Helen Harris, Devon History Society, to author, 17 November 1989. The first windmills on this location were reportedly erected by Sir Francis Drake in 1590 and 1591 (Bracken, *Plymouth and Her Neighbours*, 96).

13. Crispin Gill, *Plymouth, A New History* (Newton Abbey, Eng.: David & Charles, 1979), 2:56; Bracken, *Plymouth and Her Neighbours*, 220–21.

14. Map survey of Plymouth, 1778, by Richard Cowl, Ms. West Devon Record Office, Plymouth; Andrew Sherburne, *Memoirs of Andrew Sherburne, a Pensioner of the Navy of the Revolution* (Providence, R.I.: H. H. Brown, 1831), 80–81; Applegate, "Mill Prison," 304.

15. Cowl, Plymouth Map Survey, 1778; Sherburne, *Memoirs*, 81–82; Cutler,"Samuel Cutler's Diary," 185–86; Applegate, "Mill Prison," 304.

16. Cowl, Plymouth Map Survey, 1778; Sherburne, *Memoirs*, 81; Cutler, "Samuel Cutler's Diary," 186; Applegate, "Mill Prison," 304–5.

17. Gill, *Plymouth*, 2: 5–20; Bracken, *Plymouth and Her Neighbours*, 88–102; Worth, *History of Plymouth*, 53–61; Jewett, *History of Plymouth*, 106–12, 156–62.

18. Gill, *Plymouth*, 2: 90–91, 99–104; Bracken, *Plymouth and her Neighbours*, 233–40; Jewett, *History of Plymouth*, 589–97; Worth, *History of Plymouth*, 242–50.

19. Gill, *Plymouth*, 2:81–83, 93–94, 96–97, 108–9; Bracken, *Plymouth and Her Neighbours*, 55–56, 140–53; Jewett, *History of Plymouth*, 492–535; Worth, *History of Plymouth*, 232–34.

20. Anderson, "Treatment of Prisoners of War," 64–66; Turner, "American Prisoners of War," 201.

21. Anderson, "Treatment of Prisoners of War," 65–66; Turner, "American Prisoners of War," 201; Applegate, "Mill Prison," 304–5; Alexander, "Forton Prison" 366–67, 371–72; Adm to CSHS 13 March, 19; 21 April 1777, NMM/Adm/404. Adm to CSHS 14, 17 March, 10 July 1777. Adm 3/98/11, 98, 90, 111; Clark and Morgan, *Naval Documents. of the American Revolution* 8: 783–84; The physician received 5s per day, and the keeper was allowed to hire a dispenser of medicine.

22. John C. Sainty, *Office Holders in Modern Britain*, vol. 4, *Admiralty Officials, 1660–1870* (London: Althone Press, 1975), 25; John A. Tilley, *The British Navy and the American Revolution* (Columbia S.C.: University of South Carolina Press, 1975), 43–45. See also John Knox Laughton in *DNB*, s.v. "Montagu, John Fourth Earl of Sandwich," "Palliser, Sir Hugh," "Stephens, Sir Philip": On Lord Mulgrave's naval activities see Clark and Morgan, *Naval Documents of the American Revolution* 8: 503; 9: 555–56, 574–75.

23. Names of Commissioners for Sick and Hurt Seamen, 1777–83 taken from the *Royal Kalendar* and furnished to author by the National Maritime Museum, Greenwich, England. See also "Charles Herbert Diary," in Richard Livesey, ed., *The Prisoners of 1776: A Relic of the Revolution* . . . (Boston: C. H. Pierce, 1847), 62–65; Cutler, "Samuel Cutler's Diary," 395.

24. CSHS to Adm 29 May, 13 June 1777, Adm 3/98/11, 100, 101; Adm to CSHS 28 May 1777, NMM/Adm/404; Applegate, "Mill Prison," 304; Alexander, "Forton Prison," 369; Cutler, "Samuel Cutler Diary," 186–89. ("Extract of a Letter from Gosport," 7 May 1777, had stated that Forton Prison was to open on the next day. *London Chronicle*, 8–10 May 8–10 1777.)

25. William B. Clark, "John the Painter," *Pennsylvania Magazine of History*

and Biography 43 (1939): 1–23; M. J. Sydenham, "Firing His Majesty's Dockyard; Jack the Painter and the American Mission to France, 1776–1777," *History Today* 16 no. 5 (1966): 324–31; *Hampshire Chronicle,* 3, 10, 17 March, 1777. On 2 June 1777, J. Binstead, an Admiralty agent, wrote to the Commissioners for Sick and Hurt Seamen that he was still awaiting clarifications from the Admiralty and the solicitor general before admitting prisoners to Forton (NMM/Adm/404).

26. Cohen, "We Dare Oppose Them," 92. The words were spoken by Captain Timothy Parker, Connecticut State Navy.

27. William Avery Baker, "Vessel Types in Colonial Massachusetts," in Philip C. F. Smith, ed., *Seafaring in Colonial Massachusetts* (Boston: Anthoensen Press, 1980), 5–10; Fowler, *Rebels under Sail,* 1–3.

28. Max Savelle, Darell D. Wax, *A History of Colonial America* 3d ed. (Hinsdale, Ill.: Dryden Press, 1973), 350; Fowler, *Rebels under Sail,* 3–4.

29. Emery R. Johnson, et al.; *History of Domestic and Foreign Commerce in the United States* (Washington, D.C.: Government Printing Office, 1915), 1: pt. 1; David Hawke, *The Colonial Experience* (Indianapolis: Bobbs-Merrill, 1966), 471–75; Savelle and Wax, *History of Colonial America,* 519, 524, 534; 604–5; Fowler, *Rebels under Sail,* 4–10.

30. Jesse Lemisch, "Jack Tar in the Streets: Merchant Seamen in the Politics of Revolutionary America," *William and Mary Quarterly,* 3d. ser., 25 (July 1968): 372–80; Fowler, *Rebels under Sail,* 10–11.

31. Samuel Eliot Morison, *The Maritime History of Massachusetts* (Boston: Houghton Mifflin, 1921), 105–11; Samuel Eliot Morison, *John Paul Jones, A Sailor's Biography* (Boston: Little Brown, 1959), 22–23; Lemisch, "Jack Tar," 372–80; Fowler, *Rebels under Sail,* 11–12.

32. Neil R. Stout, "Manning the Royal Navy in North America, 1763–1775," *American Neptune* 23 (1963): 174–85; Lemisch, "Jack Tar," 381–85; Fowler, *Rebels under Sail,* 11–12.

33. Carl Bridenbaugh, *Cities in Revolt: Urban Life in America, 1743–1776* (New York: Knopf, 1955), 115–16; Lemisch, "Jack Tar," 387–400; Fowler, *Rebels under Sail,* 11–12.

34. Peter Linebaugh and Marcus Rediker, "The Many-Headed Hydra: Sailors, Slaves and the Atlantic Working Class in the Eighteenth Century," in *Jack Tar in History: Essays in the History of Maritime Life and Labour,* eds. Colin Howell and Richard J Twomey (Fredricton, New Brunswick: Acadiensis Press, 1991), 19–25; Joseph R. Frese, S.J., "Smuggling, The Navy and the Customs Service, 1763–1772," in *Seafarers in Colonial Massachusetts,* 199–212; Bridenbaugh, *Cities in Revolt,* pt. 2, "Depression, Tension and Revolt; 1760–1776"; Lemisch, "Jack Tar," 396–407; Fowler, *Rebels under Sail,* 12–14.

35. Turner, "American Prisoners of War in Britain," 205; Benjamin Quarles, *The Negro in the American Revolution* (Chapel Hill: University of North Carolina Press, 1961), 83–87, 91–93, 170. Livesey, *The Prisoners of 1776,* 243–58. (These figures are based upon Admiralty records dealing with both prisons in the Public Record Office, Kew, Adm 98/11–14, and records of the Commissioners for Sick and Hurt Seamen and the Exchange of Prisoners at the National Maritime Museum Greenwich, Adm/404/405.)

36. *DAR Patriot Index* (Washington, D.C., 1966), 1: 149; *Massachusetts Soldiers and Sailors of the Revolutionary War* (Boston: Wright & Potter, 1896–1908), 3:906; Cutter, "A Yankee Privateersman," *New England Historical and Genealogical Register* 31: 284; 32: 72.

37. Journal of Jonathan Carpenter, 1757–1837, Vermont Historical Society;

Vermont Historical Gazette 2 (Bennington, 1871): 1050; Vermont Historical Society *Proceedings* (1872) vii–viii; John K. Alexander, "Jonathan Carpenter and the American Revolution: The Journal of an American Naval Prisoner of War and Vermont Indian Fighter," *Vermont History* 36 (1968): 74–77; *Massachusetts Soldiers and Sailors of the Revolutionary War,* 3: 121; Virgil D. White, *Genealogical Abstracts of Revolutionary War Pension Files* (Waynesboro, Tenn: National Publishing Co., 1990), 1: 547; Jonathan Carpenter Journal; James N. Arnold, *Vital Records of Rehoboth Massachusetts, 1642–1896* (Providence, R.I.: Narragansett Historical Publishing company, 1897), xxvii–926.

38. Caleb Foot, "Prison Letters and Sea Journal of Caleb Foot," *Essex Institute Historical Collections* 26 (1889): 90–92; *Massachusetts Soldiers and Sailors of the Revolutionary War* 5: 836.

39. "Diary of George Thompson of Newburyport Kept at Forton Prison England, 1777–1781," *Essex Institute Historical Collections,* 76 (1940): 221–222; *Massachusetts Soldiers and Sailors of the Revolutionary War* 15: 637.

40. Clifford K. Shipton, *Biographical Sketches of Those Who Attended Harvard College in the Classes 1768–1771 (Sibley's Harvard Graduates)* (Boston: Massachusetts Historical Society, 1975), 17: 187; Letter of Nathaniel Harrington, Jr., in 1781, to his Father, in *New England Historical and Genealogical Register* 51: 322–23. The other college graduate interned at Forton was Heathcote Muirson, captain of marines on the brigantine *Angelica* and a 1776 graduate of Yale College. Muirson was committed to the prison in July 1778. See Franklin B. Dexter, *Biographical Sketches of the Graduates of Yale College with Annals of the College History* (New York: H. Holt, 1903), 3: 625–6.

41. John S. Barnes, *Memoirs of Nathaniel Fanning, An American Naval Officer,* 2d ed. (New York: New York Times, 1967), 1–7; "American Prisoners at Forton Prison, England, 1777–1779," *New England Historical and Genealogical Register* 33: 38. This list was appended by Timothy Connor to his journal.

42. "Captain Charles Bulkeley's Narrative of Personal Experience in the War of the American Revolution," in Ernest E. Rogers, ed., *Connecticut's Naval Office at New London during the War of the American Revolution* (New London: self-published, 1933), 126–27; Manuscript Narrative of Charles Bulkeley, New London County Historical Society; Clark and Morgan, *Naval Documents of the American Revolution* 7: 42.

43. R. R. Hinman, *Catalogue of the First Puritan Settlers of Connecticut: A Family Record of the Descendants of Sgt. Edward Hinman* (Hartford: Tiffany and Company, 1856), 816–17; Fowler, *Rebels under Sail,* 56–58, 96–97, 266; Clark and Morgan, *Naval Documents of the American Revolution* 3: 1088, 1206; 4: 861, 1177, 1189, 1269, 1331; 5: 63, 546, 598, 622–24, 769–70, 1230–231, 1272, 1304; 6: 171, 265, 271, 629, 640, 1201.

44. Hinman, *Catalogue of First Puritan Settlers,* 817; Fowler, *Rebels under Sail,* 147–48, 333; "List of America Prisoners at Forton," *New England Hisorical and Genenealogical Register* 33: 38; Clark and Morgan, *Naval Documents of the American Revolution* 7: 84–85, 510, 944, 950, 951, 958, 1005–1006, 1014, 1058, 1199, 1318, 1320, 8: 915, 951–52,9: 828–29.

45. "Narrative of Lieut. Luke Matthewman of the Revolutionary Navy," *Magazine of American History* 2, pt. 1 (1878): 175–79.

46. Walter D. McCaw, "Captain John Harris of the Virginia Navy: A Prisoner of War in England, 1777–1779," *Virginia Magazine of History and Biography,* 22 (1914): 160–61; Clark and Morgan, *Naval Documents of the American Revolution*

7: 239, 1065, 1114, 1131, 1216; 8: 918; 9: 19–20, 46, 104, 323–324, 696–97; "List of American Prisoners at Forton," 36.

47. Robert A. Stewart, *The History of Virginia's Navy of the Revolution* (Richmond Va.: Mitchell & Hotchkiss, 1933), 35–36; John H. Gwathmey, *Historical Register of Virginians in the Revolution: Soldiers, Sailors, Marines, 1775–1783* (Richmond, Va.: The Dietz Press, 1938), 222; *Genealogies of Virginia Families* (Baltimore: Genealogical Publishing Co., 981), 788; Clark and Morgan, *Naval Documents of the American Revolution* 5: 554, 593, 1207; 6: 1242, 1312, 1416; Benjamin Chew to Benjamin Franklin, 19 August 1778, William B. Willcox, Douglas M. Arnold, Claude A. Lopez, et al., eds, *Papers of Benjamin Franklin* (New Haven, 1988), 27: 278 (hereinafter referred to as *Benjamin Franklin Papers* or *Papers of Benjamin Franklin*).

48. Robert L. Chew, *Genealogy of the Chew Family* (Woodbury N.J.: Gloucester County Historical Society, 1982), 1–488; Eric Partridge, *A Dictionary of Slang and Unconventional English* (London: G. Routledge & Sons, 1937), 844; Francis B. Culver, "The Chew Family," *Maryland Historical Magazine* 30 (June 1935): 157–75; Clark and Morgan, *Naval Documents of the American Revolution* 6: 293; 7: 458; 8: 714; 9: 19–20, 46, 104, 323–24, 696–97; "List of American Prisoners at Forton," 36. According to Ms. Jennifer A. Bryan of the Maryland Historical Society, Robert Chew's biography (p. 218) confuses Captain Benjamin Chew with his father, also named Benjamin. Letter to author, 18 October 1991.

49. Howard, *State of the Prisons*, 3d ed., 185–87.

50. Abner Morse, *A Biographical Record of Several Families Bearing the Name Cutler in the United States* (Boston: S. G. Drake, 1867), 38; Jeremiah Colburn, "A List of the American Prisoners Committed to Old Mill Prison Since the American War . . . ," *New England Historical and Genealogical Register* 19 (1865), 74; Cutler, "Samuel Cutler's Diary," 42.

51. Livesey, *Prisoners of 1776*, 12–17, 24, 28, 30; *Massachusetts Soldiers and Sailors of the Revolutionary War* 7: 743; "List of American Prisoners, Old Mill," 142.

52. William H. Bowden, "Diary of William Wigder of Marblehead, Kept at Mill Prison, England, 1781," *Essex Institute Historical Collections* 73 (1937): 311; *Massachusetts Soldiers and Sailors of the Revolutionary War* 17: 296; Colburn, "List of American Prisoners, Old Mill," 138.

53. Ralph D. Paine, *The Ships and Sailors of Old Salem* (Chicago: A. C. McClurg & Co., 1912), 118–19; *Massachusetts Soldiers and Sailors of the Revolutionary War* 13: 705; "List of American Prisoners, Old Mill," 138.

54. Philip C. F. Smith, *Fired by Manley Zeal: A Naval Fiasco of the American Revolution* (Salem, Mass.: Peabody Museum of Salem, 1977), 5–8; Isaac J. Greenwood, *Captain John Manley; Second in Rank in the United States Navy, 1776–1783* (Boston: C. E. Godspeed & Co., 1915), 5–11; Robert E. Peabody, "The Naval Career of Captain John Manley of Marblehead," *Essex Institute Historical Collections* 45 (1909): 1–6; Fowler, *Rebels under Sail*, 14, 29–31; *Massachusetts Soldiers and Sailors of the Revolutionary War* 10: 177.

55. Smith, *Fired by Manley Zeal*, 88–89; Greenwood, *Captain John Manley*, chaps. 2–9; Peabody, "Naval Career of Capt. John Manley," 4–24; Fowler, *Rebels Under Sail*, 36–37, 269, 275–76; "List of American Prisoners, Old Mill," 138. Many references to Captain Manley during the period 1775–77 can be found in Clark and Morgan, *Naval Documents of the American Revolution* vols. 7–9.

56. Marion S. Coan, ed., "A Revolutionary Prison Diary: The Journal of Dr. Jonathan Haskins," *New England Quarterly* 17 (1944): 290–91; Clark and Morgan,

Naval Documents of the American Revolution 8: 527–28, 831, 834, 871; John K. Alexander, "Jonathan Haskins' Mill Prison 'Diary': Can It Be Accepted at Face Value?" *New England Quarterly* 40 (1967): 564.

57. Sherburne, *Memoirs,* 13–33.

58. Richard E. Winslow, III, *"Wealth and Honour": Portsmouth During the Golden Age of Privateering, 1775–1815* (Portsmouth, N.H.: Portsmouth Maritime Society, 1988), 25–26; Sherburne, Memoirs, 34–81.

59. Robert W. Neeser, ed., *Letters and Papers Relating to the Cruises of Gustavus Conyngham: A Captain of the Continental Navy, 1777–1779, Publications of the Naval Historical Society* 6 (New York, 1915), xxi–xxix; Charles O. Paullin in *DAB,* s.v. "Conyngham, Gustavus."

60. Neeser, *Gustavus Conyngham,* xxxiii–xiviii; Paullin, *DAB,* s.v. "Conyngham, Gustavus"; Fowler, *Rebels under Sail,* 139–44; "List of American Prisoners, Old Mill," 138–39.

61. Carrow Thibault, Captain from the Country, Typescript, 1–5, John Green to J. M. Nesbitt & Co., 2 November 1781, Carrow Thibault Papers, Philadelphia Maritime Museum. The "List of American Prisoners, Old Mill," 211, and the *Pennsylvania Packet,* 18 June 1782, cite the date of Green's capture as 29 June and his committal to Mill as 23 August 1781. However the *Public Advertiser* (London) for 3 August 1781, noted that *Lion* was brought into Portsmouth two days earlier, an indication that Green's letter to Nesbitt offers the more accurate dates.

62. George Ralls Narrative, Paris, 7 November 1778, New-York Historical Society; Von Bitter and Harrison to Colonel William Aylett, 2 July 1777, in "Correspondence of Colonel William Aylett," *Tyler's Quarterly and Genealogical Magazine* 1 (July 1919): 106–8; Stewart, *History of the Virginia Navy,* 22–27, 32.

63. Mary Barney, *A Biographical Memoir of the Late Commodore Joshua Barney* (Boston: Gray and Bowen, 1832), 1–26; Ralph D. Paine, *Joshua Barney, a Forgotten Hero of Blue Water* (New York: The Century Co., 1924), 3–32; Clark and Morgan, *Naval Documents of the American Revolution* 2: 51 n, 62 n, 182 242, 583, 630 n.

64. Barbara W. Tuchman, *The First Salute: A View of the American Revolution* (New York: Knopf, 1988), 4–7; "[Pennsylvania] Letters of Marque, 1778–1782," *Pennsylvania Archives,* 5th ser., 1 (1906), 655; M. Barney, *Biographical Memoir of Joshua Barney,* 26–88; Paine, *Joshua Barney,* 33–115: Clark and Morgan, *Naval Documents of the American Revolution* 3: 1263–64; 4: 597–98, 870–71, 1467; 5: 17–18; 6: 782; 7: 1017; 8: 101 n; "List of American Prisoners, Old Mill," 140. Joshua Barney's manuscript autobiography citing much of this information is in the Americana Collection, National Society Daughters of the American Revolution, Washington, D.C.

Chapter 3. The Time of Settling In

1. Jonathan Carpenter Journal, 12 May 1778; Caleb Foot, "Prison Letters and Sea Journal," 109–10. The Manuscript Division of the Library of Congress has a copy of an Admiralty order to captains of all Royal Navy ships listing a series of questions to be asked to all crewmen on captured American vessels. Lans. 1219: fo. 32.

2. Livesey, *Prisoners of 1776,* 44; Alexander, "American Privateersmen in

the Mill Prison," 318–319, "Forton Prison during the American Revolution," 367–69; Applegate, "Mill Prison," 303–4.

3. Anderson, "Treatment of Prisoners of War," 64–65, 72. Applegate, "Mill Prison," 305; Alexander, "Forton Prison," 370.

4. "Regulations Which Are to Be Observed by the Prisoners," Hartley-Russell Papers, Berkshire Record Office D/EHy 040; Adm to the CSHS, 30 April 1777. Adm./M/404/NMM.

5. "Table of Victualing," Hartley-Russell Papers, D/EHy 040; Turner, "American Prisoners in Britain," 202.

6. William J. Rose. Obituary *Chicago Tribune*, 24 Sept.1991, section 2 p. 9; Anderson, "Treatment of Prisoners of War," 77–78.

7. Cutter, "A Yankee Privateersman" (1876), 343; Alexander, "Forton Prison," 376.

8. Cutler, "Samuel Cutler's Diary," 186; Applegate, "Mill Prison," 308–10.

9. Livesey, *Prisoners of 1776*, 45, 59.

10. "Humanitas" to Lords Commissioners of the Admiralty 29 August 1777, in Clark and Morgan, *Naval Documents of the American Revolution* 9: 611–13; Adm/M/404/NMM. The letter, forwarded by the commissioners, was received by the Admiralty itself on 3 September 1777.

11. Livesey, *The Prisoners of 1776*, 62–63; "Humanitas" to Lords Commissioners of the Admiralty, Clark and Morgan, *Naval Documents of the American Revolution* 9: 612–13.

12. Sheldon S. Cohen, "The Preachers and the Prisoners," *Essex Institute Historical Collections* 126 (January 1990): 4; Barnes, *Memoirs of Nathaniel Fanning*, 2–3.

13. Coan, "Journal of Dr. Jonathan Haskins," 297; Cutler, "Samuel Cutler's Diary," 187; Cutter, "A Yankee Privateersman," (1876), 343. The similarities between the entries of Haskins and Cutler is one of several that suggest plagiarism of some sort.

14. Anderson, "Treatment of Prisoners of War," 73; CSHS to Adm, 25 November 1777, Adm /M/404/NMM; Adm to CSHS, 6, 11 December 1777; Adm 3"3/ PRO; Alexander, "Forton Prison," 366–67.

15. Livesey, *Prisoners of 1776*, 19–44.

16. Howard, *State of the Prisons*, 3d ed., 184; Anderson, "Treatment of Prisoners of War," 73.

17. Livesey, *The Prisoners of 1776*, 57–89, 136–37; Coan, "Journal of Dr. Jonathan Haskins," 424; Cutler, "Samuel Cutler's Diary," 187–88, 308, 315–16, 395–96; Applegate, "Mill Prison" 311–12; Alexander, "Mill Prison," 324–25.

18. Livesey, *The Prisoners of 1776*, 51; Coan "Journal of Dr. Jonathan Haskins," 298.

19. John Duffy, *Epidemics in Colonial America* (Baton Rouge La.: Louisians State University Press, 1971), chap. 2 (Boston figures are on p. 51); Richard H. Shryock, *Medicine and Society in America, 1600–1860* (New York: New York University Press, 1960), 71, 94, 161.

20. Turner, "American Prisoners of War in Britain," 202; Philip Stephens to the CSHS, 12 July 1777 Adm/M/404/NMM; Livesey, *The Prisoners of 1776*, 46–53; Applegate, "Mill Prison," 311.

21. *Vital Records of Newburyport, Massachusetts to the Year 1849* (Salem, Mass.: Essex Institute, 1911), 2: 112; Livesey, *The Prisoners of 1776*, 57, 244; Coan, "Journal of Dr. Jonathan Haskins," 299. On 28 June 1777 Dr. Haskins (p. 297) mentions a prisoner named Black Will employed as a nurse to the pris-

oners. For information on blacks who served on American privateers, see Quarles, *The Negro in the American Revolution,* 91–93.

22. Livesey, *Prisoners of 1776,* 26–38; Revell, *Haslar, The Royal Hospital,* 24; Alexander, "Forton Prison," 370.

23. Lewis B. Namier, *England in the Age of the American Revolution* (London: Macmillan & Co., 1930), 257–63; Dorothy Marshall, *Eighteenth Century England* (London: Longmans, 1963), 60–63, 128–29, 156; Anderson, "Treatment of Prisoners of War," 78.

24. Anderson, "Treatment of Prisoners of War," 64–66; 78; Alexander, "Forton Prison," 371–72, 375; Applegate, "Mill Prison," 305–6.

25. Cutter, "A Yankee Privateersman" (1876), 345; 29 May 1779 entry, Jonathan Carpenter Journal ; "Diary of George Thompson," 226.

26. Letter of Forton Prisoners to Commissioner of Admiralty, 17 September 1777, Adm/M/404/NMM; Barnes, *Memoirs of Nathaniel Fanning,* 9; Alexander, "Forton Prison," 371–72.

27. Cutler, "Samuel Cutler's Diary," 186, 305, 396; Coan, "Journal of Dr. Jonathan Haskins," 296, 301. Applegate, "Mill Prison," 305–6.

28. Livesey, *The Prisoners of 1776,* 50, 55; Coan, "Journal of Dr. Jonathan Haskins," 298; "Narrative of Captain John Porter, 10 June 1777," in Clark and Morgan, *Naval Documents of the American Revolution* 9: 391.

29. "Humanitas," to Lords Commissioners of Admiralty 29 August 1777, Adm /M/404/NMM; also in Clark and Morgan, *Naval Documents of the American Revolution* 9: 611–13; Livesey, *Prisoners of 1776,* 62–63; Coan, "Journal of Dr. Jonathan Haskins," 300; Cutler, "Samuel Cutler's Diary," 395.

30. Livesey, *Prisoners of 1776,* 83–91; Coan, "Journal of Dr. Jonathan Haskins," 302–3; Applegate, "Mill Prison," 305–6.

31. Cutler, "Samuel Cutler's Diary," 187; Livesey, *Prisoners of 1776,* 47.

32. Cutler, "A Yankee Privateersman" (1876), 344–46; Cutler, "Samuel Cutler's Diary," 187; Alexander, "Forton Prison," 373; Alexander, "Mill Prison," 310.

33. Cutler, "A Yankee Privateersman," (1876), 344–46, (1877), 18–19. Coan, "Journal of Dr. Jonathan Haskins," 288–309; "Samuel Cutler's Diary," 395–98; Livesey, *Prisoners of 1776,* 51–201; Alexander, "Forton Prison," 370–71; Applegate, "Mill Prison," 305, 316.

34. Cutler, "A Yankee Privateersman" (1876), 344; "Humanitas" to Lords Commissioners Admiralty, Clark and Morgan, *Naval Documents of the American Revolution* 9: 612; *Hampshire Chronicle,* 14 September 1778; Applegate, "Mill Prison," 314; Alexander, "Forton Prison," 370–71.

35. Philip Stephens to Vice Admiral Molyneux Shuldham, Plymouth, 31 May 1777, in Clark and Morgan, *Naval Documents of the American Revolution* 8: 879.

36. Thomas Haley to CSHS 21 September 1777, Adm/M/404/NMM; Clark and Morgan, *Naval Documents of the American Revolution* 8: 652–53; Livesey, *Prisoners of 1776,* 246, 249; Cutler, "Samuel Cutler's Diary," 187. A search of Admiralty dispatches revealed that no such petition of 16 September 1777 was received by the Admiralty (letter to author from Naval Historical Center, Washington D.C., 6 March 1992).

37. Philip Stephens to Admiral Sir Thomas Pye, Portsmouth, 25 September 1777, in Clark and Morgan, *Naval Documents of the American Revolution* 9: 658; Livesey, *Prisoners of 1776,* 63, 71, 84.

38. Applegate, "Mill Prison," 318; Alexander, "Forton Prison," 374–75; Livesey, *Prisoners of 1776,* 43–77; Coan, "Journal of Dr. Jonathan Haskins,"

297–303; Michael A. Quinn, *Love Letters to Mike: Forty Months as a Japanese P.O.W.* (New York: Vantage Books, 1977), 64.

39. *Town and Country Magazine* [London] (August 1777): 684, 686; Cutter, "A Yankee Privateersman" (1876), 346 n; Coan, "Journal of Dr. Jonathan Haskins," 300, 301; Livesey, *Prisoners of 1776*, 57, 58, 62.

40. Livesey, *Prisoners of 1776*, 57, 58, 77, 79.

41. Prelinger, "Benjamin Franklin and the American Prisoners of War," 263–66; Livesey, *Prisoners of 1776*, 59, 60.

42. Livesey, *Prisoners of 1776*, 74–78.

43. Fowler, *Rebels under Sail*, 273–76, 280–89; Young, "George Robert Hewes," 605–6; Lemisch, "Jack Tar," 373–77, 407.

44. Robert Middlekauff, *The Glorious Cause*, 509.

45. Moncure D. Conway, *Writings of Thomas Paine* (New York: Putnam, 1894–96), 1: 170–79; Cutler, "Samuel Cutler's Diary," 305; Coan, "Journal of Dr. Jonathan Haskins," 298; Livesey, *Prisoners of 1776*, 79.

46. Alexander, "Forton Prison," 371–73; Applegate, "Mill Prison," 306, 310, 315; Livesey, *Prisoners of 1776*, 86–210.

47. Coan, "Journal of Dr. Jonathan Haskins," 297; Livesey, *Prisoners of 1776*, 246. Charles Herbert lists Burgoyne among the escapees.

48. John Newsham to Philip Stephens, 25 June 1777, Adm/3/98/11/115; Philip Stephens to John Newsham 30 June, 2 July 1777 Adm/3/98; 116, 119–20; Philip Stephens to CSHS 25 June, 10, 12, July 1777, Adm/M/404/NMM; Admiralty to CSHS, 10 July 1777, Adm./M/404/NMM; CSHS to Admiralty 10 November 1777, Adm/3/98/11/135. An inaccurate report appeared in the *Salisbury and Winchester Journal* (9 December 1777) that all the Forton prisoners were to be confined on a warship in Portsmouth harbor.

49. Lord Stormont to Lord Weymouth, 2 July 1777, in Clark and Morgan, *Naval Documents of the American Revolution* 9: 423, 452–53; Cutter, "A Yankee Privateersman" (1876), 344.

50. Cutter, "A Yankee Privateersman" (1876), 343–47. Seaman Connor made no mention concerning a report in the *Salisbury and Winchester Journal* (9 December 1777) that a Royal Navy lieutenant had been arrested for allegedly abetting one of these escape attempts.

51. Josiah Smith to Benjamin Franklin, 4 June 1777, in Clark and Morgan, *Naval Documents of the American Revolution* 9: 377–78; Coan, "Journal of Dr. Jonathan Haskins," 297.

52. Livesey, *Prisoners of 1776*, 50–77.

53. Livesey, *Prisoners of 1776*, 54–55, 61, 77; Alexander, "Forton Prison," 382–83; Applegate, "Mill Prison," 317–18.

54. Barnes, *Memoirs of Nathaniel Fanning*, 11; Livesey, *Prisoners of 1776*, 47, 49–50.

55. Cutter, "A Yankee Privateersman" (1876), 343–48; Alexander, "Forton Prison," 373; Livesey, *Prisoners of 1776*, 49–50, 61–62, 63, 66, 72–73, 74–75.

56. William Hutchinson, *The History of the County of Cumberland*, (reprint; London: East Ardley, EP Publishing in collaboration with Cumberland County Library, 1974), 224; *Gentleman's Magazine* 58, pt. 2 (1787): 1026–27; Sheldon S. Cohen, "Thomas Wren: Ministering Angel of Forton Prison," *Pennsylvania Magazine of History and Biography* 102 (July 1979): 280–81.

57. Henry and Julian Slight, *Chronicles of Portsmouth* (London: Lupton Relfe, 1828), 81–92; Alfred Goodall, "Early Independency in Essex," *Congregational Historical Society Transactions* (1913–15): 156; Gates, *Illustrated History of*

Portsmouth, 291–92, 297–98; Hutchinson, *History of Cumberland*, 224; Cohen, "Thomas Wren," 281–282.

58. Gates, *Illustrated History*, 298; Hutchinson, *History of Cumberland*, 224; Cohen, "Thomas Wren," 281–82.

59. Portsmouth City Records Office, Records of John Pounds Memorial Church, Portsmouth, CHU 82/9–11; Hutchinson, *History of Cumberland*, 224; Cohen, "Thomas Wren," 282; Gates, *Illustrated History*, 298.

60. [John Thornton] Memorandum for the American Commissioners, 5–8 January 1778 in *Benjamin Franklin Papers*, 25: 414–19; *Gentleman's Magazine* 57 pt. 2, 1026; Cohen, "Thomas Wren," 286, 289.

61. "Memoir of the Late Rev. Robert Heath," *Theological Magazine* 9 (1801): 161–62; Sheldon S. Cohen, "The Preachers and the Prisoners," 5–6; Reverend Eliezer Jones, "An Historical Retrospect," in "A Memorial of Nonconformity" (ca. 1886), Gloucestershire Record Office, Records of Rodborough Tabernacle, D. 4248, 1417.

62. Edwin Welch, "Andrew Kinsman's Church at Plymouth," *Transactions of the Devonshire Historical Association* 97 (1965): 212–36; Jones, "Historical Retrospect," 89–90; Cohen, "The Preachers and the Prisoners," 6.

63. "Memoir of Robert Heath," 163; Jones, "Historical Retrospect," 90; Cohen, "The Preachers and the Prisoners," 6.

64. Walter Wilson, *History and Antiquities of Dissenting Meeting Houses in London, Westminster and Southwark* (London,: Privately printed, 1808), 343–50; "Memoir of Robert Heath," 163–64; Jones, "Historical Retrospect," 90; Cohen, "The Preachers and the Prisoners," 7. Charles Herbert mistakenly referred to Heath as a Presbyterian minister (Livesey, *Prisoners of 1776*, 104).

65. Cutler, "Samuel Cutler's Diary," 396–98; Cohen, "The Preachers and the Prisoners," 7. Samuel Cutler's fellow fugitive was William Morris, a nephew of the noted expatriate artist Benjamin West, who reportedly had also given the two Americans money. See Cutler, "Samuel Cutler's Diary," 397.

66. William B. Clark, "In Defense of Thomas Digges," *Pennsylvania Magazine of History and Biography* 77 (1953): 385–89; Richard Henry Lee, *Life of Arthur Lee* (Boston: H. C. Carey and I Lea, 1829), 1: 354–56.

67. John A. Sainsbury, "The Pro-Americans of London, 1769–1782," *William and Mary Quarterly* 3d. ser., 35 (1978): 443; *The Parliamentary Register or History of Proceedings and Debates of the House of Lords* (London, 1776), 10: 105–6; *Gentleman's Magazine* 47 (1777): 607; Clark, "In Defense of Thomas Digges," 390.

68. John A. Sainsbury, "The Pro-American Movement in London, 1769–1782: Extraparliamentary Opposition to the Government's American Policy" Ph.D. diss., McGill University 1975, 267–68; *The Public Advertiser* (London), 2 January 1778, 267–68; *London Evening Post*, 23–25 December 1777, *Gentlemen's Magazine* 47 (1777): 607; 48 (1778): 43; Clark, "In Defense of Thomas Digges," 390.

69. Jonathan R. Dull, *A Diplomatic History of the American Revolution* (New Haven: Yale University Press, 1985), 10, 53, 78; Samuel F. Bemis, *The Diplomatic History of the American Revolution* (Bloomington, IN: Indiana University Press, 1965), 31; Lemisch, "Listening to the Inarticulate," 13.

70. Josiah Smith to Benjamin Franklin, 4 June 1777, in *Papers of Benjamin Franklin*, 24: 118–19; John Porter to Benjamin Franklin, 6 June 1777, in *Papers of Benjamin Franklin*, 24: 130–32; Captains Lambert Wickes and Samuel Nicholson to the American Commissioners in France, 6 September 1777, in *Papers of Benjamin Franklin*, 24: 381–82, 631.

71. American Commissioners to Lord Stormont, 23 February 1777, and American Commissioners to Lambert Wickes, in *Papers of Benjamin Franklin,* 23: 360–61, 377–78; *London Chronicle* 4–6 November 1777; American Commissioners to James Thompson and Elisha Hinman, 25 November 1777, in *Papers of Benjamin Franklin,* 25: 189–91; *Public Advertiser* 11 March 1777; Captain Lambert Wickes to the Committee of Secret Correspondence, 28 February 1777, in Clark and Morgan, *Naval Documents of the American Revolution* 8: 623–24; Prelinger, "Franklin and the American Prisoners," 262–63. Examples of such cartels in America can be found in Clark and Morgan, *Naval Documents of the American Revolution* vols. 5–8.

72. American Commissioners to Lord Stormont, 2 April 1777, in *Papers of Benjamin Franklin,* 23: 548–49; Lord Stormont to Lord Weymouth, 2–3 April 1777, in Clark and Morgan, *Naval Documents of the American Revolution* 8: 735–36; Benjamin Franklin to David Hartley, 4 October 1777, John Thornton to Benjamin Franklin,4 October 1777, *Papers of Benjamin Franklin,* 25: 64–68; Prelinger, "Franklin and the American Prisoners of War," 265–66.

73. Franklin to Hartley, *Papers of Benjamin Franklin,* 14 October 1777 (25) 64–68. For the limited information available about John Thornton, see *Papers of Benjamin Franklin,* 25: 26–28. For further information on some of David Hartley's antiwar activities, see Colin Bonwick, *English Radicals and the American Revolution* (Chapel Hill: University of North Carolina Press, 1977), 105–7.

74. American Commissioners: Instructions to John Thornton, 11 December 1777; Benjamin Franklin to Sir Guy Cooper, 11 December 1777, in *Papers of Benjamin Franklin,* 25: 269–76; Prelinger, "Franklin and the American Prisoners of War," 266.

75. John Thornton to the American Commissioners, [17] December 1777, John Thornton, Memorandum for the American Commissioners, 5–8 January 1778, David Hartley to Benjamin Franklin, 25 December 1777, in *Papers of Benjamin Franklin,* 25:299, 350, 415–18, Prelinger, "Franklin and the American Prisoners of War," 267–69.

76. Thornton Memorandum, 413–18; Prelinger, "Franklin and the Prisoners of War," 267–69.

77. Dull, *Diplomatic History of the American Revolution,* 77; Thornton Memorandum, 416–19; Cohen, "Thomas Wren," 288, 296. Thornton may have been engaged as a British spy during his trip, but the memorandum gives no indication of this possibility.

78. Thornton Memorandum, 415–16; Livesey, *Prisoners of 1776,* 84–85, 87–90.

79. *New Hampshire Gazette,* 3 September 1778; Cutter, "A Yankee Privateersman," (1876), 347; Adm to CSHS, 6 December 1777 Adm/M/404/NMM; Alexander, "Forton Prison," 370.

80. Thornton Memorandum, 415–19; Prelinger, "Franklin and the American Prisoners of War," 269–71.

81. David Hartley to Benjamin Franklin, 3 February, 13 February, 18 February 1778, in *Papers of Benjamin Franklin,* 25: 578, 663, 690.

Chapter 4. First Fruits of Perseverance

1. David Hartley to Benjamin Franklin, 3 February 1778, *Papers of Benjamin Franklin,* 25: 578. Copies of some of David Hartley's correspondences to Benja-

min Franklin are also held by the Hartley-Russell family, Bucklebury, Reading, England, and the Berkshire Record Office.

2. Gilbert Chinard, ed., *The Treaties of 1778 and Allied Documents* (Baltimore: The Johns Hopkins Press, 1928), ix–xxv, 3–71; Dull, *Diplomatic History of the American Revolution* 91–99; Middlekauff, *The Glorious Cause,* 404–5; Mackesy, *War for America,* 160–61.

3. Richard B. Morris, *The Peacemakers: The Great Powers and American Independence* (New York: Harper & Row, 1965), 13–16; Christopher Hibbert, *Redcoats and Rebels: The American Revolution Through British Eyes* (New York: W. W. Norton 1990), 207–8; Dull, *Diplomatic History of the American Revolution* 99–100; Middlekauff, *The Glorious Cause,* 407–10.

4. John Drinkwater, *Charles James Fox* (New York: Cosmopolitan Book Corporation, 1928), 167–68; Cobbett, *Parliamentary History of England* 19: 672–83; *Annual Register 1778,* 21, chaps. 5, 6; *Gentleman's Magazine* 48: 91–92, Hibbert, *Redcoats and Rebels,* 201–3.

5. John S. Watson, *The Reign of George III, 1760–1815* (Oxford: Clarendon Press, 1960), 210–11; *Annual Register 1778,* 21, 315–20; *Gentleman's Magazine* 48: 51–55; Cobbett, *Parliamentary History of England* 19:, 683–84, 745–51, 762–69, 1022–24; Hibbert, *Redcoats and Rebels,* 209–10; Mackesy, *War for America,* 159–60, 219–21.

6. Watson, *Reign of George III,* 211–13; Hibbert, *Redcoats and Rebels,* 204–6; Cobbet, *Parliamentary History of England,* 19: 1031–59, 1176–79; XX: 1–42, 139–44; *Gentleman's Magazine,* 48: 92–93, 138–39; *Annual Register, 1778,* 21: chap. 6, also pp. 127–29; *Annual Register, 1779* 22: chaps. 4, 5.

7. Middlekauff, *The Glorious Cause,* 406–7, 419–36; Hibbert, *Rebels and Redcoats,* 216; Mackesy, *War for America,* 181–83; Watson, *Reign of George III,* 211.

8. William M. James, *The British Navy in Adversity* (London: Longmans & Co., 1926), 102–8; 166–67; Middlekauff, *The Glorious Cause,* 423–28, 430–32; Hibbert, *Rebels and Redcoats,* 223–26, 231–33.

9. Middlekauff, *The Glorious Cause,* 435–36; Alden, *History of the American Revolution,* 409, 439–40.

10. James, *The British Navy,* chaps. 6–8, pp. 138–43; Hibbert, *Rebels and Redcoats,* 22–30. Dull, *Diplomatic History of the American Revolution* 107, 110; Mackesy, *War for America,* 200–11.

11. Morison, *John Paul Jones,* 133–62; Fowler, *Rebels under Sail,* 150–57; James, *The British Navy,* 143.

12. Fowler, *Rebels under Sail,* 281–84; Young, "George Robert Hewes," 606; Cutter, "A Yankee Privateersman" (1879), 37–39; "List of Americans Committed to Old Mill," 137–41, 209–11.

13. Livesey, *Prisoners of 1776,* 99; Coan, "Journal of Dr. Jonathan Haskins," 306; Cutter, "A Yankee Privateersman" (1876), 350.

14. Cutter, " A Yankee Privateeersman" (1876), 349; (1877), 20; (1878), 167; Barnes, *Memoirs of Nathaniel Fanning,* 12; Livesey, *Prisoners of 1776,* 190.

15. Livesey, *Prisoners of 1776,* 98, 103–4, 113–14, 195; Coan, "Journal of Dr. Jonathan Haskins," 305–6; *Annual Register, 1778,* "Chronicle," 161–216; *Annual Register, 1779,* "Chronicle" (through March), 193–204; *Gentleman's Magazine* 48 (1778), 49 (through March).

16. Livesey, *Prisoners of 1776,* 118.

17. 12 May 1778 entry, Jonathan Carpenter Journal; Cutter,"A Yankee Privateersman" (1876), 352; (1877) 19–20.

18. Alexander, "Mill Prison," 322–5; 30 July 1778 entry, Jonathan Carpenter Journal; Cutter, "A Yankee Privateersman," (1877), 287; (1878), 70; Livesey, *Prisoners of 1776*, 150–51. Coan, "Journal of Dr. Jonathan Haskins," 429.

19. Cutter, "A Yankee Privateersman" (1879), 37–39.

20. Livesey, *Prisoners of 1776*, 247–57; "List of American Prisoners Committed to Old Mill," 137–39; Cutter, "A Yankee Privateersman" (1877), 284–85.

21. See Cutter, "A Yankee Privateersman," entries for June 1777-June 1779, 30–32 (1876–1878).

22. Livesey, *Prisoners of 1776*, 86–225, 181; Coan, "Journal of Dr. Jonathan Haskins," 294–309, 424–41, 436.

23. Livesey, *Prisoners of 1776*, 182; Anderson, "Prisoners of War in Britain," 67–68 (French officers were usually on parole); Livesey, *Prisoners of 1776*, 14. Also note Abell, *Prisoners of War in Britain*, chap. 3.

24. 29 June 1778 entry, Jonathan Carpenter Journal; Admiralty to Philip Stephens, 12 August 1777. Adm 3/98/11/234, Admiralty Ms. Records, PRO.

25. Cutter, "A Yankee Privateersman" (1876) 348; Livesey, *Prisoners of 1776*, 97, 117.

26. "Commissioners for Sick and Hurt Seamen and the Exchange of Prisoners," in *Royal Kalendar, 1777–1778*, National Maritime Museum, Greenwich (letter to author, 14 October 1991); Anderson, "Prisoners of War in Britain," 77–80; Applegate, "Mill Prison," 305–6; Alexander, "Forton Prison," 371–72.

27. Alexander, "Forton Prison," 374–75; CSHS to John Newsham, 27 August 1778, Adm/M/404, NMM.

28. Barnes, *Memoirs of Nathaniel Fanning*, 17; Admiralty to John Newsham, 16 February 1779, Adm/M/404, NMM.

29. Barnes, *Memoirs of Nathaniel Fanning*, 12; CSHS to John Newsham, 22 October 1778, Adm/M/404, NMM.

30. George Ralls Narrative, 7 November 1778, Ms., New-York Historical Society. The often unreliable narrative was written in Paris following Ralls's escape and was submitted to the American commissioners. Coan, "Journal of Dr. Jonathan Haskins," 301, 439.

31. Livesey, *Prisoners of 1776*, 154, 198, 203–4.

32. Barnes, *Memoirs of Nathaniel Fanning*, 15–16.

33. 8 September 1778 entry, Jonathan Carpenter Journal; Cutter, "A Yankee Privateersman" (1877), 18, 20, (1878), 71; John Newsham to Admiralty, 27 January 1779, Adm 3/98/11/443–44, PRO.

34. Livesey, *Prisoners of 1776*, 153–54, 183–84; Coan, "Journal of Dr. Jonathan Haskins," 430, 436–37.

35. Cutter, "A Yankee Privateersman" (1876) 351–52; (1877), 19, 212; (1878), 166–67; Livesey, *Prisoners of 1776*, 94, 154, 183–84; Alexander, "Forton Prison," 372; Applegate, "Mill Prison," 305.

36. Barnes, *Memoirs of Nathaniel Fanning*, 11–12; Alexander, "Forton Prison," 372–373.

37. 25 March 1777 entry, Jonathan Carpenter Journal; "Diary of George Thompson," 227; "Prison Letters and Sea Journal of Caleb Foot," 110; Barnes, *Memoirs of Nathaniel Fanning*, 12.

38. Livesey, *Prisoners of 1776*, 86–225; Coan, "Journal of Dr. Jonathan Haskins," 294–309, 424–41; Cutter, "A Yankee Privateersman," entries January 1778–June 1779, 30–32 (1876–78).

39. Barnes, *Memoirs of Nathaniel Fannin*, 11, 17; Cutter, "A Yankee Priva-

teersman" (1876), 352; (1877), 213; 19 June 1778–25 June 1779 entries, Jonathan Carpenter Journal.

40. Livesey, *Prisoners of 1776*, 117, 140, 143, 164, 212; Coan, "Journal of Dr. Jonathan Haskins," 303–9, 424–41.

41. Livesey, *Prisoners of 1776*, 108, 143–44, 196.

42. "Cutter, "A Yankee Privateeersman," 20 January 1778–30 June 1779 entries, 31–32 (1877–78), also (1878), 72; On Americans in Haslar Hospital, see 27 March 1779 entry, Jonathan Carpenter Journal.

43. John Howard, *State of Prisons* (3d. ed.), 184; Livesey, *Prisoners of 1776*, 197.

44. George Ralls Narrative; Livesey, *Prisoners of 1776*, 121, 131, 169, 176, 179, 196, 198, 218; Coan, "Journal of Dr. Jonathan Haskins," 307, 424.

45. James, *British Navy*, 81–86; Mackesy, *War for America*, 175–77; Fowler, *Rebels under Sail*, 286–87; Anderson, "Treatment of Prisoners of War in Britain," 67–72; Benjamin Franklin to David Hartley, 21 March 1779, in *Papers of Benjamin Franklin*, 29: 176.

46. "Cutter, "A Yankee Privateersman," (1878), 281, 282; 17 December 1778, entry Jonathan Carpenter Journal.

47. "Diary of George Thompson," 225; John Newsham to Admiralty, 27 January 1779, Adm 3/98/11 443–44, PRO.

48. Livesey, *Prisoners of 1776*, 155–56, 171–72.

49. Ibid., 176–77, 215–16.

50. Livesey, *Prisoners of 1776*, 243–58; Cutter, "A Yankee Privateersman" (1879), 36–40; Anderson, "Treatment of Prisoners of War," 71–72; Lemisch, "Listening to the Inarticulate," 17 n; Alexander, "Forton Prison," 385, 384 n.

51. Carey, *A Sailor's Songbag*, 120; Barnes, *Memoir of Nathaniel Fanning*, 9–20; 12 May 1778–30 June 1779 entries, Jonathan Carpenter Journal; Lemisch, "Listening to the Inarticulate," 26–28; Alexander, "Forton Prison," 388.

52. Livesey, *Prisoners of 1776*, 141–42, 155–156, 172.

53. Livesey, *Prisoners of 1776*, 44–228; Cutter, "A Yankee Privateersman," entries 13 June 1777–30 June 1779.

54. David A. Foy, "*For You the War Is Over: American Prisoners of War in Nazi Germany* (New York: Madison Books, 1984), 27–33; chaps. 5, 11; Ben Goldman, "German Treatment of American Prisoners of War in World War II" (master's thesis, Wayne State University, 1947), 1–121; "American Prisoners of War in Germany," U. S. Department of State, *Bulletin*, 15 April 1945, 683–84.

55. Livesey, *Prisoners of 1776*, 199.

56. 12 January 1779 entry, Jonathan Carpenter Journal; Barnes, *Memoirs of Nathaniel Fanning*, 13–18; Cutter, "A Yankee Privateersman," entries 15 February 1778–11 January 1779.

57. Ann Bridge, *Portrait of My Mother* (London: Chatto & Windus, 1955), 32–33; Cutter, "A Yankee Privateersman" (1877), 19, 287; (1878), 73, 281; (1879), 38; R. R. Hinman, *Catalogue of the First Puritan Settlers*, 817–18; *Papers of Benjamin Franklin*, 27: 276 n.

58. Cutter, "A Yankee Privateersman" (1877), 287; 1878, (73); Stewart, *History of Virginia's Navy*, 179–80; *Papers of Benjamin Franklin*, 22: 461, 469 n. 470–71, 23: 452–53; Rene-Etienne-Henry Vic Gaiault de Boisbertrand, Memorandum for the American Commissioners, 5 September 1778, 27: 356–57.

59. Barnes, *Memoirs of Nathaniel Fanning*, 13–14. The *Hampshire Chronicle* for 14 September 1778 cites details about the prisoners' method of tunneling that are similar to those mentioned by Fanning.

60. Admiralty to CSHS, 11 September 1778, Adm/ M/404, NMM; Barnes, *Memoirs of Nathaniel Fanning,* 10.

61. Cutter, "A Yankee Privateersman" (1876), 348–49; (1878), 283; (1879), 36; John Watson and John Swain to Franklin and Arthur Lee, 17 January 1779, in *Papers of Benjamin Franklin,* 28: 388–89.

62. Thomas Greenleaf to John Adams, 16 July 1778, in Robert J. Taylor, Gregg L. Lint, Celeste Walker, eds., *The Papers of John Adams* (Cambridge, Mass.: Belknap Press, 1953), 6: 293; Clark, "In Defense of Thomas Digges," 421; Webb, "An Early Victorian Street," 13; Gates, *Illustrated History of Portsmouth,* 291–92; Barnes, *Memoirs of Nathaniel Fanning,* 18.

63. Cutter, "A Yankee Privateersman" (1876), 348–49; Barnes, *Memoirs of Nathaniel Fanning,* 18; Livesey, *Prisoners of 1776,* 107, 196; *Portsmouth Guide 1775,* 76.

64. Clark, "In Defense of Thomas Digges," 392–93, 405; Thomas Digges to Benjamin Franklin, 18 September 1778, *Papers of Benjamin Franklin,* 27: 420; *London City Directories* 1777–79, Guildhall Library, London.

65. Barnes, *Memoirs of Nathaniel Fanning,* 18 n; *Papers of Benjamin Franklin,* 28: 295 n; Olive Anderson, "American Escapes from British Naval Prisons during the War of Independence," *The Mariner's Mirror,* 45 (1955): 239; Bridge, *Portrait of My Mother,* 33–34.

66. "Alphabetical List of the American Prisoners who, having escaped from the Prisons of England, were furnished with Money by the Commiss[ione]rs of the US. at the Court of France to return to America." Ms. American Philosophical Society, hereinafter referred to as APS; copy in Papers of Benjamin Franklin; *Papers of Benjamin Franklin,* 25: 495 n; 26: 13, 156, 284, 656, 660, 685–86; 27: 480; 27: 89, 120, 510, 522. Also see Thomas Digges to Benjamin Franklin, 18 September 1778, *Papers of Benjamin Franklin,* 27: 420–21.

67. Conversation between the author and the Reverend John Sturges (ret.) 5 August 1987; H. Sargent, "A History of Portsmouth Theatre," *Portsmouth Papers* (1971): 3–7; Webb, "An Early Victorian Street," 12–13.

68. David Welsh to Benjamin Franklin, 18 June 1778, in *Papers of Benjamin Franklin,* 26: 658–59, see also 27: 30, 339–41; Cutler, "Samuel Cutler's Diary," 397; Cohen, "The Preachers and the Prisoners," 10; Livesey, *Prisoners of 1776,* 123, 252.

69. Livesey, *Prisoners of 1776,* 94–221.

70. CSHS to Adm., 5 January 1779, Adm/98/11/398–411; Livesey, *Prisoners of 1776,* 203–4. The Admiralty ordered an inquiry into the escape on 6 January 1779.

71. John Channing to Benjamin Franklin, 24 August 1778, Tristram Barnard to American Commissioners, 9 October 1778, *Papers of Benjamin Franklin,* 27: 295, 526–27; Shubael Gardner to American Commissioners, 22 December 1778, *Papers of Benjamin Franklin,* 28: 260–61, 295–96.

72. Alexander, "Forton Prison," 375, 383, 387–89; Lemisch, "Listening to the Inarticulate," 20–28.

73. Barnes, *Memoirs of Nathaniel Fanning,* 14–15; Alexander, "Forton Prison," 374–75, 383, 384, 388–89; Lemisch, "Listening to the Inarticulate," 20–23.

74. Livesey, *Prisoners of 1776,* 108, 133, 148, 151–54, 161, 166, 174, 175, 190, 202, 210.

75. Cutter, "A Yankee Privateersman" (1876), 349; (1878), 283; 5 April 1779 entry, Jonathan Carpenter Journal; Livesey, *Prisoners of 1776,* 210, 222; Coan, "Journal of Dr. Jonathan Haskins," 424–41.

76. McCaw, "Capt. John Harris," 167–68, 170; John Harris to Benjamin Franklin, 14 July 1778, in *Papers of Benjamin Franklin,* 27: 93; Cohen, "Thomas Wren, Portsmouth's Patron," 14, 16; Thomas Wren to David Hartley, 19 November 1778, Hartley-Russell Papers , D/EHy/040; Cutter,"A Yankee Privateersman" (1878), 281; Cohen, "The Preachers and the Prisoners," 17.

77. David Hartley to Benjamin Franklin, 3 February 1778, Benjamin Franklin to David Hartley, 12 February 1778, Thomas Wren to Benjamin Franklin, 24 March 1778, in *Papers of Benjamin Franklin,* 25: 578, 650–53, 26: 165; Thomas Wren to David Hartley, 7 February, 19, 20 March, 13 May 1778, Hartley-Russell Papers, D/EHy/040; Cohen, "Thomas Wren, Portsmouth's Patron" 13.

78. Cutter,"A Yankee Privateersman" (1876), 344, 350–52; (1877), 19–20, 213, 285, 287; (1878), 70–72, 165–68, 280–84; Barnes, *Memoirs of Nathaniel Fanning,* 19; Cohen, "Thomas Wren, Portsmouth's Patron," 13–14; Cohen, "Preachers and the Prisoners," 17.

79. Barnes, *Memoirs of Nathaniel Fanning,* 19; Memorandum to David Hartley from twelve prisoners at Forton, June 1779, Hartley-Russell Papers, D/EHy/040, 10a; "Diary of George Thompson," 232; 18 May 1779 entry, Journal of Jonathan Carpenter; Cohen, "Thomas Wren, Portsmouth's Patron," 13–14; Cutter, "A Yankee Privateersman" (187), 350–52; (1877), 19–20, 213, 285, 287; (1878), 70–72, 165–68, 280–84.

80. Miles Saurey's profession as a linen draper in Plymouth is mentioned in the city directories for this period (letter to author from West Devon Record Office, Plymouth, 14 July 1987).

81. Livesey, *Prisoners of 1776,* 134, 197; Coan, "Journal of Dr. Jonathan Haskins" 424–25.

82. Livesey, *Prisoners of 1776,* 90–196, 209, 225.

83. Ibid., 104, 186.

84. *Papers of Benjamin Franklin,* 25: 64–68, 485 n, 580–81; 26: lxvi–lxvii, 57–58, 61–62, 526, 539–40; 27: 43 n, 129; 28: 16–17, 21, 247, 361, 600 n; 29: 18–21, 165; "Alphabetical List of the American Prisoners."

85. American Commissioners to the American Prisoners, [19] September 1778, American Commissioners to Officers and Prisoners at Forton, 20 October 1778, in *Papers of Benjamin Franklin,* 27: 422–23, 576–77; Benjamin Franklin to David Hartley, 12 February 1778, in *Papers of Benjamin Franklin,* 25: 650–52. See also 25: 272, 274–75, 417–19, 571; 26: 165–66, 526; 27: 190–91, 278–79.

86. Prelinger, "Franklin and the American Prisoners," 269–71; Benjamin Franklin to Vergennes, 24 April 1778," in *Papers of Benjamin Franklin,* 26: 334–37.

87. David Hartley to Benjamin Franklin, 29 May 5 June 1778; American Commissioners to Lord North, [6] June 1778; Benjamin Franklin to David Hartley, 25 May, 6 June, and 16 June 1778, in *Papers of Benjamin Franklin,* 26: 528, 529–30, 539–40, 592–93, 600, 626; Prelinger, "Franklin and the American Prisoners," 271–73.

88. David Hartley to Benjamin Franklin, 16 July 1778, in *Papers of Benjamin Franklin,* 27: 94–95; Prelinger, "Franklin and the American Prisoners," 272–73.

89. See n 85. on letters to the American prisoners; Benjamin Franklin to David Hartley, 29 November 1778, in *Papers of Benjamin Franklin,* 28: 169; Prelinger, "Franklin and the American Prisoners," 273; Thomas Wren to David Hartley, 19 November 1778, Forton prisoners Memorandum to David Hartley, June 1779, Hartley-Russell Papers, D/EHy/040.

90. Antoine-Felix Wybert, Joseph Lunt, Edward MacKellar to Benjamin

Franklin, 2 October 1778, in *Papers of Benjamin Franklin,* 27: 491–92; Thomas Wren to David Hartley, 13 May, 19 November 1778, Hartley-Russell Papers, D/EHy/040; Cutter, "A Yankee Privateersman" (1876), 350; (1877), 18–20, 212–13, 284–88; (1879), 165–68, 280–83; 6 July-10 December 1778 entries, Jonathan Carpenter Journal; Prelinger, "Franklin and the American Prisoners," 274–75. Wybert was released from Forton on 11 January 1778. Cutter, "A Yankee Privateersman" (1878), 282.

91. Letter by John Archer from Mill Prison, England, 25 September 1778, *Essex Institute Historical Collections* 6 (1864): 113–14; Livesey, *Prisoners of 1776,* 93, 113, 135, 153, 160, 173, 175.

92. David Hartley to Benjamin Franklin, 10 December 1778, in *Papers of Benjamin Franklin,* 28: 218–19; Livesey, *Prisoners of 1776,* 214, 217; Prelinger, "Franklin and the American Prisoners," 275.

93. Benjamin Franklin to David Hartley, 1 January 1779, in *Papers of Benjamin Franklin,* 28: 321. Also see *Papers of Benjamin Franklin,* 28: 129 n, 271, 479–80, 512, 587–88; 29: 9 n, 23–24; Prelinger, "Franklin and the American Prisoners," 275–76.

94. Livesey, *Prisoners of 1776,* 227–28; *Papers of Benjamin Franklin,* 29: 20, 23 n, 233–34.

Chapter 5. The Inconstant Waves of Dame Fortune

1. Ian R. Christie, *The End of North's Ministry, 1780–1782* (London: Macmillan & Co., 1958), 3–48; Ian R. Christie, *Wilkes, Wyvill and Reform; The Parliamentary Reform Movement in British Politics, 1760–1785* (London: Macmillan & Co., 1962), 68–124; Ian R. Christie, *Wars and Revolutions, Britain, 1760–1815* (Cambridge Mass.: Harvard University Press, 1982), 135–36; Watson, *Reign of George III,* 227–36; Hibbert, *Redcoats and Rebels,* 259–61; Mackesy, *War for America,* 245–47, 264–65, 301–5, 359–63; Bonwick, *English Radicals and the American Revolution,* 106, 136–38; Drinkwater, *Charles James Fox,* 177–203.

2. Watson, *Reign of George III,* 213–15, 233–40; Christie, *The End of North's Ministry,* chap 2, pt. I; Alden, *History of the American Revolution,* 421–22; Mackesy, *War for America,* 359–62; Drinkwater, *Charles James Fox,* 197–202.

3. Morris, *The Peacemakers,* 13–17, 165–68, 172; Bemis, *Diplomatic History of the American Revolution,* 84–87, 113, 155–62, Dull, *Diplomatic History of the American Revolution,* 91–92, 107–9, 124–30; *Annual Register* 23 (1780), 375–78.

4. Mackesy, *War for America,* 249, 268–69, 310–16, 359–63, 381–82, 385; Watson, *Reign of George III,* 240–42; *Annual Register* 22 (1779), 105–7; 23 (1780), 15–37.

5. Middlekauff, *The Glorious Cause,* 442–49, 452–57, 461–62; Alden, *History of the American Revolution,* 410–16, 419–20; 458–59; Hibbert, *Redcoats and Rebels,* 244–247, 265–68, 280–85.

6. James, *The British Navy,* 147–211; Tuchman, *The First Salute,* 168–70, 173–76; Mackesy, *The War for America,* 275–78, 294–97, 310–34, 347–58.

7. Fowler, *Rebels under Sail,* 79–96, 106–121; Paullin, *The Navy of the American Revolution,* 181–200, 203–9.

8. Morison, *John Paul Jones,* 227–40; Fowler, *Rebels under Sail,* 165–68; Paullin, *The Navy of the American Revolution,* 296–97; Middlekauff, *The Glorious Cause,* 532–34.

9. John H. Sherburne, *Life of John Paul Jones* (New York: Adriance, Sher-

man & Co., 1851), 134–40; John S. Barnes, ed., *The Logs of the Serapis, Alliance, Ariel, under the Command of John Paul Jones 1779–1780* (New York: De Vinne Press, 1911), 3–20; Morison, *John Paul Jones,* 196–97.

10. "Diary of George Thompson," 230; Paine, *Ships and Sailors of Old Salem,* 124. Newspapers from London included the *London Chronicle* and the *London Evening Post.* The *Hampshire Chronicle* was published in Winchester.

11. See chap. 2, n. 38, 45, 52, 54, 55, 60, 61.

12. 5 April 1779 entry, Jonathan Carpenter Journal; "Diary of George Thompson," 227; Cutter, "A Yankee Privateersman" (1878), 284. (Apparently, Jean-Daniel Schweighauser, American agent at Nantes had informed Franklin of the prisoners arrival on 3 April 1779, *Papers of Benjamin Franklin,* 29: 282.)

13. Benjamin Franklin to David Hartley, 4 May 1779, in *Papers of Benjamin Franklin,* 29: 425–28 (Franklin may have entrusted the personal delivery of this letter to Thomas Digges, who was then in Paris); *Papers of Benjamin Franklin,* 29: 469 n.

14. David Hartley to Benjamin Franklin, 21 May 1779, in *Papers of Benjamin Franklin,* 29: 468–70, 531–32; Clark, "In Defense of Thomas Digges," 396–97.

15. Benjamin Franklin to the Committee for Foreign Affairs, 26 May 1779, Benjamin Franklin to Thomas Digges, 31 May 1779, Thomas Digges to Benjamin Franklin, 11 June 1779, in *Papers of Benjamin Franklin,* 29: 548–53, 576–77, 666–67; Clark, "In Defense of Thomas Digges," 397–98; Prelinger, "Franklin and the American Prisoners," 276.

16. David Hartley to Benjamin Franklin, 24 June 1779, in *Papers of Benjamin Franklin,* 29: 732; "Diary of George Thompson," 228.

17. 25 June 1779 entry, Jonathan Carpenter Journal; Forton Prisoners to David Hartley, 26 June 1779, Hartley-Russell Papers, D/EHy/040.

18. Barnes, *Memoir of Nathaniel Fanning,* 19–20.

19. Ibid., 20.

20. Thomas Digges to Benjamin Franklin, 6 July 1779, in Robert H. Elias and Eugene D. Finch, eds., *Letters of Thomas Attwood Digges, 1742–1821* (Columbia: University of South Carolina Press, 1982), 69; Clark, "In Defense of Thomas Digges," 398.

21. 2 July 1779 entry, Jonathan Carpenter Journal; Cutter, "A Yankee Privateersman" (1878), 285.

22. Carey, *A Sailor's Songbag,* 1–164; Cutter, "A Yankee Privateersman" (1878), 285.

23. Carey, *A Sailor's Songbag,* 78.

24. *Ibid.,* 128. The opening words of this popular chanty begin, "As I was walking down Paradise Street / Weigh, hey, blow the man down / A lovely young damsel I chanced to meet."

25. *Ibid.,* 110.

26. *Ibid.,* 90.

27. Paine, *Ships and Sailors of Old Salem,* 129; *Hampshire Chronicle,* 19 April, 24 May, 9, 16, 23 August, and 6 September 1779; "Diary of George Thompson," 228, 230–31; Mackesy, *War for America,* 289–96.

28. Royal Kalendar, 1779, 1780, Ms., National Maritime Museum; Watson, *Reign of George III,* 213; Mackesy, *War for America,* 241–42; Sainty, *Office Holders in Modern Britain,* 4: 25; Tilley, *The British Navy & the American Revolution,* 43–44, 128–32.

29. 29 May 1779 entry, Jonathan Carpenter Journal.

30. *Ibid.*

31. "Diary of George Thompson," 229; "Prison Letters and Sea Journal of Caleb Foot," 100.

32. Paine, *Ships and Sailors of Old Salem,* 120–29; Neeser, *Gustavus Conyngham,* 169–73; Greenwood, *Captain John Manley,* 117–19; Peabody, "The Naval Career of Capt. John Manley," 24; Bowden, "Diary of William Wigder," 311.

33. Paine, *Ships and Sailors of Old Salem,* 128; "List of Prisoners in Old Mill Prison," *New England Historical & Genealogical Register* 19: 139.

34. Thomas Digges to Benjamin Franklin, 12 October 1779, *Papers of Benjamin Franklin,* 30: 526; John Dalton, et al., to Benjamin Franklin, 11 November 1779, Ms. APS, Copy, Benjamin Franklin Papers, Yale University Library; Neeser, *Gustavus Conyngham,* 168–73, Paine, *Ships and Sailors of Old Salem,* 121–29.

35. Alexander, "Forton Prison," 383; Lemisch, "Listening to the Inarticulate," 20–22.

36. 29 May 1779 entry, Jonathan Carpenter Journal.

37. Paine, *Ships and Sailors of Old Salem,* 125. George Pike reportedly was committed to Mill Prison on 22 March 1779 ("List of Mill Prisoners," [19], 138–39).

38. "Prison Letters and Sea Journal of Caleb Foot," 95, 97, 109.

39. Robert Birrell to Benjamin Franklin, 29 January 1780, Ms. Pennsylvania Historical Society, hereinafter referred to as PHS, Forton Prisoners to Franklin, 7 February 1780, Ms. PHS, William Hodgson to Franklin, 23 November 1779, 28 January, 10 March, 28 March 1780, Thomas Mehany to American Commissioners, 13 August 1780, Ms. APS, copies, Papers of Benjamin Franklin.

40. Neeser, *Gustavus Conyngham,* 173; Paine, *Ships and Sailors of Old Salem,* 121; Gustavus Conyngham to Benjamin Franklin, 18 November, 1 December 1779, Ms. APS Mill Prisoners to Benjamin Franklin, 2 November 1779, Ms. PHS, copies, Papers of Benjamin Franklin.

41. James Adams to Benjamin Franklin, 3 November 1779, 27 May 1780, Ms. APS, Copy, Papers of Benjamin Franklin.

42. CSHS to Admiralty, 22 November 1780, Adm 98/13/136–39.

43. Howard, *State of Prisons,* 3d ed., 185–86; Royal Kalendar, 1778, 1780; James Adams to Benjamin Franklin, 27 May 1780, Ms. APS, copies, Papers of Benjamin Franklin.

44. Howard, *State of Prisons,* 3d ed., 185–86; "Diary of George Thompson," 232; Forton Prisoners to Benjamin Franklin, 7 February 1780, Ms. PHS, Copy, Papers of Benjamin Franklin.

45. Howard, *State of Prisons,* 3d ed., 185–87.

46. Neeser, *Gustavus Conyngham,* 166; "Prison Letters and Sea Journal of Caleb Foot," 95–96, 100; Howard, *State of Prisons,* 3d ed., 187.

47. *The Scots Magazine* 41 (1779): 219–20, 271–72; 305–8; Mackesy, *War for America,* 250, 280, 288, 302–9, 330–31; Hibbert, *Redcoats and Rebels,* 261; Anderson, "Establishment of British Supremacy at Sea," 82, 89.

48. John Manley to Jonathan Williams, 16 July 1780, Ms. APS, copy, Papers of Benjamin Franklin; Prelinger, "Franklin and the American Prisoners, 275, 281"; Anderson, "The Treatment of Prisoners of War," 71–72.

49 Benjamin Franklin to David Hartley, 21 March 1779, Benjamin Franklin to Thomas Wren, 26 February 1780, Ms. Library of Congress, hereinafter referred to as DLC, American Prisoners at Forton to Benjamin Franklin, 7 February 1780, Ms. PHS, Gustavus Conyngham to Benjamin Franklin, 1 December 1779, Ms. APS, copies, Papers of Benjamin Franklin.

50. "Diary of George Thompson," 225, 228, 230, 232; Admiralty entry, 19 December 1780, Adm 98/13/161; Paine, *Ships and Sailors at Old Salem*, 125.

51. "Letters and Sea Journal of Caleb Foot," 100; Adm to CSHS, 23 November, 5 December 1780, Adm/M/404 NMM; "Diary of George Thompson," 225.

52. CSHS to Adm, 14 November 1780, Adm/98/13/139–41; Davies, *Documents of the American Revolution*, vol. 16 Calendar (1779–80), 439.

53. Thomas C. Parramore, "The Great Escape from Forten [sic] Gaol: An Incident of the Revolution," *North Carolina Historical Review* 45 (1969): 353–56; Barnes, *Memoirs of Nathaniel Fanning*, 13–14; "Narrative of Lieut. Luke Matthewman," 181–82.

54. "Diary of George Thompson," 233.

55. "Letters and Sea Journal of Caleb Foot," 111.

56. Paine, *Ships and Sailors of Old Salem*, 127; Neeser, *Gustavus Conyngham*, xlix–l, 190; Gustavus Conyngham to Benjamin Franklin, 18 November, 1 December 1779, Ms. APS, copies, Papers of Benjamin Franklin.

57. Paine, *Ships and Sailors of Old Salem*, 124–25; John Manley to Jonathan Williams, 16 July 1780, John Dalton et al., to Benjamin Franklin, 11 November 1779, Ms. APS, copies, Papers of Benjamin Franklin.

58. Fareham Justices to CSHS, 29 September 1779, Adm/M/404 NMM; CSHS to Adm, 22 November 1780. Adm 98/13/138–41; Lemisch, "Listening to the Inarticulate," 19.

59. Neeser, *Gustavus Conyngham*, 173; William Cowdry to Admiralty, 9 November 1779, Adm/98/12/258.

60. Fareham Justices to CSHS, 29 September 1779; CSHS Report, 6 June 1779. Adm/98/12/36, Adm/M/404 NMM.

61. "Diary of George Thompson," 232.

62. Thomas Digges to Benjamin Franklin, 13 November 1780, Ms. PHS, copy, Papers of Benjamin Franklin; Clark, "In Defense of Thomas Digges," 421.

63. Jeremiah Pierce to Benjamin Franklin, 8 June 1779, *Papers of Benjamin Franklin*, 29: 646–48; "Letter of Nathaniel Harrington Jr.," 322.

64. Neeser, *Gustavus Conyngham*, 190; Clark, "In Defense of Thomas Digges," 405–6; Gustavus Conyngham to Benjamin Franklin, 18 November 1779, Thomas Digges to Benjamin Franklin, 9 November 1779, Ms. PHS, copies, Papers of Benjamin Franklin.

65. Clark, "In Defense of Thomas Digges," 394–96, 406; Thomas Digges to Benjamin Franklin, 10 November 1779, Ms. PHS, copy, Papers of Benjamin Franklin.

66. Morison, *John Paul Jones*, 195–96; Jonathan Williams, Jr., to John Paul Jones, 7 April 1779, Benjamin Franklin to John Paul Jones, 14 March, 28 April 1779, Franklin to the Commissioners for Foreign Affairs, 26 May 1779, Franklin to Sartine, 23 April 1779, in *Papers of Benjamin Franklin*, 29: 119, 226–27, 276–77, 366–67, 386–88, 547–53.

67. Barnes, *Memoirs of Nathaniel Fanning*, 23; Morison, *John Paul Jones*, 196–97; Barnes, *Logs of the Serapis, Alliance Ariel*, 3–20; Sherburne, *Life of John Paul Jones*, 134–38.

68. Benjamin Franklin to Pierre Landais, 24 April 1780, in *Papers of Benjamin Franklin*, 29: 372; Barnes, *Memoirs of Nathaniel Fanning*, 23; Prelinger, "Franklin and the American Prisoners of War," 277–78.

69. Sheldon S. Cohen, "Thomas Wren, Portsmouth's Patron of American Liberty," *Portsmouth Papers* 57 (1991): 13, 15–16, 18, 20; Bartholomew Raredon to Benjamin Franklin, 13 September 1779, *Papers of Benjamin Franklin*, 30: 330:

Benjamin Franklin to Thomas Wren, 26 February 1780, Ms. DLC, copy, Papers of Benjamin Franklin.

70. Thomas Digges to Benjamin Franklin, 28 January, 25 August, 18 September, 10 October 1779; Elias and Fitch, *Letters of Thomas Digges,* 151, 226, 256, 299; Cohen, "Thomas Wren, Portsmouth's Patron," 13; Alexander, "Forton Prison," 378–79.

71. Geddes, "Portsmouth during the French Wars," 11–19; Cohen, "Thomas Wren, Portsmouth's Patron," 16, 18; Thomas Wren to David Hartley, 4 October 1779, Mary Walters [?] 1780 to David Hartley, Hartley–Russell Papers, D/Ehy/040.

72. Thomas Digges to Benjamin Franklin, 8, 30, October 1779, *Papers of Benjamin Franklin,* 30: 491, 622; Cohen, "The Preachers and the Prisoners," 8–10; Clark, "In Defense of Thomas Digges," 405–6; Neeser, *Gustavus Conyngham,* 190; Thomas Digges to Benjamin Franklin, 30 October, 26 November, 4, 17 December 1779, in Elias and Fitch, *Letters of Thomas Digges,* 99, 105, 114, 123, 126.

73. William Hodgson to Benjamin Franklin, 10 March 1780, Ms. APS, copy, Papers of Benjamin Franklin; Thomas Digges to Benjamin Franklin, 20 September, 30 October, 1779, 10 March, 18 August, 1780, Elias and Fitch, *Letters of Thomas Digges,* 86, 101, 173, 249.

74. Clark, "In Defense of Thomas Digges," 395–98; Benjamin Franklin to David Hartley, 4 May 1779, in *Papers of Benjamin Franklin,* 29: 425–28; Thomas Digges to Benjamin Franklin, 10 May, 18 May, 21 May, 31 May, 1 June 1779, Elias and Fitch, *Letters of Thomas Digges,* xlvii–xlviii, 40–42, 46–55.

75. Clark, "In Defense of Thomas Digges," 398–411; Thomas Digges to Benjamin Franklin 30 October 1780, 28 June 1780, Elias and Fitch, *Letters of Thomas Digges,* 99, 101, 151; Thomas Digges to David Hartley, 26 June 1780, Hartley-Russell Papers, D/Ehy/040.

76. Thomas Digges to Benjamin Franklin, 20 September, 30 October 1779, Elias and Fitch, *Letters of Thomas Digges,* 86, 100; Thomas Digges to David Hartley, 2 September 1779; Hartley-Russell Papers, D/EHy/040.

77. See Thomas Cooper, *DNB* s.v. "Hodgson, William"; Thomas Digges to Benjamin Franklin, 26 November, 3 December 1779; 10 March 1780; Elias and Fitch, *Letters of Thomas Digges,* 114–15 n, 119; Clark, "In Defense of Thomas Digges," 404, 410.

78. Thomas Digges to Benjamin Franklin, 10 March, 29 December 1780, Elias and Fitch, *Letters of Thomas Digges,* 173–74, 345 n, 4, 5; William Hodgson to Benjamin Franklin, 20 March 1781, Ms. APS, copy, Papers of Benjamin Franklin; Clark, "In Defense of Thomas Digges," 411, 413, 418–27.

79. Thomas Digges to Benjamin Franklin, 10 March, 14 April 1780, Benjamin Franklin to Thomas Digges, 14, 26 February 1780, Benjamin Franklin to David Hartley, 2 February 1780, Mss. APS, PHS, DLC, copies, Papers of Benjamin Franklin; "Alphabetical List of the American Prisoners," Ms. APS; Thomas Digges to David Hartley, 26 January 1780; Hartley-Russell Papers, D/EHy/040; Prelinger, "Franklin and the American Prisoners," 283–89.

80. Clark, *Ben Franklin's Privateers,* 22, 77–78, 140–44, 153, 169–70, 174–76; Stephen Marchant to Benjamin Franklin 25 July 1779, *Papers of Benjamin Franklin,* 30: 142–44; David Hartley to Benjamin Franklin, 18 September 1779, *Papers of Benjamin Franklin,* 30: 622; Thomas Digges to Benjamin Franklin 30 October 1779; Elias and Fitch, *Letters of Thomas Digges,* 99; Prelinger, "Franklin and the American Prisoners," 276.

81. Franklin's Instructions to John Paul Jones, [28 April 1779], *Papers of Benjamin Franklin,* 29: 387; John Paul Jones to Benjamin Franklin, 11 October 1779, *Papers of Benjamin Franklin* 30: 520–21; Morison, *John Paul Jones,* 245, 251–52; Prelinger, "Franklin and the American Prisoners," 277–78; Clark, "In Defense of Thomas Digges," 404.

82. Benjamin Franklin to David Hartley, 19 October 1779, David Hartley to Benjamin Franklin, 26 October 1779, Thomas Digges to Benjamin Franklin, 30 October 1779, *Papers of Benjamin Franklin,* 30: 559–60, 595–97, 620; (The 19 October 1779 letter is also in Hartley-Russell Papers, D/Ehy/040); Clark, "In Defense of Thomas Digges," 404.

83. William Hodgson to Benjamin Franklin, 23 November 1779, Ms. APS, copy, Papers of Benjamin Franklin; Morison, *John Paul Jones,* 258, 263; Prelinger, "Franklin and the American Prisoners," 279; Clark, "In Defense of Thomas Digges," 404; Letter on the Proposed American Exchange to John Bell, 10 November 1779, Adm 98/12/262.

84. William Hodgson to Benjamin Franklin 28 January 1780, Ms. APS, copy, Papers of Benjamin Franklin; Prelinger, "Franklin and the American Prisoners," 279.

85. Thomas Digges to Benjamin Franklin, 10 February 1780, Elias and Fitch, *Letters of Thomas Digges,* 159; Clark, "In Defense of Thomas Digges," 406–9; Benjamin Franklin to James Lovell, 16 March 1780, Ms. DLC, copy, Papers of Benjamin Franklin; Adm to CSHS, 31 December 1779, Adm/M/404 NMM; Officers at Mill Prison to Admiral Lord Shuldham, 5 November 1779, Adm/1/806/235.

86. Henry Laurence et al. to Benjamin Franklin, 2 November 1779, Ms. University of Pennsylvania Library, hereinafter referred to as PU, Robert Birrell et al. to Benjamin Franklin, 29 January 1780, copy of petition sent to Admiral Lord Shuldham, Ms. PHS, copies, Papers of Benjamin Franklin; Prelinger, "Franklin and the American Prisoners," 280–81; "Prison Letters and Sea Journal of Caleb Foot," 97; Paine, *Ships and Sailors of Old Salem,* 128.

87. Benjamin Franklin to William Hodgson, 20 January 1780, Benjamin Franklin to Thomas Wren, 26 February 1780, Mss. DLC, copies, Papers of Benjamin Franklin; Prelinger, "Franklin and the American Prisoners," 279–80.

88. John Bell to David Hartley 28 February 1780, Hartley-Russell Papers, D/EHy/ 040; David Hartley to Benjamin Franklin, 26 October, 16 November 1779, 1 March 1780; Jonathan Hopes to Benjamin Franklin, 23 March 1780, Mss. APS, PHS, copies, Papers of Benjamin Franklin; Prelinger, "Franklin and the American Prisoners," 280–81. (On 11 December 1779 the Admiralty had initially ordered the compilation of a list of Americans for release at both Mill and Forton, Adm/ M/404 NMM.)

89. Franklin to Sartine, 13 February, Sartine to Franklin, 24 April 1780, Mss. DLC, copies, Papers of Benjamin Franklin; Prelinger, "Franklin and the American Prisoners," 280–81; Clark, "In Defense of Thomas Digges," 410–11.

90. David Hartley to Benjamin Franklin, 27 March 1780, William Hodgson to Benjamin Franklin, 28 March, 12 May, 11 August 1780, Mss. APS copies, Papers of Benjamin Franklin; Thomas Digges to Benjamin Franklin, 24 May, 18 August 1780. Elias and Fitch, *Letters of Thomas Digges,* 210, 249; Prelinger, "Franklin and the American Prisoners," 280–81.

91. "Letters and Sea Journal of Caleb Foot," 99; John Manley to Jonathan Williams, 16 July 1780, Ms. APS, copy, Papers of Benjamin Franklin.

92. William Hodgson to Benjamin Franklin, 20 September, 4 December 1780,

Mss. APS copies, Papers of Benjamin Franklin; Prelinger, "Franklin and the American Prisoners," 282.

93. James L. Banks, *David Sproat and Naval Prisoners in the War of the Revolution* (New York: The Knickerbocker Press, 1909), 6–27; Henry R. Stiles, ed., *Letters from the Prisons and Prison-ships of the Revolution* (New York: Privately Print., 1865), 1–49; Henry Onderdonk, Jr., *Revolutionary Incidents of Suffolk and Kings County* (New York: Leavitt & Company, 1849) 207–49; Lemisch, "Listening to the Inarticulate," 9–10, 13; Dandridge, *American Prisoners of the Revolution*, chaps. 24–46.

94. Neeser, *Gustavus Conyngham*, 179–80; Ann Conyngham to Benjamin Franklin, 22 September 1779, (annotated note and letter), *Papers of Benjamin Franklin*, 30: 385–86.

95. Ann Conyngham to Benjamin Franklin, 22 September 1779, *Papers of Benjamin Franklin*, 30: 385–86.

96. Abram W. Foote, *Foote Family, Comprising the Genealogy and History of Nathaniel Foote of Wethersfield Connecticut and His Descendants* (Rutland Vt.: Marble City Press, The Tuttle Company, 1907), 1: 541; "Letters and Sea Journal of Caleb Foot," 104–5.

97. "Letters and Sea Journal of Caleb Foot," 96–97.

98. Samuel Harris to Benjamin Franklin, 12 June 1781, Ms. APS, copy, Papers of Benjamin Franklin; Prelinger, "Franklin and the American Prisoners," 282–84.

Chapter 6. Farewell to All That

1. Paine, *Ships and Sailors of Old Salem*, 128.

2. Middlekauff, *The Glorious Cause*, 559–70; Hibbert, *Redcoats and Rebels*, 315–30; Alden, *History of the American Revolution*, 467–76; Tuchman, *The First Salute*, 245–90.

3. Mackesy, *War for America*, 460–70; Hibbert, *Redcoats and Rebels*, 333–37; Middlekauff, *The Glorious Cause*, 571; Tuchman, *The First Salute*, 296–98; Watson, *Reign of George III*, 242–43; Christie, *The End of North's Ministry*, chaps. 3–4, pt. II; Christie, *Wilkes, Wyvill and Reform*, 137–42; Prelinger, "Franklin and the American Prisoners," 290; Cobbett, *Parliamentary History of England*, 22: 988–89, 1064–1105; Raithby, *Statutes at Large*, 15: 255.

4. Dull, *Diplomatic History of the American Revolution*, 137–51, 159–63, 170–74; Morris, *The Peacemakers*, 261–465; Middlekauff, *The Glorious Cause*, 571–75; Watson, *Reign of George III*, 249–56.

5. James, *The British Navy in Adversity*, 335–47; Mackesy, *War for America*, 446–59; Tuchman, *The First Salute*, 294–96.

6. Fowler, *Rebels under Sail*, 87–90, 121–26, 169–70; Paullin, *The Navy of the American Revolution*, 208–27, 230–38; Clark, *Ben Franklin's Privateers*, 174. Some seamen from the Continental Navy, such as Stephen Gregory of the captured frigate *Confederacy*, were still sent to English gaols. See Stephen Gregory to Benjamin Franklin, 3 September 1781, Ms. APS, Copy, Papers of Benjamin Franklin.

7. Bowden, "Diary of William Wigder," 73: 311–47, 74: 22–48, 142–58; *Hampshire Chronicle*, January 1781–May 1783. Wigder stated that the news of Cornwallis's surrender was brought to them on 25 November 1781, and they celebrated the news two days later, "Diary of William Wigder," 74: 156–57.

8. Benjamin Golden to Benjamin Franklin, 2 December 1781, Ms. APS, copy,

Papers of Benjamin Franklin; Adm/M/404/405/1777–1783, NMM; Adm 98/13/14, PRO.

9. Paine, *Ships and Sailors of Old Salem,* 129–40; Sherburne, *Memoirs of Andrew Sherburne,* 77–99. The manuscript letters of Captain John Green from September 1781 through June 1782 also offer some valuable insights into captive life at Mill.

10. "List of Prisoners Committed to Old Mill Prison," 140–41, 209–12. According to this list, sailors from eighty different ships were committed to Mill during 1781. CSHS to Adm, 14 May 1782, Adm/98/14/170.

11. CSHS to Adm, 29 January 1782, Adm/98/14, 75–76, PRO; John Green to Henry Laurens, 17 February 1782, Captain John Green letterbook. In October 1781 the possibility of removing American prisoners from Forton to Shrewsbury to relieve overcrowding was discussed, but not implemented. Attorney general to earl of Hillsborough, 17 October 1781. Davies, *Documents of the American Revolution,* 19: 195. Jonathan Elkins, a former rebel soldier captured near his Vermont home in 1781 and taken initially to Canada, was one example of the several nonmariners who were transferred to British gaols at this time. For a short account of Elkins' incarceration in Mill (February–June 1782), see "Reminisces of Jonathan Elkins; From a Manuscript in the Possession of the Vermont Historical Society," *Proceedings of the Vermont Historical Society,* 1919–20 (1921): 207–9.

12. Bowden, "Diary of William Wigder," 73: 347; CSHS to Adm, 27 August, 16 October 1782; 11 February 1783, Adm/98/14/237, 262, 301.

13. Adm to CSHS, 21 April 1782, Adm/M/405/NMM; CSHS to Adm, 25 March 1783, Adm /98/14/317–18.

14. Paine, *Ships and Sailors of Old Salem,* 138–39; John Green to Thomas Digges, 20 April 1782, Captain John Green letterbook. Green also complained to American officials about Cowdry's alleged misbehavior. See John Green to Henry Laurens, 5 April 1782, Henry Laurens Papers, University of South Carolina.

15. Sherburne, *Memoirs of Andrew Sherburne,* 86.

16. Bowden, "Diary of William Wigder," 73: 328–35, 336, 338; 74: 30, 37, 41, 42, 45, 142, 145. If Wigder's portrayal is accurate, Keeper Cowdry's mellowing toward the Americans might also have been the result of increasing antiwar sentiment then pervasive throughout much of Britain. It might also be due to the large number of non-English speaking nationals that the keeper now had to supervise.

17. Benjamin Golden to Benjamin Franklin, 2 December 1781, William Hodgson to Benjamin Franklin, 7 June 1782, Mss. APS, copies, Papers of Benjamin Franklin.

18. Adm to CSHS, 30 July, 10 August, 17 October, 2 November 1781, Adm/M/405 NMM ; John Allyer, John Grant, William Sheffield to Adm, 13 August 1781; Captain William Fitzwilliam to Adm, 2, 12 November 1781, Adm 98/13/427–28, 503, 512, PRO.

19. Bowden, "Diary of William Wigder," 73: 336, 338, 341, 342, 344, 74: 22, 37, 45, 144, 153, 155.

20. Adm to CSHS, 3 April 1782 Adm/M/405 NMM; Golden to Franklin, 2 December 1781, Ms. APS, Copy, Papers of Benjamin Franklin.

21. Sherburne, *Memoirs of Andrew Sherburne,* 86–87.

22. Paine, *Ships and Sailors of Old Salem,* 135, 139.

23. Bowden,"Diary of William Wigder," 74: 30, 38, 156.

24. Thomas Wren to William Hodgson, 8 January 1781; Samuel Hubbard to Benjamin Franklin, 12 February 1781; Samuel Harris to Benjamin Franklin, 12 June 1781; William Hodgson to Benjamin Franklin, 9 January, 18 September,

1781; 15 January, 22 February 1782; Mss. APS, copies, Papers of Benjamin Franklin; "List of Mill Prisoners," 136.

25. Paine, *Ships and Sailors of Old Salem,* 129 n, 139; Sherburne, *Memoirs of Andrew Sherburne,* 80–81.

26. Bowden, "Diary of William Wigder," 73: 314, 322, 343, 344; 74: 24, 26, 29, 39–40, 143.

27. Adm to CSHS, 23 June 1781, Adm/M/405 NMM; CSHS to Adm, 25 June 1781, Adm/98/13/ 353, 371–73, PRO; Bowden, "Diary of William Wigder," 74: 23, 28.

28. William Hodgson to CSHS, 4 December 1781; CSHS to Adm, 27 May 1782, Adm/98/14/13, 176–77, PRO; Hodgson to Franklin, 9 January, 18 September 1781, Mss. APS, copies, Papers of Benjamin Franklin.

29. John Green to Robert Heath and Miles Saurey, 12 April 1782, Captain John Green letterbook; CSHS to Adm, 23 September 1782, 11 February 1783, Adm/98/14/ 251, 301; Jacob Smith to Benjamin Franklin, 24 January 1783, Ms. APS, copy, Papers of Benjamin Franklin. Smith, from Philadelphia, was taken aboard a privateer named *Franklin* ("List of Mill Prisoners," 212.)

30. Paine, *Ships and Sailors of Old Salem,* 129 n; Sherburne, *Memoirs of Andrew Sherburne,* 85–86. In his letterbook Captain John Green also gives occasional mention of building ship models.

31. Mill Prisoners Petition to Adm, 1 June 1781, CSHS to Adm 25 June 1781, Adm 98/13/353, 371–73. PRO; Adm to CSHS 23 June 1781, Adm/M/405. NMM; Bowden, "Diary of William Wigder," 74: 23, 28.

32. Sherburne, *Memoirs of Andrew Sherburne,* 83.

33. CSHS to Adm, 25 June 1781, Adm 98/13/371–73; Howard, *State of Prisons,* 3d ed., 187. For descriptions of prison ship confinement, note these works, some of which have already been cited: Danske Dandridge, ed., *American Prisoners of the Revolution;* Albert G. Greene, ed., *Recollections of the Jersey Prison-Ship,* (Providence R.I.: H. H. Brown, 1829); Jesse Lemisch, "Listening to the Inarticulate"; Oliver Anderson, "The Treatment of Prisoners of War during the American War of Independence"; Henry Onderdonck, *Revolutionary Incidents of Suffolk and King's Counties* (New York: Leavitt & Company, 1849).

34. William Hodgson to CSHS, 4 December 1781, Adm 98/14/13; CSHS to Adm, 4 July 1781, Adm 98/13/381; Mill Prisoners Petition to Adm, 1 June 1781, Adm 98/13/353; CSHS to Adm, 27 May, 16 October 1782, Adm, 98/14/176–77, 258–59 PRO; Adm to CSHS, 23 January 1781, 2 March 1782, Adm/M/ 405 NMM. Dr. Farquharson had been the medical member of the Commissioners since 1778, letter to author from National Maritime Museum, 14 October 1991; Alexander, "Forton Prison," 380, 380 n; Paine, *Ships and Sailors of Old Salem,* 128, 130; Bowden,"Diary of William Wigder," 74: 40.

35. Adm to CSHS, 10 January 1782 Adm/M/405 NMM; CSHS to Adm, 11 February 1783, Adm 98/14/301 PRO.

36. Bowden, "Diary of William Wigder," 73: 326, 341, 346; 74: 40, 42, 44. It is difficult to estimate the exact percentage of illnesses among the captives at any one time.

37. Paine, *Ships and Sailors of Old Salem,* 134–35; John Green to Thomas Digges, 7 June 1782, Captain John Green letterbook.

38. Sherburne, *Memoirs of Andrew Sherburne,* 90–96.

39. Adm to CSHS, 5 June 1781, Adm/M/405 NMM; Nicholas Rogers, "Liberty Road: Opposition to Impressment in Britain during the American War of Independence," in *Jack Tar in History,* eds. Howell and Twomey, 53–75; James, *The*

British Navy in Adversity, chaps. XIX–XXI; Tilley, *British Navy in the American Revolution,* 277–78, 280–81.

40. Figures on the number of defectors are based on lists sent by the Commissioners for Sick and Hurt Seamen to the Admiralty and noted in Adm 98/13 and Adm 98/14 PRO, and in pardons forwarded by the Admiralty to the Commissioners, Adm/M/405 NMM.

41. Shubal Clark pardon, Adm to CSHS, 2, 20 March 1782 Adm/M/405 NMM; Charles F. Jenkins, "John Claypoole's Memorandum-Book," *Pennsylvania Magazine of History and Biography,* 16 (July 1892): 186. Another exception was a few captives who sought to serve on East India Company ships. See for example, CSHS to Adm, 28 November 1781, Adm/98/14/9, PRO.

42. Benjamin Golden to Benjamin Franklin, 2 December 1781, Samuel Harris to Benjamin Franklin, 12 June 1781; Gustavus Conyngham to Benjamin Franklin, 21 June 1781; Mss. APS, copies, Papers of Benjamin Franklin.

43. Paine, *Ships and Sailors of Old Salem,* 125, 126; Sherburne, *Memoirs of Andrew Sherburne,* 83, 87.

44. Bowden, "Diary of William Wigder," 73: 331, 74: 43, 146, 148.

45. Adm to CSHS, 16 February 1782, Adm/M/405 NMM. The number of escape attempts is based on those listed for this time period in Adm/98/13 and Adm 98/14 PRO.

46. Raithby, *Statutes at Large,* 15: 255, 282–83; CSHS to Adm, 12 April 1782, Adm/M/405 NMM.

47. Paine, *Ships and Sailors of Old Salem,* 130; Bowden,"Diary of William Wigder," 73: 342; CSHS to Adm, 12 November 1782, Adm/98/13/504–5, PRO; Adm to CSHS, 25 August 1782, Adm/M/405 NMM.

48. Michael Bright, Champon Wood, Levy Younger, Bartholomew Cashman to Benjamin Franklin, 24 February 1782, Ms. APS, copy, Papers of Benjamin Franklin; Lemisch, "Listening to the Inarticulate," 18–20; Anderson, "American Escapes from British Naval Prisons," 238–40.

49. "Narrative of Lieut. Luke Matthewman," 181–83; Parramore, "Great Escape from Forten Gaol," 354–55; CSHS to Adm, 9 January 1781, Adm/98/13/181–82, PRO.

50. Sherburne, *Memoirs of Andrew Sherburne,* 87–88; Paine, *Ships and Sailors of Old Salem,* 128–40; Jenkins, "John Claypoole's Memorandum-Book," 179, 188. Neigus, formerly captain of the Dunkirk cutter *Marquis of Marbeck,* had been commited to Mill in October 1781. Colburn, "List of American Prisoners, Old Mill," 211.

51. Bowden, "Diary of William Wigder," 73: 335, 337, 340, 341–46; 74: 22–23, 37, 45–46, 143; Jenkins, "John Claypoole's Memorandum-Book," 179, 189.

52. Bowden, "Diary of William Wigder," 74: 22–23; Neeser, *Gustavus Conyngham,* xlx.

53. Barney, *Memoirs of Commodore Joshua Barney,* 89–105; Paine, *Ships and Sailors of Old Salem,* 131–33; Bowden, "Diary of William Wigder," 343.

54. Barney, *Memoirs of Commodore Joshua Barney,* 87–89.

55. Barney, *Memoirs of Commodore Joshua Barney,* 89; Bowden, "Diary of William Wigder," 73: 343.

56. Barney, *Memoirs of Commodore Joshua Barney,* 90.

57. Bowden, "Diary of William Wigder," 73: 328, LXXIV, 24; Colburn, "List of Mill Prisoners, Old Mill," 140; Jenkins, "John Claypoole's Memorandum-Book," 179, 189. In early 1782, Captain Kemp made a successful escape. See

Francis Coffyn to Benjamin Franklin, 23 April 1782, Ms. APS, copy, Papers of Benjamin Franklin.

58. "Narrative of Luke Matthewman," 182–83; CSHS to Adm, 13 August 1781, Adm/98/13/427 PRO.

59. Joshua Goss, et al. to Benjamin Franklin, 8 April 1782, Ms. APS, copy, Papers of Benjamin Franklin; Adm to CSHS, 2 March 1782. Adm/M/405 NMM.

60. Edwin Welch, "Andrew Kinsman's Churches at Plymouth," *Transactions of the Devonshire Historical Association* 97 (1965): 212–36; Barney, *Memoirs of Commodore Joshua Barney,* 90–105.

61. "Narrative of Lieut. Luke Matthewman," 183; Parramore, "The Great Escape from Forten Gaol," 355.

62. "Narrative of Lieut. Luke Matthewman," 183; Clark, "In Defense of Thomas Digges," 428. The trial was held for Captains Edward Macatter, John Kelly, and Luke Ryan who commanded American commissioned privateers. Apparently some of their crew members were also tried (see note 89).

63. John Adams to Benjamin Franklin, 19 October 1781, Ms. APS, copy Papers of Benjamin Franklin.

64. Sherburne, *Memoirs of Andrew Sherburne,* 83.

65. Paine, *Ships and Sailors of Old Salem,* 128–29; Bowden, "Diary of William Wigder," 73: 319, 324, 339, 74: 48.

66. Bowden, "Diary of William Wigder," 74:, 40, 148.

67. Ibid., 73: 326, 341–42, 346, 74: 40, 148, 156.

68. Quinn, *Love Letters to Mike,* 73–74, 163, 242–43; Bowden, "Diary of William Wigder," 73: 347. See also Lemisch, "Listening to the Inarticulate," 5–6.

69. Paine, *Ships and Sailors of Old Salem,* 129; John Green to Lieutenant General [William] Haviland, 20 October 1781, John Green letterbook. Similar mention of the remark in Parliament was made by William Wigder. See Bowden, "Diary of William Wigder," 73: 323.

70. Thomas Wren to Benjamin Franklin, 5 December 1782; Benjamin Franklin to William Hodgson, 10 December 1783; Benjamin Franklin to Thomas Wren, 26 February 1780; Thomas Wren to William Hodgson, 8 January, 13 February, 27 February 1781, Mss. APS, DLC, copies, Papers of Benjamin Franklin; Cohen, "Thomas Wren, Portsmouth's Patron," 18–20. Wren also kept in contact with prisoners at Mill. See, for example, John Green to Thomas Wren, 19 September 1781, Captain John Green letterbook.

71. Thomas Wren to William Hodgson, 13, 27 February 1781, WR [Thomas Digges] to Benjamin Franklin, 29 December 1780; Benjamin Franklin to Thomas Digges, 5 December 1780; William Hodgson to Benjamin Franklin, 20 March, 8 May, 29 June, 21 December 1781, Mss APS, PHS, Copies, Papers of Benjamin Franklin; Clark, "In Defense of Thomas Digges," 424–31; Prelinger, "Franklin and the American Prisoners," 288–89.

72. Paine, *Ships and Sailors of Old Salem,* 128, 136, 140; Bowden, "Diary of William Wigder," 73: 321–22, 329, 74: 26, 46, 47; John Green to Thomas Digges, 18 June 1782, Captain John Green letterbook; John Green to Henry Laurens, 19 February 1782, Henry Laurens Papers. Visiting ship captains and local residents also continued providing aid to the Mill and Forton captives.

73. Cohen, "The Preachers and the Prisoners," 7–11; William Hodgson to Benjamin Franklin, 10 March 1780, Ms. APS, copy, Papers of Benjamin Franklin.

74. Paine, *Ships and Sailors of Old Salem,* 128, 136, 140; Bowden, "Diary of William Wigder," 73: 320–22, 329, 74: 39, 45; Miles Saurey to William Hodgson, 10 February 1781, Ms. APS, copy, Papers of Benjamin Franklin; Miles Saurey to

David Hartley, 5 March 1782, message appended to a 3 March 1782 letter of John Green to Henry Laurens, Henry Laurens Papers.

75. Sir Lewis Namier and John Brooke, eds., *The History of Parliament: The House of Commons, 1754–1790* (New York: Oxford University Press, 1964), 2: 592–93; David Hartley to Benjamin Franklin 11, 12, 21 March 1782; Benjamin Franklin to David Hartley, 5 April, 13 May 1782, Mss. Massachusetts Historical Society, hereinafter referred to as MHi, and APS, copies, Papers of Benjamin Franklin; Thomas Digges to John Adams, 2 March, 2, 9, 16, 23 April 1782; Elias and Fitch, *Letters of Thomas Digges,* 362–64, 371–77.

76. Namier and Brooke, *The History of Parliament,* 2: 594; *Papers of Benjamin Franklin,* 22: 200 n; CSHS to Adm, 16 April, 1, 8 June, 1781. Adm/98/13/313 PRO; Bowden, "Diary of William Wigder," 73: 328; 74: 23, 28; Paine, *Ships and Sailors of Old Salem,* 139.

77. Thomas Digges to Benjamin Franklin, 29 December 1780; William Hodgson to Benjamin Franklin 9 January, 20 March 1781, Mss. PHS, APS, copies, Papers of Benjamin Franklin; Clark, "In Defense of Thomas Digges," 425–27; Elias and Fitch, *Letters of Thomas Digges,* 343–45.

78. Benjamin Franklin to William Hodgson, 1, 25 April 1781; William Hodgson to Benjamin Franklin, 12 April, 8 May, 29 June, 20 July 1781, Mss. DLC, copies, Papers of Benjamin Franklin; Clark, "In Defense of Thomas Digges," 427–37; Prelinger, "Franklin and the American Prisoners," 288–89; Bowden, "Diary of William Wigder," 73: 347, 74: 150.

79. William Digges to David Hartley [? 1782], in Hartley-Russell Papers, D/EHy/040, 27a; Benjamin Franklin to David Hartley, 5 April 1782, DLC, Copy, Papers of Benjamin Franklin; Elias and Fitch, *Letters of Thomas Digges,* 367–76; Clark, "In Defense of Thomas Digges," 431–36.

80. Clark, "In Defense of Thomas Digges," 436–37; Elias and Fitch, *Letters of Thomas Digges,* 377; CSHS to Adm, 31 May, 17 July, 1782, Adm 98/14/178, 211–12 PRO.

81. Thomas Digges to John Green, 11 June 1782; Elias and Fitch, *Letters of Thomas Digges,* 378–79; Clark, "In Defense of Thomas Digges," 435–36; Benjamin Franklin to Robert Livingston, 25 June 1782, Ms. National Archives, hereinafter referred to as DNA, copy, Papers of Benjamin Franklin. One example of the disrespect that American agents had for Thomas Digges can be found in a letter dated 21 May 1782 from Francis Coffyn in Dunkirk to Moses Young (Henry Laurens's secretary) in Brussels. In the letter Coffyn declares that Digges had not delivered books that Young had given the Marylander to take to Franklin's agent in Dunkirk (Hartley-Russell Papers D/EHy/040, 18a).

82. William Hodgson to Benjamin Franklin, letters from 20 March 1781 to 18 April 1783 (letter on Witherspoon's release 4 September 1781); Benjamin Franklin to William Hodgson, letters from 1 April 1 1781 to 14 January 1783, Mss. APS, PHS, copies, Papers of Benjamin Franklin; Prelinger, "Franklin and the American Prisoners," 289–90; Harrison, *Princetonians,* 2: 355–56.

83. CSHS to Adm. 31 October, 4 December 1781, Adm/98/13/493, Adm/98/14/13, PRO; Adm to CSHS 12 September 1781, 23 April 1782, Adm/M/405 NMM; William Hodgson to Benjamin Franklin, 22 March, 9, 14 April, 10 May, 7 June, 13 July 1782; Benjamin Franklin to William Hodgson, 26 April, 27 May 1782, Mss. Public Record Office Kew, and APS, PHS, copies, Papers of Benjamin Franklin; Bowden, "Diary of William Wigder," 73: 47, 143. Prelinger, "Franklin and the American Prisoners," 290.

84. William Hodgson to Benjamin Franklin, 13 July, 1782, Ms. PHS, copy, Papers of Benjamin Franklin.

85. Shipton, *Sibley's Harvard Graduates,* 15: 220, Sherburne, *Memoirs of Andrew Sherburne,* 84–85; Bowden,"Diary of William Wigder," 74: 43.

86. Considerable correspondence between Benjamin Franklin and Coffyn, Williams, and Bondfield relating to the prisoners can be found in published and manuscript Papers of Benjamin Franklin. John Adams in Amsterdam also had dealings in these matters with the agents. See, for example, Francis Coffyn to John Adams, 2 October 1782, John Adams Papers, Massachusetts Historical Society.

87. Page Smith, *John Adams* (Garden City N.Y.: Doubleday, 1962), 1: chap. 35; L. H. Butterfield and Marc Friedlander, eds., *Adams Family Correspondence* (Cambridge Mass.: Belknap Press, 1973), 4: 258–61; John Adams to Benjamin Franklin, 18 October 1781, Ms. APS, copy, Papers of Benjamin Franklin.

88. Prelinger, "Franklin and the American Prisoners," 288–91; "Alphabetical List of the American Prisoners," Ms. APS, copy, Papers of Benjamin Franklin.

89. Mary Macatter and Amy Kelly to Benjamin Franklin, 12 September 1782, Ms. APS, copy, Papers of Benjamin Franklin; Clark, "In Defense of Thomas Digges," 436–37. Edward Macatter and Luke Ryan, who commanded another of Franklin's privateers, were tried in London for piracy, found guilty, and sentenced to death but were pardoned after the intercession of the French government. John Kelly was perhaps a crewman on Macatter's privateer, who was also confined in London. Apparently his name was not an alias for Luke Ryan. See Clark, *Benjamin Franklin's Privateers,* 174–75.

90. Daniel Edwards, Joshua Goss, et. al. to Benjamin Franklin, 8 April 1782, Ms. APS, copy, Papers of Benjamin Franklin.

91. Michael Bright, Champon Wood, Levy Yonger [Younger], Bartholomew Cashman to Benjamin Franklin, 24 February 1782; Nathaniel Fanning to Benjamin Franklin, 23 November 1782, 27 January 1783. (Fanning claimed he was imprisoned by a false charge of "pillaging a neutral vessel.") Mss APS, copies, Papers of Benjamin Franklin.

92. Hector St. John Crèvecoeur to Benjamin Franklin, 27 August, 26 September 1781, Mss. APS, copies, Papers of Benjamin Franklin. See also Stanley T. Williams in *DAB,* "Crèvecoeur, Michel-Guilloume Jean de."

93. Petition of Mill Prisoners, 1 June 1781, CSHS to Adm, Adm/98/13/353 PRO; Gustavus Conyngham to Benjamin Franklin, 21 June 1781, Ms. APS, copy, Papers of Benjamin Franklin; Bowden, "Diary of William Wigder," 74: 36.

94. Francis Coffyn to Benjamin Franklin, 10 March, 29 July, 29 December 1781; John Adams to Benjamin Franklin, 18 October 1781, Mss. APS, copies, Papers of Benjamin Franklin; Prelinger, "Franklin and the American Prisoners," 282–83.

95. Committee for Foreign Affairs to Benjamin Franklin, 9 May 1781; James Lovell to Benjamin Franklin, 9 May 1781; William Hodgson to Benjamin Franklin, 4 September 1781; Benjamin Franklin to William Hodgson, 8 August 1781; Benjamin Franklin to Dr. John Witherspoon, Jr., 11 September 1781; Benjamin Franklin to James Lovell, 5 November 1781; William Temple Franklin to John Witherspoon, 13 September 1781; Mss. APS, DLC, DNA, copies, Papers of Benjamin Franklin.

96. William Hodgson to Benjamin Franklin, 28 March, 12 May, 11 August 1780, 18 September, 30 October 1781, 15 January 1782; Thomas Digges to Benjamin Franklin, 24 May, 18 August 1780; Benjamin Franklin to William Hodgson, 5, 19 November 1781, Mss. University of Michigan, William Clements Library,

hereinafter referred to as MiU-C, APS, PHS, DLC, copies, Papers of Benjamin Franklin; CSHS to Adm, 20 August, 11 September, 31 October 1781, Adm/98/13/ 439–40, 455, 493 PRO; Adm to CSHS, 12 September, 12 November 1781, Adm/ M/405 NMM; Greenwood, *Captain John Manley,* 120; John Green to David Strachen & Co., 17 January 1782, Captain John Green letterbook.

97. Benjamin Franklin to William Hodgson, 5, 19 November 1781, Mss. DLC, MiU-C, copies, Papers of Benjamin Franklin; CSHS to Adm, 4 December 1781, Adm/98/14/13 PRO.

98. David D. Wallace, *The Life of Henry Laurens* (New York: G. P. Putnam's sons, 1915), 358–94; "A Narrative of the Capture of Henry Laurens," South Carolina Historical Society, *Collections,* 1 (1857): 19–59; Moses Young to Benjamin Franklin, 5 February, 8 July 1782, Mss. APS, copies, Papers of Benjamin Franklin.

99. Wallace, *Life of Henry Laurens,* 391–95; "Laurens Narrative," 61–68; Paine, *Ships and Sailors of Old Salem,* 136; Sherburne, *Memoirs of Andrew Sherburne,* 89; Adm to CSHS, 27 February 1782, Adm/M/405, NMM; John Green to Henry Laurens, 8 April 1782, Captain John Green letterbook; John Green to Henry Laurens, 3, 27 March, 5 April 1782; Henry Laurens to John Green, 2 May 1782, Henry Laurens Papers.

100. Benjamin Franklin to Robert Livingston, 4 March 1782; Benjamin Franklin to John Adams, 21 April 1782; Benjamin Franklin to William Hodgson 5, 22, 24, 26 April 1782; William Hodgson to Benjamin Franklin, 22 March, 9, 11, 14, April, 10 May 1782; Lord Shelburne to Benjamin Franklin, 7 April, 21 May 1782, Mss. APS, DNA, DLC, MHi, PRO, MiU-C, copies, Papers of Benjamin Franklin; *Parliamentary History of England,* 22: 1103–5; Raithby, *Statutes at Large,* 15: 255; Prelinger, "Franklin and the American Prisoners," 290; CSHS to Adm, 19 April 1782, Adm 98/14/146–49 PRO; Adm to CSHS, 11 May 1782, Adm 405/ M/NMM.

101. Evan Nepean to William Hodgson, 7 April 1782 in Davies, *Documents of the American Revolution,* vol. 19 Calendar, 280; Benjamin Franklin to William Hodgson, 13, 26, April 1782; William Hodgson to Benjamin Franklin, 9, 14, April, 10 May 1782, Conditions of the exchange of Prisoners with America, 8 May 1782, Mss. APS, PRO, copies, Papers of Benjamin Franklin; John Green to Magnus Miller, 16 May 1782, Captain John Green letterbook. In a letter to Henry Laurens dated 24 May 1782, Captain Green claimed that 654 Americans were then jammed into Mill. See Henry Laurens Papers.

102. William Hodgson to Benjamin Franklin, 7 June 1782; Benjamin Franklin to Robert Livingston, 25 June 1782, Mss. APS, DNA, copies, Papers of Benjamin Franklin; CSHS to Adm, 15, 27 May, 5 June 1782, Adm 98/14/171, 176–77, 182–83 PRO; Adm to CSHS, 2 March 1782, Adm/M/405, NMM; Paine, *Ships and Sailors of Old Salem,* 139–40; John Green to Thomas Digges, 18 June 1782; American prisoners to the Duke of Richmond, 19 June 1782, Captain John Green letterbook; Prelinger, "Franklin and the American Prisoners," 290–91.

103. Paine, *Ships and Sailors of Old Salem,* 139–40; Adm to CSHS, 16 March 1782, Adm/M/405 NMM. A month before this exchange, William Hodgson noted that two of the Americans held at Mill wished to remain in Britain, while twenty-three others "who were taken in French ships. . . . wish to go to France to settle business." See William Hodgson to Evan Napean, 18 May 1782, in Davies, *Documents of the American Revolution,* vol. 19, Calendar, 299.

104. William Hodgson to Benjamin Franklin, 13 July 1782, Ms. HSP, copy, Papers of Benjamin Franklin.

105. Mill Prisoners to Lord Shelburne, 1 September 1782, Manuscript Division, Library of Congress, Lans. 1219: fo. 61; CSHS to Adm, 28 August, 23 September, 16 October 1782, Adm 98/14/240, 251, 262 PRO.

106. CSHS to Adm, 22 July, 16 October, 28 October 1782, 27 February 1783, Adm 98/14/214, 262, 271, 308 PRO.

107. William Hodgson to Benjamin Franklin, 14 October, 14 November, 12 December 1782, Mss. APS, copies, Papers of Benjamin Franklin.

108. William Hodgson to Benjamin Franklin, 8 January 1783, Ms. APS, copy, Papers of Benjamin Franklin.

109. Benjamin Franklin to William Hodgson, 14 January 1783, Ms. APS, copy, Papers of Benjamin Franklin.

110. CSHS to Adm, 11 February 1783, Adm/98/14/301 PRO; Jacob Smith to Benjamin Franklin, 24 January 1783, Ms. APS, copy, Papers of Benjamin Franklin.

111. Adm to CSHS, 3 March 1783, Adm/M/405 NMM; CSHS to Adm, 25 March 1783, Adm/98/14/317–18 PRO; William Hodgson to Benjamin Franklin, 25 March 1783, Ms. APS, copy, Papers of Benjamin Franklin.

112. CSHS to Adm, 21 April, 10 June, 1783. Adm /98/14/346, 355–56 PRO.

113. Doyle, *Voices from Captivity,* 10–11; John Charretie to Benjamin Franklin, 17 January 1784; James Leveux to Benjamin Franklin, 2, 30 March 1784; Benjamin Franklin to James Leveux, 8 March 1784; List of Escaped Prisoners, 10 July 1785; Benjamin Franklin to Schweighauser and Dobree, 16 August 1783; Jonathan Williams, Jr., to William Temple Franklin, 10 July 1785; Andrew Limozin to Benjamin Franklin [c. 1786], Mss. APS, copies, Papers of Benjamin Franklin.

Chapter 7. Epilogue

1. CSHS to Adm, 21 April, 18 June 1783, Adm/98/14/346, 358 PRO; James Walsh to Benjamin Franklin, 4 January 1783; John Butler to Benjamin Franklin, 15 July 1783; John Audley to Benjamin Franklin, 26 July 1783, Mss. APS, copies, Papers of Benjamin Franklin. New Hampshire seaman Eli Bickford made the inaccurate claim that he was not released from an English prison until after the Paris Peace Treaty was signed in September 1783 (Dandridge, *Prisoners of the American Revolution,* 179.)

2. *Hampshire Chronicle,* 14 April 1783; CSHS to Adm, 21 April, 20 August 1783; CSHS to Adm, 21 April, 20 August 1783, Adm/M/405, NMM.

3. Deborah E. Carr, *Index to Certified Copy of Lists of American Prisoners of War, 1812–1815* (Washington D.C.: n.p., 1924), 1–23; General Entry Books for American Prisoners of War, 1812–1815, Adm 103 ser. Plymouth, 268–70 PRO; Ms. Elisabeth Stuart, Senior Assistant Archivist, Devon Record Office, to author, 5 September 1990; Paul Brough, Senior Assistant Archivist, Devon Record Office, to author, 7 September 1992. Ira Dye, who has examined prisoner of war records for the years 1812–15, estimates that approximately ninety-four hundred Americans were held captive in Britain during this period. Of this number, only two to three hundred were detained at Mill (Ira Dye to author, 9 January 1993.)

4. Diane Venables, "Forton Barracks, 1807–1923," *Gosport Records* 12 (1976): 20–24. Additional information concerning Forton Prison was supplied through the courtesy of Sarah Quail, Portsmouth City Records Office.

5. Cornelius Ryan, *The Longest Day: June 6, 1944* (New York: Simon and Schuster, 1959), 36–38, 40, 41, 67, 70; John Keegan, *Six Armies in Normandy:*

From D-Day to the Liberation of Paris (New York: Viking Penguin, 1984), 65–66; Julie Gardiner, *Overpaid, Oversexed, and Over Here: The American GI in World War II Britain* (New York: Abbeville Press, 1992), 28, 113, 116, 202.

6. Isaac Kramnick, *The Rage of Edmund Burke: Portrait of an Ambivalent Conservative* (New York: Basic Books, 1977), 129–96; Frank O' Gorman, *Edmund Burke, His Political Philosophy* (Bloomington, Ind.: Indiana University Press, 1973), chap. VI; George H. Guttridge, *David Hartley M.P.: An Advocate of Conciliation* (Berkeley: University of California Press, 1926), 301–32; Owen Sherrard, *A Life of John Wilkes* (New York: Dodd, Mead & Co., 1930), 302–9; Namier and Brooke, *The History of Parliament,* 2: 152–53, 592–94, 3: 640.

7. G. F. Russell Barker in *DNB,* s.v. "Lennox, Charles, Third Duke of Richmond"; J A. Hamilton in *DNB,* s.v., "Bertie Willoughby, Fourth Earl of Abingdon"; Paine, *Ships and Sailors of Old Salem,* 138–39.

8. Thompson Cooper in *DNB,* s.v. "Hodgson, William." Saurey's note was attached to a letter sent by Captain John Green to Henry Laurens on 5 April 1782. See Henry Laurens Papers.

9. Clark, "In Defense of Thomas Digges," 436–38.

10. Cohen, "The Preachers and the Prisoners," 2–26. (The Bible passage is 1 Jn. 2:10.) Searches in England have uncovered no information concerning the postwar career of Miles Saurey, Deacon Heath's colleague.

11. Cohen, "The Preachers and the Prisoners," 11–12.

12. Cohen, "Thomas Wren, Portsmouth's Patron," 20–23; Cohen, "Thomas Wren, Ministering Angel," 296–98.

13. Richard Price to Marquis of Lansdowne, 10 November 1787, Ms. Bowood, National Library of Wales; "4 November 1787 entry Richard Price's Journal," *National Library of Wales Journal* 21 (1980): 391; Cohen, "Thomas Wren, Portsmouth's Patron," 3, 23; *Gentlemans' Magazine* 57, pt. 2: 1026–27. Wren's will, probated in May 1788, left his estate to his sister, Sarah Frearson of Ulverston (Public Record Office, Chancery Lane, London).

14. John Bigelow, *The Life of Benjamin Franklin* (Philadelphia: J. P. Lippincott Company, 1905), 3: chaps. 7–13; Alfred O. Aldridge, *Benjamin Franklin, Philosopher and Man* (Philadelphia: Lippincott, 1965), chaps. 34–37; Verner W. Crane, *Benjamin Franklin and a Rising People* (New York: Little Brown, 1954), 192–204; Esmond Wright, *Franklin of Philadelphia* (Cambridge, Mass.: Harvard University Press, 1986), 338–60.

15. Page Smith, *John Adams* (New York: Doubleday, 1962), vol. 2, 628–30; Robert A. East, *John Adams* (Boston: Twayne, 1979), 64–100; Gilbert Chinard, *Honest John Adams,* vol. 2, 1784–1826.

16. E. James Ferguson, John Catanzariti Smith, Mary A. Gallagher, eds., *The Papers of Robert Morris, 1781–1784* (Pittsburgh: University of Pittsburgh Press, 1975), 2: 45–46 n; Jonathan Williams, Jr., *Papers of Benjamin Franklin,* 1: "Genealogy," lvii; *Papers of Benjamin Franklin,* 24: 403 n; Mildred E. Lombard in *DAB,* s.v. "Williams, Jonathan, Jr."; Francis Coffyn to Benjamin Franklin, 11 October 1783; Benjamin Franklin to Mme. de Mollien, 4 March 1784; J. Ingen Housz to Benjamin Franklin, 11 June 1785, 1 January 1787; J. Ingen Housz to Samuel Vaughan, Jr., 1 January 1786, 20 May 1787, Mss. APS, copies, Papers of Benjamin Franklin; *Columbian* (Massachusetts) *Centinel,* 15 July 1795.

17. Barney, *Memoirs of Commodore Joshua Barney,* chaps. 10–19; "[Pennsylvania] Letters of Marque, 1778–1782," 654; Edward Breck in *DAB,* s.v. "Barney, Joshua."

18. Neeser, *Gustavus Conyngham,* 203–22; Paullin, s.v. "Conyngham";

Greenwood, *Captain John Manley,* 126–40; Peabody, "Naval Career of Capt. John Manley," 24–27.

19. Samuel Woodhouse, "The Voyage of the *Empress of China," Pennsylvania Magazine of History and Biography* 63 (January 1939): 24–36; William B. Clark, ed., "Journal of the Ship *Empress of China" American Neptune* 10 (1950): 83–107; Thibault, "Captain from the Country," 5–12, Carrow Thibault Papers.

20. Ms. Will of George Ralls, February 1799 probate, Loudon County Will Book F. 1797–1803, 474–75; *Virginia Gazette,* 14 August 1779; William W. Hening, *The Statutes at Large, Being a Collection of All the Laws of Virginia,* (Richmond: Samuel Pleasants, Jr., 1823), 13: 580–81; Stewart, *History of Virginia's Navy,* 28–33; Coan, "Journal of Dr. Jonathan Haskins," 290–91. Dr. John Witherspoon, Jr., who may have been temporarily detained at Mill, reportedly died at sea in the summer of 1795. Harrison, *Princetonians, 1769–1775,* 356.

21. Morse, *Genealogical Record of Several Families Bearing the Name Cutler,* 38–40.

22. Livesey, *Prisoners of 1776,* 13–16.

23. Bowden, "Diary of William Wigder," 73: 311–12; Paine, *Ships and Sailors of Old Salem,* 120, 147–48.

24. Winslow, "Wealth and Honour," 57–58; Sherburne, *Memoirs of Andrew Sherburne,* 104–286.

25. Abraham Foote, *Foote Family,* 1: 541; "Letters and Sea Journal of Caleb Foot," 90, 99 n 114–20; Shipton, *Sibley's Harvard Graduates,* 17: 167; "Diary of George Thompson," 221.

26. Bridge, *Portrait of My Mother,* 34–36; Hinman, *Catalogue of the First Puritan Settlers,* 816–18; Barnes, *Memoirs of Nathaniel Fanning,* xix–xx, 31–103.

27. Rogers, "Capt. Charles Bulkeley's Narrative," 125, 127–29; Ms. narrative, Charles Bulkeley, New London County Historical Society.

28. "Narrative of Lieut. Luke Matthewman," 184–85.

29. American Antiquarian Society, *Index of Obituaries in the Massachusetts Centinel and the Columbian Centinel, 1784–1840* (Boston: G. K. Hall, 1961), 1: 888; Delwyn Associates, Substitutes for Georgia's Lost 1790 Census, Typescript (Albany Ga., 1975), 42; Ms. Affidavit of James Innes, Williamsburg, Va., 9 February 1784; Virginia State Library's McCaw Catalogue, "John Harris of the Virginia Navy," 171–72; Gwathmey, *Historical Register of Virginians in the Revolution,* 222; Stewart, *History of Virginia's Navy,* 180.

30. "A Report of the Records Commissioners of the City of Boston," *Boston Town Records , 1778–1783* (Boston: Municipal Printing Office, 1895), 306; Department of Commerce and Labor, *Heads of Families at the First Census of the United States Taken in the Year 1790, Massachusetts* (Washington D.C.: Government Printing Office, 1908), 191; Edward W. Hanson, Massachusetts Historical Society to author, 27 April 1993; John Alexander, "Jonathan Carpenter and the American Revolution: The Journal of an American Naval Prisoner of War and Vermont Indian Fighter," *Vermont History* 36, no. 2 (1968): 74, 85–90; *Vermont Historical Society Gazetteer* 1: 1050.

31. Lemisch, "Listening to the Inarticulate," 9–10.

32. Paine, *Ships and Sailors of Old Salem,* 120, 147; Sherburne, *Memoirs of Andrew Sherburne,* 109–14.

33. Doyle, *Voices from Captivity,* 1–295; Lemisch, "Listening to the Inarticulate," 1–29. Other previously cited scholars who have contributed excellent writings on this topic include Olive Anderson, Catherine Prelinger, and John Alexander. A worthwhile though more general work on the subject of American

war prisoners during the conflict is William R. Lindsey, "Treatment of American Prisoners of War During the Revolution," *The Emporia State Research Studies* 22, no. 1 (Summer 1973): 5–32.

34. Livesey, *Prisoners of 1776,* 68, 90, 107, 115–16, 145–46; Abell, Prisoners of War in Britain, 284–86; Bowden, "Diary of William Wigder," 73: 343, 345, 74: 22, 31–32; Sherburne, *Memoirs of Andrew Sherburne,* 83, 85–87. For a description of similar self-regulating bodies among American prisoners in a later war, see Arthur A. Durand, *Stalag Luft III, The Secret Story* (Baton Rouge La.: Louisiana State University Press, 1987).

35. Cohen, "Thomas Wren, Portsmouth's Patron," 14–16; "Diary of George Thompson," 225, 229; CSHS to Adm, 27 January 1779, 98/11/442–44 PRO; Adm to CSHS, 16 February 1779, Adm/M/404, NMM.

36. Livesey, *Prisoners of 1776,* 45–47, 52–53, 56, 62–63; Sherburne, *Memoirs of Andrew Sherburne,* 87–88.

37. Barnes, *Memoirs of Nathaniel Fanning,* 15; Carey, *A Sailor's Songbag,* 24–153.

38. Barnes, *Memoirs of Nathaniel Fanning,* 10, 12; Cutler, "Samuel Cutler's Diary," 186.

39. Jonathan Carpenter Journal, 29 May 1779; Bowden, "Diary of William Wigder," 74: 41–42, 47.

40. Bowden, "Diary of William Wigder," 74: 142; John Green to Lieutenant General [William] Haviland, 20 October 1781, Captain John Green Letterbook, Carrow Thibault Papers. For other details regarding prisoner escape attempts, see chaps. 3–6.

41. "Alphabetical List of the American Prisoners." See chaps. 3–6 for related information about prisoner escapes.

42. Livesey, *Prisoners of 1776,* 93; Carey, *A Sailor's Songbag,* 24–153.

43. Middlekauff, *The Glorious Cause,* 296, 342, 419, 498, 508, 510; Lemisch, "Listening to the Inarticulate," 17.

44. Morison, *John Paul Jones,* 166; Greene, *Recollections of the Jersey Prisonship,* 180; Lemisch, "Listening to the Inarticulate," 19.

45. Charles C. Tansill, ed., *Documents Illustrative of the Formation of the Union of the United States* (Washington, D.C.: Government Printing Office, 1927), 875; Max Ferrand, ed., *The Records of the Federal Convention of 1787* (New Haven: Yale University Press, 1911), 2: 208.

46. Cohen, "Thomas Wren, Portsmouth's Patron," 3; Fowler, *Rebels under Sail,* 246–99; Reverend John Sturges, (ret.) John Pounds Memorial Church (Portsmouth) to author, 10 February, 1987; Elisabeth Stuart to author, 6 September, 1990. The articles referred to and previously cited in the text are those by John Alexander, Jesse Lemisch, and Catherine Prelinger.

Appendix

1. Bowden, "Diary of William Wigder," 73: 312–47, 74: 22–48, 143–58.

2. Alexander, "Jonathan Carpenter and the American Revolution," 75–76.

3. John K. Alexander, "Jonathan Haskins' Mill Prison Diary: Can It be Accepted at Face Value?" *New England Quarterly* 40 (1967): 561–64.

Bibliography

Printed Sources

Articles

Alexander, John "American Privateersmen in the Mill Prison During 1777–1782, an Evaluation." *Essex Institute Historical Collections* 102 (October 1966): 318–40.

———. "Forton Prison During the American Revolution: A Case Study of British Prisoner of War Policy and the American Response to that Policy." *Essex Institute Historical Collections* 103 (October 1967): 365–89.

———. "Jonathan Carpenter and the American Revolution; The Journal of an American Naval Prisoner of War and Vermont Indian Fighter." *Vermont History* 36 (Spring 1968): 74–90.

———. "Jonathan Haskins' Mill Prison 'Diary': Can It Be Accepted At Face Value?" *New England Quarterly* 40 (December 1967): 561–64.

Anderson, Olive "American Escapes from British Naval Prisons during The War of Independence." *The Mariners' Mirror* 41 no. 3 (1955): 238–40.

———. "The Establishment of British Supremacy at Sea and the Exchange of Naval Prisoners of War, 1689–1783." *English Historical Review* 75 (January 1960): 77–89.

———. "The Treatment of Prisoners of War in Britain During the American Revolution." *Bulletin of the Institute of Historical Research* 28 (January 1955): 63–83.

Applegate, Howard "American Privateersmen in the Mill Prison During 1777–1782." *Essex Institute Historical Collections* 97 (October 1961): 303–20.

Bowden, William H. "Diary of William Wigder of Marblehead, Kept at Mill Prison, England, 1781." *Essex Institute Historical Collections* 73–74 (October 1937–January April 1938): 311–47, 23–48, 142–57.

Brown, Gerald S. "The Anglo-French Naval Crisis 1778: A Study of Conflict in the North Cabinet." *William and Mary Quarterly* (January 1956): 3–25.

Clark, William B. "In Defense of Thomas Digges." *Pennsylvania Magazine of History and Biography* 77 (October 1953): 381–438.

Clark, William B. "John the Painter." *Pennsylvania Magazine of History and Biography,* 62 (January 1939): 1–23.

Coan, Marion S., ed. "A Revolutionary Prison Diary, the Journal of Dr. Jonathan Haskins." *New England Quarterly* 17 (June–September 1944): 290–309, 424–42.

Cohen, Sheldon S. "The Preachers and the Prisoners." *Essex Institute Historical Collections* 126 (January 1990): 1–26.

Cohen, Sheldon S. "Thomas Wren, Ministering Angel of Forton Prison." *Pennsylvania Magazine of History and Biography* 102 (July 1979): 279–301.

Cohen, Sheldon S. "We Dare Oppose Them; The Connecticut State Navy in the American Revolution, 1775–1780," *The Connecticut Historical Society Bulletin* 47 (July, 1982): 74–96.

Colburn, Jeremiah "A List of American Prisoners Committed to Old Mill Prison" *New England Historical and Genealogical Register* 19 (April–July 1865): 136–141, 209–13.

Cutter, William, ed. "A Yankee Privateersman in Prison in England." *New England Historical & Genealogical Register* 30–33 (July 1876–January 1879): 343–52, 18–20, 212–13, 284–88, 70–73, 165–68, 280–86, 36–40.

"Diary of George Thompson at Newburyport Kept at Forton Prison, England, 1777–1781." *Essex Institute Historical Collections* 76 (July 1940): 221–42.

Foot, Caleb "Prison Letters and Sea Journal of Caleb Foot." *Essex Institute Historical Collections* 26 (April–June 1889): 90–122.

Jenkins, Charles F. "John Claypoole's Memorandum-Book." *Pennsylvania Magazine of History and Biography* 16 (July 1892): 178–90.

Lemisch, Jesse "Jack Tar in the Streets; Merchant Seamen in the Politics of Revolutionary America." *William and Mary Quarterly* 3d ser. 25 (July 1968): 371–407.

Lemisch, Jesse. "Listening to the Inarticulate: William Wigder's Dream and the American Prisoners' Response to that Policy." *Journal of Social History* 3 (Fall 1969): 1–29.

Lindsey, William R. "Treatment of American Prisoners of War During the American Revolution." *The Emporia State Research Studies* 22 (Summer 1973): 1–32.

McCaw, Walter D. "Captain John Harris of the Virginia Navy: A Prisoner of War in England, 1777–1779." *Virginia Magazine of History and Biography* 22 (April 1914): 160–72.

"Memoir of the Late Rev. Robert Heath." *Theological Magazine,* 9 (May 1801): 160–67.

Montgomery, Thomas L., ed. "[Pennsylvania] Letters of Marque, 1778–1782." *Pennsylvania Archives* Fifth Ser., 1 (1906): 613–59.

Moyne, Ernest J. "The Reverend William Hazlitt. A Friend of Liberty in Ireland During the American Revolution." *William and Mary Quarterly* 3d ser. 21 (April 1964): 287–97.

"Narrative of Lieut. Luke Matthewman of the Revolutionary Navy." *The Magazine of American History* 2 (March 1878): 175–85.

Parramore, Thomas C. "The Great Escape from Forten Gaol; An Incident of the Revolution." *North Carolina Historical Review* 45 (October 1968): 349–56.

Patterson, A. Temple "Portsmouth, A French Gibraltar?" *The Portsmouth Papers* 10 (September 1970): 3–17.

Peabody, Robert E. "The Naval Career of Captain John Manley of Marblehead." *Essex Institute Historical Collections* 45 (January 1909): 1–27.

Prelinger, Catherine M. "Benjamin Franklin and the American Prisoners of War in England During the American Revolution." *William and Mary Quarterly* 3d ser., 32 (April 1975): 261–94.

"Reminiscences of Jonathan Elkins; from a Manuscript in the Possession of the

Vermont Historical Society." *Proceedings of the Vermont Historical Society for the Years 1919–20* (1921): 187–211.

Sainsbury, John A. "The Pro-Americans of London, 1769–1782." *William and Mary Quarterly* 3d ser., 35 (July 1978): 423–54.

"Samuel Cutler's Diary." *New England Historical & Genealogical Register:* 32 (January–October 1878): 42–44, 184–88, 305–8, 395–8.

Turner, Eunice H. "American Prisoners of War in Britain, 1777–1783." *The Mariner's Mirror* 45 no.3 (1959): 200–06.

Venables, Diane "Forton Barracks and the Royal Haslar Hospital." *Gosport Records* 12 (September 1976): 1–27.

Webb, John "An Early Victorian Street—The High Street Old Portsmouth." *The Portsmouth Papers* 26 (March 1977): 3–22.

Welch, Edwin "Andrew Kinsman's Churches at Plymouth." *Transactions of the Devonshire Historical Association* 97 (1965): 212–36.

Williams, G. H. "The Western Defenses of Portsmouth Harbor." *The Portsmouth Papers* 30 (December 1979): 3–73.

Books

Abell, Francis *Prisoners of War in Britain, 1756–1815.* London: Humphrey Milford, 1914.

Allen, Gardner *Massachusetts Privateers of the Revolution.* Boston: Massachusetts Historical Society, 1927.

Banks, James L. *David Sproat and Naval Prisoners in the War of the Revolution.* New York: The Knickerbocker Press, 1909.

Barnes, John S. *Memoirs of Nathaniel Fanning an American Naval Officer.* New York: The New York Times, 1967.

Barnes, John S., ed., *The Logs of the Serapis, Alliance Ariel.* New York: De Vinne Press, 1911.

Barney, Mary *A Biographical Memoir of the Late Commodore Joshua Barney.* Boston: Gray and Bowen, 1832.

Bonwick, Colin *English Radicals and the American Revolution.* Chapel Hill: University of North Carolina Press, 1977.

Bowman, Larry *Captive Americans; Prisoners during the American Revolution.* Athens: Ohio University Press, 1976.

Bracken, Charles *A History of Plymouth and Her Neighbours.* Plymouth, Eng.: Underhill, 1931.

Bridge, Ann *Portrait of My Mother.* London: Chatto & Windus, 1955.

Carey, George, ed. *A Sailor's Songbag: An American Rebel in English Prisons, 1777–1779.* Amherst: University of Massachusetts Press, 1976.

Chew, Robert L. *Genealogy of the Chew Family.* Woodbury, N.J.: Gloucester County Historical Society, 1982.

Christie, Ian R. *The End of North's Ministry, 1780–1782.* London: Macmillan & Co., 1958.

Christie, Ian R. *Wars and Revolutions; Britain, 1760–1815.* Cambridge, Mass.: Harvard University Press 1982.

Christie, Ian R. *Wilkes, Wyvill and Reform; the Parliamentary Reform Movement in British Politics, 1760–1785.* London: Macmillan & Co., 1963.

Clark, William B. *Ben Franklin's Privateers, a Naval Epic of the American Revolution.* Baton Rouge: Louisiana State University Press, 1956.

Clark, William B., and William J. Morgan eds. *Naval Documents of the American Revolution.* 9 vols. Washington, D.C.: U. S. Government Printing Office, 1961–86.

Cobbett, William, comp. *The Parliamentary History of England from the Earliest Period to the Year 1803,* XIX–XXIII. London: Longman & Co., 1814.

Crane, Verner W. *Benjamin Franklin and a Rising People.* New York: Little, Brown, 1954.

Dandridge, Danske *American Prisoners of the Revolution.* Baltimore, Md.: Genealogical Publishing Co., 1967.

Davies, K. G., ed. *Documents of the American Revolution* IX–XIV. Dublin: Irish Academic Press, 1975–76.

Dorn, Walter L. *Competition for Empire, 1740–1763.* New York: Harper & Bros., 1940.

Doyle, Robert C. *Voices from Captivity, Interpreting the American POW Narrative.* Lawrence: University of Kansas Press, 1994.

Drinkwater, John *Charles James Fox.* New York: Cosmopolitan Book Corporation, 1928.

Dull, Jonathan R. *A Diplomatic History of the American Revolution.* New Haven: Yale University Press, 1985.

Ehrman, John *The Navy in the War of William III, 1689–1697.* Cambridge, Eng.: Cambridge University Press, 1953.

Elias, Robert H., and Eugene D. Finch, eds. *Letters of Thomas Attwood Digges, 1742–1821.* Columbia: University of South Carolina Press, 1982.

Ferrand, Max, ed. *The Records of the Federal Convention of 1787.* 2 vols. New Haven: Yale University Press, 1911.

Foote, Abram W., *Foote Family Genealogy.* Rutland, Vt.: Marble City Press, The Tuttle Company, 1907.

Force, Peter compiler, *American Archives,* ser. IV, V. Washington, D.C.: M. St. Claire Clarke and Peter Force, 1837–43.

Fowler William M., *Rebels under Sail; the America Navy During the Revolution.* New York: Scribner, 1976.

Gates, William G. *Illustrated History of Portsmouth.* Portsmouth, Eng.: Charpentier & Co., 1900.

Gill, Crispin *Plymouth, A New History.* Newton Abbey, Eng.: David & Charles, 1979.

Greene, Albert G., ed. *Recollections of the Jersey Prison Ship, from the Manuscript of Capt. Thomas Dring.* reprint; New York: Corinth Books, 1961.

Greenwood, Isaac J. *Captain John Manley; Second in Rank in the United States Navy, 1776–1783.* Boston: C. E. Godspeed & Co., 1915.

Guttridge, George H. *David Hartley M.P., an Advocate of Conciliation.* Berkeley: University of California Press, 1926.

Harrison, Richard A. *Princetonians, 1769–1775; A Biographical Dictionary.* Princeton, N.J.: Princeton University Press, 1987.

Hibbert, Christopher *Redcoats and Rebels, the American Revolution Through British Eyes.* New York: W. W. Norton & Co., 1990.

Hinman, R. R. *Catalogue of the First Puritan Settlers of Connecticut: A Family Record of the Descendants of Sgt. Edward Hinman.* Hartford: Tiffany and Company, 1856.

Howard, John *The State of the Prisons in England and Wales, with Preliminary Observations and an Account of Some Foreign Prisons.* Warrington, Eng.: W. Eyres, 1780, 1784.

Howell, Colin and Richard J. Twomey eds. *Jack Tar in History: Essays in the History of Maritime Life and Labour.* Fredricton, N.B.: Acadiensis Press, 1991.

James, William M. *The British Navy in Adversity.* London: Longmans & Co., 1926.

Jewitt, Llewelleyn *A History of Plymouth.* London: Simpkin, Marshall & Co., 1873.

Johnson, Allen and Dumas Malone, eds. *Dictionary of American Biography* I–XX. New York: Charles Scribner's Sons, 1928–36.

Kamikow, Marion, and Jack Kaminkow *Mariners of the American Revolution.* Baltimore: Magna Carta Book Co., 1967.

Labaree, Benjamin W.; William B. Willcox; Barbara Oberg et al., eds. *The Papers of Benjamin Franklin.* Vols. 1–30. New Haven: Yale University Press, 1959.

Lambert, Sheila, ed. *House of Commons Sessions Papers for the Eighteenth Century.* Wilmington, Del.: Scholarly Resources, 1975.

Livesey, Richard, ed. *The Prisoners of 1776; A Relic of the Revolution.* Boston: C. H. Pierce, 1854.

Mackesy, Piers *The War for America, 1775–1783.* Cambridge, Mass.: Harvard University Press, 1965.

Maclay, Edgar S. *A History of American Privateers.* New York: D. Appleton and company, 1899.

Massachusetts Soldiers and Sailors of the Revolutionary War. Vol. I–XIV. Boston: Wright & Potter Printing Co., 1896–1908.

Metzger, Charles H. *The Prisoner in the American Revolution.* Chicago: Loyola University Press, 1971.

Middlebrook, Louis F., *History of Maritime Connecticut during the American Revolution, 1775–1783.* 2 vols. Salem, Mass.: The Essex Institute, 1925.

Middlekauff, Robert *The Glorious Cause; the American Revolution, 1763–1789.* New York: Oxford University Press, 1982.

Miller, Nathan *Sea of Glory; A Naval History of the American Revolution.* Annapolis: Naval Institute Press, 1992.

Morgan, William, J. *Captains to the Northward; the New England Captains in the Continental Navy.* Barre, Mass.: Barre Gazette, 1959.

Morison, Samuel E. *The Maritime History of Massachusetts.* Boston: Houghton Mifflin Company, 1921.

Morison, Samuel E. *John Paul Jones, a Sailor's Biography.* Boston: Little Brown, 1959.

Morris, Richard *The Peacemakers, the Great Powers, and American Independence.* New York: Harper & Row, 1965.

Morse, Abner *A Biographical Record of Several Families Bearing the Name Cutler in the United States.* Boston: S. G. Drake, 1867.

Namier, Sir Lewis B., *England in the Age of the American Revolution.* London: Macmillan & Co., 1930.

Namier, Sir Lewis, and John Brooke eds. *The History of Parliament, the House of Commons, 1754–1790*. New York: Oxford University Press, 1964.

Neeser, Robert W., ed. *Letters and Papers Relating to the Cruises of Gustavus Conyngham, a Captain in the Continental Navy, 1777–1779*. New York: De Vinne Press, 1915.

O'Gorman, Frank *Edmund Burke, His Political Philosophy*. Bloomington, IN: Indiana University Press, 1973.

Paine, Ralph D. *Joshua Barney, a Forgotten Hero of Blue Water*. New York: Century Co., 1924.

Paine, Ralph D. *The Ships and Sailors of Old Salem*. Chicago: A. C. McClurg & Co., 1912.

Paullin, Charles *The Navy in the American Revolution; Its Administration Its Policy and Its Achievements*. Reprint; New York: Haskell House Publishers, 1971.

The Portsmouth Guide, or a Description of the Ancient and Present State of the Place. Portsmouth, Eng.: R. Carr, 1775.

Quarles, Benjamin *The Negro in the American Revolution*. Chapel Hill: University of North Carolina Press, 1961.

Raithby, John, ed. *The Statutes at Large of England and Great Britain*. London: Eyre and Strahan, 1811.

Richmond, Herbert W. *The Navy in the War 1739–1748*. Cambridge, Eng.: Cambridge University Press, 1920.

Rogers, Ernest E., ed. *Connecticut's Naval Office at New London during the War of the American Revolution*. New London: Self-Published, 1933.

Sainsbury, John *Disaffected Patriots; London Supporters of Revolutionary American, 1769–1782*. Kingston,Ont.: McGill-Queens University Press, 1987.

Sainty, John *Office Holders in Modern Britain, IV, Admiralty Officials, 1660–1870*. London: Althone Press, 1975.

Sherburne, Andrew *Memoirs of Andrew Sherburne; a Pensioner of the Navy of the Revolution*. Providence, R.I.: H. H. Brown, 1831.

Sherburne, John H. *Life of John Paul Jones*. New York: Adriance, Sherman & Co., 1851.

Sherrard, Owen *A Life of John Wilkes*. New York: Dodd, Mead & Co., 1930.

Shipton, Clifford K. *Biographical Sketches of Those Who Attended Harvard College in the Classes 1768–1771* (17). Boston: Massachusetts Historical Society, 1975.

Slight, Henry, and Julian Slight *Chronicles of Portsmouth*. London: Lupton Relfe, 1828.

Smith, Page *John Adams*. 2 vols New York: Doubleday, 1962.

Stephens, Leslie and Sidney Lee, eds. *Dictionary of National Biography* I–XXII. London: Oxford University Press, 1921–38.

Stewart, Robert A. *The History of Virginia's Navy of the Revolution*. Richmond, Va.: Mitchell & Hotchkiss, 1933.

Syrett, David *Shipping and the American War, 1775–1780*. London: Althone Press, 1970.

Taylor, Robert J.; Gregg L. Lint; Celeste Walker; et al., eds. *The Papers of John Adams*. Cambridge, Mass.: Belknap Press; 1953.

Thompson, Mark A. *The Secretaries of State, 1681–1782*. Oxford: Clarendon Press, 1932.

Tilley, John *The British Navy and the American Revolution*. Columbia: University of South Carolina Press, 1975.

Tuchman, Barbara *The First Salute, A View of the American Revolution*. New York: Knopf, 1988.

Wallace, David D. *The Life of Henry Laurens*. New York: G. P. Putnam's Sons, 1915.

Watson, John S. *The Reign of George III 1760–1815*. Oxford: Clarendon Press, 1960.

White, Leonard F. W. *The Story of Gosport*. Southsea, Eng.: SWP Barrell, 1966.

White, Virgil D. *Genealogical Abstracts of Revolutionary War Pension Files*. Wayneboro, Tenn.: National Historical Publishing Co., 1990.

Winslow, Richard E., III *"Wealth and Honour": Portsmouth during the Golden Age of Privateering, 1775–1815*. Portsmouth, N.H.: Portsmouth Maritime Society, 1988.

Magazines, Newspapers

The Annual Register: A Review of Public Events at Home and Abroad, London, 1777–83.

Columbian (Massachusetts) *Centinel*.

The Gentleman's Magazine and Historical Chronicle, 1756–83, vols. 27–54.

Hampshire (England) *Chronicle*, 1776–83.

London (England) *Chronicle, 1777–79*.

London (England) *Evening Post,*1776–79.

New Hampshire Gazette, 1777–79.

Salem (Massachusetts) *Gazette*, 1775–78.

The Salisbury and Winchester Journal, (England) 1777–79.

Town and Country Magazine (London) 1777–78.

Manuscript Materials and Repositories

American Philosophical Society

Berkshire (Reading, England) Record Office

British Library, Map Room and Newspaper Division, Colindale

Connecticut Historical Society

Essex Institute, Salem, Massachusetts

Dr. Williams's Library, London

Gloucestershire (England) Record Office

Gosport (England) Museum

Guildhall Library, London

Hampshire (England) Record Office

Hartley-Russell Papers, Reading (England)

Harvard University Library, Archives

Historical Society of Pennsylvania

Library of Congress, Washington, D.C.
Loyola University of Chicago, Cudahy Library
Maryland Historical Society
Massachusetts Historical Society
National Maritime Museum, Greenwich (England)
Naval Historical Center, Washington, D.C.
Newberry Library, Chicago
New England Historical and Genealogical Society
New Hampshire Historical Society
New London (Connecticut) Historical Society
New-York Historical Society
Northwestern University Library
Philadelphia Maritime Museum
Portsmouth (England) City Record Office
Public Record Office, Kew and Chancery Lane (England)
University of Pennsylvania Library
South Carolina Historical Society
University of South Carolina, Henry Laurens Papers
Vermont Historical Society
Virginia State Library
West Devon (Plymouth, England) Record Office
Yale University Library, Benjamin Franklin Papers

Index